PRAISE FOR THE FIRST EDITION OF

PUTIN'S RUSSIA

"Lilia Shevtsova is in a class by herself as an analyst and explicator of Russian politics, and her mastery is fully on display in *Putin's Russia*. She combines investigative skills with hard-headed judgment and narrative verve. Her portraits of the main actors are textured and convincing. Not only is this a superb book by a powerful author, it has an additional significance in the context of Russia's evolution as a normal modern country: As recently as 15 years ago, this sort of gimlet-eyed look at what goes on in and around the Kremlin was available only from dissidents, emigrants and Western specialists. It's a testament to how far Russia has come from Soviet times—and it augurs well for Russia's future—that someone of Shevtsova's intellectual integrity, independent convictions, and relentless honesty, based at a Moscow think tank, can help all of us understand what's happening—and why—in the leadership of her country."

—**STROBE TALBOTT**, president, Brookings Institution

"Winston Churchill said that Russia is a mystery inside an enigma. Having been in Russian politics for the past twelve years, I can attest that Lilia Shevtsova in her latest book has brilliantly succeeded in unwrapping the Russian enigma. As for the mystery, it will finally be solved only by history."

—**GRIGORY YAVLINSKY**, head of Russia's Yabloko party

PUTIN'S RUSSIA

OTHER BOOKS BY
LILIA SHEVTSOVA

GORBACHEV, YELTSIN, AND PUTIN: Political Leadership
in Russia's Transition (*edited with Archie Brown*)

YELTSIN'S RUSSIA: Myths and Reality

*To read excerpts and find more information on these and other publications
from the Carnegie Endowment, visit*
www.CarnegieEndowment.org/pubs

PUTIN'S RUSSIA

REVISED AND EXPANDED EDITION

LILIA SHEVTSOVA

Translated by
ANTONINA W. BOUIS

CARNEGIE ENDOWMENT FOR INTERNATIONAL PEACE
Washington, D.C.

Carnegie Endowment for International Peace
1779 Massachusetts Avenue, N.W., Washington, D.C. 20036
202-483-7600, Fax 202-483-1840
www.CarnegieEndowment.org

To order, contact Carnegie's distributor:
The Brookings Institution Press
Department 029, Washington, D.C. 20042-0029, USA
1-800-275-1447 or 1-202-797-6258
Fax 202-797-2960, Email bibooks@brook.edu

Cover photo: Russian president Vladimir Putin at the Kremlin during the three-day hostage siege at a Moscow theater in October 2002 (AP/Wide World Photos).

Interior design by Naylor Design. Composition by Oakland Street Publishing.

Library of Congress Cataloging-in-Publication Data

Shevtsova, Lilia Fedorovna.
    Putin's Russia / Lilia Shevtsova ; translated by Antonina W. Bouis.—Rev. and expanded ed.
        p. cm.
    Includes bibliographical references and index.
    ISBN 0-87003-213-5 (pbk.)
    1. Russia (Federation)—Politics and government—1991- 2. Putin, Vladimir Vladimirovich, 1952- I. Title.

    DK510.763.S492 2005
    947.086'092--dc22   2004029072

---

10   09   08   07   06   05   1   2   3   4   1st Printing 2005

CONTENTS

FOREWORD

Russia continues to matter. Major world challenges—the war on international terrorism; confronting Islamic fundamentalism; preserving European and world security; stabilizing volatile energy markets; fighting the proliferation of weapons of mass destruction; and dealing with regional conflicts, including the Middle Eastern quagmire—cannot be met without Russia's constructive participation. To secure Russia's integration into the international community is becoming one of the most ambitious challenges for the West in the twenty-first century.

It is true that Russian leader Vladimir Putin has made a pro-Western shift since the terrorist attacks of September 11, 2001. Russia became a U.S. ally in the antiterrorist campaign without asking for any reciprocity and without the usual horse trading Soviet leaders demanded for any concession to the West. There are times when history makes leaders. In the fall of 2001, the attacks transformed a hitherto cautious and tentative politician into a leader who surprised the world by proposing a new role for Russia, one almost unprecedented in history: unconditional support for the West.

Yet, as events after 1945 remind us, a wartime alliance will only survive the end of war if it embodies shared interests and values. Are both the West and Russia prepared to grow from their current anti-terrorist alliance into a constructive strategic partnership, including Russia's full-fledged integration into the West? The answer depends first of all on domestic developments in Putin's Russia, on how soon Russian elites and Russian society embrace liberal democratic rules of the game.

So far, Russia remains an area of ambiguity. Both optimists and pessimists can find arguments to support their views. On the one hand, one can see that Putin has restarted economic reforms that had stalled under his predecessor Boris Yeltsin and has led a foreign policy revolution in opening Russia to the West. He has introduced a new type of political leadership—pragmatic, rational, with a more predictable type of governance.

On the other hand, the Russian leader has demonstrated a profound mistrust of the key elements of liberal democracy: political pluralism, an independent opposition, and free media. He has attempted to base his rule on a mix of economic liberalism, pragmatic authoritarianism, and a pro-Western orientation. The combination may have been enough to modernize a peasant country. But it can hardly help Russia deal with the challenges of the postindustrial era. Sooner or later, the limitations of one-man rule—even in a more pragmatic wrapping—will become clear.

Dramatic events in Russia during 2004 have demonstrated that political stability has not been achieved and that Russia has to cope with the outcomes of the Chechen war and with a growing terrorist threat. Facing new uncertainties, President Putin has chosen to strengthen his authoritarian rule. His political moves raise serious concerns about Russia's future and the nature of its foreign policy.

The question therefore remains open: When and how will Russia be ready for its major breakthrough: dismantling personified power and establishing independent institutions and the rule of law? Only then can the new Russia become a real partner of the West.

Putin's Russia, first published in 2003, is the first comprehensive account of Russia's troubled transformation, its new leadership, and its relations with the West. This revised edition of a book that is already a classic in its field includes new analysis of the consequences of Putin's first term and of the beginning of his second. Its author, Lilia Shevtsova, a senior associate in the Carnegie Endowment's Russian and Eurasian Program, has long been a keen observer of Russia's politics, dividing her time between Moscow and Washington. She is one of the most respected of the political analysts in Russia and the West who closely follow Russia's postcommunist transformation. Her previous landmark study, *Yeltsin's Russia*, was also published by the Endowment.

We are grateful for the support provided to the Endowment's Russian and Eurasian Program by the Carnegie Corporation of New York, the Starr Foundation, and the Charles Stewart Mott Foundation.

Jessica T. Mathews
President
Carnegie Endowment for International Peace

ACKNOWLEDGMENTS

T his political diary would have never appeared in print without the support and friendship of a terrific group of people. It would not have been published without the constant support and encouragement of Jessica Mathews, the president of the Carnegie Endowment. Both vice presidents of the Endowment, Paul Balaran and George Perkovich, are also partially responsible for this story about Putin's Russia. Paul created the warm atmosphere that has always surrounded me in Moscow and Washington. George read the revised edition of the book and helped me with his insights and ideas. I am also indebted to Thomas Carothers, who helped me prepare the book for a Western audience.

Special thanks go to Strobe Talbott, who was my first reader, both for his good advice and extensive comments and for the thoughts he generously gave to me.

Robert Nurick, the former director of the Carnegie Moscow Center, read the manuscript and helped me with matters of style and logic. I am grateful to Andrew Kuchins, the Center's current director, who provided invaluable comments and moral support. I must thank Anders Åslund, director of the Carnegie Endowment's Russian and Eurasian Program, for his help and encouragement.

My greatest thanks go to my friends Angela Stent, Arnold Horelick, Daniel Yergin, Peter Reddaway, Archie Brown, David Kramer, and Igor Kliamkin, who shared their thoughts and knowledge with me.

I am indebted to Antonina Bouis, the translator, who found my voice and gave part of herself to the book as well.

I am grateful to Alice Phillips, who edited the first edition of this book. Alfred Imhoff made final editorial corrections of the manuscript, edited the revised edition, and gave astute comments.

I must thank Carmen MacDougall, vice president of the Carnegie Endowment, for giving this book high priority and enthusiastically promoting it. My thanks to Trish Reynolds, the Endowment's director of publications, with whom I have worked on two books about Russia, and to Sherry Pettie, who coordinated the editorial and production process for three of my books, including the first edition of *Putin's Russia*. My thanks go also to Matt Boyle, who managed the production of this edition.

Caroline McGregor and Faith Hillis, junior fellows at the Carnegie Endowment, and Dmitri Borshchevsky, coordinator of the Russian Domestic Politics and Political Institutions Program at the Carnegie Moscow Center, helped me prepare the manuscript for publication.

I am grateful to my friends and colleagues at the Carnegie Endowment and outside the Endowment—in both Moscow and Washington—for being there, grateful that I can see them and argue, agree and disagree, and we still remain friends. They all, perhaps without realizing it, help me keep my political diaries.

And finally, my thanks to my family—mother, husband, and son—for their patience and for understanding that thinking and writing about Russian politics is a habit that can't be kicked.

PUTIN'S RUSSIA

PROLOGUE

On December 31, 1999, Yeltsin's Russia became Putin's Russia. Boris Yeltsin—a political maverick who until the end tried to play the mutually exclusive roles of democrat and tsar, who made revolutionary frenzy and turmoil his way of survival—unexpectedly left the Kremlin and handed over power, like a New Year's gift, to Vladimir Putin, an unknown former intelligence officer who had hardly ever dreamed to become a Russian leader.

Yeltsin—tired and sick, disoriented, and having lost his stamina—apparently understood that he could no longer keep power in his fist. It was a painful and dramatic decision for a politician for whom nonstop struggle for power and domination was the substance of life and his main ambition. His failing health and numerous heart attacks, however, were not the main reasons behind his unexpected resignation.

The moment came when Yeltsin could not control the situation much longer and—more important—he did not know how to deal with the new challenges Russia was facing. He had been accustomed to making breakthroughs, to defeating his enemies, to overcoming obstacles. He was not prepared for state building, for the effort of everyday governance, for consensus making, for knitting a new national unity. By nature he was a terminator, not a transformational leader. It was time for him to graciously bow out and hand over power to his successor. And Russia had to live through a time of real suspense while the Kremlin was preparing the transfer of power.

The new Russian leader Vladimir Putin has become a symbol of a staggering mix of continuity and change. For part of Russia, he symbolized a link with Yeltsin's past; for another part, he was a sharp break from it. The new Kremlin boss has been shrewd enough to let people think what they want and to see what they long for.

Outwardly, with Putin's ascendancy to power, the style of Russian leadership has changed dramatically. He was unusually young for a Russian leader when he first entered the Kremlin, a 48-year-old dynamic yet ascetic-looking man, such a contrast to the pathetic Old Boris at the end of his rule. Putin has succeeded not only in taming Russian elites and arrogant tycoons, but also has maintained an amazing 70 percent approval rating for several years.

Putin does not even try to play monarch. He wants to be accepted as a pragmatic manager. During his first term in the Kremlin (2000–2004), he succeeded—at least outwardly—in achieving order and stability. He began a pro-Western revolution in foreign policy. He pushed forward economic reforms that had stalled under Yeltsin. Yet at the same time, he demonstrated a deep distrust of the major democratic institutions and an open desire to keep tight control over society. Unlike Yeltsin, who knew how to survive in an atmosphere of spontaneity and acquiescence, the new Russian leader preferred subordination and loyalty. But still, during his first term, Putin seemed unsure how to balance political freedoms and the centralization of his power, authoritarianism and dialogue with both society and political forces.

Not only its leader and leadership pattern but Russia itself in those years suddenly changed, as if someone closed one chapter and started another. The country—only recently torn between extremes, anticipating an apocalyptic scenario, in a desperate search for its new self—drifted into a lull, dominated by longing for calm private life, by disgust for any great ideas, and by fear of new shake ups. President Putin became an embodiment of this longing for stability and tranquillity. He would have never ascended to the top if the country had wanted to continue its revolution.

During his first term, Putin demonstrated that he had an agenda for Russia: authoritarian modernization and partnership with the West. His administration's amazing macroeconomic consolidation and friendly relations with Western powers appeared to confirm that he was on a good course, that he had finally found what Russia needed. But the slowing pace of economic reforms in 2003–2004, deepening social problems, the continuing war in Chechnya and the danger of spillover to other North

Caucasus republics, and finally the tragic escalation of terrorist acts in Russia together tested Putin's leadership—and he failed. This Russian leader has been confronted by new challenges, and his reaction has been the traditional answer for all Russian and Soviet rulers: He has embarked on the path of centralization, clamping down on all autonomous actors and political freedoms. For any observer of recent Russian developments, his use of personified power was the major reason underlying endemic corruption, powerful vested interests that prevented further reforms, the failure of the decision-making process, and the lack of information at the top about the real condition of society. By choosing hypercentralization, Putin has pushed Russia further into the trap.

The events of 2004 proved that the appearance of calm in Russia is deceptive. Too many questions continue to pile up: How sustainable is the Russian political system? Will Russia preserve at least some of the political freedoms from Gorbachev's and Yeltsin's legacies? How will Putin be able to combine his authoritarian ways with economic liberalism and pro-Western policy? How will a succession struggle and the redistribution of property affect Russia's future? Will Russia move toward dictatorship, or will Putin or any other force try to stop this process?

Putin's epoch is not over, and both the president and Russia may baffle us with their answers to these questions. Putin's Russia is still an unfinished story.

This book shows how Russia under Vladimir Putin has tried to define its new identity internationally and domestically, moving forward and backward from optimism and hope to anguish and resentment. It is a book on transitional ambiguity. On the one hand, this ambiguity helps to preserve continuity with Yeltsin and the pre-Yeltsin past and acts as a soothing drug for those who want to live in the past—and thus it has become the major stabilizing factor. On the other hand, it prevents Russia from making a more vigorous transformation, with its inevitable new tensions. Every country in transition has been facing its own dilemma between stability and breakthrough. For Russia, this dilemma is complicated by the fact that a radical transformation might trigger developments that Moscow would not be able to control.

In the second term of his presidency, it appears that Vladimir Putin has started to limit the ambivalence of his own course, switching from a

Western-imitation policy to more authoritarian ways and showing more suspicion toward his Western partners. This turn certainly will be painful for liberal-democratic forces in Russia. But Putin's going straight also means less deception and fewer illusions. Society will see the results of his authoritarian rule and will stop hoping that the "iron hand" will save Russia.

This is also a book about the paradoxes of transition. It is intellectually intriguing but politically alarming to watch how the holdovers from the past in action—the Communists are fighting for parliamentary democracy, and the liberals are defending authoritarianism and personified rule. It's perplexing to see how former KGB colonel Putin has led Russia's pro-Western shift. It's stunning that Russia's participation in the antiterrorist alliance with the West helps Russia preserve its traditional state and power. And the list of puzzles is not complete. Here is one more paradox: Ordinary Russians are much readier to modernize than are Russian elites, who are dragging their feet, being totally unable to rule democratically.

This is also a book on leadership. Starting in 2000, leadership enabled Russia to reenergize itself. Yet the fact that leadership is the only viable political institution prevents Russia from becoming a modern state and liberal democracy. In fact, since 2004, its leadership may have become the most serious obstacle to the country's future transformation.

This is not a book for those who are looking for quick and definite answers. It is for those who are ready to look behind the evident, who want to understand the reasons for vacillations, who can imagine how difficult it is to fight depression and dismay, especially when the political class is not up to the dramatic tasks at hand.

This is not simply a book on a country and its leader. It is a story of constant overcoming, of challenges and opportunities, of the ability to learn by losing and making blunders. If I succeed in provoking your interest in trying to solve Russian puzzles, my mission will be fulfilled.

Chapter 1

THE KREMLIN'S
POWER PLAY

———— ❧ ————

Yeltsin on the wane. The Primakov formula. Who runs Russia?
The Kremlin seeks an heir. The Bank of New York scandal.
Enter Putin. Russia wants order. The uses of war.

I t is Moscow in the spring of 2000, less than half a year since Vladimir Putin emerged in the Kremlin as the new leader of Russia. Oligarchs, once arrogant and bullying but now living in fear of a visit from secret police in black masks, have already moved their money and their families abroad and are keeping a low profile.[1] Only notorious tycoon Boris Berezovsky, one of those who orchestrated Putin's ascent, desperately tries to build an opposition to challenge the new Kremlin boss; but no one will dare to join him. Russia's governors and other regional lords, many of whom ran almost independent fiefs under Putin's predecessor, Boris Yeltsin, now look to Moscow in servile fashion. The corridors of the Kremlin are full of people with a military bearing and nondescript faces.

Women, particularly middle-aged ones, swoon over President Putin, lifted from obscurity and named prime minister, victor in the March presidential election, champion of the "strong hand" in Chechnya and of "verticality of authority" (a term coined by Russian elites to describe a top-down system of governance based on subordination and a domineering role for the executive branch). Some declare their love for their slender, athletic leader in television interviews. Putin, with his tireless activity and determined air, baffles observers accustomed to watching a chronically ailing leader and speculating about who rules Russia. This new president stirs anxiety among various groups; after all, no one is sure what is on his mind.

Editors in chief and heads of major television networks censor the mass media, steering clear of any topic that might disturb the new boss in the Kremlin. The intelligentsia returns to the kitchen to berate the authorities over a cup of tea or a glass of vodka, their criticism driven back inside, as in the long-forgotten Brezhnev years. Ordinary Russians just lie low.

Remembering too well Yeltsin's final phases, I keep wanting to pinch myself. Just six months ago, Russia was a different country. By the end of the 1990s, Yeltsin had lost control of it and himself. Berezovsky whispered his plans for Russia into the ear of the president's sweet daughter, and she and a few friends elevated and toppled high officials and made government policy. Oligarchs kicked open the doors of government offices and ran for their own benefit the remnants of the economy, which had been decimated by long-standing weaknesses and the August 1998 financial collapse. Regional leaders ruled over their provinces like little tsars, either paying no attention to the Kremlin or blackmailing the Moscow courtiers and the president himself.

The Russian state eroded, losing its power and the ability to perform elementary functions of government.[2] Russia sank deeper and deeper into social and economic crisis: falling life expectancy (for men, from 64.2 years in 1989 to as low as 57.6 years in 1994); a resurgence of contagious diseases that had been eliminated in the Soviet Union; decaying schools; hundreds of thousands of homeless children; millions of migrants; a shrinking economy that during Yeltsin's tenure contracted in real terms by 40 percent; and finally, rampant lawlessness and corruption that had become a lifestyle passing for "normal." Ordinary people had lost both the past and the future, and the present was confusing for many. But neither the president nor elites seemed to notice—they were busy pretending to rule, struggling for a place at the top, robbing the state.

The newspapers attacked Yeltsin ruthlessly, but ordinary people had wearied of their unprecedented freedom to criticize the government, because it brought about no improvement. The president was regarded with both pity and scorn. The authorities were blamed for everything from failed hopes for a normal life after the fall of communism to people's feelings of helplessness. The Kremlin had totally lost the aura of sacredness and mystery that had surrounded rulers of Russia through the ages, revealing itself as a marketplace where everything could be bought and sold.

In another dispiriting development, the Russian presidency seemed to have reverted to the Soviet pattern of gerontocracy, in which one old man hung on as leader until he died, only to be replaced by another old man. President Yeltsin, once powerful and charming, with an astonishing strength of will that had enabled him to destroy the Communist Party and the Soviet empire, now hid from the world, shuttling between dachas outside Moscow. Few besides his family and physicians had access to him. His physical decline was tortured. It was not only his heart condition—though he later admitted he had had five severe heart attacks. He seemed to have problems with everything, including walking, holding himself erect, concentrating, and even comprehending what he was being asked about. When he was shown to the public, his doctors alone knew the effort it took for him to hold himself together. And he was not that old as we watched him deteriorate; he was still in his late sixties.

Like Yeltsin, the other denizens of the Kremlin were more and more removed from society and its ills. Neither constant charges of corruption nor crushing national problems worried them; they thought only of holding on to their power and perquisites. Those who formed the Kremlin entourage were reckless, sure of themselves and their control of the game. They seemed to have no premonition that the game might end.

At the end of the 1990s, in fact, no one was really running the country. Beginning in 1996, the political class was preoccupied with when Yeltsin would step down and who would rule Russia after him. How did Tsar Boris look today, was he compos mentis or not? How long would he last? Everything else was secondary. Society settled in for what it assumed would be the patriarch's prolonged good-bye, while Russia continued its political and economic decay.

Who then had even heard of Vladimir Putin? Who outside a tiny circle in Moscow knew his name even in early 1999? The few who had met him had trouble later recalling the man or remembering that Yeltsin had made him head of the Federal Security Service (FSB), formerly the KGB. In 1998 or much of 1999, a suggestion that Putin would be the next president of Russia would have elicited bewilderment, if not laughter.

The slow crumbling of governmental authority seemed well-nigh irreversible then, and rapid assertion and consolidation of central control highly unlikely, but very soon those and other expectations would be stood on their heads. It seemed that Yeltsin would never leave office voluntarily, much less before his term was over—that he would sit (or lie) in the Kremlin until he died. It seemed that there would be a vicious struggle among the main "power clans," or interest groups; the heads of some were already imagining their victories and gloating. It seemed clear that the two leading contenders for Yeltsin's throne were Moscow mayor Yuri Luzhkov, who successfully competed with federal authorities for power and money, and recent prime minister Yevgeny Primakov, experienced apparatchik, former head of the Federal Intelligence Service (SVR), and current foreign minister. Finally, whatever the result of the power struggles at the top, many assumed that the Russian people had gotten used to a free and spontaneous life, to constant political bickering, to the unruliness of elites, and would reject any return of the "iron hand." But those who thought so turned out to know little of the Russian soul, or of how panic and fear can suddenly change the political mentality of millions.

As the 1990s drew to a close, economic and social emergencies and the febrile mood they created among the populace were ready to speed up events in Russia. In 1998, Russia moved inexorably toward a financial crash. Russian stocks were plummeting. State bonds were paying 130 to 140 percent. The Central Bank was trying desperately to keep the ruble stable. On August 19, the Ministry of Finance had to cover 34 billion rubles worth ($5.7 billion before devaluation) of GKOs (state short-term bonds). The treasury did not have that kind of money, nor could it borrow it anywhere. The $22 billion International Monetary Fund and World Bank credit granted to Russia—under heavy pressure from U.S. president Bill Clinton—had vanished to parts unknown.

During what for many ordinary people was a painful postcommunist transformation, Russians had become used to labor strikes, hunger strikes, suicide, and self-immolation driven by despair and hopelessness.

But the situation grew more volatile in 1998. Desperate miners from state-owned mines, who had not been paid for months, began blocking railroad tracks. Their representatives came to Moscow and set up a tent city in front of the White House, where the Russian cabinet sits. The miners demanded not only back pay but also Yeltsin's resignation. I remember the men, stripped to the waist in the broiling sun, sitting in the street and rhythmically beating their miners' helmets on the hot cobblestones. I remember their angry looks at officials' limousines with closed and shadowed windows hurtling past. Moscow was suddenly back in the throes of class hatred dredged up from long ago. The hungry Russia of the provinces had come to Moscow to remind the capital of its existence, and the wake-up call was ominous. In the late 1980s, it had been the miners—when they wanted Yeltsin in the Kremlin—who had rattled the throne beneath Gorbachev. Now they wanted him out. The power in the Kremlin was registering seismic movement again.

The miners were left unmolested, however, and mayor Yuri Luzhkov gave orders that they be allowed to demonstrate and even had them fed. As a pretender to the highest Kremlin post, Luzhkov had an interest in keeping the miners in Moscow as long as possible: They could hasten a new distribution of power, and he was the first waiting in line to claim his prize.

Russia cried out for leadership at this critical juncture, but neither the president nor the cabinet nor other political figures had the answers to the country's problems. The doddering Yeltsin had almost disappeared from view, making occasional public appearances only to confirm that he was still alive. "Working on documents," the official explanation for his absences from the Kremlin, drew a skeptical smile from Russians. Even usually sure-of-themselves liberals seemed to have lost their nerve. The 37-year-old prime minister, Sergei Kiriyenko, dubbed by the press "Kindersurpriz" (after a chocolate popular with Russian children), looked perplexed. When elevated to prime minister shortly before, he had brimmed with self-assurance. Now, in an apparent attempt to hide his confusion, he talked nonstop. His words, like persistent, boring rain, meant nothing.

Left to deal with a deepening financial crisis, Kiriyenko didn't have time—much less the ability—to gauge its seriousness. His experience as a Komsomol (Communist Youth League) leader and then a provincial banker in Nizhny Novgorod until coming to Moscow the year before had not prepared him for this. I remember the reaction of officials at international organizations who dealt with Kiriyenko. "My God, how will he cope?" they asked, clutching their heads. "He doesn't even know which buttons to push."

Before the end of 1998, treasury officials had to find 113 billion rubles ($18 billion) to pay the interest on GKOs and OFZs (state loan bonds). Moscow also had to pay salaries and pensions for public-sector workers, and the nonpayments had been accumulating since the beginning of the year. Tax revenues would not exceed 164.6 billion rubles ($22.5 billion). The fragile Russian banking system was on the verge of collapse. The economy was disintegrating. The West could no longer help. Russian citizens were still being patient, but that could end at any moment. And then—no, no one wanted to contemplate what could happen in Russia then.

Some of the members of Yeltsin's team quickly figured out that the financial chaos, with millions of rubles streaming out of the country, presented a unique opportunity for enrichment for people who kept their heads. In any case, everyone in power in 1998 not only survived the crash but continued to do well financially, even better than before. Russian history has shown how much advantage can be extracted from a crisis, especially if you are the one managing it.

After some hesitation, on August 17, 1998, the Kiriyenko government declared Russia bankrupt, deciding to go for default and devaluation at the same time—this after Yeltsin's promise that there would be no devaluation. The small circle that reached the decision on bankruptcy included leading reformers Anatoly Chubais and Yegor Gaidar. The previous day, Kiriyenko and Chubais had flown to Yeltsin's dacha with proposals that the president had been forced to approve, having no other solution. A demoralized Yeltsin had lost control over events.

Acknowledging the influence of the powerful oligarchic clans, Kiriyenko met with their representatives late that night to give them a report on what had happened. Most likely, Yeltsin's oligarchs knew what was coming. Grigory Yavlinsky, the leader of the democratic movement Yabloko, openly accused Kiriyenko of acting on behalf of the tycoons, saying, "The financial collapse was Kiriyenko's fault, because his actions had been ineffective and, most important, favored certain oligarchic groups." In any case, all the tycoons had gotten their money out of the failing banks in time, and soon they established new banks and continued to prosper, while ordinary Russians lost their savings in the collapse and had to start from scratch.

Yet the Kiriyenko government was not fully accountable for the August 1998 financial crisis. The emergency was partly a reaction to the Asian economic meltdown that had begun the year before. Moreover, the preconditions had been established in Russia under the government of prime minister Victor Chernomyrdin, who had survived for quite a long while in the time of Yeltsin's permanent cabinet reshuffles. Appointed premier in 1992 after Gaidar's dismissal, he was fired in 1998 only because Yeltsin suspected him of harboring an interest in the president's job—which Chernomyrdin definitely did. (One of the catalysts for his firing was a visit to the United States, during which he met with his old negotiating partner Vice President Al Gore and Gore treated "Cherno" like a future leader of Russia. Yeltsin could not tolerate that.)

What had led to the financial collapse were parliamentary populism and the premier's craven behavior. Instead of fighting for a workable budget, Chernomyrdin chose to create the GKO pyramid—to borrow money at a high rate of interest. As for the parliament, which pumped unsecured rubles into the budget, we know that venting and caving in to populist demands for fiscal irresponsibility are always among the functions of parliaments. In the case of Russia, that populism gets more play because the Duma, the lower house of the parliament, does not form the government and is not responsible for its actions. That was true in Yeltsin's era, and it is still true in Putin's.

Nor was Kiriyenko's government blameless. Kiriyenko had enough financial know-how to have realized he could avert catastrophe by devaluing the ruble gradually, but he did not do so. Either he panicked or he was certain that his luck would hold. Or else he was working in the interests of certain oligarchs, as Yavlinsky suggested.

Russians rushed to save their money, desperately trying to withdraw funds from private banks. But many lost everything. Foreigners lost their money as well. Most of them closed their offices and left the country. The Moscow gold rush seemed to be over for good. After some vacillation, Yeltsin fired the government of Kindersurpriz Kiriyenko and decided to bring back Victor Chernomyrdin, whom he trusted, hoping that that political heavyweight would find a way out. Yeltsin himself remained at his dacha, unable to face his people as their country slid toward the abyss.

Yeltsin's absence during the crisis gave rise to rumors about his stepping down. CBS News in the United States reported that the Russian president had signed a letter to be read after the parliament approved Chernomyrdin's candidacy, in which Yeltsin resigned from office and handed over all power to his successor. Chernomyrdin's close associates assiduously spread that rumor, hoping to push events in that direction. Journalists hurried to update their political obituaries of Yeltsin yet one more time.

Finally, when rumors of his resignation had become the top news story of the day, Yeltsin appeared in public. On August 21, the ailing president made a point of inspecting Russia's Northern Fleet and visiting the nuclear-powered battleship *Peter the Great*. It was a warning—"Don't touch me, I have military might behind me." Yeltsin was accompanied, as Brezhnev had been in his day, by an entire hospital. But even though at that moment he could barely speak, Yeltsin could still create a lot of trouble. The old bear had the power to fire people, to shuffle and reshuffle the cabinet, to use force if necessary. God alone knew what an unpredictable Kremlin boss could do when threatened or feeling depressed or angered, or when at a loss as to what to do.

On August 28, Yeltsin gave a television interview, his first in a long time. Much care must have gone into preparing and editing it. Nevertheless, Yeltsin looked extremely ill and old during the interview; it was hard for him to talk and, it appeared, even harder for him to think. He grew animated just once, when he declared firmly, "And I won't retire." Only then did he come alive, the old stubbornness in his eyes. The interview had been done for the sake of that one phrase, when the president suddenly awoke.

Events took another unpleasant turn for Yeltsin when the parliament rejected Chernomyrdin. The country was without a government and burdened with a collapsing economy. Yeltsin could have insisted and proposed Chernomyrdin again, and yet again, and if the deputies had rejected his candidate for prime minister three times he could have dissolved the parliament and called new elections. That meant war with the parliament. But the president could no longer operate with any certainty that society, the power structures (the army and navy, the intelligence services, and internal affairs—*siloviki*, as they are called in Russia), and regional elites would support him. Now real panic set in at the Kremlin. Its inhabitants, so cocky yesterday, were suddenly paralyzed with fear, unable to cope with the growing disarray.

Television viewers got another look at General Alexander Lebed—who had long frightened Russians with his dictatorial aspirations—when he arrived in Moscow with the clear hope of being invited to take charge. Several years before, Lebed had been one of the most influential politicians in Russia. In the presidential election of 1996, Lebed came in third; and as a reward for calling on his supporters to vote for Yeltsin in the second round, he was given the post of secretary of the Security Council (the body coordinating the activity of the power structures). Lebed was the one who signed the Khasavurt peace treaty with Chechnya that ended the first Chechen war (1994–1996). He could not quiet his presidential ambitions, and in late 1996 Yeltsin fired him. After that, the irrepressible general won election as governor of one of Siberia's richest regions, Krasnoyarski Krai, and became a regional tsar.[3]

The general could not suppress a triumphant grin as he descended the aircraft's stairs upon arrival. His whole demeanor seemed to say, "Well, it looks as if I'll have to save this country!" Lebed's appearance in Moscow was supposed to signal the Kremlin's readiness to use force to hold onto the power that was draining away from it. But it was a rather desperate ploy, because the general, as everyone knew, had vast ambitions and had never been on a leash. He could not be trusted. If Lebed ended up in the Kremlin as Yeltsin's savior, the best Yeltsin and his team could expect was to be pensioned off the very next day.

The year 1999, decisive for the future of Russia, showed how far the country had moved beyond the monolithic, autocratic power traditional for Russia and yet how much it still lived by it, even when power was transferred to a new leader through democratic mechanisms. It was a strange and disturbing mixture of continuity and change, this fusion of governance à la Old Russia with elements of liberal democracy. The degeneration of Yeltsin's presidency and the crumbling of his power that accelerated after the financial collapse revealed the essence of the regime that Yeltsin had created to be an *elected monarchy*. In fact, Yeltsin, a revolutionary of a sort, who had delivered a fatal blow to the Soviet empire and to communism, helped preserve—without meaning to—aspects of the "Russian System" that had perpetuated itself down through the long centuries, surviving tsarism and the Bolshevik Revolution.

The Russian System is a specific type of governance structure whose characteristics include paternalism, the state domineering over the individual, isolation from the outside world, and ambitions to be a great power. The heart of the system was the all-powerful leader, above the law and a law unto himself, concentrating in his hands all powers, without a balancing accountability, and limiting all other institutions to auxiliary, administrative functions. The Russian System did not need fixed rules of the game; it needed fixers.

Yeltsin's ascent to power through victory in a free and fair election fatally undermined the Russian System, introducing into politics in Russia a new kind of legitimation, which destroys the sacred and irrational character of power and makes power dependent, at least partially, on society. As president, Yeltsin weakened the Russian System by opening society to the West and turning away from at least some of the great-power complexes. But by preserving one-man rule, Russia's first noncommunist leader preserved the inertia of the Russian System, not only in the people's mentality but in the style of presidential rule, in the relations between authorities and society.

Russia's experience in the 1990s proved that the one-man regime could function relatively well in a stable environment but could not manage in a crisis, especially when the leader was physically incapable of performing a leader's routine tasks, had no support in society, and could not rely on the army and other instruments of coercion. In the absence of mature institutions, Yeltsin inevitably had to share power with his most trusted and loyal people. Naturally, the most trusted and loyal people turned out to be members of his family and friends of the family.

Yeltsin's political family (known in Russia as "the Family") was a mixed group that included the president's younger daughter Tatyana (Tanya) Dyachenko; her closest pal and, it appeared much later, boyfriend, Valentin Yumashev (they married after Yeltsin resigned); Yeltsin's chief of staff, Alexander Voloshin; and oligarch Roman Abramovich. The infamous oligarch Boris Berezovsky, the master of intrigue, was their leader and the brains of the bunch. These were the people who ruled the Kremlin in the late 1990s, and they continue to exert their influence on Russian politics.

It is a story that has been repeated in many countries in many periods: The strong leader who has worked so long to gather all power into his own hands becomes a hostage of his court as he ages. From inside that trap, he watches his power and his character degrade. Sometimes he understands that he is becoming a weakling and even a laughingstock. Often he doesn't.

It was hard to discern in the shell of a man left by the late 1990s the Boris Yeltsin who had ridden the democratic wave in the late 1980s and the beginning of the 1990s and who could elicit unconditional support from crowds merely by his presence. The leader who had made his mission Russia's return to Europe and its transformation into a flourishing democratic state ended up a politician completely dependent on his Kremlin servants, stooping to primitive intrigue and manipulation to survive.

Yeltsin's every appearance outside the Kremlin threatened to compromise him and his country. Russia and the world knew of his outlandish behavior: Here a drunken Yeltsin conducted a band in Germany; there he crawled out of his airplane, puffy-faced and staggering, after missing an official meeting with the Irish prime minister. We can only guess at scenes the cameras of Western correspondents failed to capture. As Yeltsin grew weaker physically, the ostensibly superpresidential system became obviously disabled, devolving into a half-hearted Impotent Omnipotence.

Yeltsin's primary means of exercising power as his second term wore on was the personnel merry-go-round that never stopped. In the eight years of his presidency, he changed prime minister seven times and prosecutor general six times, went through seven heads of his old agency, the FSB, and had three ministers of foreign affairs. Permanent cadre revolution became his major instrument for holding onto power. Shakeups of his team made it seem for the next week or two as if he were still in control, and created an artificial need for him to play coordinator and arbiter. It was an illusion of governance.

Having lost the reforming impulse, the elected monarchy turned into a source of instability. Under the Russian Constitution that Yeltsin had edited after he dismantled the parliament in 1993, the parties elected to the parliament had no opportunity to form a cabinet, and the rubber-stamp parliament had no real opportunity to affect the policies of the government. Thus the regime procured for Russia an irresponsible parliament with an irresponsible multiparty system. Both the parties and the parliament kept themselves alive by means of constant attacks on the executive branch. The cabinet, formed by the president and subordinate to him, was even less accountable. It consisted almost entirely of representatives of influential groups and existed to serve their interests. Such a regime could not deal successfully with the challenges Russia faced. At best, it could guarantee stagnation.

For Yeltsin personally, the important thing in early 1999 was to find a candidate for the prime minister's job who would be acceptable to the parliament yet pose no threat to himself. Moscow mayor Yuri Luzhkov seemed to think his time had come to ascend the Russian throne. For that, he first had to become prime minister. Under the Russian Constitution, the prime minister's best chance to take over the presidency comes if the president resigns for reasons of health. In such a case, the prime minister organizes new elections—and in Russia, that gives him the resources for organizing his own victory at the polls.

Even some members of Yeltsin's team bet on Luzhkov, indicating a certain defeatism within the ranks. But for Yeltsin—or rather, for his political Family—Luzhkov was unacceptable. Independent and headstrong, Luzhkov ruled Moscow godfather-style. But the biggest headache for the Yeltsin team was the mayor's entourage. Even a dull observer noticed the hostility between the Kremlin court and the Moscow court, which sometimes broke into open warfare.

When foreign minister Yevgeny Primakov's name came up, Yeltsin decided right away that he was his choice for premier. The first to suggest the idea was Grigory Yavlinsky, leader of the democratic party Yabloko. Yavlinsky saw Primakov as a lesser evil than other possible candidates for the job and thought he would not want to go on to be president but would be merely a transitional figure who would help Russia escape coups or political upheaval in any form during the inevitable transfer of power from Yeltsin to his successor.

Primakov was an experienced Soviet apparatchik who knew how to keep up good relations with all important groups. He had managed to get through the collapse of the Soviet Union without alienating either Gorbachev or Yeltsin. He succeeded in simultaneously being friends with Iraqi president Saddam Hussein and U.S. secretary of state Madeleine Albright! Primakov always avoided conflicts and knew how to wait. He also understood how to be loyal without servility. This was a man who could be supported by the most varied groups—a moderate conservative who at the time was the perfect symbol of the stability that the majority of Russians desperately wanted and needed.

Yeltsin offered the prime minister's post to Primakov. "I refused categorically," Primakov wrote in his book *Years in Big-Time Politics.* On leaving Yeltsin's office, however, he ran into the president's younger daughter, Tatyana Dyachenko, and family friend Valentin Yumashev—that is, the people who ruled the Kremlin. They managed to persuade him to accept Yeltsin's job offer. Primakov explained his turnaround this way: "For a moment, reason took a back seat and feelings won out."

Yeltsin, by taking on Primakov as prime minister, obtained a reprieve for himself. And in early 1999 an informal double-rule gradually prevailed in Russia, with political weight shifting to the cabinet. The new prime minister brought in his people and made the cabinet a major decision-making body that did not wait for advice or endorsement from the presidential staff—a development hardly welcome to the Yeltsin Family. A new "ruling party" began to form around Primakov, and interest groups that had not been satisfied with their roles signed on.

It was the second time in a decade in postcommunist Russia that a quest for the redistribution of power in government had begun. The first attempt took place during the clash between the president and parliament in 1991–1993, when the two branches of government contended to see which would be the more powerful. That conflict had ended dramatically, with the dissolution of the parliament and Yeltsin's order to fire on the White House, the former parliament building in Moscow. A peaceful separation of powers had been unlikely then, because both sides wanted a monopoly on power and neither was prepared to impose any limitations on itself.

In 1999, a redistribution of political resources initiated by Primakov began within the executive branch. It included a strengthening of the cabinet, which had never been independent or strong in Russia, and the prime minister's taking over of the economic agenda. The rest of the governance, including security policy and control over the power structures, remained in the hands of Yeltsin's staff. It was an informal re-division of power within the executive, making the split among president, cabinet, and prime minister much more even than it had been. Influential political forces—the Communists, and also major representatives of regional elites—openly supported the idea of constitutional reform that would remove the president's excessive powers and legally endorse the change of rules that Primakov had initiated. The main proposals for reform came down to the idea that Russia must switch to a hybrid premier–presidential regime, under which the president's personal power would be lessened and the parliament and the cabinet would have a larger role.

Russian liberal reformers, especially those close to Gaidar and Chubais, had from the start been against a system of counterbalances to the president, because they believed it could slow economic reform. Their position was understandable, given that the left wing dominated the parliament; strengthening the legislative branch, and especially forming the cabinet on the basis of the majority in the parliament, could mean trouble for reform policies. So for the sake of economic results, the liberal reformers rejected an extremely important principle of liberal democracy: checks and balances, provided by strong institutions.

Russia had fallen into a historical trap. What it boiled down to was that those who called themselves liberals did not trust the representative institutions or society, fearing the unleashing of populism. They preferred to leave governing exclusively in the hands of the leader, making him the sole center of power. The liberals' fears of populism were not unfounded. But rule through a superpresidency did not speed the course of economic transformation in Russia; on the contrary, the reform measures introduced by presidential decree lacked legitimacy and were often boycotted by numerous bureaucrats and by social groups that felt the decrees endangered their interests. Moreover, the president's unusually extensive powers created the temptation at the top to move toward frank and harsher authoritarianism. Yeltsin did not go that way. But his successor might try.

In addition, the weakness of institutions meant that the president was drawn into day-to-day management, which would have been taxing for even a much hardier person than Yeltsin. The existence of a prime minister allowed the president to evade responsibility for the work of his cabinet; when his policy failed, he simply fired cabinet members. Or he fired the prime minister, who in that era was only a presidential appointee with no strong party support in the parliament. So the model of power in the Yeltsin years, during which the cabinet was intentionally weak—and was in fact an extension of the president's staff—created room for the leader's erratic behavior.

In early 1999, Primakov's government, backed by the Duma, put through the most liberal budget in Russia's history, which reduced government spending and made control of inflation a goal. And the most amazing thing was that the Communist Party supported fiscal austerity. It seemed that the left wing, forced to bear responsibility for the government, had to curb its appetite.

The "Primakov formula," however, was not to be incorporated into the Constitution. On May 12, 1999, Primakov was forced to resign, and the experiment with separation of powers in Russia—particularly reapportionment of executive power—failed again. Eighty-one percent of those polled immediately afterward by the Public Opinion Foundation disapproved of the firing, whereas a mere 8 percent approved. Twenty-two percent of those polled said they would vote for Primakov if he ran for president—15 percentage points ahead of Communist Party leader Gennady Zyuganov, 11 ahead of Yavlinsky, and 7 ahead of Luzhkov. It appeared that Primakov had become quite popular and had a good chance to be more than a transitional figure. And that did not fit with the plans of Yeltsin and his entourage.

Naturally, Primakov is not a democrat or a liberal, and never was. He is an adherent of bureaucratic capitalism. He is known to hate personal criticism and to be suspicious of reporters.[4] He would have been unlikely to tolerate freedom of opposition if he had gained power. He also distrusted the West, especially the United States. The former premier was famous for his "Primakov loop"—learning of the March 1999 NATO bombing of Yugoslavia while en route to the United States, Primakov had the pilot turn the plane around and fly back to Moscow. That loop immediately made him a hero in Russia.

But we should not spend much time lamenting Primakov. He might have pushed constitutional changes curbing the enormous power of the Russian president. But bearing in mind the influence of left-wing and centrist forces in the country, such changes could have slowed economic transformation even more. Nor do we have good reason to believe that Primakov would have begun building independent institutions after his ascent to the top Kremlin post. Finally, we might come to the conclusion that Primakov would never have made the pro-Western shift that Putin accomplished in 2001. That by itself allows us not to regret Primakov's exit.

Why didn't the Primakov experiment succeed? It was not simply because Yeltsin could not bear for the prime minister's office to become the hub of government activity. That was certainly a factor, but much more important was that under the Primakov formula the Yeltsin Family's hold on power was not guaranteed. An independent prime minister supported by the Duma and with his own power base within the state apparatus and power ministries would not allow the Yeltsin crowd to name anyone else as Yeltsin's successor. And the Family did not want to see the too powerful, independent Primakov, who was not obligated to the Family, as the heir.

An old Russian tradition came into play as the succession issue loomed: failure to establish the mechanisms for a legitimate and truly constitutional transfer of power. A lack of such mechanisms had condemned Russia to the palace coups under the tsars and the putsches that brought in new general secretaries of the Communist Party. Even the passing of power from Gorbachev to Yeltsin in December 1991 was accompanied by the fall of the state and took the form of a coup run by three republic leaders, one of them Yeltsin. Eight years later, as Yeltsin faded and the shadow network formed around him, the question of how to resolve the succession took a dramatic turn. And the solution must acknowledge yet another challenge: integrating the ruling class's desire for self-perpetuation with the new democratic mechanisms in Russia, particularly elections.

The Yeltsin team wanted not only to receive assurances of future security but also to retain control over the power and property that its members and the tycoons close to them had amassed during Yeltsin's rule. Primakov could guarantee the president's safety. But he was unlikely to promise a peaceful life to the entire Yeltsin entourage—especially because after being appointed prime minister he had dared to proclaim a war on corruption, thus challenging the mighty oligarchs close to the Kremlin. Rumors flew around Moscow that special forces loyal to Primakov had prepared a list of potential victims. At the top of the list, according to the rumors, was the name Boris Berezovsky, friend and adviser of Yeltsin's daughter Tatyana and oligarch extraordinaire. Drawing Berezovsky's hostility was dangerous even for an experienced political wolf like Primakov.

Several other kinds of Yeltsin supporters found Primakov unsettling. The technocrats and bureaucrats who had been winners in Yeltsin's distribution of power and property were as interested as he was in maintaining the shadow networks by which they were able to arrange sweet deals behind the scenes, and as leery of Primakov's anticorruption stance. Primakov also worried the liberal-leaning with his dubious attitude toward political freedoms, especially freedom of the press. The liberals could not forgive his distrust of the West, or even his assertiveness toward the Western powers. Thus Primakov was unable to consolidate the support of Yeltsin voters, who included not only oligarchs and liberals but all those who had benefited from Yeltsin's rule.

But it was Primakov's challenge to Yeltsin's clique that signed his polit-ical death warrant. Yeltsin's entourage could not forgive the prime minis-ter for his accumulation of power or for the threat emanating from him that he would use that power against some members of the Kremlin power clan. It was clear from the way Yeltsin behaved at meetings with his premier that he did not like or trust him. Yeltsin later admitted that he had never planned to give Primakov power and looked on him as a tempo-rary figure. "Yevgeny Maksimovich willy-nilly helped me achieve my main political goal—to bring the country peacefully to 2000 and to the elections. Afterward, as I thought then, we would together find a young and strong politician and hand him the political baton," Yeltsin wrote of Primakov, rather disingenuously, in his book *Presidential Marathon*.[5]

In the last months of Yeltsin's rule, the president and his team became openly hostile toward their independent premier. When the two leaders appeared on television together, Yeltsin looked grim, unable to hide his irritation, and he avoided eye contact with Primakov. The prime minis-ter made an effort to appear calm, but it was obvious how much it cost him. In *Presidential Marathon*, Yeltsin explained his displeasure by saying that Primakov had rallied around himself elites who dreamed of a "return to the old ways." But what Yeltsin found unforgivable was that in the eyes of many Russians, Primakov had become a candidate for successor with-out Yeltsin's approval.

Yeltsin's plans to get rid of Primakov were accelerated by the impeachment vote in the parliament, scheduled by the Communists for May 14, 1999. The Kremlin was afraid that Yeltsin's possible impeachment by the Federation Council—the upper chamber of the parliament, which had grown increasingly hostile toward the president—would empower the second most influential figure in Russia past recall.

The experienced fighter in Yeltsin decided on a preemptive strike. Two days before the impeachment vote by the Federation Council, he fired the prime minister without warning. Seemingly exhausted, weak, and unable to speak coherently, Yeltsin was reanimated by danger. His politi-cal sense of smell sharpened at such moments; he was still capable not only of defending himself but also of attacking—especially a rival. Yeltsin couldn't stand to have anyone next to him—he wanted to be complete-ly alone at the top.

Primakov—unlike several other prime ministers and almost all of Yeltsin's other subordinates who had found themselves in similar situations—did not plead with Yeltsin to keep him on. "I accept your decision. You have the right to do so under the Constitution. But I consider it a mistake." That was all Primakov said in farewell to Yeltsin before he left the room. He retired with dignity, not asking anyone for anything.

Primakov's departure did not spark protests in Russia, though the Kremlin was worried about such a reaction. But it was a heavy blow for the entourage that had formed around the prime minister and had dreamed of future positions. Primakov's political Family started looking around for other shelter, and some of its members even tried to get back into Yeltsin's good graces. When the leader is the major source of power and politics, the only survival skill worth having is the ability to see which way the power is flowing. Under such circumstances, it is difficult to remain loyal to people or principles.

———————— ❧ ————————

The attempt to impeach Yeltsin was a failure. Primakov's firing left the potential opposition to Yeltsin without steam. That helped create a new atmosphere inside the Kremlin, giving the presidential team a new feeling of determination and vigor. They again felt sure of themselves. All their energy was directed toward settling a single issue: finding a political heir loyal to Yeltsin and themselves. In the spring of 1999, Yeltsin seemed to be considering leaving the political area prematurely. His entourage was having more and more trouble controlling his behavior and maintaining the charade that he was in charge.

Yeltsin was a very sick man by that time. He had intervals when he was more like his old self and thought rationally, but one suspected that such periods were created by doctors and medication. Tsar Boris was becoming a ruin. His decay roused both fear and pity. After all, he was formally the leader of a state possessing nuclear weapons. Watching him, you felt that you were seeing the political funeral of a once great and powerful politician. Hardly anyone could have predicted at that time that the first Russian president would ever reemerge on the political scene.

Yeltsin would indeed amaze us—and not only once. But that would happen much later, after he left his post.

As Yeltsin faded, he relied even more on the people around him, most of all on his younger daughter Tatyana, then in her mid-thirties. He admitted in *Presidential Marathon* that Tatyana played a major role in the Kremlin: "Tanya by her humble presence and occasional bit of advice really did help me."

That was too modest an appraisal of his younger daughter's contribution. In actual fact, in the last years of Yeltsin's second term, Tatyana became the virtual ruler of the country. The sweet young woman, practically a girl, with limited life experience, found herself in the thick of political events. In early 1996, when the fight was on to keep Yeltsin for a second term, family friend and journalist Valentin Yumashev had the idea of bringing Tanya into the election campaign to serve as a direct channel between the campaign team and the president. Shy and timid at first, Tanya entered politics as an "information channel" and stayed on.

When Brezhnev was fading, the person who had the most influence on him was his nurse. With Yeltsin, it was his younger daughter, but it could have been a nurse, a driver, or a cook. Before the Family became the main influence on Yeltsin, the gray cardinal of the Kremlin was Yeltsin's bodyguard, Alexander Korzhakov.[6] In a one–man political show, especially in a weak one like Yeltsin's, the absence of independent institutions when the leader goes into decline means that power can fall into other hands most randomly.

After 1996, Tanya gradually took control of all important political appointments. A grimace of dislike on her face was enough to get someone fired, while an approving smile could speed someone else up the ladder of success. All vivid personalities in the Yeltsin entourage were removed, to be replaced by faceless people who preferred to operate behind the scenes, or by out-and-out ruthless individuals who did not even conceal their nature. Yeltsin's last team, the one that prepared the Successor Project, was selected by his daughter and her intimate friends.

Tatyana's friends became heads of government institutions and received huge chunks of state property. Tanya decided when and how the president would be shown to the public and prepared drafts of his speeches. She managed the emotions and eventually the behavior of her father, who grew more helpless every day. Yes, Yeltsin was stubborn and egocentric. But he loved Tatyana and let her do almost whatever she wanted with him; he turned into her puppet. Russian tradition and the weakness of civil society had brought the country to such a pass that it could do nothing but sit back and watch the drama of the collapse of power and the state, and the degradation of the president's personality.

In the late 1990s, Russia entered the era of the political Family: rule by the president's daughter and chums of hers undistinguished by expertise, brains, or talent. The situation with the next ruling team, however, would be even bleaker, which proves that governance based on loyalty and mutual obligations never brings bright and responsible people to the top. The names of Tanya's major associates—Valentin Yumashev, Alexander Voloshin, Roman Abramovich—meant nothing to anyone. Only Berezovsky, Tanya's adviser, the leading intriguer of the tsar's court, was known, and only because he liked being in the spotlight. In the later years of the Yeltsin administration, Berezovsky was crowded out by younger people whom he had introduced to Tatyana and with whom she felt more comfortable—people like Abramovich and Voloshin, with a strange, even dubious, past, implicated in shady dealings.[7] Perhaps these characters who suddenly surfaced and were attracted to the president's daughter were good friends to her, spoke her language, and had the same interests. It is also very likely that they provided various services to the Yeltsin family that tied the family to them.

As the Kremlin brotherhood grew accustomed to armored limousines and official bodyguards, to having every door open for them and no one monitoring their behavior, they lost all sense of limits. They began discrediting potential opponents and economic rivals; as in Soviet times, only the servile survived. It is a good thing that the Family was driven mainly by greed. Its members were not interested in foreign policy or relations in the post-Soviet space. They did not indulge in state building. They were capable of nothing more than moving pieces on the political chessboard. But they achieved perfection in that game. They ran an extended intrigue intended to create the appearance of activity on the part of the president, a sick old man, who in turn, and perhaps unaware, provided cover for them. From their position deep inside the Kremlin, this corrupt cooperative of friends and business comrades-in-arms created a giant vacuum to suck money out of Russia and into their own pockets.

———————— ❦ ————————

The moment came when the question of a successor was more important to the Kremlin circle and its closest associates than to Yeltsin himself. The weaker the president grew, the more acute became the Family's need to find a successor they could rely on after his departure. Survival and the perpetuation of their power preoccupied the Yeltsin team throughout 1999. The heir had to be prepared, legitimated through service as prime minister, so that the political class would get to know him. Leaping straight onto Yeltsin's throne, the Kremlin's team realized, was hardly possible for their candidate, for even patient Russian society would not tolerate that.

Actually, Yeltsin himself had been giving some thought to his successor for a while. But before 1997, his objectives had been different—then he was apparently interested in finding a leader who would continue his mission, who would pursue his reforms. Starting in 1997, though, he began to look at the people around him, pondering those he might be able to entrust with his political inheritance. For a while, he seemed particularly fond of Boris Nemtsov, governor of Nizhny Novgorod, a young, flamboyant liberal who would become one of the leaders of the Union of Right Forces (SPS). After Nemtsov, Yeltsin closely observed the work of General Nikolai Bordyuzha, for some time his chief of staff.

In many ways, however, Yeltsin's search for a potential heir was a game with Machiavellian overtones. The president was provoking potential pretenders so that he could gauge their attitude toward him. Anyone who dared apply for the role of successor was destroyed. Thus Yeltsin fired Prime Minister Chernomyrdin, who considered himself the heir in 1997 and 1998. The search for a successor was also a search for rivals to be neutralized or, better, erased from the political scene. But by 1999, Yeltsin could not rule, and therefore the succession issue had to be solved.

On May 19, 1999, Sergei Stepashin became the new Russian prime minister.[8] He was a Yeltsin loyalist who had moved from post to post—he had been director of the Federal Counterintelligence Service (predecessor of the FSB), minister of justice, and minister of internal affairs. Stepashin had had a paradoxical career—at one time he had been a democrat, and then in 1994 he had been entrusted with the pacification of Chechnya. Such sharp switches were typical for politicians drafted by Yeltsin. Temperamentally, Stepashin was a cautious man who never tried to play leading roles. That Yeltsin was appointing representatives from the power structures (*siloviki*) to the office of prime minister revealed the thought process of the ruling group. The Kremlin must have believed that the prime minister of a transitional cabinet should be someone who controlled the army or other power structure. He might be needed to defend the Kremlin from rivals.

However, in May 1999 there was no final clarity on the optimal candidate for regent. Yeltsin subsequently said, in *Presidential Marathon*, "Even as I nominated Stepashin, I knew that I would fire him." That Yeltsin's team had not yet decided on the final appointee is the only explanation for the constant presence in the president's inner circle during that period of Victor Aksyonenko, minister of transportation, who was fighting for the position of first loyal subject. In comparison with the crude and rascally Aksyonenko, who had long been suspected of financial machinations, the other candidates to the throne, including foreign minister Igor Ivanov, interior minister Vladimir Rushailo, and Putin, seemed like intellectual giants and models of conscience.

Gradually, Yeltsin and his clique came to prefer Vladimir Vladimirovich Putin. In his memoirs, Yeltsin wrote that as early as 1997, the year Putin moved to Moscow, he had his eye on him. Yeltsin was "amazed by Putin's lightning reflexes." The president had the feeling that "this young . . . man was ready for absolutely anything in life, he would respond to any challenge clearly and distinctly." In this case, Putin's relative youth (he was then 45) seemed to matter to Yeltsin, who must have felt that Russia needed dynamism rather than stabilization. If Yeltsin is to be believed, he did not dare propose the unknown Putin while Primakov retained his influence, and so he used Stepashin as a buffer between Primakov and the real heir. But most likely it was not that complicated—the Kremlin Family was still vacillating over its choice.

In his narrative, Yeltsin paints himself as savvy and sharp, in control of the process, picking out candidates and rejecting others, elaborating on the consequences of his choices. Reality was more pathetic: Yeltsin would never have quit his post and never have looked for an heir if he had been in command.

Stepashin was not fated to be the successor. But he did not know that. He threw himself into his role as prime minister with total sincerity. He even tried to form his cabinet, rejecting advice from the Kremlin. What unforgivable carelessness! He failed to understand that to survive in his position he had to lie low. Even more important, the Kremlin wasn't sure that Stepashin would protect his benefactors. So, on August 9, less than three months after his appointment, Stepashin was sent packing in the most humiliating manner.[9] The Kremlin was in a hurry. The entourage must not have been certain how long Yeltsin would last. It was time to present the real heir to the public. By early August, the main candidate for successor had been selected.[10] The game of prime ministerial poker was drawing to a close.

Vladimir Vladimirovich Putin appeared on the national stage unexpectedly. The political class as well as the public was surprised to see him, but everyone was so exhausted by the moves leading up to this that the new holder of the prime minister's office roused no opposition. He was seen as just one more premier in a long line, most likely an accidental figure. No one realized that this was the true heir. The unlikely choice and Putin's personality lulled suspicions. Many people simply paid no attention to him or considered his appointment something of a joke.

Who was this Mr. Nobody? He was a KGB officer who had served in East Germany. It wasn't clear what he had done there—gathered intelligence or spied on his fellow citizens. Putin retired in the rank of colonel, which meant that he had not had a brilliant career in the KGB. The Fates then made him a close aide of the liberal mayor of Saint Petersburg, Anatoly Sobchak. The trajectory—from the special service to the liberals—was not at all unusual in the early post-Soviet era; Putin's predecessor as prime minister, the short-lived Stepashin, had followed the same course in reverse. During Yeltsin's presidency, many people performed extraordinary somersaults, moving from camp to camp and rising to and falling from power.

Having become Sobchak's shadow, Putin turned into an effective manager. His relationship with his boss is exceptionally significant in understanding his future ascendancy. Putin proved he could be loyal and faithful and showed that allegiance to bosses and friends was extremely important to him. He followed the rules and could be relied on. The latter, we admit, was and still is a rare quality for Russian politicians and managers. Putin behaved decently toward the people with whom he had ties and to whom he was obligated. He quit his job immediately after Sobchak lost the gubernatorial election in July 1996, even though he could have stayed on working for the new governor of Saint Petersburg, Vladimir Yakovlev. After Putin managed to move to Moscow and unexpectedly jumped up the career ladder when Yeltsin appointed him director of the FSB, he demonstrated his loyalty to his former boss one more time. But more about that later.

Outwardly, Putin was an unexpected choice for a leader: hardly good-looking, rather short, with an inexpressive face and an awkward manner in public. He certainly was not charismatic. Next to the tall and powerfully built Yeltsin, he looked like a boy. He did not belong to the Yeltsin entourage—he was merely in its orbit to execute orders. Putin never pushed himself forward, keeping to the sidelines. In the beginning, he appeared shy and withdrawn. He was definitely not a public figure. Even the most sophisticated Kremlinologist was unlikely to see in him the future ruler of Russia. He was faceless and bland, either by nature or by training as an intelligence officer who had been taught not to stand out. There was nothing memorable about him except for his interest in the martial art of judo; that suggested he was not as simple as he seemed but possessed an inner strength and hidden ambitions.

When Yeltsin asked Putin whether he was prepared to become prime minister, he replied at once, according to Yeltsin in *Presidential Marathon*, in the military manner: "I'll work wherever you assign me." The answer pleased Yeltsin. On August 16, 1999, the Duma confirmed Putin as prime minister. The confirmation went smoothly precisely because no one took Putin seriously. Many saw his appointment as a sign that the Kremlin was giving up the power struggle. Luzhkov and Primakov must have been pleased with Yeltsin's choice—inconspicuous and shallow-looking Putin certainly did not seem to be a serious threat to their presidential ambitions. What poor judgment on the part of those old-timers in politics!

In his memoirs, Yeltsin goes on about his affection for his successor. Here is how Yeltsin (or the author who ghostwrote Yeltsin's memoirs) describes Putin: "Putin has very interesting eyes. It seems that they say more than his words. . . . I had the feeling . . . that this man, young by my standards, was absolutely ready for everything in life, and could respond to any challenge." However, the declarations of love in Yeltsin's book, which was published after Putin became president, are more likely an attempt by the Yeltsin Family to keep Putin in their embrace, to explain publicly that he had been their choice, and to impress on him that he owes them for it.

It wasn't Putin's eyes and precise answers that convinced Yeltsin to make him his final choice. Something about the man—in his behavior, in his life experience—encouraged Yeltsin and his closest associates to entrust him not only with the country but with their lives. After a long and tortuous selection process involving the testing of numerous pretenders to the throne, the ruling team saw in Vladimir Vladimirovich something that made it believe he would not sell them out, that they could trust him and be assured of their future. And they had ample reason to worry about the future—because of the allegations of corruption, because they had acquired many enemies, because they were blamed for all the country's ills.

One event in Putin's life could have reassured them significantly in this regard. Putin helped Anatoly Sobchak, his former boss, who was suspected of abuse of power and corruption in Saint Petersburg, to get to Paris secretly. That saved Sobchak from a trial and perhaps from being thoroughly discredited if he had been found guilty of misdeeds. Getting Sobchak into France was a military operation that involved the special services, a chartered plane, and the covering of tracks. In Paris, Sobchak was probably under the protection of Putin's agency. To put it baldly, Putin used his position as head of the FSB to help a witness and potential suspect escape justice. Yeltsin considered that a good deed; he had "great respect" for the man who would do such a thing, he said in his memoirs. Here we have a window into the way both the former and current Russian presidents relate to the law. The Sobchak story must have convinced Yeltsin and his entourage that Putin would not give them up, even if it endangered his career.

Sobchak died unexpectedly on February 1, 2000, after his former assistant had already become the Kremlin boss. Putin attended his funeral and did not hide his tears from the television cameras. One could see that he was not acting; he was sincerely grieving over the death of his boss. Russia saw that the new leader was humane, and his behavior struck a chord in Russians' hearts. In some way that could not have been predicted, Putin succeeded not only in being accepted by the ruling Family but in being liked by society as well.

Putin confirmed his capacity for loyalty in the spring of 1999, when he defended Yeltsin during his conflict with then–prosecutor general Yuri Skuratov. At that time, a great many elites had turned their backs on Yeltsin, and it looked as if the president was about to be toppled. It was then that Putin first appeared in the spotlight, playing the role of Skuratov's exposer in order to defend the president.[11] Putin burned his bridges, taking Yeltsin's side at a time when even Yeltsin's staunchest supporters were distancing themselves from the Kremlin (partly because Yeltsin was playing dirty). The ruling Family saw then that Putin could be trusted, that one could rely on him.

The most important argument in Vladimir Putin's favor as Yeltsin's successor was that he was completely obligated to Yeltsin for his advancement. Putin had nothing of his own—no supporters, no charisma, no ideology, no popularity, no experience—nothing that made him an independent figure. He had been created by the people around Yeltsin; naturally they expected gratitude and allegiance from him.

There may, however, have been other circumstances in Putin's life history that guaranteed his dependence on his creators. We can only speculate about what those could be, but a heftier security deposit than Putin's promises of fidelity must have been required by Yeltsin's people. That, however, is only a guess; there is no proof for it. Though there were obvious cynical reasons for this choice of successor, Yeltsin may still have considered Putin—a man who had a liberal period in his past and who belonged to a younger generation—someone who could carry on his work.

The appointed heir had time to prove his loyalty not only to Yeltsin and his Family but to some of the leading oligarchs as well. Boris Berezovsky recalled later: "Primakov intended to put me in prison. It was my wife's birthday. . . . And quite unexpectedly, Putin came to the party. He came and said, 'I don't care in the least what Primakov will think of me. I feel that this is right at this moment.'" That act of Putin's, when Berezovsky's fate was uncertain, can be seen as evidence either of Putin's human decency—supporting a person he knew who was in trouble—or of his pragmatism—supporting a person who still had enormous influence. Most likely the episode showed that Putin was capable of devotion to people with whom he had been thrown together. Putin came to a party hosted by a man who might have ended up in jail; in other words, Putin clearly was no coward. However, he might have known that Primakov's days were numbered and he could safely visit. If Putin only knew that Berezovsky would soon become his worst enemy!

That Putin had no political ties but did have roots in the power structures was important for the ruling team. It was better, the team reasoned, to have military protection during the volatile period when Yeltsin disengaged and the successor took over. That Putin had no ties to any political group was a plus in the new Russia, for it might mean that no interest group had claims on him. And that the final candidate for the role of successor had no political past at least guaranteed that, as a completely new face, he had not yet bored his audience. The absence of ideological engagement made it possible for the ruling team to shape Putin's image in whatever way they desired. Thus he could be presented as a liberal, a conservative, or a patriot.

However, for the new premier—barely known outside the Moscow Ring Road—to be taken seriously as Russia's leader, there had to be a perceived need among the Russian public that Putin would step in to fill. The need was clear after the financial crash of 1998 and from the moment Primakov took office. Weak Russia needed a strong state and a leader with a tough image who was ready to stop the rot. Ironically, at just the same time, in August 1999, an international scandal broke that gave yet more impetus to Russia's move toward a stronger rule. The Bank of New York was implicated in the alleged laundering of $4.2 billion from Russia.[12] Russian government officials and people close to them allegedly played a role in the money laundering as well. The world press made Russian money and Russian corruption the top story of the day.

The Bank of New York scandal violently upset ruling circles in Russia. It was one thing for law enforcement authorities in tiny Switzerland or even Italy to suspect high officials and members of the Yeltsin Family of laundering money and taking bribes. It was quite another when the secret services of the United Kingdom and the United States fastened on the idea. The scandal widened, leading to hearings in the U.S. Congress, the threat of sanctions against Russian businesses, and the possibility of investigations into the financial dealings of Russian politicians.

The passions and fears loosed by the scandal increased the feeling of vulnerability among Russia's elites.[13] Some elites who had engaged in dubious activities and financial manipulations and who had been involved in illegal deals now realized that they could lose the safe harbors they had prepared in Western countries, to which many of them had already sent their families. Now they were forced to deal with their own survival inside Russia. A strong leader who could defend their interests was what they urgently needed.

At the height of the uproar over money laundering, evidence of fresh scandal created a sensation: the credit cards reportedly provided by the Swiss company Mabetex to Yeltsin and members of his family.[14] The Russian president, who until then had kept silent, called U.S. president Bill Clinton with just one aim: to deny the allegations about his and other family members' "Swiss connections." Evidently, Yeltsin really cared what kind of reputation he had in the West. But why did he and his family need credit cards from Mabetex? They had an enormous country at their disposal.

Meanwhile, the anxiety of the political class was not enough to create a mandate for a "strong-arm" regime in Russia; the masses needed to feel the need for a new and authoritarian rule as well. An occasion quickly arose: the invasion of the Russian republic of Dagestan by separatists from neighboring Chechnya on August 2, 1999. The separatists supposedly took advantage of the confusion in Russian political life to attempt to create a radical Wahhabite Islamic state in Chechnya and adjacent regions. But by a strange coincidence, they attacked Dagestan when preparations were already under way in Moscow for a transfer of power. And why didn't Moscow stop the invasion? Why did the Russian power ministries calmly watch the open massing of armed separatists in border regions? Moreover, a brigade of Interior Ministry troops that had been protecting the border between Chechnya and Dagestan was quickly removed just before the invasion.

Some Russian journalists wrote openly that people close to the Kremlin, primarily Berezovsky, might have pushed the Chechen fighters to attack Dagestan to increase the Russian people's sense of vulnerability and pave the way for a change of rule.[15] "Why did Chechnya happen before Yeltsin's reelection? Why is there now Dagestan before these elections?" asked the magazine *Profil'* on August 30, referring to the parliamentary elections scheduled for December. "Who ordered a war in Dagestan, and why?"[16]

In any other country, such questions would have called for court hearings and a mass firing of officials. But in Russia they were merely shrugged off. Such is the effect of living with continual scandals, and of the still-powerful ingrained fear of the authorities.

The Chechen invasion prompted in Russian citizens the very feelings that are vital for the formation of a new type of order—fear and a sense of vulnerability. The next month, August 1999, several residential buildings in Moscow and other Russian cities were blown up, killing about 300 civilians and sending shock waves throughout the country.[17] The explosions put society in a mood that could be described as demanding a "strong hand." In September, just after the blasts, Russian citizens considered "personal safety" a higher priority (40 versus 28 percent) than "social guarantees"—a major issue after the loss of the Soviet social security net that had previously obsessed them. "Crime" and "instability" topped the list of concerns (47 and 46 percent, respectively). Even before opening an investigation, the Kremlin announced that there was a "Chechen trace" in the crimes. Police began rounding up anyone who looked remotely Chechen. The terrorists, however, were never found, which gave rise to suspicion about the involvement of Russian secret services in the explosions.

The conspiracy theory is too simple an explanation for the watershed change in Russian public opinion. In the confusion that reigned in Russia, with the constant leaks of information from the top, even the secret services would have had difficulty carrying out such an operation without leaving many clues and witnesses behind. In any case, there are no secrets in today's Russia—all that is hidden is revealed sooner or later. But at the same time, we must admit that to this day there are no satisfactory answers to numerous questions stemming from that period. Nor does one sense any desire by the Kremlin to conduct a thorough investigation of the events that would lead to the capture of the perpetrators, thereby putting an end to all the rumors.[18]

The prime minister lost no time showing himself to be a strong and powerful politician. Speaking to the Duma after the explosions, Putin described the challenge facing Russia: "In blowing up the houses of our fellow citizens, the bandits are blowing up the state. They are undermining authority—not of the president, city, or Duma. But of authority per se." He stated that his goal was "to defend the population from bandits." He said what millions of citizens expected of a leader. When he spoke from the podium of the Duma, the Russian audience finally saw what it wanted—a determined, willful face, the springy walk of an athlete, and . . . very cold eyes. Many decided that a man with eyes like that had to be strong. And a majority of Russians wanted a strong man in the Kremlin. They were tired of watching Yeltsin fall apart.

Having done nothing yet except declare his determination, Putin received mass support from the main forces in Russian society. The accumulated fears, the disarray, the feeling of being in danger, and the very real Russian "Weimar syndrome" all pushed people toward a longing for order and a new face in the Kremlin. The sociologist Yuri Levada wrote in the last edition of *Moskovskie novosti* of 1999: "No researchers had ever seen Russian society in this state. . . . All the fears and passions that had been biding their time came to the surface and the hidden layer of our consciousness was exposed."

All the feelings that had been stored away in people's minds during the years of Yeltsin's administration now surged up as disillusionment and yet also hope for change. But that hope was reflected mainly in the search for a new leader, not in a demand to break the pattern of personalistic rule. In their mass longing for security and order, it seemed that Russians would have supported any new face as long as it appeared confident and was not that of a human wreck. Youth and dynamism were what Russians wanted in a president, and that in itself was a positive break with the tradition of declining and impotent leaders.

———————— ❧ ————————

The blasts in Russian cities were the final straw that rendered retaliatory action in Chechnya inevitable. On September 30, 1999, federal troops entered Chechnya. Large-scale war began. It was a civil war where victory is impossible and what is considered victory can easily turn to defeat. Because the military actions were labeled "antiterrorist operations," no approval from the upper chamber of the parliament, the Federation Council, or declaration of a state of emergency in Chechnya was required. Thus the war was conducted outside the framework of legality. Whatever political expediency demanded could be done unhampered in Chechnya.

Whereas in early 1999 only a madman would have contemplated a new war in the Northern Caucasus, by autumn the second Chechen war had helped unite Russian society, soothing Russians' vulnerability complex. The operation against Chechnya had been prepared under Primakov and Stepashin, but as a limited action against Chechen terrorists and criminal elements. The plan was to move the army to the Terek River to create a buffer zone between the pro-Russian and separatist regions of Chechnya, and also to mount surgical strikes on terrorist bases.

Why did Russian troops cross the Terek and go into the territory beyond? Why did the military begin mass bombing in Chechnya, leading to thousands of casualties among civilians and the creation of tens of thousands of refugees? We know that Russian generals wanted revenge for their humiliation at the hands of a small number of poorly armed fighters in the first Chechen war. Perhaps they managed to convince Putin to pursue the war to its end and were certain of victory. Perhaps Putin himself wanted that. What is known is that the prime minister himself proposed the initiative of the "antiterrorist operation." He did not hide it. Reporters once asked him, "Then the entire responsibility (for Chechnya) is yours?" He replied: "To a great degree that is so. I told myself: I have a certain amount of time—two, three, four months—to shatter those bandits. And then, they can fire me."[19] But did he know what the operation in Chechnya would be like? Once it began, it was too late to change his decision; he was hostage to the new war and the generals' ambitions.

The majority of Russians considered the first Chechen war criminal. Now it was considered criminal not to support the military crusade in Chechnya. Thus in January 1995, 54 percent of those polled wanted Russian troops pulled out of Chechnya (27 percent supported the troops' presence there, and 19 percent had no opinion). By contrast, in November and December 1999, between 61 and 70 percent of those polled approved of the operation in Chechnya. Even after the substantial losses in Chechnya became known—including thousands killed and wounded among the Russian army and civilians—in July 2000, 70 percent of respondents felt that there should be no negotiating in Chechnya but that order should be imposed on the republic with the help of the army.

After the military attack on Chechnya began, Putin no longer needed to continue the difficult struggle for power. All he had to do was point to the enemy, who were Chechens, naturally. War lifted him to the peak of the political Olympus.

Other circumstances guaranteed Putin's move to real power. First among these was the quite effective game played by the Kremlin. The people who constituted Yeltsin's political circle were not political geniuses. When threatened, however, they succeeded in finding a mechanism for their survival, which was not at all sophisticated but which worked, at least for the time being. The ruling team managed to restore control over power resources and, at least partially, over society's moods by working on people's darkest fears and ratcheting up the desire for stability at any price. Chechnya turned out to be a good excuse for consolidation because it served simultaneously as an internal and an external enemy.

After August 1999, the widespread desire for security in Russian society in effect led to consolidation Soviet-style. The planned, albeit crude, manipulation of public opinion by the state-run mass media aided the reimposition of central control. But it is important to acknowledge that many Russians at that particular moment acquiesced in and perhaps were relieved by the turn back to the old and familiar pattern of rule. They had been through lifetimes of change in a dozen years. Russian society, cut off from its traditions, uncertain of the future, disoriented and helpless, was stuck between floors in the elevator of history—between past and future. The weary, disillusioned post-Soviet citizen could find in the return to clear-cut decisions, authoritarian style, and the search for the enemy a bit of calm and comfort, if only temporarily.

To ensure Putin's ascension, the Kremlin now needed to clear the field of his main opponents, Luzhkov and Primakov, who had created their own political movements, Fatherland and All-Russia. (The two had put off working out their relationship and deciding who would be the leading challenger for the spot in the Kremlin.) The Kremlin killed Luzhkov and Primakov politically through a dirty campaign in the state-run media, pressure on members of the opposition, and bribery of members of their movements. The demoralized political class quickly reoriented itself, focusing on the strongest player: the Kremlin, once again. The habit of obeying central power reasserted itself, as those who had sworn fealty to Luzhkov and Primakov yesterday were bowing today to the Kremlin's new appointee. It was frustrating to watch the journalists, analysts, advisers, and plain hangers-on who only recently had crowded around Primakov and the Moscow mayor. Some of them vanished from the political scene. Others ran next door and began seeking access to Putin.

At last, the relevant Russian officials realized how important television is for politics. In the 1996 presidential campaign, the people at Russian television had just been learning how to manipulate public opinion, crafting an image of an active leader out of the ailing Yeltsin. Now television had become the primary political ax for destroying Putin's opponents. Sergei Dorenko, a well-known news anchor on state television, was assigned the task of demoralizing Luzhkov and Primakov. Behind Dorenko was Berezovsky, one of the shareholders of the state television's Channel 1. Every Saturday night in prime time, Dorenko poured another load of filth on the Kremlin's rivals. He accused Luzhkov of many and varied crimes: His wife transferred money outside the country, he was a thief, he had been party to the murder of an American businessman. Luzhkov couldn't wash it off fast enough. Once he finished with Luzhkov, Dorenko moved on to Primakov, using every means possible to paint him as a sick old man. The place for him wasn't the Kremlin but a retirement home, was the message on state television.

The Kremlin, using all its resources to destroy the opposition, deliberately forgot about the Communists, according them favored status. The battle among similar species was more vicious than the one between different species. The Kremlin's equanimity toward the Communist Party had a definite goal. The Yeltsin–Putin team needed a good showing by the Communists in the upcoming parliamentary and presidential elections, so that Gennady Zyuganov would be Putin's main rival. That guaranteed Putin's victory. The ruling team wanted to use again the strategy it had employed successfully in the 1996 elections, when the fact that Communist candidate Zyuganov was the main competition facing him helped Yeltsin stay in power. Left with the alternatives of the Communist past or an indefinite future with a sick leader, Russia had chosen the second option. So this time the Kremlin was even prepared to support Zyuganov, both materially and organizationally, to keep him around as the only opponent. The Kremlin team did not show much imagination, but at that moment they did not need it to have their way with the demoralized Russian electorate.

During an amazingly short period of time in the autumn of 1999, the spectrum of Russian political life shifted radically. Back in the summer, the political class would have supported Primakov as Yeltsin's successor. Society was ready then to accept an elderly, extremely cautious leader and to endorse the constitutional amendments that would have created a strong cabinet and an influential parliament. In the autumn, society and the political class, seeming to forget Primakov's existence, turned to the young unknown whose very appearance symbolized strict order and harsh personal rule.

In other words, it became clear that the Russian mindset was still flexible and unformed and could be controlled. Political institutions meant nothing. A few people in the Kremlin controlling all state resources determined the fate of the presidency and the enormous country along with it. Employing blatant manipulation and pressure, they changed the characters, sets, and content of the play. The preceding period of Yeltsin upsets had beaten down society sufficiently that it readily agreed to participate in the show the Kremlin was proposing.

The public observed this with calm resignation, even though the Kremlin intrigue was primitive and obvious. Why did Russia accept the humiliating spectacle unfolding before its eyes? Perhaps it was another manifestation of Russian fatalism—you can't do anything about it, you can't fight city hall. Only a small group of intellectuals and journalists protested. But who paid any attention? That the president's clique was appointing a successor and few people were surprised or shocked—on the contrary, most people found it natural—was telling. It showed either that the tradition of autocracy still lived or that Russians did not care much about the political regime, having become convinced that they would find ways to survive under any form of rule. And a lot of people had already come to like the new candidate for the throne.

At that moment at the end of 1999, the small steps Putin was taking as the new prime minister, especially his reliance on the state apparatus, could be interpreted as a return to the Soviet past—without communism, but with Communists. There was a sense of déjà vu. But it was too soon to draw final conclusions about the essence of the new regime. After all, Putin's life had included the Saint Petersburg period with the liberal Anatoly Sobchak, which could not and cannot be discounted. It remained to be seen how Putin coupled Soviet habits and a KGB background with the liberal principles acquired in Saint Petersburg.

The new premier had a positive reception from the country in the last months of 1999, and his ratings rose quickly. According to the All-Russian Center for Public Opinion Research (hereafter VTsIOM), in October, 65 percent approved of Putin's policies, compared with 52 percent in September and 33 percent in August. Their poll at the end of November found that 29 percent of respondents would vote for Putin for president, whereas 17 percent were for Zyuganov and 13 percent for Primakov. It became clear before the Duma elections in December that the Luzhkov–Primakov "second party of power" had no chance of success.

As for the Chechen war, in November 1999, 48 percent of Russians supported Putin's "antiterrorist operation" (29 percent demanded even harsher policies toward Chechnya, and only 7 percent thought excessive force unjustified). For the first time in many years—at least since Gorbachev came to power—Russian society had returned to the saving idea of military patriotism, which became the refuge of all in Russia who feared and who felt vulnerable.

Even the liberals joined the war camp. "Today in Chechnya it is not the question of Chechnya that is being decided, but an incomparably more important question—today in Chechnya the Russian army is being reborn," announced Anatoly Chubais, leader of the liberals and a recent favorite of the West, in November 1999. After the West accused Russia of human rights violations in Chechnya, Chubais flung back an accusation: "I consider the position taken by the West as a whole ... on Chechnya to be immoral. I consider the position of the West dishonest." Thus a leading liberal and friend of the West suddenly turned anti-Western. Well, he wanted to survive. A politician who had been considered brave and principled turned out to be weak and conformist. He could have believed what he was saying, though; many such do.

On November 14, 1999, Yeltsin publicly embraced Putin and confirmed once again that he was "the only choice for Russia." There were almost no doubts left about the scenario Russia would follow. The successor was already appointed. But the new leader still had to be tested by election—first the parliamentary elections, then the election for president.

The old resources for the legitimation of power in Russia—through the "leading party," Marxist ideology, blatant coercion—had been exhausted. The Kremlin gang turned to elections. The role of elections in Russia was now clear: They had become a mechanism for supporting the appointed monarch. Only the unexpected could stop Putin's path to the Kremlin.

Chapter 2

THE END OF
THE YELTSIN ERA

———————— ✠ ————————

The parliamentary elections of 1999. The difficult fate of Russian liberals.
The Communist Party as a still powerful element. Yeltsin amazes
everyone and departs. What Yeltsin leaves to his heir.

Elections for the Third State Duma, the lower house of the Russian parliament—the bicameral Federal Assembly—took place on December 19, 1999.[1] For Putin and the other candidates who would compete three months later in the presidential election, the parliamentary contests were akin to primaries. Not long before the balloting, to neutralize their main opponents—the Luzhkov–Primakov alliance—and to create a base in the new parliament, the Kremlin formed, in a matter of a few weeks, a movement it called Unity (or Medved, for the bear that was its symbol). One of the leading organizers of the pro-Kremlin movement was Boris Berezovsky, a media oligarch with an inexhaustible supply of ideas. It was Berezovsky who traveled to the regions and persuaded governors to support the Kremlin movement rather than the OVR (Fatherland and All-Russia) Party of Luzhkov and Primakov.

That Berezovsky—who had helped oversee the demoralization and degradation of power under Yeltsin—was one of the main people smoothing the way for Putin, Yeltsin's chosen successor, colored the undertaking, which was meant to guarantee the continuation of Russia's pattern of rule and ruling team. All of Yeltsin's Family was actively engaged in preparing for the victory of its heir: exerting pressure on the media, seeking the support of oligarchs and governors, collecting *compromat* (a Russian term for

44

compromising materials) on possible rivals. This aggressive campaign in support of Putin might mean that reciprocity on the part of the next Kremlin boss was anticipated. Could the artificially created new leader escape his puppet-masters, who included Yeltsin's daughter Tatyana and her close associates? It was natural to assume that in his desire to legitimize his power, Putin would be unlikely to tolerate his creators or any mention of those who pulled the strings. It all depended on what bound them together and to what degree Putin depended on the Yeltsin Family. It also depended on how strong, determined, and willful the new leader would be.

At first, very few people believed in the attempt to create a new Kremlin party. How could such an undertaking be serious—organizing a new movement, without even the most elementary program, just a few months before the elections? But gradually the idea was given material expression. People supposed to embody muscular force were named leaders of the new Unity movement: minister of emergency situations Sergei Shoigu; world champion wrestler Alexander Karelin; and General Alexander Gurov, who, being in the Ministry of Internal Affairs, fought the Russian mafia. It was a simple-minded public relations game, waving the heroic, macho images of rescuer, wrestler, good cop. Those images were chosen to resonate with the average Russian in need of protection and security in these uncertain times. The three types would be seen as honest and straightforward guys, salt of the earth. And they would generate excitement, however bogus. Thus its creators manufactured the movement that would serve as the base for Putin and his regime.

Among the first to join Unity were the governors who were not on good terms with the law, including Kursk governor Alexander Rutskoi, Primorye governor Alexander Nazdratenko, and Kaliningrad governor Leonid Gorbenko. The Bears also got support from regions that totally depended on Kremlin subsidies. In short, the new movement attracted dependent people and people with murky reputations.

Unity was a virtual creation. Right up to the elections, it had no ideology and no structures. It was a ghost movement. I remember the early meetings of the Bears; the nondescriptness was astonishing. One could have gotten the impression that previous political waves had exhausted the country's intellectual potential and left the Bears with the refuse of the political process. These new types of politicians shared, however, one amusing characteristic: self-confidence. They did not pretend to have wise thoughts or ideas or even ambition. They wanted only to be Putin's supporters and were sure this would guarantee them victory in the upcoming elections and afterward some role within the Kremlin network.

Of course, the creators of the Kremlin party did not need many vivid personalities or experienced politicians; they needed an obedient mass. Putin became Unity's platform and compensated for the lack of other party planks. The Bears had one shining hope: to take to the political stage on the coattails of the new leader. Their party was the latest refuge for the state apparatus that had managed to adjust and survive in every regime—from Stalin, Khrushchev, Brezhnev, and Gorbachev to Yeltsin. Now it was prepared to serve a new leader without even knowing which way he would turn.

But the new "party" could become a real power only on the condition that Putin supported it openly. He vacillated until November 24, 1999, when he declared that he would support Unity "as a citizen and friend of Sergei Shoigu," one of its leaders. Things fell into place—the new structure, still fleshless and amorphous, was perceived as "the party of Putin." In late October, Unity's approval rating was below 4 percent (according to VTsIOM, which is headed by a well-known sociologist, Yuri Levada), but by late November it had already climbed to 19 percent. The party quickly took on people who sensed an opportunity to be catapulted into power.

Simultaneously, Putin made an approving gesture—albeit a more restrained one—toward the newly formed Union of Right Forces (the SPS, established in August 1999).[2] Several liberals—Yegor Gaidar, Sergei Kiriyenko, Boris Nemtsov, and Irina Khakamada—headed the Union, but the real leader and financier was Anatoly Chubais, the "privatization tsar." Chubais and Putin had a difficult and controversial relationship: The usually aggressive Chubais, accustomed to having his own way, now had to be cautious in dealing with Putin—who hardly needed such a powerful and ambitious figure around.

For Putin, supporting Unity and maintaining a condescendingly approving attitude toward the Union of Right Forces was a bold step. If those two movements lost the parliamentary elections, Putin would likely vanish from the political arena and Yeltsin would have to find a new heir. Putin decided to go for broke. It was a risk, but the whole plan of bringing a new man without political experience to power was a risk.

The Kremlin administration swung into gear behind Putin's candidacy. It organized an active campaign against OVR and Grigory Yavlinsky's Yabloko, the political blocs sponsoring alternative presidential candidates. The goal was obvious: to destroy these blocs with a centrist and democratic agenda in the parliamentary elections and thus cripple their candidates in the presidential election. Yeltsin's team wanted to guarantee Putin's victory.

The Kremlin put extreme pressure on Russia's governors to give up Luzhkov and Primakov, Putin's major opponents. The regional leaders preferred not to resist the Kremlin and quickly left the ranks of OVR. Some regional barons proved miracles of flexibility, having spent time in every pro-Kremlin movement that functioned under Yeltsin—Yegor Gaidar's Russia's Choice, Democratic Russia's Choice, and Victor Chernomyrdin's Our Home Is Russia. After their temporary halt with OVR, they switched to Unity as if on signal.

The results of the December 1999 balloting for the parliament confirmed that Russian democracy was fully or nearly fully controllable. As a result of the Kremlin's machinations, Unity received 23 percent and the SPS, which had jumped on the "Putin train" in time, also got good results—9 percent of the vote. Those movements formed a solid base for Putin in the Duma. The Communist Party received less than usual—24 percent of the vote. OVR got 13 percent, the Zhirinovsky bloc 6 percent, and Yabloko 5 percent. They formed the following factions in the Duma: The Communists had 85 seats, its allied group the Agrarian-Industrial Bloc had 43, Unity had 83, Unity's ally the People's Deputy group had 56, the SPS had 32, OVR had 49, the progovernment group Russian Regions had 47, the Liberal Democrats had 12, and Yabloko had 17.

The other 21 seats were taken by independent deputies. (In the 1995 Duma, the Communists had a total of 157 seats; their Agrarian ally had 20; the progovernment Our Home Is Russia, predecessor of Unity and OVR, had 55; the Liberal Democrats had 51; Yabloko had 45; and Democratic Choice of Russia, predecessor of the SPS, had 9. The rest of the seats were divided among smaller factions.) This unique primary showed that Putin had a good chance of winning the presidential election: Votes for pro-Kremlin Unity and the SPS were in fact votes for a new leader.

The "antiterrorist campaign" in Chechnya that had begun in September and been embraced by the majority of Russians had a profound effect on the vote, because Unity and the SPS were its two biggest backers among the competing parties. An article in the liberal magazine *Itogi* on December 23 went further: "The Duma election campaign of 1999 enriched Russian political science with one indisputable revolutionary discovery: A large-scale military operation, it turns out, can be cold-bloodedly used as an election technique."

With strong Unity, People's Deputy, Russian Regions, and SPS factions in the new Duma for the first time, a Kremlin leader had strong support in the parliament, which had given Yeltsin no breathing room. The weakening of OVR–All-Russia, which had constructed grand plans in the summer, almost automatically meant the final defeat of Primakov, Putin's main rival in the struggle for the Kremlin. The Russian political class had made its choice in the Duma elections, and it was for Putin. The Primakov–Luzhkov faction in the Duma soon joined the Kremlin camp. Russian centrists were not ready for independent life; they needed a shadow of power to survive. In the end, they would start competing with Putin's Unity for the role of the faction most loyal to the president.

After some thought, Primakov dropped out of the presidential race, knowing he had no hope of winning. Later, he would throw his support to Putin and become a frequent visitor of the new leader. And in truth, why should he have stayed in the opposition once Putin began realizing a philosophy of power that was quite close to Primakov's own? Besides, Primakov had always survived and thrived because he connected with all of Russia's rulers.[3]

The parliamentary elections also showed that it was too soon to bury the Russian Communist Party, which had lost some of its influence but remained a powerful force. In the course of the Yeltsin years of development, the Communist Party had evolved into a fixture of the Russian System that helped preserve stability. The Communists kept the protest voters from overreacting. They also compromised with the Kremlin team at key moments. In exchange, they got a few things that helped satisfy the groups that supported them. The Kremlin always took care of the interests of the agrarian lobby, the military-industrial complex, and the regions that supported the Communist Party.

Yeltsin's successor was inheriting a fully formed left-wing opposition that had demonstrated its unwillingness to undermine the presidential regime. The Communist Party had accepted the rules dictated by the ruling team, confirming that it was no longer interested in a serious struggle for the Kremlin and would settle for the role of eternal opposition. This was convenient and not dangerous. So the Communists, once elements of the Yeltsin regime, easily fit into the Putin regime. Of course, a postcommunist system in which the Communist Party is an important element is a paradox. But it was not the only paradox in the new Russia.

Another paradox was that the Communists, despite losing some of their local administrative support, increased their voter base. It was not only pensioners who were casting their ballots for Gennady Zyuganov's party—which was the major residue of the Soviet past and ironically the most influential party in postcommunist Russia—but also doctors, teachers, and military personnel disillusioned with the reforms of the last dozen years. Such people were voting not for communism but for a more socially oriented policy. And because social stresses were unlikely to decrease in the near future, the left wing of the political spectrum would not shrink either.

It was also possible that under the influence of its new base—because there was no other alternative to the Kremlin—the Communist Party might move toward real, rather than rhetorical, opposition to the Kremlin. But with the same leaders as in the Soviet past, the Communists hardly could have become a constructive force in Russia, as did former communist parties in Eastern and Central Europe.

The very existence of an eternal opposition in the form of the Communist Party, which preserved a large measure of Sovietism and antiliberalism, increased the odds against the appearance of another opposition force in Russia, including democratic alternatives. With the Communist Party as the main opposition, the authorities could pretend they were running a liberal democracy, though in reality the government was not fully liberal and hardly democratic. The Communists helped the administration maintain a liberal image. Without the Communist Party, neither Chubais nor Gaidar, much less Putin, could have pretended to fill the liberal niche.

The liberals who had come together within the framework of the Union of Right Forces, the SPS, found themselves in a difficult position after the Duma elections. The SPS had managed to unite a large part of the reformist electorate (taking a portion of Yabloko's supporters) and had hoped to become a serious ally of Putin, if not the leading one.[4] Putin, however, did not feel obligated to the liberals, and apparently did not want to depend on anyone at all. In that, he followed the Yeltsin tradition. After the Duma elections, Putin openly ignored the SPS liberals, while making a deal with the Communists in which they divided up the Duma committee posts. Putin also supported Communist Gennady Seleznev for speaker of the lower house.

With these actions, Putin showed that ideology was not an important consideration for him; he would stick with pure pragmatism. At this point, the president's aim was to get the loyalty of the parliament, where the majority of members were from leftist and centrist groups. Putin was not worried about the sentiments of the SPS members. He was sure they would not dare create resistance and would come to accept the situation. The SPS leaders did in fact swallow their pride, and in the presidential election three months later they again supported Putin.

The leaders of the SPS, primarily Chubais and former prime minister Kiriyenko, unconditionally endorsed Putin's policy in Chechnya and his leanings toward statism. Kiriyenko—attempting to justify himself and his fellow liberals while seeking a place in the new government structures— formulated the new credo of the Russian right, replete with theoretical constructions, in the April 14, 2000, *Kommersant-Daily*.

Kiriyenko defined the new liberalism as "liberalism of lifestyle." The old version, which he termed "liberalism of outlook," had become obsolete, he insisted. Russian liberalism, he said, "is following the demands of the new generation," and the new generation is "the generation of statists and great power advocates." So the liberals should be thinking not about individuals, rights, and freedoms but about a strong state. The liberals can't oppose Putin's policy, argued the ideologue of new "liberalism." "What opposition, when there is no time left?" Kiriyenko would exclaim with feigned simplicity.

A majority of the Russian liberals united in the SPS considered their number one goal to be cooperation with the president and implementation of his policy. They proved yet again that economic priorities—the market and not democracy—were important to them. Several outspoken "liberals" (for example, Petr Aven) called on Putin to become the "Russian Pinochet," suggesting that only a dictatorship could continue the country's market reforms. Behind that simple idea was another, one more important for many supporters of the market and the oligarchs linked to them: They perceived authoritarianism and totalitarianism as the best means of protecting their positions from social backlash and from their rivals.

I remember the talk in Moscow during that period. Analysts asked one another who had gone to serve Putin and who was still waiting it out. Almost all the oligarchs and the majority of liberals who were close to privatization tsar Chubais had "lain down" under Putin. That was understandable, because the property and prosperity of the former depended exclusively on the government's attitude toward them. As for the latter, none of the leading liberals had martyrdom in mind in the fight for freedom and democracy. They were saved by the fact that Putin believed in the market; that allowed for minimal loss of face when they joined up with Unity and got jobs from the new leader.[5]

The majority of Russian liberals close to power were behaving like the technocrats in the bureaucratic-authoritarian regimes of Latin America, who were prepared to service even dictatorial regimes if they accomplished economic modernization. But the point is that in Russia, with the traditionally enormous role of the state apparatus and shadowy rules of the game, Russian liberals could become merely a front for a corrupt system. And they were too smart not to notice that.

A few SPS leaders, such as Boris Nemtsov and Irina Khakamada, seemed clearly uncomfortable with the new situation. They permitted themselves to make critical, albeit moderate, statements about the Kremlin policy. The "father" of Russian reforms, Yegor Gaidar, chose to stay silent, and that meant that he was also critical of the administration but preferred not to speak out. The dissatisfaction of individual liberals and their criticism of the Kremlin allowed them to preserve their influence on some part of the opposition groups within the society and even attempt the role of "constructive opposition" (later, SPS leaders invented the term "ruling opposition" in trying to justify their attempt to perform two mutually exclusive roles simultaneously).

Some Russian observers believed that SPS leaders intentionally divided up roles—Chubais and Kiriyenko usually praised the government and the president, while Nemtsov and some others criticized them—and in this way tried to keep incompatible parts of the electorate under the SPS's control. For the authorities' part, allowing mild venting by a dissatisfied minority that did not threaten them in any way helped them keep up a civilized image.

The SPS liberals, in their desire to be part of the government at any cost, were prepared to continue in the role of stabilizer that they had taken on during the Yeltsin administration. The SPS was in the same trap that Democratic Russia—the first Russian democratic movement formed in Gorbachev's time—had fallen into when it supported Yeltsin in his power struggles in the early 1990s. Democratic Russia, too, had tried to become the president's ally, hoping to get its share. But when Yeltsin ignored it, the movement accepted the role of unrequited ally, supporting the president despite it all.

Subsequently, the liberals of the second wave, united around Gaidar's Russia's Choice and, later, Democratic Russia's Choice, no longer made demands on Yeltsin, having become part of the government without preliminary conditions. They became an important element in Yeltsin's shadow spider web, initiating moderate reforms from time to time. Who will do it, if not us? the liberals in power asked. Ultimately they, like the Communists, became a stabilizing element of the regime. So Yeltsin's regime, now being passed on to the new leader, managed to rest on supposedly eternal and irreconcilable enemies—the SPS liberals and the Communists.

But in the final analysis, the stabilizing role of the SPS liberals within the framework of elected monarchy discredited the idea of liberal democracy. Moreover, the splintering of economic liberalism and democracy inevitably led to lawless, oligarchic capitalism; there simply could be no other kind of capitalism under such conditions, where economic freedom was not accompanied by political freedom and the rule of law, and economic freedom was limited by the manipulations of the state apparatus.

As for the only democratic (noncommunist) opposition to Putin—Yabloko—it lost more than 900,000 voters somewhere between the previous elections in 1995 and the 1999 elections. The Yabloko faction in the Duma dropped by more than half, from 45 seats in the old Duma to 17. Yabloko's defeat was the result of society's disillusionment with liberal democratic values. The movement paid for its defense of those values, including the antiwar stance of its leader, Grigory Yavlinsky. Part of Yavlinsky's base supported the war in Chechnya. Moreover, a large segment of liberal-thinking people preferred the SPS to Yabloko because, they said, "You can't keep on criticizing the government, you finally have to help the government." Yavlinsky replied to this, "If we start cooperating with an administration that will use us as cover, then we will annihilate ourselves"—and he was right. But the drama for Yabloko at that historic moment was that the niche for a democratic opposition was too narrow.

The weakening of Yabloko's influence reflected Russia's need for new forms combining the human rights movement with more constructive ways of influencing the administration. The small party of the intelligentsia, always in the opposition and never going to come to power, did not suit many ambitious people who regarded a political party as a trampoline for advancement. Besides which, the regime's consolidation around the idea of order, which appealed to society and elites, would of course not help to strengthen the opposition democratic alliance. Those who feared a new "iron fist" preferred to avoid criticizing the administration. People grew more cautious—the memory of Soviet times was too recent. Yeltsin's heir from the KGB was a reminder of Soviet repression and at the same time a factor that restrained political emotions. Russia's political arena was taking on a conformist look.

After Unity's victory in the parliamentary elections, Putin's drive to power was inexorable. But with society's unstable moods and the unpredictable nature of the Chechen war, there could be no firm guarantee of Putin's victory in June 2000, when Yeltsin's term ended. The authors of Project Putin who were at the core of Yeltsin's entourage—his daughter Tatyana, his adviser Valentin Yumashev, his presidential head of staff Alexander Voloshin, and their friends the oligarchs—worried that they might not be able to keep Putin's ratings high until June, that something could happen to spoil their plans. Putin had to be brought to power immediately.

———————— ✺ ————————

And here Yeltsin astonished the world—on December 31, 1999, when the whole country was celebrating the New Year, Russia's first president announced that he was retiring. Reading his statement to the people, he shed a tear. "I've made a decision," he said in the taped broadcast to the nation. "I've thought long and hard. Today, on the last day of the departing century, I am retiring. . . . I want to ask you all to forgive me. Because many of our dreams did not come to pass."

Yeltsin looked solemn and sentimental, even sad. New Year's Eve and the approaching new millennium turned out to be very suitable for the first postcommunist president's farewell. Russians at their festive tables with champagne glasses in hand were prepared to forgive their leader many things, including the empty promises Yeltsin so liked to make. Russians are not rancorous. The unexpected announcement did not shock the country, or cause major upset. "About time!" captures the reaction of most Russians to the Kremlin's New Year's present.[6] Yeltsin's retirement meant that Putin would be in charge of the Kremlin and Russia and of his own presidential elections. And the Kremlin need not have worried: No one tried to ruin the scenario, and no "strangers" had any pretensions to the throne.

Preparations for Yeltsin's departure resembled a secret military operation. Only a few tested and trusted people were in on it—those who had persuaded Yeltsin to make Putin his successor, first among them Tatyana. In his memoir, *Presidential Marathon,* Yeltsin, or his ghostwriters, tried to make it look as if the president himself had made the decision and had informed his entourage at the very last moment. "I didn't know anything until almost the last moment," Tatyana declared to *Kommersant-Daily.* But Yeltsin was in no condition to plan and carry out his resignation on his own. He was not the director, the producer, or the screenwriter of this performance. He was merely the aged star dressed in the tatters of his former charisma brought in to play his final part.

According to Yeltsin's book, the first conversation he had with Putin about him resigning and Putin becoming acting president took place on December 14.[7] Putin, Yeltsin recalled, had doubts. The heir was evidently ambiguous about Yeltsin's offer. Here is how Putin reacted to Yeltsin's proposal of succession, according to Yeltsin in *Presidential Marathon*: "You know, Boris Nikolayevich, to tell the truth, I'm not sure whether I'm prepared for this, whether I want it, because it is a rather difficult life." Colonel Putin apparently hesitated. That was the correct response. No need to rush things. Putin's reaction merely convinced Yeltsin that he had found the right man, one who was in no hurry to climb onto the throne. Let us not deny Putin his sincerity—apparently he truly was not sure of himself at first and wanted more time to prepare for power. But after the conversation with Yeltsin, Putin agreed to take the Kremlin job.

Had Putin known what the president would suggest on December 14? He must have. Starting in August, he must have realized his loyalty and his performance were being tested. Members of the Family held numerous preliminary meetings at their dachas, during which they discussed the details of the transfer of power. They were preparing Putin for Hour X, and he was preparing himself for it too. As a former intelligence officer, he understood—or should have understood—what was going on. Moreover, the operation relied on his cooperation, his brains, and his intelligence officer expertise.

When Yeltsin met with Putin again, on December 29, Putin knew that he was Russia's new boss. The talks between the departing monarch and his successor were a formality, a symbolic act, like the signing of a treaty. Yeltsin's entourage and Putin had already agreed on all the basic details of the project. Obviously, the ruling "Family" could not give up power just like that. Roles were assigned. The parties' mutual obligations were ratified. It was, simultaneously, a complex transfer of personal power, the perpetuation of the ruling corporation, and the endorsement of the formed-by-Yeltsin elected monarchy. The corporation had taken its time selecting the heir, expended great effort destroying its real or imagined foes, and used every means possible to reach its goals—from smear campaigns against opponents of the Chechen war to provoking society's neurasthenia. To call things by their real names, the process was a conspiracy by the Kremlin entourage to hand over power to a specific person and to ensure his success.

The parties then turned to the stage set and the creation of a semblance of legitimacy for the event of Yeltsin's resignation. They made sure the news did not get out beforehand. The videotape of Yeltsin's message to the nation, which had been recorded in the utmost secrecy, was delivered to the Ostankino television studios in an armored car accompanied by a military escort. All national stations were to begin broadcasting the tape precisely at noon on December 31, when the Russian Far Eastern time zone entered the New Year. Thus, the population of the Far East and Siberia got the news about the change of scenery in Moscow while sitting at their tables celebrating New Year's Eve.

Meanwhile, the Kremlin was busy organizing meetings. First, Yeltsin and Putin met with Patriarch Alexii, and the Russian Orthodox Church blessed the transfer of power. The Orthodox Church always satisfied the desires of the state; there was something monarchical about that. Then came the transfer to Putin of the nuclear briefcase, a symbol of power and confirmation of Russia's great-power status. This too was taped. Then came a meeting of the retiring president and his successor with the power ministers—*siloviki*. This was the most important meeting, because the transfer of power had to have the agreement of the Defense and Interior Ministries and the security services; there could be no threat from them. Then came a farewell banquet with the power ministers, and the entire company watched Yeltsin's broadcast on television.

Around one o'clock in the afternoon, Moscow time, Yeltsin shook everyone's hand. Then journalists with cameras were allowed inside, and they taped Yeltsin's last minutes in his role of the leader. Russia soon watched Yeltsin leave the Kremlin. He looked like he was having trouble speaking and moving. The cameras showed him leaving the presidential office for the last time—he stopped for a minute, gestured around the room, and turned to Putin, as if he were leaving it as a gift: Here, now you are master of all this. Slowly, treading heavily, he went out on the steps of the Kremlin and said something more to Putin. Later, we learned that he said, "Take care of Russia." Theatrical, almost touching. But Yeltsin was an actor, and a good one, especially in his best years. Everything that has a beginning has an ending, I thought, looking at the footage of Yeltsin in a new role—in the role of a pensioner.

Putin looked tense and pale throughout the invented-by-the-Kremlin ceremony that all of Russia watched. There was no expression on his face—his gaze was remote. That is how he experienced the significance of the moment. A boy from Saint Petersburg, a regular guy from a worker's family, a recent gofer, was receiving a huge country to rule—that was enough to make his head spin. But at least outwardly, he controlled his emotions, if there were any. The Yeltsin period was over. Russia rang in a new year with a new leader.

While Yeltsin was on the way to his dacha—where he had been hiding for more than a year and which became now his official residence—Bill Clinton called. The American president was true to his warm and fuzzy and slightly teary self—he felt he had to say good-bye to the man that political fate had placed beside him on the world stage. Clinton definitely liked Ol' Boris. Yeltsin, overcome by emotion and very weary, could not talk and asked to move the call to that evening.

From the point of view of guaranteeing the succession, Yeltsin's premature retirement was a well-planned and well-executed act. Yeltsin's team, which had been so pathetic and inexperienced at the beginning, had proven that it could learn the art of intrigue. In any case, the Kremlin team did succeed with Project Successor. A man in almost total isolation, who had not dealt with the outside world for at least a year, Yeltsin would have never done this alone. So even if we were to presume that Yeltsin had chosen his heir himself, it might have seemed an independent act to him while not being so at all.

To ensure Putin's victory in the presidential election, Yeltsin had to leave early. Rumors of his retirement had circulated for a long time.[8] But not everyone believed Yeltsin would be able to subjugate his ambition and pride to reason. The unexpectedness of his exit was a crucial element in the whole play and the guarantee of the planned outcome. It is difficult to say what persuaded Yeltsin—pressure from the Family or an understanding of the political realities and the desire to find a successor who could preserve his legacy or revive the moribund reforms. Did the ailing Yeltsin think about anything besides his constant illnesses? To what degree did he understand the problems he was leaving his heir? Most likely, the need to guarantee his and his family's personal safety was uppermost in whatever calculations he made. Otherwise, why would he have chosen a man who had no experience in public politics and dealing with high-level government management, who was unknown to society at large but had shown that he could be loyal to his mentors?

Putin's behavior as chief of the FSB was the determining factor for Yeltsin and the Family's choice of him as successor. Putin had been cautious and had not exhibited excessive ambition. He was precise and disciplined. He had no connections that tarnished him. (But perhaps it was just the reverse—there was something in his past that allowed the Family to control his future.) He knew how to wait, never hurried, and seemed to be a rational, pragmatic man. But most important, he had proved that he could be trusted at a difficult time for the president. It was these qualities that determined Putin's fate and the fate of the state.

There were two more things. The first was Putin's relative youth—he was 47 years old at that time. Yeltsin liked young politicians; he felt they were the future of Russia. Second was the fact that Putin had in his life a liberal period in Saint Petersburg. Of course, those who moved Putin to the top knew that without public acceptance he could not be placed on the throne. Therefore the victory of the pro–Putin movements in the parliamentary elections became a significant factor in the final choice of successor.

Yeltsin handed Putin his present, which was Russia. There was no doubt that from then on all the state's resources would be used to guarantee Putin the presidency.

Thus ended the rule of Russia's first president, Boris Yeltsin.[9] His rule began with the faith of millions in a better future for Russia, and it ended in disillusionment and insecurity. Yeltsin himself, the symbol of renewal and strength in the late 1980s, had by the late 1990s turned into a doddering old man whom many regarded as another Brezhnev. The Russian people awaited his departure impatiently and worried that the mumbling half-ruin of a man would do something unexpected before he left, like starting a new shakeup or engaging in a new political or military conflict. Enough was enough, Russians thought, with little pity and much scorn and weariness.

People could have supported almost anyone else to be rid of Yeltsin. He was doomed, not only because society did not accept him any longer but also because this proud maverick couldn't keep going after having lost his old self-assurance. Russia wanted to close Yeltsin's chapter. Ironically, very soon some of those who had wished for Yeltsin's departure, considering him a political ruin, would change their minds on his rule and start to remember his times with nostalgia—finding in his rule more and more positive signs. You have to compare to make your final judgment of people and history.

Yeltsin, who had seemed upon his arrival in the Kremlin to be breaking many traditions as well as destroying the communist empire, merely confirmed the Soviet tradition of no leader leaving in time. His predecessors had had to be carried out of the Kremlin feet first, or forced out. He himself, recently powerful and willful, proud and ambitious, stayed on until it was painful to watch him. It will be interesting to see whether Putin manages to break that tradition, and if so, how.

Yeltsin left behind a complex political structure overgrown with powerful vested interests—regional, oligarchic, bureaucratic interests. The pattern of leadership he bequeathed reflected both the strengths and weaknesses of his character and of his conception of the presidency. The regime he created had facets of suspicion and egocentricity, and combined a desire for autocratic total power with an unwillingness to use that power like a dictator. It was a continuation of Yeltsin's personality and at the same time a continuation of the ancient Russian tradition of autocratic monarchical rule. It perpetuated at least some aspects of the Russian pattern of governance—the Russian System with its reliance on the leader-arbiter's staying above the fray, its fusion of state and society, of politics and the economy, its paternalism. No matter what form of leadership Yeltsin's heir tried to build, it would be extremely difficult to destroy Yeltsin's political thinking and the habits embodied in the structures, philosophy of power, and political complexes that survived him.

Russia will return to Yeltsin's personality again and again in an attempt to understand his legacy and decide whether it was ultimately positive or negative. Society will ponder what he was for his tormented country—reformer or stabilizer, liberal or conservative, statist or destroyer of the state? Where was he directed? If to the future, what kind of future? Or did he try to slow society's forward movement and preserve part of the Soviet and pre-Soviet past, afraid of too much change too fast?

That there is no agreement in Russia in evaluating Yeltsin suggests that the study of his role may be subject to certain shifts and that much depends on what his successor becomes and how he uses Yeltsin's legacy. Yeltsin could be regarded more kindly in the future than he was at the end of his political life. The fact that after several years of Putin's presidency even former Yeltsin critics look at the first Russian president in a more favorable way points to that.

For now, one thing is clear: Yeltsin in the early 1990s became Russia's leader first of all because he combined in his personality and his rule a connection to the past and a simultaneous rejection of that past. In an amazingly analogous way, Putin began by claiming continuity with Yeltsinism and at the same time rejecting it.

Yeltsin's political style embodied rudiments of a typical Soviet politician alongside a desire to destroy the communist instincts he possessed. He could behave like a haughty boyar out of Old Russia, disdainful of subordinates. He preferred making decisions personally and behind the scenes, resorting to intrigues characteristic of the Soviet *nomenklatura* and even of feudal times. He could not function in a system with a separation of powers, striving as he always did for a monopoly in that commodity, power. He gathered power in his fist, muscling out anyone else who might lay claim to it.

At the same time, Yeltsin showed a feeling for democracy. He understood the significance of basic civil liberties and did not attack them. He could tolerate criticism, albeit with difficulty, even when it was ruthless. For instance, he never touched journalists, even those who made it their business to attack him. He knew how to appeal directly to the people in his struggle with the state apparatus and his opponents, and he understood the power of the people. He was not vengeful and never persecuted his enemies and opponents. That was new for Russia, which was accustomed to revenge in politics, not forgiveness and tolerance. Thus Yeltsin had already begun undermining the traditional Russian System of rule.

In the early years of his administration—1991 and 1992—Yeltsin unquestionably had major goals: to see Russia integrated into Europe and to make Russia a civilized, powerful democracy. Cooperating with the West and drawing a line below the communist past were paramount for Yeltsin in the beginning, though he may not have given much thought to how to achieve them. But when he began to feel resistance, which started in early 1992, and he realized that he had no clear vision of what exactly he wanted to achieve, he turned to what he had always known—fighting his opponents and strengthening his personified regime. At that moment, he began thinking of reforms only in the context of protecting his position. If reforms did not interfere with his power, he continued them; if they complicated his life, he slowed them down or rejected them completely. Outwardly, Yeltsin was still the guarantor of the new orientation toward the West and liberalization. But beginning in 1993, he stopped being the moving force behind the reform process, which was growing moribund.

Not only the style but the politics of the first Russian president was marked by contradiction. Yeltsin made anticommunism his ideology. He managed to train the political class to operate in an atmosphere of pluralism. He gave his first government to the young, unknown liberal technocrats, exploding the Russian tradition of gerontocracy that had denied the young power except for the brief revolutionary period during the 1920s. Yet he ended up returning to an almost monarchical rule. He failed to rule in a different way. His *elected monarchy* functioned as monolithic, undivided personal rule. Such has always been the way in Russia. It is true that now it requires democratic, electoral legitimization. But personal rule distorts democracy, turning it into an imitation. Besides, this old–new hybrid political structure is doomed to be internally torn, unstable and ambivalent.

———————— ✣ ————————

Yeltsin took power at a decisive moment in Russian history thanks to the contradictory nature of his politics: He was a rebel who came out of the bowels of the old system and still belonged to it when he began dismantling it. It is hard to imagine the dissident Andrei Sakharov as leader of the new Russia. Václav Havel or Lech Walesa is unthinkable as a leader of Russia. Their rise to power in Czechoslovakia and Poland reflected the previous regimes' greater experience with liberalization, which occurred even under communist rule. Russia had to undergo liberalization and democratization at the same time, and that is why it needed a leader who could unite the two parts of society: the one that was not ready to leave Soviet life and only wanted a renewal of socialism, and the one trying to escape the past, to get rid of its vestiges fully and forever. Yeltsin, still functioning in two eras, was the ideal politician to combine temporarily two incompatible desires and agendas for the future.

Theoretically, we could imagine another path for overcoming communism: a radical uprooting of all elements of Sovietism, including a replacement of the elites and the construction of new institutions. But such a radical transformation would have demanded a leader ready to use violence to neutralize the strata not prepared for decisive changes. In Russia, those strata formed the majority. Besides which, that kind of transformation demanded the presence of an organized democratic force with a plan of action and a leader with the political will to unite the groups interested in a critical breakthrough.

There were no such forces or leaders in Russia at the time of the break with communism, nor do they exist today. And even with an outwardly successful radical transformation from above, we could expect to see an eventual deformation of the new forms and institutions by the cultural milieu, historical characteristics, and traditions of Russian society. In short, Russia's revolutionary transition to the liberal-democratic rules of the game in the early 1990s was dubious. Russia did not follow the example of Poland and Czechoslovakia—a pact among the main political forces and a peaceful division of power between the old and the new elites. The anticommunist opposition in Russia was too weak and the *nomenklatura* too strong to achieve reforms on the basis of consensus. The irony and drama in Russia's postcommunist transformation were related to the fact that its engine and its base were still the old Soviet-born establishment. Continuity in the new Russia explained the nature of change. The more change, the more it was the same thing.

For an evolutionary, bloodless exit from communism when there was no national consensus regarding the past, present, or future, Russia needed a leader of a special type, a politician with an enormous amount of charisma who could serve as a substitute for the lack of new elites, structured agenda, and readiness to build new institutions. Such a leader could embody the complexes of the past and the desire to put an end to those complexes. But he could not be politically and ideologically monotonous, pure and definite—he would have to vacillate, have weaknesses, explode into conflicts, move in opposite directions. The cost of that leadership would inevitably be a delay or even U-turns in the liberal-democratic breakthrough.

The best thing for Russia would have been Yeltsin at the stage of overcoming communism and a new leader at the next stage, someone who could unite the nation on a democratic platform rather than an anticommunist one. After 1996, Yeltsin should have retired from public life, both because he was sick and not up to it and because he did not understand what he should do next and did not know how to change. He did not know anymore what goals to set other than his own survival. He should have left office so that Russia had a chance to keep moving toward further liberalization and more structured democracy, and so that he could keep his dignity and stay in history as an undoubtedly transformational leader.

Yeltsin, however, had already begun focusing on his own survival, on keeping power at any cost after 1992, when he fired Gaidar as head of his government. It was surprising how quickly he began fading, for a man who had been physically strong. Living on the edge, heavy drinking, stress, and other immoderate habits took their toll. He aged much more quickly than Gorbachev, even though they were born the same year.[10] But it wasn't so much a question of physical wear and tear as that he was losing his intuition, could not understand new problems and challenges, got confused, and then fell into depression or tried to respond with his old method of firing officials and appointing new ones.

Keeping Yeltsin in the Kremlin after 1996 led inevitably to the degradation and demoralization of power. The chance of rescue was nonexistent because the president had worked for years to destroy all possibility of alternative elites and leaders coming to the fore. That the majority of Russian liberals had bet on the leader and rejected the need for independent institutions discredited the very idea of liberal democracy in citizens' eyes. Russia was in a trap. On one hand, Yeltsin's reelection to a second term condemned government to stagnation. But on the other hand, there was no democratic alternative to him, and that was at least partially the fault of the liberals and democrats. The only alternative to Yeltsin in 1996 was the Communist Party's return to power under Zyuganov. Thus

Yeltsin had to remain on the political stage, even though there was no further need for an anticommunist consolidator and he had become an obstacle to a new stage of transformation. He was a lesser evil.

In the Yeltsin regime, the democratic-populist principle was constantly in conflict with the authoritarian-monarchical principle. The conflict between the incompatible combination of democracy and leadership through personified power led to democracy's becoming a facade hiding a completely different interior.

Autocratic leadership had existed in Russia for many centuries, changing only its ideological colors and method of legitimization. During the Communist stage, autocracy was legitimized by the Party and hid behind the mask of collective leadership, which did little to change its essence. After the collapse of communism, Yeltsin revived a tradition that had long distinguished Russia from the rest of Europe and that once again made monolithic power, this time without any "collectivist" cover, the nucleus of politics. In the 1990s again, the leader's power, not society, was the main subject of the Constitution. All the major institutions of Russian politics were functioning in the space created by central authority, as had happened for centuries. It was true that in Yeltsin's era, political actors in Russia acquired freedom and politics became spontaneous and unpredictable. For the first time, uncertainty of the outcome was introduced into the Russian political process. But this happened not because power underwent a crucial transformation and those in authority understood the rationale of political fragmentation and freedom but because authority was weak and confused. Moreover, the uncertainty of the political process was the result of the uncertain rules of the game.

Yeltsin's elected monarchy, functioning in a stratified society with a corrupt bureaucracy and weak power structures, could be nothing but a parody of the old totalitarianism and of the authoritarianism of the 1970s and 1980s. To survive, the elected monarchy had to share power with influential groups, to make constant deals and bargains, to face multiple constraints and obstacles. Consequently, the outwardly authoritarian leader who took so much power into his own hands was only quasi-authoritarian.

This type of regime resembled what Guillermo O'Donnell has labeled "delegative democracy"—a system of power based on the premise that "whoever was elected to the presidency is thereby entitled to govern as he or she sees fit."[11] For Russia, Yeltsin's "delegative democracy" in the 1990s was a definite step forward from the previous pattern of totalitarian and authoritarian rule. But because of its internal contradictions and traps, this rule could not be durable or effective. The question was how Russia could extricate itself from the trap of weak and demoralized omnipotence.

The monolithic nature of Yeltsin's rule seemed to aid the cause of economic reform. But the breakthrough into the effective and civilized market soon turned out to be illusory. It was indeed easier under presidential autocracy to implement market reforms and neutralize the resistance of social groups unprepared to give up state paternalism. At the same time, however, the return to personified power made impossible the development of a systemic politics that combined the activities of manifold independent institutions, each working on issues of concern to its members. Though in the short run market reform benefited from the superconcentration of power, in the long run it lost out because of the slow progress in creating a liberal–democratic society. And market capitalism in the absence of independent institutions, clear rules of the game (first of all, the supremacy of law), and independent individuals can be only a parody of the market.

We could be less critical of Yeltsin's work if we accepted that the number of challenges facing Russia in 1991 was huge and that ways of solving those problems on the road to liberal democracy were limited. But let us not forget that Yeltsin held many levers of power in his hands and that, before post-Soviet politics and society took definite shape, he had great influence over the course of events. There is no justification for his failure to push liberal transformation more energetically. He bears personal responsibility for the missed opportunities in Russian reforms.

Faced with the same obstacles, a leader who tried more consistently to escape the limits of autocracy and the traps of court politics, who understood more clearly Russia's challenges, could have helped the country make more determined strides toward a civilized system of governance, independent institutions, civil society, and a system of checks and balances. But here is a problem: How many leaders who had complete power had the ability and courage to share it with other forces and institutions voluntarily? Moving toward a liberal-democratic system means first of all the ability to share power.

We should give president Boris Yeltsin his due. Russia under his rule escaped destructive scenarios for itself and for the world, and there were plenty of them. Even if he did not handle it as well as might be envisioned, he presided over the rather peaceful decline of a nuclear superpower and the initial stage of its transformation. The price of this transformation for millions of Russians was huge and unbearable. But it might have been much heavier.

At the same time, just because Russia escaped apocalypse under Yeltsin and there were no other strong candidates for the presidency, we should not soften our assessment of his leadership. That after his departure society wanted an "iron hand" and longed for order is a judgment on his rule. He helped society to get freedoms, but he failed to understand the role of the rule of law and accountability, first of all on behalf of authority. If we look at the need to accomplish the democratic project and the opportunities, albeit limited, that he had, then Yeltsin was a weak, inadequate leader.

Yeltsin and his leadership were stitched together out of insoluble conflicts. He had enormous formal powers and at the same time was incapable of executing his decisions. He personally tended toward bossism but was left without mass support and was constantly forced to ingratiate himself and be a populist. He was a leader whose ideal was a superpresidential regime but who had to function in an era of disintegration. He was a politician who hated compromise and yet had to make many deals and concessions. He was a man who proclaimed the goal of democracy and oversaw the creation of an elected monarchy. He was a president who won two elections only to become a screen for the clans behind the throne. He was a model of a powerful, dynamic personality who ended up fighting his own uncertainty and weakness.

Yeltsin turned out to be a revolutionary who made permanent revolutionary shakeups his means of surviving. The more uncertain he felt in a new situation, the more he turned to revolutionary rhetoric and actions. Revolution for him became a means of preserving the status quo, the pattern of rule he got used to—one more paradox of the transition reality. He was the destroyer of communism, yet thanks to him the Communist Party became an important factor in the functioning of his regime. And that regime—established at the beginning of the 1990s with high hopes and many good intentions—ended up souring a significant part of the nation on democracy.

Yet Yeltsin made a return to communism in Russia an impossibility. He habituated the political class to a relatively civilized method of dealing with international issues. Since his presidency, it is harder for Russia—perhaps impossible—to return to a cold war with the West. In many ways, he guaranteed the peaceful dissolution of the USSR and the appearance of independent states on its territory. He taught the political class to exist in an atmosphere of pluralism and free expression. (Although the course of events under Putin will show that some back-tracking is not ruled out.) And finally, Yeltsin made a return to a planned, centralized economy an impossibility.

There is another result of his administration that I feel is worthy of approval: Yeltsin's weak, chaotic, often helpless leadership forced a significant part of society to think for itself, to depend on its own strength, and to come out of the shadow of the state. Frustration with the leader made people learn to walk on their own. That fact may help Russia survive under any leader.

Russia will have to pay a high price to rid itself of the disabled, half-hearted form of autocracy that Yeltsin revived. But first we must see whether Putin will manage to make Yeltsin's quasi-autocracy work. If it turns out that he cannot (which is likely), society will have to pay for the mistakes of both the father of the regime and his heir who tried to keep the hybrid torn from within the regime alive. It may be that Yeltsin's success as transformer will be determined by how quickly his elected monarchy can be dismantled and by how enduring the democratic habits and the new mentality that Russia acquired under him will prove to be.

That is the legacy Boris Yeltsin left to Vladimir Putin. The very act of handing over power to Putin, as regent and heir, highlighted the principle of elected monarchy inherent in the system Yeltsin created. Yeltsin's early retirement had little to do with democracy; on the contrary, it demonstrated the imitative quality of Yeltsin's conception of democracy. His departure was preferable to the slow fading of the politician, but the artificial advance of elections, the way they were manipulated, had only one goal: to guarantee rule by a single political group.

So Putin's taking power, still in the role of acting president, confirmed the logic of Yeltsin's regime. Now Putin had a chance to show how flexible that regime was and how much it could evolve and in what direction. The new Russian leader had to survive several harsh trials, the first of which was a test of his gratitude—reciprocity with the old ruling team.

Before Yeltsin's retirement in December 1999, Putin played the role of obedient appointee ideally. He did everything to show that he had no ambitions of his own. At the moment, he really might have had none. He seemed to be trying not to cast a shadow; he wanted to be a mere functionary rather than a notable person or a leader. Perhaps he was still wary of responsibility and was afraid of his own inexperience. He may have been worried that at the last moment Yeltsin would change his mind and name a new heir.

Right down to the wire, there could be no certainty that this heir would be the last. Who knew what the sick man or his daughter might think of next? So Putin had to be obedient, not attract attention, and patiently bide his time. Perhaps this was a natural role for him, in keeping with his career in intelligence work. He had always been in supporting roles and found public life difficult. He had not yet learned how to function in it. Or we might be bad shrinks; we cannot rule out the notion that Putin did not much care whether he would be the new monarch or not.

With Yeltsin's retirement, Putin was front and center. There was no doubt that Putin would win the presidential election scheduled for March 2000. But it remained to be seen whether he would follow the logic of Yeltsin's legacy or begin changing it. Regardless of how Putin felt about the Yeltsin regime, he would have to live with it for a long time, either in peaceful coexistence or in conflict. And Russia will spend a long time clarifying its attitude toward the man who left the stage unexpectedly on the eve of the year 2000.

Chapter 3

PUTIN, THE NEW
RUSSIAN LEADER

—————————— ❧ ——————————

Presidential elections without a choice. What course to take? The new
Kremlin spider web. Formation of the government. Taming of the governors.
Whom to rely upon. The intelligentsia is concerned.

Immediately after the New Year 2000 celebrations, Putin, as acting
president, promulgated his first decree, which granted Yeltsin immunity.[1] Under the decree, Yeltsin could not be prosecuted for criminal
or administrative wrongdoing for any of his actions as president.
Moreover, Yeltsin's aides (his daughter Tatyana and the rest of his inner circle) were declared as having been responsible only to him—that is, they
were absolved of legal responsibility. Putin's decree created a zone of
immunity around the former president that could be extended at will to
the members of Yeltsin's entourage.

As foreign observers noted, Putin's decree "gave foundation to all the
charges laid against Yeltsin by his enemies."[2] Many Russian observers felt
the same way. But we had to admit that in Russia a guarantee of immunity to the departing leader was the only way of assuring that the old ruling group would leave the stage without a fierce battle.

In the meantime, Prime Minister Putin's popularity and the administrative levers he had inherited made the outcome of the presidential election, set for March 26, 2000, inevitable. According to the Constitution,
the presidential election is supposed to be held in June. But Yeltsin's early
retirement made it possible to reschedule the election for an earlier date
to guarantee Putin's victory while he was still popular.

There were ten other candidates besides Putin. Some of them were the usual suspects who had been competing with Yeltsin during the previous elections, among them the Communist leader Gennady Zyuganov, the leader of the democratic Yabloko Grigory Yavlinsky, and the leader of the nationalistic Liberal Democratic Party, political clown Vladimir Zhirinovsky. The rest of the presidential hopefuls entered the race without the slightest chance not only of winning but even of getting substantial support. They wanted publicity and television coverage so that they could pursue other goals afterward.

In any case, participation in the presidential campaign would never be a liability. Konstantin Titov, Ella Pamfilova, Sergei Govorukhin, Yuri Skuratov, Alexei Podberezkin, and Umar Dzhabrailov (in the order of votes received) all ran in the name of running, not in the name of winning, as if demonstrating that the goal is nothing and process is everything. Everyone knew that no one but Putin had a chance, because the entire might of the state was working on his behalf.

The second Chechen war allowed Putin to play the strong, determined leader, but there were other, no less crucial, factors that assured his success. On one hand, Putin was Yeltsin's official successor, blessed by the first Russian president, which guaranteed the support of the bureaucracy and a smooth transition. On the other hand, his image as a hard-edged, stern leader was a positive contrast to the impotent, feeble Yeltsin. This successor could be acceptable both to the portion of the public that was loyal to the regime and to the protest voters—to those who wanted an arranged, seamless succession and continuity and those who demanded change at the top and break with the past.

Most important, Putin had become the optimal way of getting rid of Yeltsin, both for the ruling class and for society as a whole, which was fed up with the erratic leader. Even his former close lieutenants and staunch supporters were thinking: Enough is enough!

The vagueness of Putin's political image made him a tabula rasa on which everyone could write what he or she wanted. It may not have been conscious on Putin's part in the beginning, but he tried to be all things to all people. Every social and political group could hope that in the long run he would support its formula for bringing order to Russia. He combined the determination and clarity always associated with the military in people's minds with a certain amorphousness. This vagueness allowed Everybody's Man to appeal to all strata of society and to avoid precise answers to the questions that were worrying Russia. For someone beginning his political career and preparing for elections for the first time, this was a sound strategy.

The ruling class unequivocally supported Putin, hoping that the new leader would preserve the current rules of the game; in backing him, it endorsed the status quo, which it benefited from extensively and wanted to continue.[3] Then there were those who hoped that Putin, as a representative of the security services, would return society to the way it had been in Soviet times, or offer a pure authoritarian regime. Some of the liberals hoped that Putin, with his market-oriented past in Saint Petersburg, would continue the long-stalled economic reforms. But the overwhelming desire among the political class and Russians in general was that Putin prove himself a leader who could bring order to Yeltsin's chaos and end the unpredictability of the Kremlin.

Before the election, Putin refused to elaborate on his credo, attempting to maintain credibility with his disparate supporters. But he could not keep silent forever. So far, he had spoken only once on the direction of Russia's development, in an article with the pretentious title "Russia on the Cusp of the Millennium" that appeared on December 30, 1999. In it, Putin leaned too much toward the past. He called for melding universal human values with Russian traditions, patriotism, collectivism, statism, and social justice.[4] Those principles had been truly popular in Russia in Soviet times, when the country was trying to mark out its own "special path." But with the fall of communism, the Russian alternative and claims of uniqueness were all void. Putin—whether he realized it or not—was trying to revive an idea that had been proven to have no future. Perhaps he was trying to impress conservative-minded Russians. But either he or his advisers made a mistake here.

Putin brought down on himself the criticism of liberals and the pro-Western contingent. He could have overlooked their displeasure, for these groups were in the minority in Russia. It was apparently far more important for him to win understanding and support among statists—those who supported a strong Russian state, a much larger group. But because he knew that liberals were powerful in the mass media and among entrepreneurs, he quickly adjusted his position, rendering it even more amorphous.

In an open letter to voters in February 2000, Putin and his staff showed that they had learned their lesson: This time, they tried to avoid any ideas that could inspire attack or even criticism. Yeltsin's successor attempted to eliminate all ideological accents and mentioned only consensual values that even competing forces—liberals, the left wing, or statists—could not reject. It all came down to an increased role for the state (without specifying where the increase would come), further market reform, and a revival of the idea of social justice.

At the same time, Putin tried out a critical stance toward the Yeltsin administration. "Our first and most important problem is the weakening of will. The loss of state will and persistence in completing started affairs. Vacillation, dithering, the habit of putting off the hardest tasks for later," he wrote, attempting to distance himself from Yeltsinism and appealing to people critical of Yeltsin's policy.[5]

Putin basically refused to campaign for the March election, stressing his duties as prime minister and acting president, which were covered extensively on television and by the other media, which followed the prime minister's every step. His team wisely chose to present him not as a charismatic leader but as just like everyone else, the "man on the street." Looking at Putin—with his plain face, ill-cut clothes, and straightforward, slightly awkward manner—every ordinary Russian could imagine himself as president. Even Putin's occasional use of street slang (for instance, his promise to "wipe out" the Chechen terrorists "in the john"), which shocked the intelligentsia, impressed the rest of the country with the new leader's folksiness.

The psychological factor was also important in Russians' attitude in the months leading up to the election. Russian society includes a large "wandering mass" of people who have supported someone new in each election, in search of a hero. In the 1996 elections, they supported General Alexander Lebed. Then they rushed to the support of Yevgeny Primakov in early 1999. Their new hero was Putin. His jump in the ratings was tied in large part to a drop in support for other politicians. Those guys had been around for ten years, some even longer, and they were becoming annoying. Putin was a new face, and people went for the freshness. They would have been attracted to any alternative to the rotting Yeltsin regime. But the irony was that they supported an alternative handpicked by Yeltsin's circle. Russian citizens, it seemed, were not ready to support someone from the opposition. They were neither frustrated enough nor angry enough to make their own independent choice not approved by the ruling team.

The last polls before the balloting for president, conducted by VTsIOM, showed Putin as the almost certain victor. At that point, 53 percent of voters intended to vote for the acting president (down from 58 percent a bit earlier). Putin's rating was beginning to slide, but not dangerously. Zyuganov, the head of the Communist Party, was stuck at 21 percent; and Yavlinsky of the liberal Yabloko was the choice of just 6 percent of the electorate.

When asked what Russia needed, 71 percent of those polled replied "a strong leader" and 59 percent "a strong state." "Democratic institutions" were not a priority—only 13 percent of respondents named them. Society was backhandedly passing judgment on the Yeltsin era, associating it with a weak leader and a weak state. But it was disturbing that Russia was once again trying to escape the crisis of Yeltsinism by searching for a new savior and not through the forming of enduring institutions.

Also disturbing was the fact that Russians did not believe Putin would come to power honestly, whether because of others' machinations or his own—and that many who thought so planned to vote for him anyway. People were frustrated by the Russian-style election, which was used to legitimize choices made through sweet deals. But at the same time, they accepted these choices. The majority of those polled—54 percent—felt that Putin's presidential campaign was dishonest, and 72 percent thought there would be chicanery when the votes were counted.

On the eve of the election, 63 percent were reported to trust Putin fully, down from 76 percent two weeks earlier (though only 25 percent were bothered by the fact that he had worked for the KGB-FSB). According to VTsIOM polls, the biggest factors in the drop in Putin's ratings were the confirmation of his ties to the oligarchs (58 percent) and the continuing war in Chechnya (57 percent). Fifty-five percent worried about his lack of a definite program. But despite all that, people did not see any other option.

The portrait sociologists created of the typical "Putinist" on the basis of these polls showed that the acting president's main backing came from young people and those more than 60 years old. He had more female than male loyalists. People with a middling education gave him the strongest backing; those who were leery of him most often had attained higher levels of education, were between the ages of 30 and 50, and lived in large cities. Support for Putin was weaker in Moscow, always more dynamic, sophisticated, and advanced than the rest of the country.

A VTsIOM survey on March 9, two weeks before the election, showed that a very large percentage of voters who supported Putin rejected the idea of extending the presidential term from four years to seven. Only 24 percent backed term extension, while 65 percent were against it (11 percent had no opinion). This showed that Russians no longer approved of lifelong rule and suggested that the longing for stability based on one leader might have been transitional.

Yeltsin's early resignation did not give Putin's opponents time to prepare for the rescheduled election or the public time to get sick of Putin. The other candidates in the presidential contest made it look something like a real race, allowing Putin to legitimize through an electoral victory his appointment by Yeltsin's circle. In this situation, Putin needed only to turn his de facto presidential powers into de jure ones. Vladimir Vladimirovich was doomed to win because he could not lose—there was no one to lose to, and he could not lose. Even if he had wanted to.

Right up until election day, the ruling group and its candidate managed to sustain an image of a strong, effective leader that was built on almost nothing. The image was created solely on the strength of Putin's continual trips around the country and other manifestations of his physical activity. The public remained totally uninformed of his real plans. When a reporter asked him what his program would be, he replied cagily, "I won't tell." This outrageous statement was the essence of the Putin election campaign—say nothing concrete, promise nothing. For those accustomed to Western political standards, the statement was a challenge of sorts, as well as an expression of disdain for public opinion—"You know you'll elect me even without a program." He was right.

On March 26, Putin won the presidency in the first round with the support of almost 53 percent of voters. His main rival, Zyuganov, got

29.2 percent; the leader of the democratic opposition, Yavlinsky, finished with 5.8 percent. Governor Aman Tuleyev got 2.95 percent; professional nationalist Vladimir Zhirinovsky, 2.7 percent; and governor Konstantin Titov, 1.47 percent. The rest of the candidates together got even less than 1 percent, and "none of the above" got 1.88 percent.

A huge factor in Putin's victory was that he was the only candidate sponsored by the ruling group, which had employed "administrative resources" to neutralize his opponents and organize support for him. The central and local authorities on all levels did everything possible to get him the win—"everything possible" being a multitude of methods, from persuading and pressuring voters to harassing other candidates to assuring a "correct" count of the vote.

Russian sociologists Lev Gudkov and Boris Dubin, explaining Putin's victory, noted Russians' desire to join and support the victor's camp, embodied now by Putin. No one seemed to care about the new leader's aims and ideology. The important thing was that he had already been sitting in the president's chair and was supported by the power structures—the army, Interior Ministry, and intelligence agencies, which were the only Russian institutions (besides the Orthodox Church) that were still fairly well regarded and thought to be relatively free from corruption.

Thus in the presidential election, Putin got the votes of 12 percent of Communists, 40 percent of Yabloko supporters, 40 percent of Zhirinovsky's Liberal Democratic Party, more than two-thirds of the Union of Right Forces (SPS) liberals, and 70 percent of the Primakov–Luzhkov Fatherland and All-Russia Party. These voters supported Putin because they believed he would win and because he and his team stood for order and demonstrated strength. And in new unruly Russia, people were longing for order and respected strength.[6]

The election for the first Russian president, in 1991, won by Yeltsin, was an election for radical change. The elections of 1996, which Yeltsin also won, were a vote to draw the communist past to an end. In the 2000 presidential election, Russia was voting for stability. There was no widespread desire for radical change. Society was tired and wanted peace and security. The desire for order was not absolute, however, because people clearly did not want to lose the liberties Gorbachev and Yeltsin had granted. The new leader had to find a new correlation between freedom and order.

The inauguration of the second president of Russia took place on May 7. The eclectic style of the new leadership was in evidence; the Kremlin tried to give the public elements of ceremony borrowed from different epochs: tsarist autocracy, Soviet times, and the anticommunist period. It was too much for good taste: Yeltsin and Putin watching the parade from the porch where the tsars had stood to greet their people; a typically Soviet style of attendance lists for guests, who were divided according to their rank and ordered to stay in their assigned hall; and the new leader taking the oath of office on Yeltsin's Constitution. The ceremony reflected the hybrid style and substance of the new ruling group, which embraced seemingly incompatible features—the KGB past of the new Kremlin boss, his liberal activity, and his nearly monarchical ascendancy to power orchestrated by anticommunists and revolutionaries!

The "postmodernism" of Putin's rise to power would continue to be displayed in his administration, which contains echoes of various eras. Tsarist-style intrigues and succession, elements of Soviet-type loyalty, new-age utilitarianism and pragmatism—all would become an impetus for mutually exclusive trends and possibilities. We will see how this man—who by training has to be unambiguous and determined, have no doubts, and seek definite solutions—will live and rule in a pluralistic, fragmented, and contradictory environment. Postcommunism in Russia was obviously not a sharp break with the past—neither pre-Soviet nor fully post-Soviet. Those who understood that and could move in the atmosphere of mixed signals and bows to seemingly incompatible principles had a chance of staying on top.

Putin looked nervous during the inauguration. The scenario called for him to take a long walk through the halls of the Kremlin to reach the room where the ceremony was to be held. As he climbed the endless Kremlin staircase, the television cameras showed his tense, pale face, his sturdy yet small figure all but lost in the vastness of the Kremlin's opulence. In his ill-fitting suit, he seemed wildly out of place in the monarchic ritual. A staff officer of the KGB, an assistant to Saint Petersburg's mayor, a nondescript member of a presidential administration—a person accustomed to being in the shadows, permanently behind the boss, running errands—found himself master of the Kremlin. This was breathtaking.

The guests were gathered in various ballrooms, depending on their place in the hierarchy as determined by the Yeltsin ruling group. Thus the main room held a very motley crowd: oligarchs, children of oligarchs, "gray cardinals," retired prime ministers, and pretty young women who did not seem to have a direct connection to the proceedings. Neither Luzhkov nor other political heavyweights could be seen in this room. But Gorbachev had been invited, on Putin's personal initiative. This at least was a good sign—Putin was bringing Gorbachev back into politics.

This was Yeltsin's last official appearance, and all eyes were on him—how did he look, could he speak, how did he walk, what did he feel in his new role? Yeltsin tried to give a memorable speech, but it was too long and lecturing. Putin, standing next to him, began giving him impatient looks. Then Putin delivered his own speech, brief and energetic, without a single hitch. Putin's very appearance underlined the difference between himself and the patriarch next to him, and the difference was for many reassuring.

The new Russian leader was in an exceptionally good position; Yeltsin might have envied him. Vladimir Putin had no opponents who threatened his power. The ruling class seemed loyal to him, even servile. The public regarded him hopefully, but their hopes were not excessive. That was also good for Putin, for if the hopes were not realized, there would be no mass disillusionment.[7]

Russia's economic situation in early 2000 was rather stable. Moreover, the country had even achieved some economic growth. In February 2000, monthly inflation was running at only 0.7 to 0.8 percent. Production had increased by 11.0 percent during the past year. The budget showed a surplus. And the price of oil was steady and relatively high at $21.50 a barrel, which was good for the economy's basic revenue stream.

The Chechen war, despite the obvious fact that it was a dead end, still had the support of the public, which wanted the Russian army to go on fighting until the separatists were crushed. All this meant that Putin had a lot of room to maneuver in setting his course.

At the same time, having seemingly unusual freedom of action, the new president was severely constrained by the system of power he had inherited from Yeltsin. Under the logic of the superpresidential regime, the president has to manage even the details. If he stops pushing the buttons, even for a short while, the system goes off into unguided flight. Besides, failures of the administration, even at the local level, damage the president's legitimacy, because in the people's eyes he is the one who controls all the levers of power and is responsible for everything.

At the same time, the system fosters the president's irresponsibility, because even if there are errors and failures, it is very hard—perhaps impossible—to remove him from office. In addition, the new leader inherited a bureaucracy and power structures (the Interior and Defense Ministries and security services) that had become overgrown with vested interests, whose aim was to preserve the former shadow rules of the game, and which waited and watched, prepared either to support Putin or to sabotage his policies. The newcomer had to learn the logic of the system he took over and decide whether he would follow it or fight it.

A no less serious problem for Putin was the merger in Russia of power and capital, politics and economics, the public and the private—a Soviet tradition Yeltsin had not only failed to break but in some areas had even reinforced. Beyond triggering the dire enough consequence of the corruption and degradation of the Russian state, the fusion of power and business had preserved and even expanded the gray zone. In that shadowy space, huge quantities of goods and services were produced and sold with no one paying a kopek in taxes. Now not only corrupt officials and some wheeler-dealers but a significant portion of the population had settled there. Millions of people worked in the gray zone. And at that time, up to 30 percent of the country's gross domestic product was produced there.

The gray zone had become the safety net for the officially unemployed, the underpaid, and those owed back pay by the government. The zone thus helped society to survive the transition. The state missed out on gigantic sums in taxes, and criminal elements profited. Yet if the state tried to destroy the zone, the loss of this workplace—where so many earned the money they needed to survive in postcommunist Russia—could undermine social stability, unless fresh legal venues for economic vitality were simultaneously created. And not only the economy but politics too had moved into the shadows, with fundamental decisions made behind closed doors and under pressure from powerful lobbies. The gray zone could not be controlled, and it contained a threat to the leader's power, if he did not want to obey its rules.

Nor did the positive economic background to Putin's administration have a solid foundation. Just as before, during the communist period, revitalization was due to high oil prices. Without structural reforms, massive investment, and the development of other sectors of the economy, the apparent economic well-being could crumble if oil prices dropped.

It was not difficult for Putin to see that the majority in the political class feared a continuation of market liberalization. His own entourage presented a problem for economic policy. Its members espoused various schools of thinking, and from the start, each competed to win him over; they did not form a cohesive professional team that could urge him to implement decisive reforms. The majority of the oligarchs from the Yeltsin era, who retained much influence, were strongly against changing the status quo and first of all breaking the fusion between power and business, for any alteration would cut into their profits and possibly topple them. In early 2000, only 15 percent of the population backed an unfettered free market, and they were a disparate bunch, incapable of providing substantive support to the regime. Fifty-two percent of Russians supported state-owned property and the priority of state regulation. The rest made up the always doubting "swamp."

Some vacillating Russians were moving toward rejection of the market. Thus in 1993, 27 percent supported private ownership of major enterprises, but by 2000 only 20 percent did. As for the state fixing firms' prices, the 45 percent who were in favor in 1993 increased to 51 percent in 2000; only 10 percent disapproved of all state interference in price setting. In 1993, 13 percent of Russians thought foreigners should be allowed to own large properties, whereas by 2000 the figure had fallen to 5 percent.[8] These were disturbing signs for any reform-minded leader.

Putin must have realized that the window of opportunity would not be open forever. If he wanted to push through any major liberalization measures, he had to hurry. Popularity and trust are highly unreliable commodities, inclined to shrink.

Further poll results suggested to Putin the political direction he should take. Thirty-nine percent of respondents did not like the new leader's ties to Yeltsin and his entourage. Clearly, Putin had to think about how to cut the old ruling team's leash. Only 12 percent criticized him for lacking a clear political line.[9] Because the figure was low and Putin's avoidance of definite policies had won him support among varied social groups, he could keep on as he was for a time. It was possible that inertia could guarantee him a quiet existence for his full term, and even reelection in 2004 if the economy held up.

But buoyed by his initial approval ratings and favorable circumstances, Putin could still make incremental yet telling changes on the economic and political fronts. In fact, he would lose an important opportunity and probably regret it if he did not undertake structural reforms for the sake of the benefits they would bring Russia. It was also possible that making radical changes without forming political backing might have toppled him, as had happened with Gorbachev and his *perestroika*. The status quo and stagnation often are more instrumental for preserving power than is revolution.

Putin embarked on his new job with a minimum of political experience and years of career habits that might work against him. The highest office in the country had fallen into his lap after a "training period" of four months as prime minister. He did not have (nor could he have acquired in his previous posts) his predecessor's political sensitivity or bureaucratic mastery. He was not a public figure with the ability to appeal to the masses in case of need. He had to learn on the job, starting with the basics of managing a national political apparatus and making presidential decisions. His work in the KGB had taught him to follow orders and to be a subordinate; now he had to wield power and exercise leadership. His only personal decision early in his administration was to begin the "antiterrorist operation" in Chechnya, which indicated a readiness to apply simple remedies to complex problems. This decision may have been the result of political immaturity, or of following certain principles, or of placating Russia's large conservative contingent—or it might have been his KGB conditioning in action.

They say, with good reason, that working in the secret services, especially in the Soviet KGB, is not a profession but a way of thinking. That way of thinking is usually characterized by hostility toward dissent of any kind, an inability to tolerate variety in the environment, the rejection of everything alien or not easily understandable, an excessive suspiciousness, and a tendency to make decisions in secret. People with such a mindset feel comfortable and secure only in their narrow circle of initiates. How characteristic that clannish way of thinking was of Putin Russians had yet to see. One could take hope in the fact that he had worked in Saint Petersburg for the liberal mayor Anatoly Sobchak and had found his way in the new atmosphere of risk, striving, and tolerance of other views.

In unfamiliar areas, Putin displayed caution and did not rush; he waited, pondered, and tried to get to the heart of the issues. His desire to understand the details, to touch everything personally, to hear out his interlocutors—these are certainly among his positive qualities. He expanded his audience, inviting people from all walks of life to the Kremlin, attentively posing questions and amiably listening to the answers. I know many people who were wary of, if not downright skeptical about, Putin until they met him, and then became his active supporters. He knew how to recruit friends. He created alternative sources of information, and he was not isolated the way Yeltsin had been.

In a situation where strategic decisions must be made quickly, however, Putin's assiduity and persistence, his desire to get at every detail, could keep him from seeing the main points. Besides, a leadership style that insists on monitoring all problems daily is exhausting, and for all his stamina and relative youth, Putin was unlikely to keep up the pace for long. Yeltsin had tried at first to be involved in every detail of management, until he realized that was impossible. Sooner or later, Putin would have to decide between strengthening institutions and redistributing some responsibilities to the cabinet and parliament, or yielding some of his responsibilities to people close to him, following Yeltsin's example.

In his first months in office, Putin did not make haste, and his hesitation made him appear bewildered. But looking back, one sees that such cautiousness was the only way to secure his position. Putin had no one at first to lean on except for the Yeltsin team that held him in its grasp. But somehow he had to begin doing things, to demonstrate his ability to control the decision-making process. He had to learn the art of governance. It was not an easy task. Unlike many others and all his predecessors, he had to become a politician after taking the job. And there were no guarantees that even if he became a politician he would go further and become a leader.

Many people characterize Putin as pragmatic and intelligent, a quick study. Early on, he demonstrated an ability to think and speak logically and precisely. He figured out how to communicate with a wide audience and even added a certain charm to his pallid personality. He learned to talk to the press and give thoughtful answers. He was extremely hardworking, and very soon he acquired huge quantities of information about various areas of governance. He had a brilliant memory, just like Yeltsin in his best years. The new leader proved to be both amazingly methodical and intellectually curious, and he turned those qualities to the task of understanding the inner workings of Russian power.

Putin said perfectly reasonable things, and soon he began to take steps in the right direction—if we consider moving Russia toward a more effective market economy the right thing to do. He recruited the liberals German Gref, Andrei Illarionov, and Alexei Kudrin, and others whom he knew from Saint Petersburg, and he brought them into the government. He asked Gref to develop a new strategy for the country's development and to prioritize economic reform tasks. The presence of these liberals, whom Putin made part of his circle, suggested that he would not permit antimarket overreactions, even if the public was growing more statist. He had grown accustomed to market thinking and could function in the framework of a market economy.

Undoubtedly, the new Russian leader had positive potential. That potential could be used for the greater good, but the exigencies of survival—or even Putin's personal complexes and prejudices—could bury it. He had only started to build his presidency.

Already a trait of Putin's stirred anxiety: He divided everyone up into friend or foe. His colleagues and comrades in arms from the Yeltsin entourage were accorded the presumption of innocence (for instance, former administration head Pavel Borodin, frequently accused of corruption).[10] Putin did not extend the same right to those who disagreed with his policies or did not show enough obedience. He soon demonstrated this with tycoon Vladimir Gusinsky and his media empire Media-Most, and then with his "godfather" Berezovsky.

Putin's attitude toward freedom of the press caused perhaps the most consternation. The new leader gradually began to regard every criticism of his policies as a challenge to the state and did not lose any opportunity to strike back at the critics. The first victim of his dislike of media independence was Andrei Babitsky, a reporter for Radio Liberty who criticized Moscow's Chechnya policy in his battlefield reports during 1999 and 2000. Babitsky bore the brunt of the Russian judicial and repressive machinery. He was charged with spying for Chechen rebels, held in an isolation cell, interrogated, and even exchanged like a terrorist for Russian soldiers and handed over to an armed Chechen group. His interrogators apparently wanted him to vanish without a trace.

The Babitsky incident can be defined as a *syndrome of totalitarianism in a pluralistic society*—a return to a typically Soviet way of treating independent journalists who had the courage to confront authority with views differing from the official line. The security services persecuted Babitsky, apparently with Putin's knowledge. Putin had to have known, because the Babitsky case became the topic of the day in the Russian media. In a group letter of protest, journalists wrote:

> Not once since the start of perestroika have the authorities permitted themselves such blatant lawlessness and cynicism toward representatives of the mass media. If the journalist Babitsky has committed an illegal act from the point of view of the authorities, then the question of his guilt or innocence must be decided in an open judicial trial. If the actions against Babitsky are a reaction to the

contents of his reports from Chechnya, this is a direct violation of the principle of freedom of the press guaranteed by the Constitution.[11]

The Kremlin did not dare keep Babitsky in prison or execute him, apparently concerned by the reaction from the international community and inside Russia. Babitsky was let free, and the charges against him were dropped in the end. This forced restraint by the security services signaled their recognition of the new political reality. Babitsky went abroad. The rest of the media community learned its lesson: Russia was not becoming a friendly place for independent journalists. And the fact that the persecution—unthinkable in Gorbachev's or Yeltsin's time— occurred at all was enough to rouse anxiety about the new Kremlin residents' attitude toward the press.

A crucial factor in any administration—and one that is much more important when the executive is strong and balancing institutions are weak—is the people with whom the leader surrounds himself and to whose advice he listens on policy and politics. In Putin's new Kremlin, the ties of the Yeltsin era continued to bind, and old courtiers held onto some or most of their power.

After the election, Putin was unable to rid his team of members of Yeltsin's entourage (for example, the head of the presidential staff, Alexander Voloshin). The new president proclaimed his "equidistance" from all the oligarchs. But the oligarchs' representatives remained part of his inner circle, exercising significant—though not open, as before—influence on important decisions. New oligarchs even began to rise to power, among them Sergei Pugachev, who had known Putin from his Saint Petersburg days. Pugachev's discreet presence in the Kremlin's corridors sent a signal that the new leader was not preparing to root out the class of oligarchs entirely; he was simply dividing them into loyal and disloyal ones.

Out of gratitude, but more, perhaps, for practical reasons, Putin continued functioning within the "paradigm of loyalty"—a system of mutual obligations within a certain circle, based sometimes on friendship and previous connections but more often on deals and fear of compromising materials. Perhaps it was this paradigm that kept him from severing old ties and that explained his unwillingness, and perhaps inability, to break with the past at this point. Once he became part of the circle of cronies hand-cuffing him, it would be difficult or even impossible for him to rid him-self of the Yeltsin entourage and other dubious hangers-on unless he cre-ated his own base and learned the very specific art of Russian governance. In early 2000, the impression was that Putin was not ready to break free.

Gradually, the president began bringing old colleagues into the Kremlin, people he knew from Saint Petersburg and whom he could trust. For the most part, however, they were people with connections to the power structures, mainly to the security services. Among them were those who had persecuted dissidents. That alone was enough to trouble democratically minded Russians and human rights activists. And their concern was justified: Given the weak democratic mechanisms and the influx of former KGB people into the higher levels of the administra-tion, some return to totalitarian behavior seemed inevitable.

For some time, even before he became president, Moscow society had been trying to determine who was "in" with Putin. It seemed that the man was surrounded by a constantly shifting kaleidoscope of new and old faces, all trying to find a spot as close to him as possible, familiar fig-ures mixing with totally unknown characters in the inevitable black suits and white shirts. Gradually, order came to the Brownian motion: Many people from the Yeltsin era gradually moved to the sidelines and took on an entreating look. In the center were new people who looked more and more confident and were becoming proficient at finding their way around the Kremlin's corridors. Things quieted down, and several circles formed around Putin.

The first circle was made up of people from the old Yeltsin political group. Preeminent was Voloshin (again, the head of the presidential staff). It was obvious that Putin kept Voloshin on not out of a sense of grati-tude but because he knew how to get things done and had gradually become quite a skillful fixer and in this capacity was still irreplaceable. Voloshin was continually hand in glove with the former members of Yeltsin's entourage and was often visited by Tatyana Dyachenko and Valentin Yumashev, leading lights of the Yeltsin Family.

The second group in Putin's entourage was the liberal technocrats, most of them from Saint Petersburg. German Gref, Leonid Reiman, Ilya Klebanov, and Alexei Kudrin were members of the government, holding key positions on its economic staff. In Moscow, they were considered people of Anatoly Chubais, long one of the preeminent Russian liberals and a permanent member of Yeltsin's team. Chubais had left the political arena in good time, but he continued lobbying behind the scenes. The relationship between Chubais and Putin was not without its dark spots and mutual suspicions. The new boss of the Kremlin would not be very likely to tolerate such a powerful and willful politician in his circle. Moreover, Putin certainly had been informed that it was Chubais who in 1999 had first objected to Putin's appointment as prime minister and, therefore, as Yeltsin's successor. Chubais knew that with an energetic president he would no longer be needed as gatekeeper and crisis manager. As for Chubais's people, they were happy to switch to Putin.

The third group in Putin's entourage was his people—those who had become friends in his Saint Petersburg phase or had been colleagues in the KGB. These *siloviki*, as they were called in Russia, were the only ones he could trust and rely on. They were, first of all, Sergei Ivanov, at the moment head of the powerful Security Council, which was coordinating the policies of the power ministries; Victor Cherkesov, a colleague from the Federal Security Service (FSB); and Nikolai Patrushev, the head of the FSB. A significant portion of the Russian public had positive feelings about the appointment to high office of people from the special services. Thus, 44 percent saw it in a positive light (21 percent as totally positive) and 35 percent in a negative light (a mere 9 percent as extremely negative).[12] The phenomenon was probably a consequence of Russians' disillusionment with the groups that arose under Yeltsin and their desire to cleanse the ruling class, because the people coming from the special services were perceived as less corrupt than others.

Along with the secret service officials were young people who had worked with Putin for Sobchak in Saint Petersburg, including Dmitry Kozak, Igor Sechin, and Dmitry Medvedev. The internal struggle between the Saint Petersburg liberals and the Saint Petersburg secret service people allowed the old Yeltsin entourage, which had brought Putin to power and had equal numbers for the corridor battles, to maintain their influence.

These groups were incompatible in their origins. But for the time being, Putin needed them all to perform their different functions. Members of Yeltsin's team continued to handle internal political conflicts. Still, they were acting as chief screenwriters. The liberals ran economic policy. Putin's secret service colleagues tried to handle, not always skillfully, the more delicate projects dealing with the consolidation of Putin's power. At the same time, they studied Kremlin intrigues. Soon we'll see that they were not very successful in learning the art of sweet deals. But they were the ones with the direct access: Putin let them in on his plans, and they could help determine where he would strike next. It was obvious that these teams of Putin's would hold differing views and strive toward different goals and that the winners would influence Putin's behavior. Maneuvering behind them, several oligarchic groups, among them Petr Aven and Mikhail Fridman's Alfa and Gazprom, exploited the battle of the political "elephants" to promote their people and create their own niches in Putin's entourage.

The time had come for Putin to show the character of his presidency. The main test, which would demonstrate not only the intentions but also the content of the new administration, was the formation of the government. Putin had two options. He could select an independent cabinet headed by a political heavyweight that would have total responsibility for economic policy and let the president take charge promoting internal stability, foreign policy, and relations with the regions. That would have been optimal for Russia because it divided the executive power and gradually moved the country toward an independent government and parliament. The second option was the creation of a totally dependent cabinet headed by an obedient prime minister and the continuation of the practice in which the president formulated all cabinet policies yet avoided all responsibility.

Putin put an end to his doubts and presented a candidate for prime minister to the Duma. The candidate was Mikhail Kasyanov, who had been first deputy prime minister in Yeltsin's government and before that Yeltsin's deputy minister of finance. Kasyanov's appointment could be interpreted as Putin's decision (probably forced) to maintain the influence of the Yeltsin political Family. It was widely known that Kasyanov was close to Yeltsin's clan.

Quite a few rumors circulated about Kasyanov. Allegedly, he had been incriminated in dubious deals involving Russian and Soviet debts. That was how he had gotten his nickname, "Misha Two Percent": It was said that he took 2 percent off the top of every debt deal he helped organize. He ignored the accusations and rumors, preferring to pretend he knew nothing about what the Moscow political world was whispering. Of course, we must give Kasyanov his due—he was also known as an experienced negotiator with Western financial institutions. And he soon showed himself to be a good administrator who knew how to survive in the shark-infested Kremlin pond.

The choice of Kasyanov signaled which model of power the new president intended to build: the obedient cabinet headed by an obedient prime minister. Putin selected the "leash" model of governance, perpetuating Yeltsin's model of the cabinet that got orders from the presidential staff and at the same time was responsible for all the president's errors— "a boy for beating," as they say in Russia.

Putin was forming a new cabinet with a strong whiff of the old. Kasyanov was immediately confirmed by the equally obedient Duma, and Putin's first government was formed.[13] It retained odious figures accused of corruption, such as Minister of Atomic Industry Yevgeny Adamov and Minister of Transportation Nikolai Aksyonenko. Putin kept the cabinet a coalition of the various groups of influence. Kasyanov represented the interests of the old Kremlin team, while Deputy Prime Minister Kudrin represented the Chubais group. Other clans, notably the group of Yuri Maslyukov, a visible Communist Party activist and representative of the Soviet defense establishment, also had a presence. The cabinet retained the old power bloc, with the exception of the head of the Foreign Intelligence Service—for the moment, the heads of the Defense Ministry, Internal Affairs Ministry, and security services were people appointed by Yeltsin. This was the result of an agreement between Putin and Yeltsin—Putin had promised not to replace them for a year.

The composition of the government showed that the new president could not yet defend his own people. Thus Gref, who had wanted a central role in the cabinet, ended up with a secondary post as director of the Ministry of Economic Development and Trade. Despite some independent moves, the new president still had to coordinate his appointments with the Yeltsin people.

A government like this, built to reflect the balance of power in the Kremlin entourage rather than to address political and economic priorities, could not be expected to be effective. The cabinet could be likened to a landmine, its members occupied not with implementing coordinated policies but with struggling to advance the interests of their groups or of their strategies.

In this context, the oversight agencies—the presidential staff and the Security Council took on a special role: They became the key decision making bodies—first in the field of domestic politics and second in the foreign policy area. The former was still headed by Voloshin and the latter by Putin's man and personal friend Ivanov. Given their composition and their vaguely defined powers, the two agencies were bound to have conflicts. The configuration of the center being built by Putin recreated the system of informal checks and balances that had existed under Yeltsin. The president's constant conciliating presence was necessary to keep the struggle among the group interests from becoming destructive. With a weak parliament and judicial system and the absence of local self-government, the president had to play the role of judge and arbiter.

While the members of the new ruling circle entered their orbits around the president, he kept silent, creating the impression that he did not know what to do next. "Putin is a puppet," the mass media joked. It was hard to avoid feeling that the president had allowed his team to turn him into the product of a public relations campaign: He read prepared speeches and used rehearsed gestures that hid his personality and made it difficult to distinguish the artificial Putin from the real one. It began to look as if the "man of muscle" created by his image makers was in truth baffled by mounting problems and emergencies.

In the summer of 2000, if anyone still labored under the illusion of Putin's independence, or wondered who really ran Russia, their doubts were settled once the prosecutor general was appointed. This was a key position. Much depended on the person in that post, including whether the oligarchs and the people in the Yeltsin contingent would feel comfortable. It was in the interests of Yeltsin's Family to have a manageable person as prosecutor general. When Putin tried to propose Kozak, his close ally, the Yeltsin entourage exerted unprecedented pressure on the president to change his mind. Papa himself—Yeltsin—was called in, according to a story in the *Obshchaya gazeta* of May 25–31. Yeltsin called Putin in the middle of the night and applied force until Putin rewrote the decree appointing Kozak, naming instead the acting prosecutor general, Vladimir Ustinov. The decree was sent to the upper house of the parliament for its approval with indecent haste and without the proper paperwork.

This business made Putin look pathetic. All Moscow was abuzz, saying that the new Kremlin boss had tried just this once to be independent and had not been allowed. The incident was the first major blow to the new president.

The president not only gave up his choice for prosecutor general but in the end did not support his own candidate for governor of Saint Petersburg, then–deputy prime minister Valentina Matvienko, whom Putin himself sent to run in his home city. When Putin saw that incumbent governor Vladimir Yakovlev—his personal enemy, who had wrested power from Sobchak and thus cost Putin his Saint Petersburg job—was likely to win the gubernatorial contest, he stopped backing Matvienko. That looked like weakness. Yeltsin would have jumped into the fray. Putin, coming upon an obstacle, retreated and waited. His training in the secret services or his characteristic indecisiveness was showing. At the time, it was not clear whether a new move would follow. But it soon became evident that, with few exceptions, the new leader was not looking for a fight and would rather avoid confrontation. The macho appearance that Putin had thus far tried to cultivate seemed misleading.

To somehow make up for his defeat in forming his cabinet, Putin redoubled his efforts to cement his superpresidential regime by limiting the independence of Russia's regions. He must have thought that he would meet less resistance there. The idea of creating new relations between the center and regions and curbing the power of the local barons had long been discussed in Putin's circles. Putin had waited for the right moment to launch his attack on the governors who were too sure of themselves.

In May 2000, the moment had come. Putin, who was inaugurated as president May 7, felt himself ready to show his initiative. He was definitely tired of being accused of being weak and indecisive. He thought it was time to act. He promulgated a decree (on May 13, 2000) on the formation of seven federal *okrugs*, or regions (whose borders happened to coincide with those of the military *okrugs*), among which the 89 republics and other components of the Russian Federation were divided. The creation of the *okrugs* was meant to improve the center's control over the activities of the regional leaders and newly formed regional elites. Representatives of the president were named to head the *okrugs*, of whom five out of seven were from the power structures—*siloviki*—and were close to Putin.[14]

The public reacted to Putin's initiative with confusion, but not fervent resistance. Putin then sent to the Duma for approval three new laws that weakened the role of both the regional leaders and the parliament's upper chamber, the Federation Council, the legislative body for the regional governors and heads of the regional legislative bodies.[15] Putin's goal was to overcome the broad federal tendencies in Russia's development and build a stricter system of subordination of the regions to the center—in fact returning to Moscow the powers that Yeltsin gave up to the regions in his day.

These first steps in neutralizing the regional leaders were successful. The governors and republican presidents never did organize to resist Putin's attack. Even the education of the regions in the center's deviousness attempted by Berezovsky—who by that time had left the Kremlin camp and was trying to create an opposition to Putin among the regional leaders—failed. The local bosses had decided to fight for survival separately—which is what destroyed them. Putin played his hand well, depriving the Federation Council of its role as counterbalance to the president, and depriving the governors of a sizable chunk of their power. In a way, he was taking his revenge for not being allowed to form his cabinet independently.

The political establishment gradually rebounded from the shock Putin's initiatives caused, and it became evident that its members had mixed feelings. Only recently, the president had been accused of delayed reaction, and now he was accused of overreacting. Putin had begun changing the mechanism of power, the regime itself. And that would affect many groups. But the observers were not sure that Putin's "revolution" would achieve its goal—the creation of the smooth and reliable superpresidential regime. Yeltsin before Putin had tried to do the same and failed.[16]

No one disagreed that the regions' feudal lords had long been in need of curtailing or that local legislation had to be brought into line with the Constitution. Of the Russian Federation's 21 republics, the constitution of only one, Udmurtia, fully complied with the national Constitution. Up to 30 percent of local acts adopted by the republics went against norms established in the Constitution, according to the May 16, 2000, *Vedomosti*. But the problem could have been solved in two ways: by emphasizing bureaucratic control, or by strengthening judicial control over the work of the regional administrations and using the financial and economic instruments of pressure that the center had available. Putin chose the former.

Of course there were reasons for adopting the bureaucratic solution other than Putin's desire to increase his own power. Creating a system of judicial and financial control over the provinces required time, whereas building a system of control through cadres loyal to the president was much faster. But Putin must have forgotten—or he did not yet know—that bureaucratic control always hides elements of anarchy and uncontrollability.[17]

The creation of the federal *okrugs* raised the most questions. Many observers doubted that the president's representatives could exercise effective control over the regions if they lacked the right to use financial transfers as carrots or sticks or to control the power structures. If, conversely, Putin gave the representatives in the *okrugs* those powers, he ran the risk of making them into influential figures. Where was the assurance that one of them would not turn into a new Yeltsin?

Moreover, there was also a feeling that the presidential envoys were intentionally being appointed to take on the responsibility for what happened regionally. Putin could always pass the buck to his representative and say, "Talk to him, he's accountable for everything." That helped the president to retain his reputation, but it did not help make the governance more efficient.

The possibility of Putin being able to fire governors seemed to his critics like giving away too much power to the center. The Kremlin's desire to form the Federation Council by appointing political nobodies—many of whom had never been to the regions they were supposed to represent—elicited a unanimous negative reaction. It was hardly a way to make the upper chamber work effectively in fulfilling responsibilities like vetoing Duma decisions, acting as a buffer between the president and the Duma, and deciding questions of war and peace. It did not take a constitutional scholar to realize that the existence of an upper chamber of the parliament in which representatives of the executive body convene ex officio and function as a legislative branch is contrary to the principle of separation of powers. But at the same time, with the Duma so compliant, the Federation Council was the only barrier on the path to strengthening the authoritarianism of the leader. Critics disliked even more the Kremlin's decision to liquidate local self-rule, making it dependent on the moods of the governors.

The regional leaders' acceptance of the new rules could be explained by their unwillingness to engage in battle with the center and by their hope of negotiating concessions separately. Bearing in mind the ancient tradition of fighting under the carpet and the apparatchik arts of the regional bosses, an attempt to block the Kremlin's initiatives was to be expected. I remember a conversation with the powerful leader of a rich Russian donor region (a region that contributed more to the federal budget than it got). When I asked why the members of the Federation Council had surrendered voluntarily to Putin, he replied with a smile, "The best way to survive in Russia is not resistance, but sabotage." To me that meant the provincial bosses were hoping to wait it out, paying lip service to the president while continuing their former policies at home.

Putin did not stop with the bid to fortify the center's control over the regions. Now that he had felt his strength a little, he was apparently sure of himself and ready to fight his real or perceived enemies in the open. In October 2000, the Kremlin forced Berezovsky to give up control of the major Russian First television channel. Berezovsky sold his shares to the state. Then Putin struck a blow at the media empire of one of the most powerful oligarchs, Gusinsky, who had supported his opponents (Luzhkov and Primakov, and then Yavlinsky) in the elections. The new leader had had all he could stomach of the popular broadcasts on the NTV television channel, the radio station Ekho Moskvy, the journal *Itogi*, and the periodical *Segodnya*—all controlled by the ambitious and arrogant Gusinsky.

On May 11, four days after Putin's inauguration, police raided the headquarters of the Media-Most holding company that controlled NTV and Gusinsky's other media. Then the government took over Gusinsky's Most-Bank (which, however, had been in trouble for a long time). Putin's proponents concluded that the president had begun an attack on the oligarchs. But that was not the whole truth, because the police did not touch other oligarchs who had ties to the Kremlin. It was clear that the Kremlin attack was selective in nature.

If Gusinsky had supported Putin and his media outlets had not attacked the Kremlin team, and if Gusinsky had not tried to demand preferential treatment from Putin, Gusinsky would not have been touched. The Most affair showed that the Kremlin had begun taking on its critics or potential competitors. The fate of the Media-Most empire was a test of the degree of political freedom that Putin would allow, and gave a taste of the rules he would impose on the game with the influential groups.

Years after it was all over, one of the leading Russian news anchors, Vladimir Pozner, gave his interpretation of the motives behind the Kremlin's campaign against Gusinsky. "I am convinced that all NTV problems were the result of personal animosity between Gusinsky and Putin. Gusinsky tried to dictate to Putin: either you support me or I'll show *compromat* (compromising materials) on you. I don't think that the president has the right to seek his vengeance. But presidents are human beings after all." Personal animosity might have triggered conflict between Gusinsky's media and the Kremlin. But the fundamental cause was much deeper and had to do with the fact that independent media did not fit into the plan of presidential personified rule.

Another test was the fate of the Channel 3 television station, which was under the influence of Luzhkov, one of Putin's two main rivals in the presidential election, who financially supported it. The Channel 3 team also was intimidated by the Kremlin. The impression created was that the ruling group was going to stoop to traditional Russian methods—suppressing or at least scaring off enemies and even just potential political opponents.

This time, the attack was directed against the media groups that were under the influence of Putin's former rivals. The Kremlin found support for such a policy not only among the *siloviki* but among the portion of the public that saw free mass media as channels of influence for the oligarchs—which in fact was true to some extent. In November 2000, VTsIOM polls found that only 7 percent of Russians thought that the main networks were independent, 79 percent thought they were dependent on the oligarchs, and 18 percent thought they were dependent on the state. Thus the struggle against independent mass media was perceived by a large portion of the population as a struggle against the tycoons, who were especially disliked and even hated in Russia.

Putin's political handwriting was becoming clearer, as was his plan of expanding presidential power. His previous silence might have been just a tactic, wary as he was of resistance. The reform of the Federation Council and of the center–periphery relations showed that Putin intended to construct his own system of governance. Yeltsin's successor was gradually morphing into the terminator of the Yeltsin regime. Putin had sent a clear signal that he was planning to liquidate the basis of Yeltsin's power, which had been the mechanism of mutual back-rubbing and tolerance. Maybe the authoritarian at heart had been pretending to be the old guard's tame creature and hesitating guy while in fact he had known all along what he wanted. But more likely Putin had a more complicated personality that combined stubbornness and indecisiveness, sense of purpose and lack of vision, suspicion and distrust of everything and the longing to rely upon faithfulness. Russia's ride with him promised to be an unpredictable adventure.

The new leader began building his power edifice on the foundation of another principle: subordination. The president was at the very top, above everyone else, from which vantage point he sent down directives to his subordinates, who passed them down lower. Direct subordination and compliance ensured a flawless connection between management floors. The mechanism of subordination did not require an active parliament or opposition or a developed multiparty system or independent mass media. Management through subordination must have impressed Putin, as a man from the secret services and a technocratic manager. Leaning on executive power allowed him to implement decisions quickly, without wasting time on endless coordination. Besides which, this management style gave him the resources of power he needed, so that he was no longer dependent on the old clans.

In fact, the state Putin was trying to re-create was the one that had always existed in Russia, except for the brief Yeltsin interregnum. By consolidating power and trying to take it all into his own fist, he was also strengthening the Russian System—a system based on power personified. That state, however, built as it was on vertical subordination, lacking communication from the bottom up, was weak and exceptionally inefficient because its energy went into the constant generation of fear, enforcing of discipline, and supporting of the vertical chain of power. The previous version of that state had collapsed in 1991. Sooner or later, a new version of the Russian System based on the "transmission belt" would collapse under its own weight, especially if it lacked a strong mechanism of repression.

The new ruling team, especially the Saint Petersburg newcomers, could not understand that an efficient state has a more complex structure that includes numerous horizontal supports and a network of counterbalances. By the way, such a state is also more conducive to its leader's survival, because he does not have to worry about preserving his inaccessibility or finding an heir who will not throw him in prison when he loses power. But for the time being, Putin was not thinking about such things. He started down the more familiar path, perhaps urged on by insecurity, by a desire to protect himself, or by the inertia of Yeltsin's legacy. Perhaps he saw no trustworthy partners out there with whom he could build institutions. He might have been fascinated by the idea of turning Russia into a huge corporation based on vertical ties, with himself in the role of chief executive officer. But Russian society was already a more complicated entity that couldn't obey rules mechanically imposed from above and didn't want to be compartmentalized by junior managers. Sooner or later, the president had to realize that.

At this point in time—1999 and 2000—Putin, like Yeltsin, was evidently not concerned with questions of how to combine the market and democracy, political and economic freedoms. Just like his predecessor, he began creating a system relying on his instincts and what felt comfortable to him. But Yeltsin was wise and experienced. He knew Russia, and his intuition told him that Russia had changed. Therefore, after some attempts to discipline the country, he had preferred to rule by allowing all the forces in Russian society to develop and not hindering anyone who was not a direct threat to his power.

Yeltsin, like Chinese leaders, let a thousand flowers bloom. Putin wanted to sow the entire field in one vegetable. His instincts, honed in the power structures, provided simple guidance: control everything, trust no one, be strong because power is the only thing people understand. Those were the political bricks with which regimes in Russia had always been built. With the public's astonishing approval ratings—more than 60 percent of respondents backed him—they seemed to be telling Putin, "We want what you want. We want to obey, keep going." But it was still unclear to what degree people who had grown accustomed to Yeltsin's freedom would be willing to line up again. Then, too, the regime of subordination went against Putin's goal of building an efficient market economy, which demands freedoms and initiative. Government is always a balancing act, and balancing authoritarianism and the market is an even trickier one.

At the same time, the new leader defied the attempts to put him into a definite ideological cluster. He proved that he was ready for complicated policy design. Leaning toward traditionalism in the process of shaping his rule, he put a new mark on Russian foreign policy. Even before the presidential election, he invited Lord George Robertson, secretary general of NATO, to Moscow, reviving Russia's relations with the alliance. He did this despite the resistance of the Russian military. He invited U.K. prime minister Tony Blair to Saint Petersburg and persuaded him that he wants to pursue warmer relations between Russia and the West.

Putin's intention was to rebuild bridges to the West after their deterioration during the later years of the Yeltsin administration, and especially after the spring of 1999 saw both NATO enlargement and the NATO bombing of Kosovo, which chilled relations between Russia and the West. It was also clear that Putin was worried by the negative reaction in the West to the war in Chechnya. He demonstrated that his goal was to join the international club, that he wanted civilized relations with the West. He understood the importance of the West in solving Russia's economic problems.

One could assume that as a member of the intelligence community and with his KGB experience, deep in his heart Putin might harbor distrust of the West. It is possible that, like many of his colleagues, he would secretly accuse the West of trying to weaken Russia and exploiting Russian weakness for its own profit, and of having a double standard in its policy toward Russia. In any case, at the beginning of his presidency, Putin still used in his rhetoric the idea of a multipolarity promoted by his predecessor Primakov, albeit more cautiously—which meant that he still cherished the illusion of Russia's "special path," or that he was unsure about the new Russia's identity and development agenda, or that he was not ready for more decisive breakthrough—for the time being. But realistically, one had to wonder which countries or groupings a weakened Russia could attract as one of the poles. In the beginning, Putin may have hesitated in setting an agenda, but with his new policy toward NATO and Europe, he was clearly turning toward the West.

Putin faced an even more complicated task, that of choosing his base of support, or the groups he would rely upon. The selection in Russia was limited: large private businesses, in the persons of the so-called oligarchs; the state apparatus, with its numerous ministries, government committees, and other institutions that constitute the backbone of the system of governance; the regional elites; the power structures, meaning the Defense and Interior Ministries and the intelligence services; medium-sized and small businesses; and society.

Selecting that base was not easy. With his statist orientation, Putin could not entirely trust big business, which had demonstrated its vested interests and inability to curb its greed. Still, the new leader could not or did not want to distance himself fully from some oligarchic groups, at least for the time being. But he hardly considered sharing power with them.

As for the state apparatus, it shared Putin's desire for centralization. Moreover, the apparatus could easily forge a union with the power structures; such a union, after all, was long the basis for the Russian regime. But relying solely on that union was even more dangerous for Putin than an alliance with the oligarchs and big business. He knew that such support could lead to an excessive emphasis on the grinding of administrative gears, slowing down the development of the free market and increasing isolationism in foreign policy. The apparatus and *siloviki* in Russia still could support the repressive dictatorial regime. Putin was at least outwardly in favor of preserving the civilized rules of the global game, and as we have seen, there were signs that he leaned toward establishing normal relations with the West. If he kept on this course, he had to cut his links with the apparatus and *siloviki*.

Society had not developed sufficiently to provide a base of social groups that could lend liberal support for an administration. Small and medium-sized businesses in Russia, which of all groups had the strongest interest in equal rules and fair competition and in ousting the oligarchs, were as yet too weak to be a pillar of the new rule. The intelligentsia was tired and frustrated, having been disappointed by the previous reform effort. As for civil society at large, it was still unstructured and amorphous after a mere decade of postcommunist evolution, and thus not a powerful pressure source.

It came down to a choice between the main political forces in Russia: the oligarchy and the state apparatus. Naturally, the two forces were entwined. During Yeltsin's presidency, the state apparatus helped enrich the oligarchy, earning a bit for its cooperation. However, the apparatus, traditionally powerful in Russia, had won much less from the transformation than had the oligarchs, so revenge and domination were very much on its members' minds.

The apparatus and the oligarchy had clashed several times in the postcommunist era. The first involved the skirmish between the faction of Alexander Korzhakov, Yeltsin's former chief of security, and the oligarchs (Berezovsky, Gusinsky, and others) during the 1996 elections. The two groups fought not only for control over Yeltsin but for different paths of development for Russia. The bureaucrats and military men in Yeltsin's entourage tried to persuade the president to cancel the elections and hold on to power by force, which would have made him hostage to them. The oligarchs, conversely, were in favor of going ahead with the elections, which would keep more freedoms and thus allow them to survive. In this case, the interests of the oligarchs and democracy coincided. In the spring of 1996, the oligarchs and the liberal technocrats who joined them—in the person of Chubais and his group—won.

The next clash between the oligarchy and the apparatus came in 1997, in the "bank war." In the course of the fighting, which centered on the privatization of Russian communications giant Svyazinvest, roles were reversed, and the liberal technocrats—Chubais and his people—became statist bureaucrats attempting to rein in the appetites of the oligarchs of the Berezovsky-Gusinsky group.[18] During Primakov's time as prime minister, the third open clash of interests occurred, with the state apparatus and Primakov on one side and the oligarchs, led by Berezovsky, on the other.

With Putin's accession, there were signs of a new conflict. They were blurred because some influential oligarchs remained in Putin's camp and this time the attack was on two representatives of big business, Gusinsky and Berezovsky, who were trying to play an independent role in politics. But the bureaucratic and power-structure supports of the regime were demanding that Putin also push the other oligarchs out of the Kremlin orbit. In forming his base, Putin seems to have chosen the variant that corresponded best to his psychology—not betting everything on one card, avoiding direct confrontation especially with powerful foes, and gradually weakening everyone by slowly narrowing their space for maneuvering. The president stressed the bureaucratic-power component but left untouched those oligarchs who had sworn fealty to him. He obviously wanted to create a system of power in which each influential group found its own place but no one group could claim to have a special role or influence in the Kremlin and so leave its allotted niche.

The problem was that none of the fundamental forces in the president's entourage—state apparatus, oligarchy, or power structures—was interested in consistent reform. It was not clear whether the president would manage to stay above the fray and avoid being captured by some political force. The much more experienced Yeltsin had not managed to remain an arbiter.

In the new context, the situation of the liberal technocrats, especially those from the Union of Right Forces (SPS), provoked mixed feelings. Under Putin, the majority of liberal technocrats moved to progovernment positions. It is unlikely they felt comfortable there, when the regime's basic supports were apparatchiks and power structures. The liberal technocrats had hoped to influence the Kremlin under the Putin administration. Under Yeltsin, albeit for a brief period, Yegor Gaidar did determine the vector of economic development. In this connection, the story of "Putin's Gaidar"—German Gref, head of the Center for Strategic Development— is edifying.

In 2000, Gref proposed a new concept of liberal reform to the president. But Putin could not give Gref carte blanche to realize his ideas, just as Yeltsin before him could not give Gaidar free rein. One sees that neither the oligarchic nor the bureaucratic-power structure version of rule allows the liberal technocrats independence. They were relegated to an auxiliary role when the oligarchs were in power, and that looked likely to be the case under bureaucratic domination as well. Liberals still could not become soloists in Russia. It was true they were able to slowly advance some reform measures, like the 13 percent flat income tax that they had succeeded in implementing under Putin. But being in the minority, they were forced into numerous battles that often ended in compromises that eviscerated reforms.

While the oligarchs and the bureaucrats fought over primacy, the Kremlin began constructing a new political stage. There were signs that a search was on for ways to break up the Communist Party and create a left-center movement that would be loyal to the Kremlin. At the same time, preparations were under way for a new law on parties, intended to create a tame multiparty system. As for the pro-Putin Unity Party— which had announced its aim of transforming itself from a movement into a more structured party with individual membership after the presidential election—it was beginning to look more like the former ruling Communist Party of the Soviet Union. The process of turning Yeltsin's political chaos into a "democracy" controlled by the center had begun.

One of the leaders of the SPS liberals, Boris Nemtsov, called this democracy "castrated." The old colleagues Putin had brought in from the security services, once they became acclimatized, starting acting more harshly than the old Yeltsin cadres. They did not hesitate to intimidate independent media in the regions, and they openly used the courts and prosecutor's office to crack down on politicians and groups that expressed their dissatisfaction with the new regime.

Thus in late May and June 2000, weeks after his inauguration as president, Putin overturned his early reputation as a slow-moving politician. He must have decided that it was time to create his own system. He wanted independence. But like most offspring, he still was unable to sever all ties to the old regime.

The outward calm and tranquility of the political scene were giving way to still-spontaneous spots of dissatisfaction. The first to become agitated were the independent mass media and the human rights activists. For them, the Putin regime was taking on more and more obvious authoritarian traits. A collective editorial by the editors and journalists of the liberal newspaper *Obshchaya gazeta* on May 25 was the first to call what Putin was building a "dictatorship." "The impression is being created," wrote the journalists of *Obshchaya*, "that the consolidation of ever more power in the hands of the president is not a means for implementing some policy (the president has not announced any clear political priorities unrelated to this consolidation of power) but an aim in itself."[19] The democratic segment of the membership of the SPS, in the persons of the old human rights activist Sergei Kovalyov and Yabloko members, spoke out against Putin's reshaping of power, accusing him of trying to reinforce robber capitalism and give it a dictatorial impulse.

Putin could not present a counterargument—after all, having initiated his top-down system of governance, he retained special-interest clans that had arisen under Yeltsin, represented by all the oligarchs still sitting in strong positions in the Kremlin. Now, with his effort to concentrate major power resources in his hands, he gave the democrats reason to suspect him of acting more harshly in the interests of the narrow groups of influence—old and new—that occupied the Kremlin. Even if he was power hungry solely on his own account, the question arose: What next?

For the time being, the Russian president proved only one thing: that he was not a democrat. But neither was he a dictator.

There was no mass resistance to Putin's initiatives, nor could such resistance appear. There were several reasons for that: media controlled by the central authorities; the lack of a strong opposition; society's passivity and fatalism; the hope that Putin would pursue honest politics; and a reluctance to criticize him. The president continued to be above criticism in Russia. Russians behaved as if they could not afford to lose hope in their new leader. Therefore, the Kremlin could disregard the scattered hotbeds of dissatisfaction among intellectuals and a few stubborn liberals.

Society followed the leader, but its loyalty and support were conditional—as always in Russia.

Chapter 4

THE MOMENT
OF TRUTH

Putin repeals the taboo on persecution of the oligarchs.
The victor in the boring wilderness. A harsh August and a feeling of suffocation.
Reinforcing the superpresidential regime. Military reform.

It is the summer of 2000. Putin's first attack on the largest independent Russian media empire, Media-Most, failed. The Kremlin so far had succeeded in taking over its bank, but the rest of the media holding belonging to the oligarch Vladimir Gusinsky survived. Gusinsky mobilized public opinion in Russia and the West in support of his company. But the president's men retreated only to regroup. A new assault on the media conglomerate was inevitable, everyone realized. The print and, especially, the electronic media independent of the state constituted a serious obstacle for Putin on the path to building his pragmatic authoritarianism. The president understood the role of the mass media in the political struggle. During the run-up to the parliamentary and presidential elections in late 1999 and early 2000, television had been the decisive force in transforming Mr. Nobody into Mr. President, and Vladimir Vladimirovich did not want this powerful political resource in the hands of his opponents—or even his mildest critics.

Putin's personal animosity toward the ambitious Gusinsky, whom he knew rather well, may have contributed to the president's attitude toward the oligarch's media outlets, particularly the highly popular network NTV. The media tycoon was arrogant enough to believe that he could influence Putin and even dictate rules of the game to him. This the president could not abide. Putin was also outraged by the lack of respect shown him in NTV's broadcasting. The popular NTV program *The Puppets* made the Kremlin boss a caricature, pitiful and even vicious at times. Journalists from NTV, accustomed to saying whatever they wanted under Yeltsin without fear of the Kremlin's wrath, did the same under Yeltsin's successor. They had not noticed that times had changed and that Putin had no intention of tolerating the free-for-all. Yeltsin would not watch television programs that criticized him. Apparently Putin tuned in.

In June, the thunder roared—Gusinsky was arrested. The move would have been almost unthinkable in the Yeltsin era; then the oligarchs had been untouchable. That was Yeltsin's understanding of democracy. He could be displeased by one or another representative of big business. But to arrest him? I believe the first Russian president saw arrests and persecution as basically communist means of governance, and therefore he loathed them. Later, after the oligarchs helped him retain power in 1996, it became impossible for him to take such action. Yeltsin knew how to show gratitude. Besides, he never destroyed anyone, not even his worst enemies.

The last political arrests in Russia went back to 1993, when Yeltsin had put in prison his rivals, vice president Alexander Rutskoi and speaker of the parliament Ruslan Khasbulatov. They had mounted opposition to him that flared into armed insurrection among thousands of followers after Yeltsin dissolved the parliament and ended with the president ordering the army to fire on the parliament building. But Yeltsin was the one who let Rutskoi and Khasbulatov out of jail and refused to prosecute them further. He tried to forget them. Most likely, Yeltsin was merciful to his opponents because he did not consider them a threat to him.

As for his mild reaction toward the tycoons, it is quite possible that Yeltsin regarded the oligarchy as the natural base for his regime. And perhaps he realized that the oligarchy made not only the market but also nongovernmental—that is, free—media possible in Russia. Yeltsin had respect for the freedom of mass information. From time to time, he grew irritated or angry when journalists or politicians treated him poorly or made him the target of crude, even brutal criticism. Sometimes, he called editors in chief on the carpet in the Kremlin and tried to give them orders. But he never persecuted anyone for criticism or personal attacks. The first Russian president remembered that his rise was made possible by the freedom of the press and freedom of expression. He behaved as if all critics and opponents for him were nothing more than annoying gnats, and his reaction was simple—shut the window so you wouldn't see or hear them. Apparently, he also felt that free speech in Russia was important evidence that the country had abandoned communism—his life's goal.

Putin, as soon became apparent, was quite different. He perceived a threat differently. He considered critics and the unruly to be enemies of the state, and therefore his enemies, because he identified the state with the president—that is, himself. He could have said after Louis XIV, "L'Etat, c'est moi"—"I am the state." And they were enemies, as he saw it, to be plucked or squeezed out of the political scene, not given the freedom to speak their minds. At least in his view of politics and power, Putin was more like a Soviet leader than a postcommunist one, and he could act more like one where his critics were concerned. Besides, he wanted the consolidation of the state, which called for more reliance on subordination and discipline. The story of the independent media showed that Putin retained some traits of the Soviet elites that Yeltsin seemed to have been lacking, among them distrust and suspicion. As for vindictiveness—this feature has a more universal character.

Note that the charges against Media-Most were not political but economic: nonpayment of debts to the state. Media-Most did have overdue debt with Gazprom, the state-owned natural gas utility, which reflected its dubious relations with the state. Gusinsky's independent media empire, which included one of the most popular Russian television networks, NTV, could not have been created without close ties to the state. The Kremlin had awarded Gusinsky broadcasting rights for channel 4 as payment for the extremely active participation of all his empire—radio and television stations, newspapers, and magazines—in Yeltsin's 1996 reelection campaign (which the NTV journalists later regretted). Gradually, Gusinsky created professional news on television—a new phenomenon in Russia. But he did it with the help of millions of dollars in loans that again could not have been received without the close cooperation of the authorities. The state monopoly Gazprom guaranteed loans for him from state banks and Western creditors. And there were doubts whether Gusinsky intended to repay the money—most likely not.

The prehistory of the other oligarchic empires in Russia was similarly murky. All the oligarchs had debts with the state, and most were mixed up in fishy deals and machinations. But the authorities continued to regard them benignly, allowing them the occasional serious misdeed. The other broadcasting companies had even greater debt—foremost among them state-owned ORT and RTR—which they had no intention of repaying. The blow fell on Gusinsky because he had violated the system of loyalty and tried to become a political force in his own right.

It is highly likely that Putin personally approved the arrest of the media oligarch. In any case, it couldn't have happened without his knowledge. As he apparently saw it, the arrest was a major step in bringing order to Russia and showed all potential critics that this president would not joke around when it came to maintaining political stability as he saw it. Thus he did away with one of the fundamental taboos of the Yeltsin regime: the prohibition against persecuting both an independent media and the oligarchs.

The Kremlin did not expect Gusinsky's arrest to create the negative reaction it did among Russian democrats and especially in the West. The Media-Most journalists destroyed every attempt by the Kremlin to justify Gusinsky's arrest. Others—politicians and oligarchs—came to Gusinsky's defense for the good reason that they saw a threat to themselves in what had happened to him. The West got involved again. The Western press made the Kremlin's crackdown on Gusinsky's media its lead story, and Western leaders prominently raised the issue with Moscow officials, which was the most unpleasant aspect for Putin. In the end, Gusinsky was released from prison and the charges against him were dropped—as it turned out, only temporarily.

The Gusinsky affair signaled that the authorities would now be using the prosecutor general's office for political ends. The prosecutor's office was being turned into a guard dog of the new regime. The president's warning was clear: No one had immunity anymore, and his critics could find themselves in an extremely unhappy situation. The prosecutor's office and the courts stood behind Putin, prepared to demonstrate that opposing the regime was futile. After Yeltsin's permissiveness, this was indeed a new tendency in Russian politics.

The signal sent by the Kremlin was received by the press and the political world. Gradually, the reaction inside Russia to the continued attack on Gusinsky's media and most of all on NTV began to diminish. People, still remembering not-so-distant Soviet times, decided not to provoke the president. "God knows what is on his mind and how far he might go if he is threatened—better not to test his patience," they were thinking. It was true that in the West, where Putin was being closely watched, observers voiced concern. But Putin must have felt that Western governments would deal with him under any circumstances. He was probably correct.

Putin sent another message as well. If one of the richest and most powerful men in Russia could be arrested and kept in prison just like that, without a fair trial, what could ordinary people expect? The Russian human rights community was seriously concerned. But this small group had little influence now. They were regarded as incurable romantics and idealists. That most of their funding came from the West was a reason for many other Russians to regard them, as they had in Soviet times, as an instrument of Western, primarily American, influence, which only increased their isolation in Russia.

It was soon revealed why Gusinsky had been released—an unseemly story. Gusinsky was forced to sign an agreement with representatives of the state (created by Gazprom's own organization dealing with the media, Gazprom-Media) that in essence traded his property for his freedom. He agreed to sell Media-Most, so disliked by the new regime, on the condition that all charges against him were dropped and he was released from prison. The agreement took the form of a special protocol and was signed by Mikhail Lesen, the minister of the press, television, and mass communications. The state behaved like an out-and-out racketeer. It put Gusinsky in prison, but as soon as he agreed to give up his troublemaking property, he was released without a trial. Under the cover of legal institutions, a cynical deal was concluded.

All this had nothing to do with the "dictatorship of the law"—the principle coined by the president and said to be the foundation of his system of governance, which supposedly demanded strict obedience to the law. Analogous blackmailing using law-and-order agencies was tried out on several other oligarchs and mostly succeeded. Thus Vladimir Potanin, one of the initiators of the "loans for shares" auctions (in the course of which the oligarchs who had helped reelect Yeltsin got property at half price), was forced to pay several million dollars in taxes to avoid an investigation. He was the first in line who experienced the new scare tactics of the law enforcement agencies. Soon he would be followed by others. All the Russian oligarchs had received property because of their access to the Yeltsin entourage. Now the new regime wanted to restore control over them and their activity by blackmailing big business.

Gusinsky was no fool. As soon as he was released, he went public about the terms of his agreement with the Kremlin. He also announced that he had signed the agreement "at gunpoint" and therefore did not intend to comply with it. The state did not get his property. We can imagine the reaction at the Kremlin to Gusinsky's "treachery"—yet all he was doing was playing by the rules the new ruling team set. Putin's team and Media-Most entered into a new unequal battle. The state, including the prosecutor's office and judges and the law enforcement agencies, openly declared a war against a private broadcasting company. The NTV network was the major object of the state attack.[1]

Meanwhile, the moods within society began to change. A large portion of the Russian political world and quite a few journalists supported the government against Gusinsky this time around. There were several reasons. Many found Gusinsky annoying personally and resented NTV's role during the Yeltsin administration, especially its great impact on Yeltsin's reelection in 1996. Others stressed the financial aspect of the conflict between Media-Most and the government, insisting that debts need to be paid and refusing to see the political component of the conflict.

Still others were afraid of drawing down the wrath of the authorities and tried to show their loyalty in every way. There were people in journalism and in politics who understood that the NTV case was about destroying the freedom of the media under cover of talk about repayment of debt but who did not have the courage to admit it. Some people were irritated by the resistance the NTV team put up. One episode in Russian political reality became a gauge of the current level in Russia of public understanding of political issues, and of human decency.

The summer of 2000 was a triumph for Putin. He succeeded in everything—taming the governors, fighting the oligarchs, liquidating the independence of the Federation Council, pocketing the Duma, weakening all the other political institutions, and cowing the press. It is true that he didn't succeed against Gusinsky—not yet. But after his political victories in Moscow and in the regions, he had no influential political opponents, no political rivals left. Even the traditional critics of the authorities like Grigory Yavlinsky, leader of Yabloko, stopped baiting the Kremlin, seeing that society was quite happy with Putin and that people were irritated with any criticism of his actions. Yavlinsky announced a personal moratorium on criticism of Putin until the new president's policies on other issues were clearer.

Nothing threatened the president on the political stage. He was the only force around, the only real source of power and influence. All the other forces, groups, and institutions reacted to what he did rather than acting in their own right. Putin became the sole embodiment of politics and power in Russia. The rest were too insignificant and even pitiful.

The causality is important here. Putin increased his power so much not because he was striving to become omnipotent—Yeltsin probably was by nature far more authoritarian—but mainly because Russian society at that moment was longing for simplicity and security. People were too tired to think, much less to choose from among the choices that political pluralism and democracy suggested. The list of available politicians was too short, and those who were available did not inspire much hope or trust. And besides, the people were fed up with them.

Those who only yesterday had mocked Putin as a politician who would never crawl out of Yeltsin's pocket were now expressing concern about where the president's excessive powers might lead. It was beginning to look as if Vladimir Putin, having gained confidence and while his approval ratings were high, wanted in one fell swoop to destroy all groups of influence that did not depend on him and to fortify the supports of his personal authority. If things continued this way, Putin would literally have no opponents in four years, and his reelection would be guaranteed. And no other influential people would be left in the political arena.

Someone in Putin's entourage—I believe it was Alexander Voloshin—noted, "Everything we do succeeds. How boring. . . ."

Indeed, in comparison with the Yeltsin years, the Putin era was growing boring. The political conflicts of every variety that had constantly exploded on the Russian stage had disappeared. Almost all the independent political actors were gone, leaving only those who sucked up to the president—Kremlin courtiers rather than political actors. The style and rhetoric of power had changed—now there were positive, affirming words and intonations harking back to the era before Gorbachev. If politics is a combination of independent institutions and organizations, channels of influence, and mechanisms for regulating conflict, this was, if not the end of politics, the extinction of many of its aspects. Not only had the struggle for power disappeared, but the struggle to maintain power had become unnecessary. "He's come for a long stay, perhaps forever," said even recent democrats and liberals, fretting about finding a niche that would help them survive in the new climate.

Putin, in the meantime, switched to international affairs. After all, activity in the global arena would boost his legitimacy, his recognition factor, and his acceptance as a player in the world political club. The summer 2000 meeting in Okinawa of the Group of Eight industrial nations (G-8) turned into a coming-out party for him. He spoke well. The members of the world club liked his calm, modest, businesslike demeanor. It wasn't hard to please them—after Yeltsin, any Russian president who could stand without help would be considered a success. Putin had a successful debate with U.S. president Bill Clinton on the Americans' possible abrogation of the 1972 Anti–Ballistic Missile Treaty, feeling the approval of France and the understanding of Germany behind him. The meeting demonstrated Putin's quick reactions and down-to-earth, technocratic approach.

Just before the meeting Putin had gone to North Korea, where he had heard from its leader, Kim Jong Il, a suggestion of his willingness to trade away the Korean missile program for Western money. Putin skillfully introduced the idea at the G-8 meeting. But Kim made a U-turn and withdrew his idea, embarrassing Putin. The new Russian leader had to learn that he must be cautious and avoid becoming a card in somebody else's game. But the embarrassment with North Korea did not change the generally positive impression that world leaders gained of Russia's president. German chancellor Gerhard Schröder suggested that in the future no G-8 meetings should be held without Putin. In other words, Putin joined the highest international league and carried it off with dignity.

Polls in Russia continued to show unprecedented popularity for the new leader. In July 2000, according to VTsIOM, 73 percent of Russians approved of Putin (17 percent disapproved of him, and 10 percent had no opinion). At the same time, 60 percent endorsed concentrating all power in one man's hands as a means of solving Russia's problems (27 percent supported the independence of the branches of government, and 13 percent had no opinion). Russians supported their new president, hoping that he would deal with Yeltsin's chaotic legacy, though they were still not confident that anyone could bring order to the country. At the same time, people agreed that they did not know the leader and his agenda. Fifty-nine percent admitted that they knew little about Putin, only 23 percent felt they had learned a lot about him, and a mere 10 percent felt that they knew what kind of a leader he was.[2]

Russian politics do not stay boring for long. The person who spoiled Putin's triumphal march was another media oligarch—Boris Berezovsky, the master of Kremlin intrigue for much of the Yeltsin era, and one of the smartest political animals in Russia. Berezovsky had been a moving force behind Project Putin. He had helped mold Putin, prepared him for the highest office. But after Gusinsky's arrest, he sensed that his creation was turning on him and other oligarchs whom he could not control. Berezovsky was among the first to realize that the president was beginning to act on a plan to free himself from the more odious part of the Yeltsin entourage. Knowing he would be at the head of those kicked out of the Kremlin, Berezovsky switched to the opposition before being shown the door.

The other oligarchs also felt the change in Putin, but they just laid low. Yet the gray cardinal and leading Kremlin spin-doctor could not tolerate being tossed aside without a word of thanks. Beyond mere feelings, Berezovsky came to the conclusion that if Putin was not stopped from gathering all power to himself soon, he would leave no room for any independent political actors, even those to whom he was obligated. He was sensing danger emanating from the new leader that he had failed to notice before. The rebellion of the country's main intriguer was a desperate attempt to stop the steamroller that could mean oblivion or political death for some, particularly himself. Besides, Berezovsky also had a business empire to save.[3]

Berezovsky was the first to openly protest Putin's reform of the Federation Council. Soon afterward, he began daily attacks on the president using his media resources, first of all his newspapers. The political silence had ended. Someone had begun criticizing the leader who had managed to hypnotize everyone, proponents and opponents alike. Berezovsky pointedly resigned from the parliament in July to protest Putin's policies. That might have seemed a foolish gesture, for parliamentary deputies had immunity from prosecution. But Berezovsky was not a petty player.

As Putin's major critic, Berezovsky could now claim to be a defender of democracy.[4] If Putin suddenly began investigating Berezovsky's machinations, the latter could point to his halo marking him as a persecuted victim of the regime. That would assure him support or even political asylum in the West in case of need. He would need it sooner than he might have expected.

Though the most restive tycoon said all the right things about the threat to the gains of democracy, no one in Russia thought he was sincere. Everyone remembered his role in the evolution of the Yeltsin regime and assumed he was only trying to save himself and his empire now. The fact that Putin's main critic turned out to be this oligarch who had more shady baggage than almost anyone strengthened the president's standing with Russians. Ordinary citizens reasoned simply that if Berezovsky was unhappy, Putin was doing the right thing. What irony: When there was a real threat to democratic freedoms in Russia, their most energetic defender was a manipulative tycoon with a suspicious reputation.

Berezovsky went further and attempted to create a "constructive opposition" to Putin. He was beginning to look at his battle with his former friend Vladimir as a personal vendetta. He might have wanted to prove that once again—as with the reelection of Yeltsin in 1996 and the organizing of Putin's own ascendancy in 1999—he could do the impossible. However, his well-publicized campaign to create an opposition failed. At the press conference he called to announce his intentions, Berezovsky was joined by people who seemed randomly selected: a second-rate actor, a columnist, a playwright, and a writer who lived abroad. It was pathetic. This time, the great intriguer was out of luck— the prosecutor general's office began investigating his deals, and he was forced to emigrate.[5]

Berezovsky's defeat showed how much the mood of Russian elites had changed. A short time before, everyone would have answered the call of that demon of Russian politics. Now Boris Abramovich was politely heard out but got no response. No one wanted to become his ally. Oligarchs could be supported and joined only when they were acting on orders from the regime. It seemed there was no independent role for either the oligarchy or the opposition in Putin's Russia.

The Kremlin godfather's vendetta against the president was the beginning of an unpleasant chain of events for the Kremlin just when it had seemed on the verge of invincibility and all its plans were successfully fulfilled. A powerful explosion went off in the underpass below Pushkin Square, in the center of Moscow, on August 8, 2000. The fiery blast knocked people off their feet, killing dozens. Many agonized for days from burns before dying. The blast was attributed to Chechen separatists. And once again, the Moscow police started endless antiterrorist "special operations," which naturally yielded no results. "We must get used to the fact that something can happen at any time in any place," the Russian newspapers wrote. That was the mood of ordinary Russian people, who had longed for stability and a quiet life with Putin's ascendancy to power and found themselves facing new insecurities.

The explosion on Moscow's main street was only the beginning of Russia's disasters. On August 12, the atomic submarine K-141-*Kursk*, the pride of the Russian fleet, sank in the Barents Sea during naval exercises. It became the fraternal grave for 118 crew members. It was only learned from a dead crew member's note, after his body was brought up, that after the submarine sank, some of the crew lived and hoped for aid that never came. For hours after the accident, they banged out an SOS on the walls, and this banging was actually heard by the Russian divers who finally discovered the submarine. Then the signals stopped. Russian attempts to save the crew, started too late—on the sixth day after the accident—and executed extremely unprofessionally, were a failure. The Russian rescuers had none of the equipment needed to open the submarine hatches. The country that launched satellites and had nuclear missiles that could destroy the world could not open the hatch of its own submarine.

Russians, who had grown accustomed to the constant losses in Chechnya, were stunned by the *Kursk* tragedy. Perhaps we all thought about the horror of a slow death by suffocation, the tapping in code, and the slow realization that the rescue would not come. Someone put it very well, describing the emotion that gripped the recently callous nation: "Today we are all in the *Kursk*, and we know that no one will save us." Every day when there was news about the submarine, people stopped what they were doing to listen closely to the radio or watch the television, trying to find a glimmer of a reason to hope that the country that still considered itself great would be able to save its seamen.

It was a rare moment of unity at a national moment of catharsis. Even during the putsch of August 1991 in Moscow, people had not been really united—the democrats and Muscovites had supported Yeltsin, but the rest of the country had calmly watched the events as onlookers at their nation's crisis. Now grief brought Russians together. The tragedy awakened not only feelings of compassion but also an understanding of the impotence of the authorities and the vulnerability of ordinary people in the country where the state never cared about the life of an individual.

Putin can consider that tragic week his first serious failure. While the remaining crew members were knocking in code on the submarine wall, the president was vacationing in the Black Sea resort of Sochi. On occasions like this, Western leaders behave very differently. At almost the same time, President Clinton interrupted his vacation to meet with firefighters battling wildfires in the western United States. Chancellor Schröder interrupted his vacation to attend memorial services for the Germans who had died in the Concorde crash outside Paris. Putin continued his holiday. The country looked at television and saw the confused faces of bureaucrats. Then came clips of Putin receiving guests in Sochi, calm, tanned, and confident in a white T-shirt. He quickly hid a satisfied smile, but the cameras had captured it. Putin was surrounded by happy guests and his beaming lieutenants; they had been talking about something pleasant after a good meal.

The television footage was a disaster for the president. He definitely did not know how to behave; he was not experienced, or cynical, enough to play convincingly and pretend. Perhaps he did not feel the gravity of situation, or he did not care. He might have thought that he should remain cool and confident of himself, not emotionally involved, detached. Much later, it became known that exactly that was the advice of Putin's people.

In the meantime, the military's top brass quit. The minister of defense, Igor Sergeyev, vanished from the scene. The remaining officials blatantly put out mountains of lies attempting to absolve themselves of responsibility for delays in organizing a rescue operation and for rejecting foreign help. As usual, they had been waiting for an order from the very top. But the order was not coming. The Kremlin continued to deliberate on whether a superpower could seek foreign help. The Soviet tradition was to let your people die quietly and keep their death a state secret. The problem nowadays was that to keep secrets in Russia was impossible.

Alan Hoskins, the leader of a group of British submarine officers, revealed that the British armed services had offered to aid the Russian ship immediately after the accident. But Moscow kept silent, then asked for help when it was too late, and finally for unknown reasons turned to the Norwegians. "Apparently, Russia had some political reasons for hesitating to save the crew of the *Kursk*," Hoskins was quoted as saying in the August 31 *Obshchaya gazeta*.

The Norwegians discovered that the Russians had hidden the truth about the conditions and details of the operation, creating suspicion that they did not want the Norwegians to be more successful than they. At some point, Vice Admiral Einar Skorgen, who was coordinating the operation for the Norwegian side, threatened to pull his divers out if the Russians continued to sabotage (he used the exact word) and interfere with their efforts. "There was a total informational chaos. We were besieged by so much false or distorted information that it endangered the safety of our divers," he was quoted as saying in despair, in the August 29 issue of the journal *Itogi*. But on the ninth day after the accident, the

Norwegians did open the hatch of the *Kursk* and get inside, revealing that all men on board were dead.

While the Russian authorities lied, the press—both Russian and Western—screamed headlines about the tragedy. "Putin's silence in the first long days of the crisis shows that he was in a state of confusion, probably bewilderment," an August 28 article in the *Times* of London said. Definitely, the Russian president lost his self-confidence—the *Kursk* case appeared to be more dramatic, for him as well, than he had probably thought at the beginning.

"Putin's reputation sank to the bottom with the submarine *Kursk*," wrote a Russian journalist. Putin kept silent for almost a week after the loss of the submarine. He must not have expected a country accustomed to the loss of lives and permanent disasters to feel such pain over the fate of this submarine. And he did not know how to react to that pain. Only recently so confident, sure of himself, he now did not know what to do, which words to use, how to address his nation.

But as soon as Putin got over his confusion, he started looking around for people to blame. Meeting with relatives of the seamen, he announced that the guilty parties in the tragedy were Big Capital and the press, the latter paid off by the former: "The newspapers and others defend the interests of those who support them (the oligarchs). They are vilely exploiting this tragedy to settle a score with the authorities. ... Why? Because we are pushing them against the wall. For robbing the country, the army, and the navy."[6] It was obvious that the president was furious about the way his behavior during the disaster had been presented in the press, which he was sure was in the hands of the oligarchs. He acted as if he was concerned only by the attacks in the media, not the fate of the seamen. He refused to see the failures of his people; he had no sense that the military and the government apparatus had behaved cynically with lives at stake. He was focused on one thing: absolving the authorities.

The search for a scapegoat did not end there. Nikolai Patrushev, director of the FSB and a close ally of Putin, announced that there had been two Dagestanis aboard the *Kursk*, hinting at a trail leading to the terrorists from the Northern Caucasus. Then the authorities revealed that one possible version was that the *Kursk* had collided with an American or British submarine. But no one could explain what happened to the second submarine after the collision—after all, it would have been damaged as well.

Putin was caught unawares first by the catastrophe itself and then by the reaction of the Russian press and public. He *was* clearly puzzled. All his statements and actions demonstrated his failure to realize that Russia had become another country, one that was accustomed to openness, and that he had to learn to tell the truth. Moreover, the mass anguish over the *Kursk* had another source: The sub had been the pride of the Russian fleet, the best ship that Russia had with the best crew. If they were doomed and nobody could rescue them, what could the rest of the country expect? That was what ordinary Russians thought. That is why they were so shocked and traumatized.

The president was not to blame for the submarine accident, of course. He was not to blame for the cowardice and hypocrisy of his subordinates—most of whom had been appointed by his predecessor. He was only guilty of being unable to get past the Soviet manner of reacting to tragedy.

Putin also showed himself lacking in a sense of the moment and an understanding of emotions, without which a leader cannot rule successfully—especially in Russia. He did not have the ability to feel compassion for the trapped seamen or the grieving Russian people, or the political intuition to catch the barely perceptible shifts in the public mood. Yeltsin had that intuition; he would have known how to react. Putin behaved as a cold, rational man. It was true that he wasn't heartless—he was unable to control his tears at the funeral of his patron and friend, Saint Petersburg mayor Anatoly Sobchak. Those tears, a manifestation of his humanity, won him the sympathy of millions. But this time, he failed to feel the public mood, or he might have been afraid that being human would be seen as being weak. Also exposed were the inexperience and unprofessionalism of his team, which advised him not to react to the August events and not to take responsibility for them.

That moment in August 2000 could have been a turning point for Putin and for Russia, bringing together regime and people at a time of crisis. Only time will tell what August taught Putin. Would that cold shower wake him up and make him more sensitive to the problems of his country? Or would that tragic experience make him even harsher, more indifferent and cynical?

Putin promised to raise the submarine. In November 2000, more bodies were brought up. One bore a note that confirmed that the men were alive after the blast and that their deaths were arduous. The country suffered yet another shock.[7]

The submarine was raised in the summer of 2001, one year after it sank. The recovery was expensive and extremely dangerous—the craft carried an atomic reactor and torpedoes that could explode at any moment. Experts saw no need to raise it. But Putin had promised his country that the submarine would be raised at whatever cost, so raised it must be. He owed it to the families of the crew. The cause of the accident was confirmed—it had been the explosion of a defective torpedo. The fleet commanders had known about that type of torpedo problem for a long time but ordered the *Kursk* into maneuvers anyway. The post-communist Russian power structures still could not break out beyond their traditional irresponsibility, carelessness, incompetence, and indifference to people's lives.

Putin finally fired the high command of the fleet but, again, in a typically Soviet way—without telling the public the real reason for the dismissals. The step did not alter the dire situation of the decaying Russian fleet. Without reconstruction and modernization, there was no guarantee that a new disaster would not occur. But before beginning to revamp its navy, Russia had to decide whether it needed to maintain such a huge fleet, symbolic of Russia's superpower status and vast imperialist ambitions, when the country couldn't guarantee safety to its seamen.

August brought bitter commentary from journalists and intellectuals. "In a sense the *Kursk* means the end of the era of Russian industrialization. Russia is tremendously worn out—morally and materially. It has used up the Soviet resources and has not created anything new," declared an article in the August 28 *Vedomosti*. Boris Vasiliev, a writer who had been a Soviet tank test driver and had seen a lot of accidents, wrote in the August 31 edition of *Obshchaya gazeta*: "What was outrageous in this story [of the *Kursk*] were the lies and amoral behavior of the president. Putin does not know how to be a leader. He is Brezhnev II. But unlike Brezhnev, he is angry inside. That's the only difference."

The mood of the military was also grim. "I'm afraid that the ship turned out to be more expensive than human lives. And what are we to make of the fact that the head of the commission on the rescue did not go to the site of the tragedy until the sixth day after the catastrophe? I would not want to be saved that way," declared General Yevgeny Podkolzin, a former paratrooper commander, in the August issue of *Kommersant-Vlast'*. What he said openly was what the rank and file and the officers of the armed services were thinking to themselves.

After the *Kursk* disaster, doubts increased about the government's ability to improve the situation in the country. Only 29 percent of Russians polled in September expressed optimism, while 34 percent felt that life in Russia would not get better, according to a VTsIOM poll. This was a verdict on the new rule.

In August 2000, the relationship between Putin and society seemed about to become much less euphoric. In July, Putin had a 73 percent approval rating (only 17 percent disapproved of his performance, and 10 percent had no opinion). In August, after the submarine accident, about 62 percent of respondents approved of Putin (28 percent disapproved, and 10 percent still had no opinion). The president had lost a sizable amount of support and gained a sizable number of critics. Forty-three percent of Russians felt that Putin had behaved "with dignity, and responsibly" during the *Kursk* incident, while 42 percent thought not. It would seem that Putin had nothing to really worry about, but the shift sent a signal that society at large was not in love with its leader—at least at that moment.

That same August, when emotions were still running high because of the submarine disaster, a fire broke out at another symbol of Soviet grandeur, the Ostankino television towers, which served all the national television channels. The dark television screens seemed to say that Russia was entering an age of catastrophes. Technical and human resources were wearing out, and something had to be done urgently.

The Ostankino fire demonstrated to the full the drawbacks of Putin's "transmission belt" of governance. For three long hours, firefighters could not start putting out the blaze because no one—not the mayor of Moscow, not the chief of the presidential staff, not the energy minister or the prime minister—wanted to take the responsibility for turning off the electricity. Only President Putin could. Similarly, the military leaders during rescue operations for the *Kursk* did nothing at all while they waited for a command from above. The concentration of power at the top bred a disinclination to take action and a desire to hide from responsibility in all levels of the administration.

Political jokes are a good indicator of the psychological state of Russian society. Here are two sad jokes from late 2000:

The first joke: Ostankino had to burn down. The FSB had lost its recording of *Swan Lake*. (Tchaikovsky's music for the ballet *Swan Lake* has very specific overtones for Russian audiences—during the August 1991 putsch against democracy, all the radio and television stations in Russia broadcast it.)

The second joke: Washington officially announced that no American towers were anywhere near Ostankino. (This joke was a reaction to official declarations by the Russian military that the *Kursk* had sunk as a result of a collision with a Western submarine.)

The appearance of such jokes suggested that Russia was returning, at least in part, to the way it had been in communist times—there had been very few political jokes in the Yeltsin revolutionary era. The return of political jokes among intellectuals especially was a reflection of both their dissatisfaction with the situation and with the authorities and their fear of expressing this dissatisfaction openly. The political joke as a form of reaction to politics and power in Russia has always been an expression of a double mentality: on the one side, resentment of politics; and on the other, an attempt not to cross the boundaries, a form of survival.

Some observers hoped that after the *Kursk* the country would stand up, dry its tears, and make the Kremlin pay—which would have sent Putin's ratings plummeting. They didn't plummet. In the end, Putin was forgiven for his clumsy handling of the crisis by many, except the victims' relatives. Observers, including Russian ones, were surprised by the people's willingness to go easy on the authorities. "Well, these things happen," many citizens sighed, fatalistically. "You can't bring back the dead." The press wrote that the authorities had been given a license to make new mistakes. Apparently, we underestimated the exhaustion factor in Russian society, which leads more to a passive acceptance of whatever life brings than to a demand for anything better. The surge of dissatisfaction with the government quickly subsided and was replaced by other feelings, foremost among them a sadness too bleak for despair and fatalism. "We just have to bear up," Russians said.

But certain conclusions were drawn. The groups of influence that were watching closely saw that the president was not as strong as he wanted to appear, did not know how to handle crises, and could become weak and disoriented. After the *Kursk* drama, a joke circulated in Moscow that the old system of power under Yeltsin was predicated on an absent president and the new system on a strong president. And everything went wrong when the strong president was absent.

The boss in the Kremlin must have realized that he had problems, because in September he began desperately working on his image. He met with people, traveled tirelessly around the country, as if trying to force Russia to forget his moments of weakness, and made gestures aimed at ordinary folk. On a trip to the Volga city Samara, he visited a dirt-poor provincial household (with a television camera crew) and ate with evident pleasure marinated mushrooms straight from the jar. Russians could enjoy their president's simplicity and trustfulness, just dropping in on a strange woman and partaking of potluck. Only those familiar with the security around the president knew the work the secret service had to do before Putin could "drop by" a random house and snack there.

But the image makers did their job. In September and October 2000, Putin restored his ratings and once again looked confident, at least outwardly. The main decision he had reached after August soon became clear: He must crush the media critics who had damaged him so badly over the *Kursk*. That meant doing whatever it took to crack down on the media conglomerates—Gusinsky's first of all.

By the end of 2000, Russia had returned to some of its old rhythms of life, as if the ten-year Yeltsin hiatus had never happened. Under Yeltsin, presidential portraits had not been in vogue. Now the Ministry of Defense ordered all military bases to buy portraits of Vladimir Putin immediately. Soon the state apparatus made a portrait of the second Russian president not only a key element of the office furniture but a symbol of personal loyalty and statist sentiments. Artists found work that looked like it might become full time. At first they didn't know how to depict the new president, because there were no instructions on that subject from above. Then the canvas size for official use was determined—2 by 3 meters—with portraits for offices somewhat smaller.

Putinomania gradually became an element of Russian life. New textbooks were introduced in the schools of Saint Petersburg, Putin's hometown, that described the childhood of little Volodya Putin. That meant something to people who had learned to read with books about the childhood of little Volodya Ulyanov (Lenin). Other Russian cities would soon follow suit with their own initiatives. In some places, the restaurant "Putin" was opened; in others, the chair and table used by the president on some occasion became a valuable item in the local museum. Putin may not have known about these initiatives, for they were probably thought up by loyal subordinates. But quite a few people heard the bugle call and got to work restoring the past.

On the political stage, players in the new production directed by the Kremlin tried to figure out which part or parts they had. When it became clear that the parliament's upper chamber, the Federation Council, would no longer be a serious institution, discussions began on what the State Council—created by Putin in September 2000 as a consolation prize for the regional bosses, or the senators, as they were calling themselves—would be doing. The bosses hoped that the State Council would be given the main functions of the upper house and even be made constitutional.

While the senators made their ambitious plans, Putin promulgated his decree on the State Council, which clarified what he wanted it to be: a consultative organ that would convene at the president's request and discuss what the president's team prepared. The governors' hopes that the president would give the State Council the right to appoint the prosecutor general and higher court judges and generally raise the body's status were dashed. And once the State Council was made the president's toy, the same fate was prepared for other political institutions.

At the first session of the State Council in November 2000, Putin proposed that its members approve the new Russian anthem. It was obvious that the Kremlin had wanted something to occupy the fledgling organ. Discussion of the anthem might have seemed like a mockery to these leaders, once omnipotent in their regions. But the governors held their peace. Instead of discussing the strategy for Russia, they began to edit verses.

They had a powerful motivation, because everybody knew that the Kremlin would get rid of all regional bosses who had not demonstrated fealty to Putin. Many of the governors were facing reelection, so the reckoning was drawing near. But even those who had tried to please the boss were not sure of the Kremlin's support.

The elections for regional head were to be held in 2000 or 2001 in almost half the republics and territorial entities. In some regions, the Kremlin had urged governors to resign "voluntarily," using the prosecutor's office and *compromat* (compromising materials) gathered on them. There was always something to be found on the governors. There was talk that Putin's electoral rival Yuri Luzhkov was thinking about retirement from his post of Moscow mayor for "health reasons," in exchange for immunity from prosecution.

After media oligarch Gusinsky, the Kremlin's second victim was Kursk governor Alexander Rutskoi, who had been vice president under Yeltsin and was a retired military pilot. Rutskoi had a controversial political biography—he had led the parliamentary mutiny against Yeltsin in 1993 and even been imprisoned. Then he reappeared as governor of Kursk, the region the ill-fated submarine was named after. No one doubted that Rutskoi, who placed family members in cushy jobs, was corrupt. But the Kremlin did not know how to get rid of him. So Putin's people chose the simplest path: The Kremlin put up its own candidate (from the security services) for the governorship and used the courts to remove Rutskoi from the race the day before the election.

Even though the democratic segment of society did not feel great warmth for Rutskoi, the manner in which he was taken out of the game—intrigue, and the executive branch telling the courts what to do—upset people. "In essence, it's the right thing, but in form, it's a mockery of democracy," observers said. And after all that, the Kremlin did not finish the job. Rutskoi was removed from the ballot, but the Kremlin's candidate did not win in Kursk; the victor was a Communist, an anti-Semite, and most likely a thief too.

Soon the practice of getting rid of people in other regions who did not suit the Kremlin, using pressure from law enforcement and threats of jail, became a popular Kremlin policy. Outwardly, the cleanup of regional government could resemble a return to legality because many of the

governors Putin's people went after were corrupt or guilty of other serious misconduct. But the Kremlin's "cleanup policy" in the regions had
nothing to do with the rule of law. Moscow was using the courts and
prosecutors in the name of political expediency to support Kremlin loyalists and weaken independent politicians and the Kremlin's foes. The
Kremlin even had a list of leaders to be discredited, details of timing and
method, and names of those in the courts responsible for passing sentence on them. In some cases, the courts did clear away corrupt politicians. But in other cases they moved, under pressure from Moscow,
against the political opponents of the center. The court system was turning into an appendage of the executive branch, as it had been in the
Soviet era.

The Kremlin, however, did not want a total purge of the regions; it
was prepared to continue the practice, instituted by Yeltsin, of making
deals in them. According to Russian law, both the president and the
regional governors were allowed only two terms. With Putin's approval
and under pressure from the presidential staff, the Duma passed an
amendment that gave 26 governors and republic presidents the right to
a third term. The number included such regional heavyweights as
Mintimer Shaimiyev, the president of the republic of Tatarstan. Putin
must have concluded that, having given the regional bosses a scare, he
could control them. Running his (that is, the Kremlin's) candidate in a
region meant getting into a fight in which the wrong people might win.
And besides, fighting meant tension, which Putin did not like. Thus, for
the sake of peace of mind, the Kremlin agreed to de facto limitless rule
for regional family clans. Later, the Constitutional Court endorsed the
ruling that gave regional bosses the right to be reelected for a third and
even fourth time, which guaranteed the preservation of semifeudal
regimes in Russian provinces.

Tatarstan is an outstanding example of how local regimes have ruled
and how they cooperated with Moscow. During the 1990s, the experienced Soviet apparatchik Shaimiyev managed to neutralize nationalist
groups in Tatarstan, to become president there, and to establish relatively
stable rule in the republic. His rule was based on the dictatorship of his
family, which controlled the republic's basic resources—oil and gas, among
others. Opposition was cruelly suppressed. Corruption and paternalism

flourished. But Khan Shaimiyev gave the center what it needed, primarily outward calm and support during elections.

At the beginning, Putin demanded that the regional feudal lords, especially Shaimiyev and Murtaza Rakhimov (the president of another Russian republic, Bashkortostan, who had built the same type of rule as Shaimiyev), curtail their appetites and bring their constitutions into line with the federal one. The regional lords grumbled and resisted at first, and even directed gentle threats at the center, but in the end they caved in. Yeltsin's successor brought a greater semblance of order to the regions, but it was still the local barons, rather than Moscow, who held sway there. Putin was apparently afraid to seriously impinge on the interests of the feudal clans that ruled most regions—especially because he planned to run again in 2004 and needed the support of the national republics and controllable regions that voted the way the local boss told them to. The new president, like Yeltsin before him, needed influential leaders who knew how to count votes in their domain.

As he began building his superpresidential regime, Putin came to understand that without preserving Yeltsin's policy of deal making in the regions, he would not survive. The price to be paid was the Kremlin's toleration of regional authoritarianism and corruption. There were no organized alternatives to the regional clans—during the Yeltsin years, after a brief period of political struggle, power in most of the regions had been seized by clans dominated by Soviet *nomenklatura* with criminal ties. Putin gradually seemed to become wary of stirring up any conflict with the ruling groups in the regions.[8]

As for the regional elections of 2000, the regions were still battlefields for the Communists and the Kremlin's "party of power." Other political movements had no chance of winning there. That was one result of Yeltsin's ten years: The power struggle locally in Russia was between the old and the new *nomenklatura*. A closer look revealed that most of the new *nomenklatura* came out of the Soviet version. The ruling class had not grown younger. The differences between the Communist governors and the governors loyal to the Kremlin were minimal. Two regions chose military men as governors—General Vladimir Shamanov, who fought in the second Chechen war, was elected in Ulyanovsk, Lenin's birthplace, on the Volga River; and Admiral Vladimir Yegorov was elected in the

Baltic port of Kaliningrad. But it would be premature to see a trend of the military coming to power. Soon it would become obvious that the governors with a military background, like General Alexander Lebed in Krasnoyarsk, his brother Colonel Alexei Lebed in Chakhasia, and Shamanov in Ulyanovsk, were far from efficient managers—they were pathetic and incompetent.

In Chukotka—in Russia's distant and underpopulated North—the new governor was Roman Abramovich, a Yeltsin oligarch who won by a large majority of votes, obtained by bribing the populace with gifts. With his billions of dollars, this young man could easily develop the resource-rich Chukotka into the Russian Klondike. It wasn't clear what Abramovich wanted with Chukotka. When asked, he said, "I feel sorry for the Chukchas." Abramovich did not seem like a man with strong philanthropic tendencies. But, ironically, he might be an improvement over the previous governor, Alexander Nazarov, a shallow and corrupt Soviet apparatchik who brought the region to complete degradation with a starving population. At least Abramovich was doing something for Chukotka—for instance, he sent all the children of the place on a seaside vacation in the South, at his own expense. Actually, he could well afford to spend several million dollars of what he had managed to borrow from the state. But the residents of Chukotka, tired of the corruption and anarchy of the previous administration, were grateful to Abramovich.

That a Kremlin insider would look for a place on the outskirts of Russia spoke volumes: Yesterday's initiators of Project Putin did not feel comfortable in the Kremlin and were looking for other "warm spots." Being a governor did not confer total immunity before the courts, but at least it lent legitimacy to one's power and was a safe harbor for waiting out political storms.

In October 2002, another oligarchic family headed by Vladimir Potanin would win regional elections in Krasnoyarski Krai, and its representative, Alexander Kchloponin, would become one more governor-tycoon. It was just the beginning. Soon other oligarchs would follow suit in trying to win local elections. A new page in Russian political history was opening as powerful financial-industrial groups were beginning to legitimize their power in the provinces through elections for the local executive branch. This time, no longer hidden in the shadows, open and legal fusion between power and capital on the regional level had a real chance to challenge the presidency and Moscow's authoritarian moods.

The Kremlin attack on the remaining independent institutions continued, and only a few were left. The next institution on the victims list was the Central Bank, headed by Victor Gerashchenko—Hercules, as he was called in Moscow. Russian liberals and Western financial people disliked Gerashchenko, considering his policy damaging for liberalization. The Kremlin loathed the powerful head of the Central Bank for being too independent and ruling his kingdom without asking for advice from the president's team. Besides, there was a real problem with the bank's transparency—nobody outside knew exactly what was happening inside. The managers of the Central Bank enjoyed salaries as high as those of Western corporate executives, which was outrageous in the eyes of Russians.

A draft was prepared of a presidential decree that stripped the Central Bank of its independence and put it under the control of the government. The Duma, loyal to Putin, would support any decision of the president's. It was true that something definitely had to be done about the Central Bank kingdom. But subordinating the bank to the government would enable the cabinet to print money at will, which would spell an end to reform.

At that moment, the Kremlin did not pursue its initiative to tame the Central Bank—it would have created too much trouble, not only among Russian liberals but in the foreign business community, which for the Kremlin was more important. Putin was intent on attracting foreign investors to Russia, and he did not need scandals. But still the idea of stripping the main Russian bank of its independence continued to be on the agenda of Putin's entourage.

Running a bit ahead, Gerashchenko was dismissed in the spring of 2002 and replaced by another man from Saint Petersburg, Sergei Ignatiev, who had a liberal background, was a good professional, and was close to the Gaidar team. There were doubts, however, whether the new head of the Central Bank would defend his institution's independent status and pursue the reform that the Central Bank's previous head had so vigorously opposed, or whether he would succumb to the pressure from the president's men. Quite a few observers in Russia shrugged skeptically as they watched the changes at the bank—they feared that with its own man there, the Kremlin would be able to use the bank for its needs, which had been hard to do under Gerashchenko. In any case, Ignatiev was an honest man, but a nominal figure rather than a political heavyweight. An irony of Russian politics is that independent people are not often reformers and liberals very often do not have independent positions.

Next on the agenda was Russia's messy multiparty system, which interfered with Putin's idea of politics and gave rise to too many irritating little parties that were difficult to control and that might someday cause problems for the "party of power." On orders from the president's team, the Central Electoral Commission prepared a new law on parties. The draft required that a party have at least 10,000 members, with organizations in 45 regions of no fewer than 100 members each, to qualify for registration. Every two years, the party would have to reregister. And if, in the course of five years, the party did not participate in an election, it would not be allowed to reregister.

The authors of the bill hoped to reduce the number of parties from 188 to fewer than 20. In essence, the law was directed against the democratic parties, which were small—first of all against Yabloko, headed by Grigory Yavlinsky. Under the new law, the Communist Party and the "party of power" had the best chances for survival, which was just the way the Kremlin's people wanted it: their "party of power" competing mainly against the permanently toned-down left-wing opposition, which scared voters into voting for the Kremlin party.[9] The law on parties was approved by the Duma, like all the other laws Putin had proposed.[10]

The Kremlin also began rooting out the other organizations it considered unnecessary or harmful. The work was being done with the help of legislation written to suit the needs of Putin's team. No one could say anymore that lawlessness abounded in Russia. "Controllable democracy" was being introduced by means of the law.

The only way an effective multiparty system could be formed was with parties depending on the result of the election participating in the creation of the government and sharing responsibility for its activity. But since the government in Russia has been formed by the president, with the parliament taking no part in its selection and parties having no influence on the executive branch, there are no impulses in society for the creation of strong parties. Besides which, the Russian authorities tried to create parties from above and foist them on the public, which could support the Kremlin-blessed movements. And it supported these poor stilted excuses for parties because there were no viable alternatives.

Soon, however, the presidential team started to realize either the flimsiness of this system or its unattractiveness to the West. And the opinion of the West was important to Putin. There were signs that the Kremlin began pondering how to make the system more civilized—or, at least, to make it *appear* more civilized. Somewhere in the team, the idea of moving to a party government ripened. But that government, as conceptualized by the Kremlin technologists, had to be formed on the basis of the Kremlin-sponsored "party of power." It looked like a return to the tradition of Soviet party government, which was based on the Communist Party's monopoly and was therefore moribund.

Finally, the president's team found time to discuss other issues. Putin began thinking about military reform, prompted by an awareness of all the signs of the degradation of the Russian army. A severe breakdown in civilian control over the military had taken place during the Yeltsin period. During the summer of 2000, the system of subordination was openly violated in the army. The unheard-of happened: The chief of the General Staff, Anatoly Kvashnin, bypassed his boss, minister of defense Marshal Igor Sergeyev, and sent the president his plan for army reform. Kvashnin behaved as if the defense minister did not exist. It was a scandal, a violation of the chain of command; suddenly, what had been under the surface became public knowledge.

The highest army command was divided into two irreconcilable camps, which could not contain their conflict any longer. Putin, as commander in chief, should have fired both the minister of defense and the chief of the General Staff. He said nothing, however, pretending nothing was amiss. He had behaved the same way in 1999, when General Vladimir Shamanov blackmailed the authorities, threatening to quit if operations in Chechnya were halted. Putin's silence then proved that he did not like open conflict and did not like making choices: Faced with alternatives, he postponed making a decision. He might not have felt strong enough to rein in the military. Thus the president faced a serious problem: not only restoring unity in the military command but also strengthening his control over the armed services, which had started doing as they pleased under Yeltsin.[11]

The problem with the chain of command was not the only problem. Russia could no longer keep 3 million people in the armed services; that was an unbearable burden for the country. The army had been placed on starvation rations. It was being sapped from within by corruption and unprofessionalism. An index of the disintegration was being kept by Chechnya, which showed the army's inability to function in hotspots. By 2000, only two or three out of a dozen divisions in Russia were battle ready. The army, which had been created for imperialist goals and superpower imagery, was now yet another confirmation of the profound crisis in the system. Not only the size but also the organization of the army were completely out of sync with the economic resources of the new Russia.[12]

Putin found the strength to announce the need for military reform. The plan he proposed in the fall of 2000 reduced the army and navy by 365,000 military personnel and 120,000 civilian workers. The reductions were to take place before 2003. By 2005, the army would be reduced by almost 600,000 people, including civilian personnel. The core of the reform in the plan was the creation of powerful battle-ready troops to be based in the basic strategic locations—Southwest and Central Asia. In a speech that fall to the leadership of the armed forces, the president adopted a harsh tone for the first time. He attacked the "parquet" generals who sat around in headquarters. He spoke critically of the weakness of the officer ranks. He started doing something that no Russian leader had ever had the courage to undertake. But would he have the courage to go the whole way until he reformed the final bastion of the empire state?

The military budget for 2001 was boosted 40 percent, thanks to increased oil revenues. But there were doubts that even a larger budget would allow radical military reform, which required heavy spending. General Andrei Nikolayev, chairman of the Duma Defense Committee, said in November, "This is a budget of stabilization. There are no clear priorities. It will improve the situation, but it cannot cardinally solve a single problem." It was true that even the expanded budget was not enough to solve the problem of retiring officers, who by law were entitled to an apartment and a retirement bonus. Experienced observers concluded that the 2001 budget would not change the situation in the army.[13] The lion's share of the budget would go for patching holes and paying off debts. No deep military reform would occur without big money.

The Russian military leadership so far had failed to meet the challenges of a new security context. On one hand, it was clear that security on Russia's southern borders with Central Asia and China had to be beefed up. On the other hand, the Russian military still considered NATO a threat and demanded fortification of the Western outposts and the retention of its nuclear potential. A weakened Russia could no longer respond to all those challenges—it had to decide on a new set of security priorities instead of continuing to build the army on the Soviet model and merely reducing its numbers.

What was the point of preserving nuclear parity with the United States? Russian observers asked.[14] According to some specialists, Russia needed no more than 500 nuclear warheads to guarantee its security. China, France, and the United Kingdom were nuclear powers with a smaller numbers of warheads. And their nuclear status cost them much less than Russia, exhausted by crises, was paying.

Moreover, about 10,000 tactical nuclear weapons were gathering dust in Russian warehouses in case of a limited nuclear war with NATO. Against whom the Russian generals intended to use them now was not clear—not even to the generals. Nevertheless, millions of dollars were spent maintaining the battle-readiness of this military rarity.

The president, undoubtedly, appreciated the difficulty of reforming the army. In late 2001, Putin approved the idea of a professional army, promising to make Russia's professional by 2010. "Neither the government nor society supports the existing draft system," Putin announced.[15] His team decided to make 2002 a breakthrough year in executing reforms and bring one airborne division to a full staffing contract. But it was unclear whether Russia had enough funds to try the experiment, which would cost about 2.5 billion rubles, or $70 million, per division. At the time, the military had 132,000 contract soldiers, down from 260,000 several years before. Putin had to admit that so far Russia had failed to make contract service attractive.[16]

The military leadership was not ready for even a partial transition to a professional army. The plans being prepared by the Ministry of Defense under Putin's comrade in arms Sergei Ivanov planned to add between 40 and 50 percent contract soldiers to the Russian armed forces in 2005–2006 and to reduce the length of service for draftees to six to eight months. But those plans remained on the drafting board. At the same time, the General Staff raised the issue of reducing the categories of draft-exempt citizens. The transition to a professional army was held back by more than lack of funds. There was another factor at work—the unpreparedness of the generals for a new model for the army, which, incidentally, required a substantial reduction in generals and a renewal of their ranks.

Besides, the creation of a new model for a modern army demanded that the political class and society answer once and for all the question: Would Russia become part of Western civilization, or continue dangling between Europe and Asia, pretending to have a "special path" of development and trying to defend itself from the West?

Chapter 5

POWER IN ONE FIST

―――――――――――― ❧ ――――――――――――

Chechnya as a trap. The government under the gun. The Soviet anthem.
Putin enters the world. Why does the president want power?

In comparison with Yeltsin's stormy rule as president, so often roiled by failures, disasters, zero-sum games, and the threat of the old man's own collapse, the first year of Putin's ascendancy, with the exception of August, was relatively smooth. The president himself might consider it successful. Only Chechnya could really spoil Putin's mood.

The sole undertaking associated with Putin's name and begun on his initiative—Russia's "antiterrorist operation" in the secessionist republic of Chechnya, already devastated by one war (1994–1996)—was a failure. No one had any doubts about that, not even in the Kremlin. From August 1999 to September 2000, according to official sources, 2,600 Russian soldiers died in Chechnya. The death toll among civilians in Chechnya was growing—no one knew whether it was in the thousands or the tens of thousands. The authorities didn't want to know. Despite the ferocity of the federal operation, the leaders of the Chechen separatist movement—Aslan Maskhadov, Shamil Basayev, Arbi Barayev, Ruslan Gelayev, and the Jordanian citizen Khattab, known for his cruelty in the first Chechen war—were all still alive (Barayev and Khattab were reported to be killed much later in 2002). Moscow's goal in the war in Chechnya—the rooting out of terrorism and terrorists—had not been attained.[1]

Moreover, after some weakening, the resistance of the Chechen fighters grew stronger toward the end of 2000. New fighters, primarily young

Chechen men, were constantly joining the forces in the field. Even Chechens who had been neutral toward the federal army and were tired of the Chechen field commanders and the continuing violence—the Chechens who had pinned their hopes for a peaceful life on the federal forces—were gradually moving toward support of the separatists as Russia's mass bombing of the civilian population killed their families and friends.

In the summer of 2000, Moscow was showing signs of confusion over Chechnya, and Russians—both the military and civilians—were feeling the strain after nearly a year of fighting. Even the proponents of a mili tary solution to the Chechen problem were forced to admit that the gov ernment was at a dead end in Chechnya. The antiwar sentiments wide spread among Russians during the first Chechen war were not a problem for the regime with this second conflict; a significant percentage of Russians was still favorably disposed toward Putin. But war fatigue was setting in.

In late August, 50 percent of those polled commented in exasperation that there was no end in sight to the war, while 41 percent pointed to the heavy losses in the federal army and 26 percent to the losses among civil ians in Chechnya. Half still felt that military action must be continued and that there was no other way out (only 39 percent wanted negotiations with the Chechens, and 11 percent had no opinion).[2] These data show that a large segment of Russian society was still prepared to put up with the war in the summer of 2000. But the sense of pointlessness, exhaus tion, and war weariness was growing.

The Russian army had occupied almost the entire territory of Chechnya, and the problem of what was to be done now was becoming much more pressing. A partisan war had broken out in the troubled republic. The Kremlin did not know how to fight guerrillas. It wasn't clear who was a fighter and who a peaceful resident. During the day, the Chechens led ordinary lives; but at night, they took up arms and shot at federal soldiers and laid landmines along the roads. Children became combatants in this "landmine war," often because the separatists paid for each mine laid and each Russian armored vehicle destroyed, and the chil dren and their families needed the money.

Russia had returned to 1996, when questions about civil resistance first arose. Federal forces did not find answers then. Yeltsin severed the

Chechen knot before the presidential election of 1996, accepting peace with the separatists and Chechnya's de facto independence. That peace meant defeat for Russia.

This time around, the problems in settling the war were compounded. Distrust between the federal authorities and the Chechens had only increased since the first conflict, which reduced the chances for peaceful negotiations. Nor could Moscow leave Chechnya. Russia's self-image had been tarnished, and few Russians were prepared to accept a new military failure. The fear was that the army would rebel before being forced to leave Chechnya ignominiously. Besides, Chechnya was not ready to build an independent state. If Russian troops left Chechnya, the field commanders—the same warlords who enriched themselves trading in hostages, drug trafficking, and selling arms—would take charge again as they had done after the first war. And the leaders then would not be the moderates like Chechen president Aslan Maskhadov but more intransigent people like Basayev and Khattab. The bandit raids into Russian territory, kidnappings, and Chechnya's disintegration into chaos would continue. But Russia could not win in Chechnya either. So at this point in history, Russia and the breakaway Chechen republic were caught in a situation with no exit.

In the meantime, normal life in Chechnya was almost impossible amid the charred and bombed buildings, abandoned military hardware at the side of the road, and people burdened with their few possessions slogging through the mud. Children were hungry and dirty, adults gaunt. Everyone was physically ailing and in need of psychological support. Journalist Anna Politkovskaya reported from the former Chechen capital Grozny after it had been bombed: "Grozny is a living hell. It is another world, some dreadful Hades you reach through the Looking Glass. There is no living civilization among the ruins—apart from the people themselves."[3]

Refugee camps in the neighboring republic of Ingushetia sheltered tens of thousands of families that had no hope of ever going home, for their homes were gone. These people had lived through two wars in six years and might never get back to normal life. In the meantime, Russia was barely handling its own problems and had no money, no compassion, no patience for rebellious Chechens. The Russian budget for 2001 included no aid to Chechnya. The only things Moscow could offer

Chechnya were isolation and oblivion, but only under the control of its troops, whom the Chechens regarded as occupiers.

The Chechens (and they were not alone) began to believe that the Russian authorities, at least the military authorities, simply did not want to end the war. "Many episodes evinced the army's unwillingness to complete a total destruction of the Chechen fighting units," said Ruslan Khasbulatov, a Chechen and a former speaker of the Russian parliament. "Apparently, somewhere in military headquarters, someone decided that continuing the war was useful." As Khasbulatov explained it, the war gave the generals constant promotion up the career ladder, financing for the military and special services, personal wealth, and growth of the power structure's political role in society.[4]

Khasbulatov seemed to be right—some of the top brass were definitely interested in continuing this war, which brought them material well-being and raised their political significance.[5] The death of enlisted men and junior officers did not worry the military and political leadership. People began to ask why, with the full power of the army deployed against them, the separatist warlords were still at large and moving freely around Chechnya—and also to ask where the rebels were getting their most advanced arms. Many called this very strange war a "contract" war, suspecting that there were secret deals between the Russian military and the separatists.

Despite all the obvious questions, Russian society still accepted, albeit already with growing resentment, that Chechnya was turning into a round-the-clock slaughterhouse. After all, this was taking place on the periphery, far from Russia's center, and people—worn out by their own problems, weary, and busy—got used to the constant bloodshed. Official Moscow stopped publishing information on the dead and wounded and tried to move Chechnya to the back burner. The army attempted to avoid responsibility for Chechnya, shifting the burden onto the internal troops, the militia. The militia said that it could not fight in Chechnya, and in fact it was not prepared for military action. In the meantime, a new generation of Chechens grew up, one that had known nothing but war, was trained to do nothing, and thought of nothing but revenge against the Russians. Those youngsters were more and more leaning toward radical Islam—Wahhabism and jihad, the "sacred war" with Russia, was becoming their life goal.

And even with the harsh controls the military placed on information coming out of Chechnya, the world was still finding out what was going on there. The face of the war was dreadful. Hundreds of Russian soldiers and Chechens alike were dying, often young boys who had not yet started living. The number of Russian cities and towns to which the dead were returned in zinc coffins from Chechnya was growing. Thousands of Chechen women were wearing black as a sign of mourning for their dead relatives. The press was also printing occasional stories about the Russian military's abuses against civilians in Chechnya, about arrests of people whose guilt was not proved but who were kept in special camps, about so-called cleansings—actions in the course of which soldiers looted Chechen property and often executed young men suspected of ties with the separatists. The Russian army acquired the virus of cruelty, and that virus could become contagious. The Russian occupation of Chechnya was triggering the blind and cruel vengeance of the separatists.

Putin clearly did not know what to do with Chechnya. He tried to distance himself from the war so that everyone would forget that it was this "antiterrorist operation" that had brought him to power. He sought opportunities to share responsibility for what was going on in Chechnya with loyal Chechens. There were very few to be found. The new Chechen leaders he appointed, like the new head of the Chechen administration, Akhmad Kadyrov, had participated in military action against the federal army or were suspected of corruption; they were not trustworthy. But there was no choice. Putin refused to negotiate with Chechen president Maskhadov. The latter had lost his former influence. But in comparison with the other separatist leaders, he had two important qualities: The Chechens had elected him their president, and his legitimacy had been conferred by Yeltsin, who as Russian president had negotiated with him.

The newspaper *Moskovskie novosti* ran an interview with Maskhadov on November 21, 2000. The editors took a risk offering their pages to him; the Kremlin might do more than chastise them for the decision. Maskhadov told the interviewer, "As a military man I can say: An army cannot stand, it must either attack, or defend itself, or retreat. When an army as large as that stops, it falls apart." And he was right—the Russian army, having lost its goal in Chechnya, without a clear and visible enemy, had started to fall apart. Maskhadov suggested that Yeltsin play intermediary in peace negotiations. But the time was not yet ripe for negotiations—the team in the Kremlin continued to talk of victory. And even if Putin understood by then that there could be no victory in Chechnya, entering into talks with Maskhadov meant returning to square one, and that was tantamount to an admission of defeat. Putin could not do that under any circumstances—at least not yet, even with the steady increase in losses and because of the steady increase in losses.

There had been a breakthrough in Russian attitudes toward Chechnya since the beginning of the year. In October 2000, for the first time during the second war, there were more opponents of the war than proponents. Only 25 percent felt that Putin was handling the Chechen problem successfully, and 36 percent didn't think Russia was having any success in Chechnya (18 percent felt that Moscow didn't know how to bring order to Chechnya).[6]

If Russian troops suffered major losses, only 34 percent of Russians said they wanted military action to continue, and 54 percent demanded negotiations. A growing number felt that war was beneficial for both the Chechen fighters and the Russian authorities. Fifty percent of those polled said so, and a significant 10 percent went so far as to say that Russia's leaders were involved in a conspiracy with the rebel leaders. This was serious. If the dissatisfaction with Chechnya was added to the other problems in Russia, the social problems and frustrations above all, Putin would have a hard time of it. That was enough to make the Kremlin worry.

Against the backdrop of the sad situation in Chechnya, the president and the still-new team in the Kremlin could take consolation in the painless passage of the budget—the first peaceful procedure in the history of relations between executive and legislature in postcommunist Russia. Under Yeltsin, discussion of the budget was always tortuous. The Duma tried to prove its independence then, because it had few other opportunities to flex its muscles. The Kremlin was forced to make concessions and even bribe entire parliamentary factions to guarantee passage of the budget bill. As a result, the budget was usually bloated and unrealistic. The government never even thought about following it. But this time around, the wheeling and dealing were minimal. The Duma approved almost every government proposal on the budget; the deputies and interest groups behind them did not dare argue or try to cut deals with the new president.

Mikhail Kasyanov's cabinet proposed to the parliament a truly revolutionary budget for 2001. The new budget apportioned 60 percent of tax revenues to the center and 40 percent to the regions. The money going to the donor regions (as was stated above, these are regions that contribute more to the federal budget than they get from it) was slashed by almost a third. Naturally, these regions were unhappy, but their feelings counted for little in Moscow. In addition, a serious problem for the localities could arise in the new year. Because the government had squeezed everything that it could out of its budget, there was no longer any guarantee that local authorities would have enough money for the social sphere, education, and health care, which were local responsibilities. Federal officials must have hoped that they would have a better chance of solving all of Russia's problems if they distributed funds from the center, as had been done in the Soviet Union.

No one appeared worried because the budget had a "hole" of about 8 percent of its total, which indicated that the government had hopes of additional revenue. But it was not clear where those funds were expected to come from. The government hoped to borrow about $5.3 billion from the International Monetary Fund and the World Bank to partially fill the "hole." But there were no guarantees that that loan would be granted. The Paris Club of creditor countries had been informed that Moscow had allocated only $5.3 billion to service its debt to the club in 2001, rather than the $14.5 billion it actually owed. Kasyanov was unilaterally restructuring the debt to the Paris Club without conferring with the members that had loaned Russia the money.[7] The cabinet could not have done it without Putin's blessing.

The budget was approved just before year's end. For the first time, Grigory Yavlinsky's Yabloko movement, which had always voted against government budget proposals, voted to approve this one. Putin could feel triumphant that the government and the Duma had begun working in harmony, as if part of the same organism. In the future, the executive branch would have no problems getting the budget through the lower chamber of the parliament; from now on, the branches of power in Putin's Russia had no source of disagreement. The unwavering obedience of the Duma was useful when it was indeed used by the government to pass reforms—but even in that case, the country needed an independent parliament to provide an evaluation of the legislation. There was no guarantee that the semiauthoritarian executive power in Russia would always propose reform solutions.

Gradually, things seemed to quiet down on the political scene, at least in Moscow, and the Kremlin dream was to finish the last year of the century peacefully. In late November, however, a new scandal broke out in Moscow. Andrei Illarionov, the president's economic adviser, suddenly launched an attack on the Kasyanov government, in his numerous interviews and public presentations accusing the cabinet of failing to take advantage of a unique economic opportunity for advancing reform.

And in fact, the economic results for the year 2000 were the best in Russia in the past quarter-century.[8] But instead of using the economic stabilization as a foundation for structural transformation, the government remained astonishingly complacent. "The intoxicating air of the unexpected well-being that has befallen Russia has played a nasty trick," Illarionov concluded. "The legislative and executive branches began dividing up additional revenues that are not related to the effectiveness of the economy."

Illarionov's comments were only the beginning; by signaling to the Russian political and intellectual community that the government was not a sacred cow, they encouraged criticism to fly on all sides. Some analysts warned that Russia was facing a possible shock in the economy. Some spoke of the inevitability of a repeat of the 1998 financial crisis.[9]

The lack of a clear economic policy and the cabinet's uncertainty had actually been evident earlier. It was apparent that neither the prime minister nor his team intended to undertake any decisive actions to reform the economy. Kasyanov avoided all responsibility; keeping his job seemed to be his lone goal. During 2000, only one really important law was approved: the flat income tax of 13 percent. But the indecisiveness of the government was due not only to Kasyanov's weakness. The Russian government was the president's cabinet, and only the president could set the tone of its activity.

The sudden attack on the government by presidential adviser Illarionov could be interpreted as evidence that Putin had suddenly realized that he had lost a year and was now scurrying to find culprits for his cabinet's inactivity. In the polemic that ensued, no one asked the questions, Where had the president been all that time, and what had he been thinking?

In the meantime, Illarionov created a new sensation. In late December, he blasted Anatoly Chubais—now head of RAO UES, Russia's electrical utility—charging him with a criminal restructuring of UES similar to the notorious, widely criticized "shares-for-loans" privatization scheme in 1996. As a result, Chubais's reform was temporarily halted. Later, after much hesitation, in the fall of 2002 Putin decided to go ahead with the UES reform and then stopped and hesitated again.

The situation—with criticism of the cabinet as a whole and criticism of Chubais's reform in particular—highlighted Putin's management style. The president allowed passions to flare up in his entourage. He gave each participant in the fight a chance to speak, and he did not defend any of them, watching the emotions and arguments from above. Outwardly, such a style may seem effective because it creates the opportunity for discussion and a clash of views. However, there was something about it that suggested that this president allowed passions to burn only because he did not know which side to choose. In other words, the openness and the apparent pluralism of views hid indecisiveness.

Moreover, it was noticeable that Putin often allowed these dogfights and squabbles to take place in his absence, which made it possible for him to distance himself from unwelcome problems once they had been aired. In the course of the debates, he promised his support to all the opponents, and everyone was sure that he had the president's backing. That was further proof of his indecision and wavering, his failure to establish a position, make a final choice, and pursue it.

Thus, at the end of 2000 it seemed that the Kremlin had not yet decided whether it should take on further economic reforms, and if so, which ones. Rows in the liberal camp between Illarionov and Chubais were disquieting. If the liberals on the president's team couldn't come to terms, how could any agreement between competing interest groups in his entourage be expected? And because the president's team was split more widely, consensus as to future development within society was hardly plausible.

The conflicts in the president's entourage also suggested that the administration, having quickly taken control of the main levers of power, was slowing down because it did not know what to do next. The struggle for portfolios and spheres of influence resumed.

Meanwhile, some substantial economic issues had to be resolved. In December 2000, German Gref, one of Putin's closest allies, admitted that in 2003 Russia would not be able to pay its foreign debts and declared that a restructuring of the Paris Club debt was urgently needed. Russia's debt to the club stood at $48 billion, and in 2003 the payments would be $17.5 billion, which could amount to as much as half the budget. That problem had been looming for a long time. What was not obvious was why the government only realized it at the end of the year. At the end of 2002, Russian authorities were already more optimistic about Russia's ability to pay its Paris Club debt. But again, everything depended on world oil prices, because oil revenues continued to be the major source of the Russian budget.

Perhaps the relative affluence of 2000 had a lulling effect on the Kremlin, making officials think that they could go on for a long time without doing anything except using up the gold and hard currency reserves. When they finally comprehended the coming challenges, they became bewildered and descended to blaming one another or shifted to a gloomy prognosis.

The behavior of the government was understandable—it was waiting for instructions from the president. That is how Russian power is programmed: Follow the one above you. Yeltsin had allowed some degree of independence and put up with the various influence groups, with a pluralism of views, and in the end even with chaos. But Putin made it clear from the start that he would not accept any movement outside the lines and that he demanded strict subordination from his lieutenants. But he was never quick enough to draw the lines, and sometimes he simply didn't know where they should be drawn because he had not decided on his positions. That justified the state apparatus in doing nothing.

Instead of speaking on the controversial economic prospects and establishing his own standpoint, Putin turned to simpler things, apparently hoping that they would not provoke emotional conflicts within society. He asked the Duma to extend its session until the deputies approved a package of new state symbols. The president evidently had decided that the country could get by without a clear strategy for economic development but absolutely must have a new seal and anthem to enter the new millennium. For the seal of the new Russia, Putin proposed the tsarist double-headed eagle, which would symbolize the succession from the tsarist empire. The Soviet anthem, originally approved by Stalin, would signify the ties to the communist period.

Yet another symbol, the tricolor flag revived by Yeltsin, was to represent the noncommunist period. The tricolor had been introduced in tsarist Russia, and the White Guards flew it when they fought the Bolsheviks in the Civil War in 1918–1920. During World War II, the tricolor was taken up by the army of General Andrei Vlasov, who was allied with Nazi Germany against the Soviet Union. Nor did President Putin forget the red flag that had symbolized the USSR—it was proposed as the flag of the Russian army. With this combination of symbols representing all the stages of Russian history, Putin proposed to show the ties of time and to give tangible form to Russia's glorious heritage. Russia would enter the twenty-first century under the banner of absurdity in its symbols.

The melding of symbols of schism and mutual hatred with a symbol of the Soviet empire was viewed by many as a mockery of history or the product of a lack of understanding of that history. Some even considered it a provocation, this attempt to unite the nation on the basis of irritants.

The president's thinking on the issue was more straightforward. My hunch is that the package was Putin's own idea, not something put together by his councilors, and that it reflected his own views. For Putin, a strong state could not exist without symbols approved by everyone. It was very important that the populace rise each morning to an anthem that inspired energy and optimism and that state buildings fly the flag of Russia proudly. It goes without saying that Putin was sincere in wanting a consolidation of society, and he apparently dreamed of becoming the leader of Russia's unification. He must have truly believed that a return to the symbols of tsarism and communism would put an end to the arduous debates that were tearing the country apart: What is the new Russia?

What should Russia take from its past and what should it reject? He wanted to bring into the new mainstream the people nostalgic for Soviet times—and there were still many of them.

Putin himself must have had at least a touch of that nostalgia, for it was clear that, personally, he liked the Soviet anthem. He did not take into account that there were people in Russia for whom a return to the past was unthinkable because it held not joy but tremendous suffering and tragedy. With his insensitivity and his obtuseness, the president gave new life to old divisive passions and reopened old wounds. He precipitated another clash between the people who wanted to obliterate the memory of the Soviet era, the deaths of millions in the Gulag, and those who continued to be proud of that period.

Russia fell into debate once again. The endless, repetitive, emotional arguments between friends and even strangers over the symbols showed how difficult it is to unite a country that has been through the fire for years and is still undergoing radical change, how intransigent were the interests of different groups—liberals, nationalists, left-oriented people—and how these groups refused to listen to one another.

The main irritant for the liberal segments of society was the Soviet anthem, whose heroic music by Alexander Alexandrov was perceived as the symbol of communism and the Soviet empire. Putin had not expected the notion of reinstating a Soviet song to cause such a storm. When the protests began, he started justifying himself with a certain ill-at-ease tone. "Let's not forget that in this case we are talking about the majority of the people," he said, referring to the results of polls on the symbols. The argument reminded many of Soviet times, when the leaders justified their actions by reference to the majority.[10] Putin humbly, albeit with hidden irony, added, covering himself, "I do allow that the people and I could be mistaken."

The long-silent Yeltsin spoke out. The former president gave a special interview in which he declared, "I am categorically against reinstating the USSR anthem as the state one."[11] But Putin, quite consciously, was appealing to that portion of society that yearned for some revival of Russia's might and glory in the Soviet style. Those were people for whom Putin felt an affinity. At least at the moment, they were his true base, not pro-Western intellectuals and human rights activists, and not anticommunists like Yeltsin. He would not disappoint his staunch loyalists and show weakness to his liberal opponents by backing down on the symbols.

In a December 8 vote in the State Duma, 381 of 450 deputies approved the change to the Soviet anthem. The white, blue, and red flag got 342 votes, and the imperial double-headed eagle 341. It was to be expected. The Duma continued to be faithful to the new president, and it approved everything he proposed; the liberal factions were firmly against Putin's symbols, but they were prevented from speaking on the issue in the parliament. The law making the symbols official included a provision requiring people to stand during the anthem. The joke went, "If you don't stand up on time, you'll do time."

A few days later, the Federation Council also approved Putin's symbols for Russia. The senators had the anthem—familiar for so long, now to become familiar again—played. Everyone obediently jumped up when the Stalin-approved music began, except for Nikolai Fedorov, president of Chuvashia, who remained in his seat. This was a harbinger of what was to come: At every official function, some would stand and others would remain seated or pretend to be tying their shoelaces. At least for the foreseeable future, it would be a constant reminder of the schism in Russian society and of the fact that the new president had encouraged it.

Journalists continued to mock the symbols the president had proposed. "He is the president of our mothers and fathers," they joked, because his choice of state symbols seemed to demonstrate that the past was more important to him than the future. Russia's leader was giving yesterday's answers to today's questions. That Russia was entering the new millennium to the strains of the Soviet anthem created a dark premonition in some people's minds.

Putin's choice of the Soviet anthem, particularly over Yeltsin's protests, also demonstrated that the president was moving away from the influence of Yeltsin and his political circle. His open disagreement with his predecessor on this subject was almost a challenge to the old ruling corporation. But it would be premature to conclude that Putin was now free of all obligations to those who had put him where he was.

Almost simultaneously, also in December 2000, another event transpired that showed Putin still felt himself under at least some obligation to the Yeltsin entourage. Despite the large amount of material turned over to it by Swiss prosecutors, the Russian prosecutor's office decided to drop the case of embezzlement by Yeltsin's presidential office, which allegedly involved the president's family. After several years of stories on the front page of Russian newspapers, "Kremlingate" was declared closed due to "insufficient evidence."

The Russian prosecutors explained that the piles of bank documents from Switzerland could not be used as evidence in a Russian court. They were copies, and not very clear ones, whereas Russian justice works only with originals. Of course, the prosecutors could have gone to Switzerland, compared the copies with the originals, made clear duplicate copies, and had them notarized if they themselves were not notaries. Instead, the prosecutors decided to shut down the Kremlingate investigation. One more scandal was hushed up, and the Yeltsin family and the high-ranking officials who fed at the same trough could sleep peacefully again. Kremlingate could never have been closed without direct orders from the Kremlin's current occupants. Clearly, the old Yeltsin circle still had influence, and Putin still felt an obligation to it.

In the meantime, the new president developed a taste for world travel. He seemed to regard his international trips as an important element in the reestablishment of Russia's prestige. Moreover, the experience—the receptions at the highest levels, spending time with global elites—seemed to give him a real sense of power. Other leaders must have similar reactions, because so many of them take up foreign policy once in office. And perhaps Putin felt that international problems were simpler to solve than domestic ones.

The Russian president flew across oceans, visiting several countries per trip. He flew from hot climes to cold and vice versa. His physical stamina was astounding. But he was young and his sports background helped; he was in excellent shape and had a lot of endurance (unlike Yeltsin). Vladimir Vladimirovich learned the secret language of diplomacy and felt comfortable and on an equal footing with the other leaders at world summits. He spoke logically and impressed people with his memory. A quick learner, he was turning into a worthy partner.

A partial list of Putin's travels in 2000 would include Belarus, Brunei, Canada, China, Cuba, France, Germany, India, Japan, Libya, Mongolia, North Korea, Turkey, and Ukraine. The president managed to use up his budget for international travel, and he had to seek additional funding.

That same year, a Russian foreign policy concept paper was finally developed by the Foreign Affairs Ministry. The document said quite a few reasonable things, among them that the country must drop its idée fixe of a global presence and think about promoting its economic interests. It stressed the need for improving relations with neighbors in the Commonwealth of Independent States and Europe. But at the same time, the draft incorporated thoughts that seemed to come from Cold War documents—for instance, that Russia was surrounded by hostile forces that had to be fought.

The concept paper created the impression that it was the product of a struggle between two groups, one concerned with the new image of Russia and one seeking a return to the days of confrontation with the West. The same duality could be discerned in Putin. On one hand, he announced, "We must rid ourselves of imperial ambitions." On the other hand, a painful reaction on the part of the Kremlin to the independent policies of Azerbaijan, Georgia, and Ukraine indicated that imperial moods, though weakened and less apparent, were still alive and that superpower claims were still being asserted by the Russian ruling team.

The character and frequency of Putin's contacts with Europeans evinced Moscow's desire to make relations with Western Europe the most important element of its foreign policy. Moscow clearly needed to activate contacts with European states, especially after Yeltsin, for whom no other countries besides the United States existed. Russia was genuinely interested in promoting economic ties with Europe. It had its reasons; trade between Russia and the European Union in 2000–2001 already constituted 48 percent of Russia's total trade, whereas trade with the United States made up only 5.5 to 6 percent. But one had the feeling that Putin's European orientation was to some extent a reaction to the growing coolness in United States–Russia relations.

The warmth of the personal relationship developing between Putin and several European leaders, particularly Tony Blair of the United Kingdom and Gerhard Schröder of Germany, was not, however, enough to smooth away the problems arising in Moscow's relations with the Council of Europe and its Parliamentary Assembly. Russia lost the right to vote in the Council of Europe because of its handling of the "antiterrorist operation" in Chechnya (this right was returned to Russia in 2001 after a delegation from the council visited Chechnya and concluded that Russian policy there was becoming more civilized). Nor was Moscow on good terms with the Organization for Cooperation and Security in Europe (OCSE), which Russia hoped to turn into a linchpin of European security in response to the strengthening of NATO. As a result, the Russian Foreign Ministry, unable to find a compromise with the Western countries on human rights issues, did not sign the OCSE declaration at the end of the year.

In addition to the European angle, Putin tried to restore Russia's ties with its allies from the Soviet period. That was the object of his trips to Cuba, Mongolia, and North Korea. In restoring torn ties with its former satellite countries, Moscow was not only after at least the partial restoration of Russia's world role. Economic motives were crucial: Moscow wanted to begin negotiations on the payment of old debts. Where it was impossible to get money back, Putin talked of being paid in raw materials and of an economic cooperation beneficial to Russia. The Russian president was introducing commercialization of foreign policy—a promising change on the international scene, where Russia had always been more interested in demonstrating its might, even when it meant losing economic benefits.

Moscow's attention to former allies from the Soviet period made Russian liberals wary and nationalists happy. The latter declared an end of Russia's pro-Western policies and a turn toward Asia.[12] But Putin clearly was not planning a break with the West. He applied the same method to foreign policy that he used at home—looking to each potential partner in turn, not tying himself permanently to anyone. It appeared that he wanted, with his diplomatic flurry, to remind the world about Russia after a lengthy period of foreign policy lethargy. In developing his international agenda, Russia's president definitely had some domestic priorities in mind, first of all an economic agenda. But at the same time, Putin's desire to move simultaneously in all directions created the impression that he still could not answer the question, Where does Russia belong? Or perhaps he postponed his answer for the time being.

Putin's activity on all international fronts only emphasized the cooler relations between Russia and the United States. In fact, they had begun to freeze during the Clinton–Yeltsin period. The sad irony is that it happened despite the fact that Bill Clinton was the first and so far the only U.S. leader who made Russia his foreign policy mission, who called for a "strategic alliance with Russian reform." Strobe Talbott, the deputy secretary of state during Clinton's presidency, gave an illuminating assessment of the United States–Russia relationship in the 1990s in his memoir *The Russia Hand*, revealing the hidden and dramatic clash of interests, hopes, and myths as a new era of this relationship took shape.[13]

By mid-1999, United States–Russia relations had come under considerable strain. Outwardly, the war in Kosovo and NATO enlargement had caused a major breach. The roots of bilateral discontent went much deeper, however. Both sides underestimated difficulties and constraints of Russia's transformation and of building normal ties when one state was at an unprecedented peak and the other in the process of a humiliating fall, especially when the two had been fierce rivals for so long and had been the symbols of alternative civilizations. Unrealistic hopes and an asymmetry of capabilities were serious sources of growing frustration in Russian–American relations. However, the United States had asymmetrical relations with other states that did not produce the same mutual dismay.

A strong belief among the Russian political class that a great-power role was the crucial consolidating factor in Russia, and the only way for Russia to survive as an entity, was the major cause of the growing rift between the United States and Russia. This belief was behind the stubbornness of Russian elites in pursuing the country's global ambitions, and their unhappiness with U.S. dominance and unwillingness to accept these plans. The Russian political class was not ready to redefine Russia's role in the world. Moscow still wanted to preserve the bilateral world order, with only one argument to support its pretensions: its nuclear arsenal.

In the field of security, the Clinton administration pursued a policy that Thomas Graham and Arnold Horelick described as "trading symbolism for substance."[14] It offered Moscow some concessions, such as incorporating it into the Group of Seven structure in exchange for withdrawing its troops from Eastern Europe and the Baltic Sea region. It also warded off a destructive Russian response to NATO enlargement. This policy not only helped the United States pursue its agenda but also softened Russia's transition to a more realistic international role. But in the end, the policy did not prevent the Russia–United States relationship from sliding into crisis. Symbolism and imitation partnership, which Russian elites considered to be hollow, only deepened Moscow's distrust of Washington.

In fact, the Clinton administration helped Russia manage superpower decline by assisting in resolving the security issues resulting from the collapse of the Soviet Union. But paradoxically, "superpower decline management" hardly could get support or even appreciation from Russian elites, who considered great-power status the only prerequisite of Russian statehood. Besides, the U.S. side did not always have the patience and time, and it lacked an understanding of Russian complexes, as was demonstrated by NATO enlargement, which brought such an emotional rejection in Russia.

Theoretically, Moscow and Washington could have worked it out under one condition: Russia's rejection of all claims to a superpower role and agreement to become a "normal" country that was part of Western civilization—that is, to become a new France. The bargain would also include Russia's voluntary acceptance of U.S. world hegemony. But all that seemed unlikely to happen at that time.

Because liberal democratic ideology had not become entrenched in Russia, in the 1990s great-power rhetoric remained—in the eyes of many representatives of the Russian political class—a powerful unifying factor, and no Russian leader could have held onto power without understanding that. Yeltsin, despite his deep-down pro-Western orientation, often thought that it was safe for him to play great-power advocate, which explains his zigzags in foreign policy. Keeping up the foreign policy and even the rhetoric of a superpower was doomed to be a major destabilizing factor in relations with the United States. Thus, the cooling down of the relationship between Moscow and Washington was inevitable.

The new people Putin brought into the Kremlin were sick of their country's weakness. They had been brought up believing in Russia's exceptionality and greatness. They wanted to be respected, and they wanted their country to be respected and taken into account again—and perhaps, if not feared as before, at least regarded with some wariness. The only foreign entity to which they wanted to prove something was the United States, because only in an equal relationship with it could Russia feel like a great power. However, the method of self-determination chosen by Russia's new ruling group in early 2000 was much like the old Soviet method—an exhibition of willful independence, even cockiness, a search for its own spheres of influence, an accent on what separates rather than what brings closer, and an attempt at blackmail in the threat of rapprochement with China.

The new team in the Kremlin took a series of steps to signal its coldness toward Washington. Putin indicated that he was not interested in developing a relationship with a U.S. lame-duck president but would wait to deal with Clinton's successor. When Putin and Clinton met in Moscow in June 2000, the Russian leader did not even pretend to demonstrate interest in strengthening a personal rapport with Clinton or in discussing serious issues. "It was no mystery what Putin's game was: He was waiting for Clinton's successor to be elected in five months before deciding how to cope with the United States and all its power, its demands and its reproaches. Putin had, in his own studied, cordial and oblique way, put U.S.–Russian relations on hold," wrote Talbott.[15]

One of the first signs of tougher Kremlin policy was the trial of the American businessman Edmond Pope, who was charged with espionage and attempting to buy blueprints of the Shkval, the Russian secret torpedo. More followed. At the tensest moment before the election in the United States, on November 3, Russian minister of foreign affairs Igor Ivanov informed the U.S. State Department that Russia would no longer abide by the Gore–Chernomyrdin agreement limiting Russian shipments of arms to Iran. This was a highly unpleasant gift to the Democrats at a point when presidential candidate Al Gore was defending himself against charges of secret deals with the Russians and tacit acquiescence in Russian corruption.[16] An extreme example of the new approach toward Washington was the attempt by the Russian military to lay the blame for the loss of the submarine *Kursk* on the United States.

Yet another example of the change in relations was the flight of Russian jets over the U.S. aircraft carrier *Kitty Hawk* in November 2000.

Such flyovers had not been carried out by Americans or Russians since the end of the Cold War. Putin's team in the Kremlin apparently wanted the Russian military to send the United States a message: "Beware, we are still strong and can create trouble for you!" The pilots were decorated for flying over the American ship.

The displays of arrogant self-confidence and public reminders that the love and hugs were over were a game aimed at the Russian man on the street and anti-Western elites, who faulted Yeltsin for being too friendly with American leaders. The anti-Americanism of Russian political elites had been in evidence before. But while it was veiled in Yeltsin's day, now it was mandatory for entrée into the political class. Like his predecessor, the new president of Russia enjoyed entering the circle of the "Group of Eight" and shaking hands with the U.S. leader. But at the same time, the Russian press—even the liberal papers—did not miss an opportunity to take digs at the Americans with the silent approval of some of the Kremlin's inhabitants.

Russian observer Andrei Piontkovsky hit the mark when he wrote in the December 7, 2000, *Obshchaya gazeta* about "the manic depression" syndrome of Russian elites expressing itself in relations with Washington. This syndrome could be seen on the one hand in the servility of some representatives of the Russian ruling class toward Washington. They flocked to the U.S. capital to meet with officials, speaking pleasantly, smiling radiantly, and giving them slaps on the back in the American manner. But back in Moscow, they turned on the United States. They had to keep up their image as statists, great-power advocates, for it was the fashion now. This hypocrisy concealed seemingly incompatible feelings: humiliation and impudence, a desire for revenge, and a longing to be accepted as equals.

The surge of anti-Americanism can hardly be said to have been instigated by the Russian president, who behaved in an extremely reticent and cautious way. But he never did anything to stop the mood either. It looked as if Putin was still forming his understanding of Russia's identity and Russian goals in the foreign policy field, and assessing the West and the United States and their intentions toward Russia. He apparently had worked out his own general orientation during his years in Saint Petersburg, when he had had many successful business contacts with the West. But after his unexpected ascendancy to the Kremlin, he had to make sure his orientation would not endanger his power, and he preferred to wait and see. Meanwhile, the political class took Putin's caution as his approval of a more active anti-American stance. In Russia, it is always safer to play on anti-Western feelings than on love of the West.

But Washington was not interested in Russia. In the autumn of 2000, the United States was having trouble electing a president. The electoral endgame gave rise to jokes in the Russian establishment that boiled down to one thing: One has to know how to control the election outcome. Even Putin made a remark, with a sarcastic smile, about U.S. democracy not being able to give the American people their new leader quickly. The torturous process of U.S. elections strengthened the conviction of the Russian ruling class that the Russian mechanism of appointing the president and using administrative resources to get him elected was much more convenient and dependable.

When it became clear that the United States had elected Republican George W. Bush, Russian elites first sighed in relief. They had decided that Republicans in the White House would be better for Russia than Democrats. The conclusion was based on three premises. First, Moscow was disillusioned with Clinton, who despite his good intentions toward Russia did little to help Russian reform, in the opinion of Russian politicians. The Russian ruling class had expected a new Marshall Plan—similar to the one the United States implemented in Europe after World War II—in gratitude to Russia for ending communism and the USSR. Those hopes were not satisfied. Or to be exact, they were not fulfilled completely.[17]

Second, during Clinton's presidency, Russia's international weight and influence continued to diminish, intensifying the asymmetry between the United States and Russia. Russian elites—unwilling to accept that imbalance, or to reconsider superpower ambitions and approach the world in a more realistic way—regarded Washington with increasing suspicion and irritation, accusing it of hegemonic plans and trying to weaken Russia. Any attempt by the United States to pursue its interests was perceived as directed against Russia, the continuation of a zero-sum game.

Third on their list of reasons to prefer Republicans in power in the

United States, Moscow observers recalled that under the Democrats John F. Kennedy and Jimmy Carter, relations between the United States and the Soviet Union were, in their view, rotten. In contrast, they praised the Republicans Richard Nixon, Ronald Reagan, and George H. W. Bush, who succeeded in establishing quite amicable relations with Soviet and Russian leaders. Obviously, human memory is selective; the Russian proponents of the Republicans had forgotten Nixon's toughness toward the Soviet Union and Reagan's early presidency with his hostility to the "evil empire."

What Russian elites disliked most about the Democrats was their desire to promote democracy and their concern for rights and freedoms. The new ruling team in the Kremlin did not want to be lectured, especially on democracy. In Moscow's perception, the Republicans traditionally were less given to interfering in the internal affairs of other countries and were ready to play balance-of-power games in which Russia still counted.

Moscow saw George W. Bush's election as the start of a new era in relations between Russia and the United States. Many in Russia viewed Bush as practically the American Putin. Bush and Putin were certain to like one another, analogy lovers reasoned. Both were starting out from square one, in politics and in their relationship.

Russian observers thought that both countries would play at geopolitics and enter into a dialogue on nuclear issues that Russian elites liked so much and that gave them a feeling of importance. Consequently, Russia would once again be regarded as a partner of the United States and thereby regain its superpower status. Kremlin strategists did not wish to see that Russia was no longer a priority for either Democrats or Republicans and that Washington was tired of Moscow and its constant mood swings and desire to be cuddled and cajoled. While under Clinton there had been a willingness to accommodate and soothe Moscow politicians, the new, harsher, and more pragmatic residents of the White House were not at all sentimental when it came to the Kremlin. Thus Moscow had to prepare for a more restrained, even cold, attitude on the part of the White House, which could always point to the difference in the two countries' capabilities.

Something else came between the two new presidents: U.S. plans for a national missile defense (NMD), which meant abrogation of the

Anti–Ballistic Missile Treaty that Russians viewed as a "cornerstone of nuclear stability." Almost the entire political class in Russia, including the liberals, felt that the U.S. plan for NMD would destroy the system of international security built over the years, in which Russia was an important element, and that is why it was totally unacceptable for Russia.

This stance of total rejection of NMD and refusal to seek a compromise with Washington threatened to embarrass Moscow if the United States went ahead with the unfurling of its nuclear umbrella. Russian foreign policy circles hoped to mobilize Europe and China against the U.S. plan. Clinton's refusal to push forward missile defense during his tenure was perceived in Moscow as the result of Russian pressure on the White House. And that perception was the basis for the Kremlin team's belief that the U.S. plan for NMD could be stopped by taking a hard line with the United States. That was the prevailing mood in Moscow.

Putin deserves credit for making a distinction between a bow in the direction of Russian complexes, which he performed, and not on one occasion only, and a sober understanding of the new international situation and Russia's role in it, which he demonstrated with his cautious policy at the end of 2000. He probably understood that the United States was no longer the main threat to Russia's security. But it was still hard for him to rise above the ambitions and neuroses of the elites, and at that point he had to follow their lead, though with increasing restraint.

Overall, 2000 was not an easy year, either for Russia or for its president. It saw the sinking of the *Kursk*. The war in Chechnya went on all year, taking lives every week. Nevertheless, despite those tragedies, public optimism was surprisingly high. For many Russians, 2000 was the least difficult of recent years. Typically, it was the least difficult for people in the provinces, the elderly, and the poor—those who lived simple lives. These people had begun getting their salaries and pension payments regularly under Putin, and that was enough to lead them to consider the year a success.

For the intelligentsia, people who lived in large cities, and the politicized segment of society, 2000 was much harder than 1999. Some of these people were more disappointed by what the new president did on the political scene, for they had expected more than their regular wages from him; they had expected vision and a strong sense of responsibility. Others had no hope from the beginning, having been suspicious of Putin; now, watching the president's ambiguousness, they felt that their suspicions were justified.

Of Russians polled on the year 2000, 39 percent had higher hopes than the year before (when the figure was 29 percent); 30 percent felt disappointment (the same as in 1999); and 16 percent felt fear (slightly down from the 18 percent in 1999). Another 13 percent felt confused (compared with 17 percent in 1999), and 20 percent felt angry (compared with 23 percent in 1999). The year 2000 had been calmer for Russia and could be characterized with the words of sociologist Yuri Levada: "A bit less fear and a bit more hope."[18]

But 2000 could not be considered a problem-free year for Putin, first as prime minister and acting president, then as the elected president. By the year's end, it was obvious that the Russian public considered the war in Chechnya a failure—49 percent called the president's actions there unsuccessful, as opposed to 24 percent at the beginning of the year. But there were no antiwar demonstrations or other actions in Russia. Society seemed to remain aloof from the war, waiting it out. People pretended that the events in Chechnya and the continual losses had nothing to do with them.

Gradually, Russians began judging Putin's presidency more severely. At the close of 2000, 45 percent felt that he was handling his responsibilities well, and 48 percent felt that he was not successful. The president's activity in the economic sphere was considered unsuccessful by 65 percent, whereas on the task of defending democracy, 53 percent considered him unsuccessful. In only one sphere did the majority (63 versus 28 percent) believe that the president was successful: international affairs. The respondents did not have a clear understanding of what his foreign policy actions meant; it was more that they were hypnotized by his constant international trips.

Although the majority did not consider the president's actions successful, his administration as a whole garnered the approval of 68 percent of respondents, and 40 percent were prepared to vote for him as president again. However, those data could not have made the president feel very optimistic. He still had support, but the majority expected nothing positive from his presidency. People were supporting him primarily because there was no alternative to him in the Russian political arena.

President Putin had managed to consolidate all the basic levers of power in his hands. He had managed to neutralize all the groups of influence that had been powerful under Yeltsin. He had struck a blow against the oligarchs and forced them to give up political ambitions. But to be perfectly objective, the oligarchy as a class had been weakened in Russia by the financial crisis of 1998, and it never recovered as a political force from that blow. The power of the regional elites had been undermined as well; the Kremlin demonstrated that it could easily get rid of regional leaders it did not like. And finally, political opposition had disappeared almost entirely. The State Duma was fully dependent on the Kremlin. What we saw was an almost tranquil idyll. The distribution of power had changed radically. Politicians were no longer divided into democrats and communists. Now the demarcation line was who was pro-Putin and who was against. There were very few of the latter, or they were lying very low.

How did the new Kremlin boss manage in such a short time and without a visible struggle to destroy the numerous "political flowers" that had bloomed under Yeltsin and spoiled his life? The answer was rather simple: Society still retained a fear of authority. Yeltsin was not feared, especially at the end of his term. Moreover, he was not considered rancorous or vengeful. He was treated like an old, sick bear who could be teased a bit and not taken seriously.

The second Russian president, however, elicited other feelings. He was not very well known, and people did not know where he drew the line or whether he had *any* lines on the use of power—including coercion. So even a slight criticism from the authorities, a glance or nod from the president, was enough to send people scurrying in toadying fashion.

It turned out that the central authorities in Russia, first among them the president, still had enormous power. Putin was the leader with administrative and coercive resources, with support within the political class. There was no alternative to him at the time. He was power personified. Those in opposition had no guarantee of surviving and existing or even raising their voices—their only option was vegetating on the margins of political life. One may object that Yeltsin also had administrative resources.

But the first Russian president could never get utter support and obedience. He had to constantly fight with the Duma, the Federation Council, the opposition; he had to bear attacks in the press and the mockery of opponents. In the end, he was despised and ignored.

Why did the nondescript, shallow-looking Putin manage to bend to his will the political scene in Russia, where the powerful and charismatic Yeltsin had failed? Besides fear of power and the traditional servility of the political class and society, there was exhaustion. Yeltsin ruled in a period of social upheaval, and when the upward surge ended, society continued living in disorder. This was a time of political whirlpools and struggle, fragmentation and pluralism, freedoms and spontaneity. Yeltsin whipped up that frenzy himself and extended the revolutionary cycle artificially, not knowing how to stabilize the situation. For Yeltsin, extending the revolution was a means of personal survival.

By the time Putin came along, it became clear just how tired and disenchanted society had become. Putin was possible because the masses wanted nothing but peace and order. Rocking the boat would no longer have the support of the people. Putin easily dealt with the chaos that had developed under Yeltsin, primarily because the majority of Russians wanted it dealt with. The main proponents of order were the "swamp" that bet on Putin and understood order to mean subordination to the leader. Putin was helped by the pendulum of development that had swung from the phase of disorder and liberalization to the phase of calming down and strengthening of conservative values. Putin behaved like the concentrated expression of the pendulum's movement.

Once he had consolidated all power in his hands, the president stopped at that. His obvious victories in 2000, besides building up his superpresidential regime or "verticality of authority," as it was called in Russia, were only two—the Duma's approval of the START-2 missile reduction treaty, and the new income tax code. This was practically the sum total of Putin's achievements for the year, despite extremely propitious circumstances, the likes of which Yeltsin had never enjoyed.

At first, Putin's frenzied activity—his constant peregrinations around the country and meetings with the most varied people, his continual appearances on television—created the impression of mobile, dynamic, even aggressive leadership. Gradually, though, many people began to perceive all that activity as mere bustle intended to create a simulacrum of governing. It looked at that moment as if the president followed the principle: "The movement is everything, the goal is nothing."

Putin had done almost nothing toward a breakthrough in liberal reform. Moreover, the end of 2000 revealed a loss of impulse in his presidency, a weakening of the energy of leadership. The question was repeated with increasing volume: Why did Putin want power—for the sake of the process or for reforms? Quite a few observers came to the conclusion that power had been a goal in itself for the young Russian leader.

Besides which, other things were gradually revealed. It turned out that not one of the Kremlin boss's actions had been brought to its logical conclusion. The oligarchs had been given a scare. But those who agreed to be faithful to the regime were granted almost total freedom to act and get rich. Only the most recalcitrant had been attacked. So Putin's anti-oligarch revolution stopped midway. The fusion of power and business was retained.

The governors were lined up in a row, like soldiers, and pacified. However, the Kremlin could not achieve its goals in the regions and obtain total obedience. Very quickly, the Kremlin had to begin doing what Yeltsin had always done: offer the governors deals and compromises.

Despite all the pressure from the Kremlin on the independent media, they continued to exist. As 2000 ended, NTV was still criticizing Putin. All attempts to imprison Gusinsky, the owner of Media-Most, and to wrest control over the media from him had led to nothing.

In other words, Vladimir Vladimirovich had managed to achieve impressive results in taming Russian politics. But it turned out that he was far from having politics on a leash. Russian society, outwardly giving the impression of being tamed, continued on its own way. The Putin team was using fear. As the president put it, he had only "shown the cudgel." For the nervous and easily frightened, that was enough. But there were others in society—those who decided to wait, to observe the regime, or not to give up. There were not many, but they existed. Losing his former aggressiveness and now encountering silent and still-invisible resistance, Putin the humble newcomer began hesitating more frequently.

Yeltsin had had his own dance—one step forward, two steps back. Putin continued dancing, taking a step forward, then stopping, sometimes even retreating; it was a halting, jerky dance. That did not mean he lacked the decisiveness to entirely break the dissatisfied elements in society and complete his construction of a "manageable democracy." Perhaps he was just biding his time and gathering his strength. But it is no less possible that he did not know what to do next. Perhaps the year 2000 was only a warm-up before the jump. But a jump in which direction?

The sources of Putin's power became clear. The first was high oil prices, which created economic stability and made possible the payment of wages and pensions. Journalists joked that though Putin was formally Yeltsin's heir, he was actually much closer to another leader—Leonid Brezhnev. It was in the period of Tsar Leonid that the USSR survived on high oil prices. As soon as prices fell, the Soviet economy collapsed like a house of cards.

The second source of Putin's power was his amazingly high approval ratings, which stayed high despite the emerging disillusionment with him among some social groups. But oil prices and ratings were too unstable to serve as bases for a presidency. At the end of 2000, oil prices were slowly coming down. As for Putin's ratings, he had become hostage to them. That was reflected in his policies; the president had to reject or postpone necessary but clearly unpopular actions, such as housing and utility reform, because they threatened to wreck his high ratings.

It looked as if the Kremlin started its day with an analysis of the president's ratings. If support was faltering in some social group, the Kremlin began working on it—"turning its face to it." The president suddenly began making speeches that would resonate with that audience. If he needed to flirt with the left, he began attacking oligarchs. If the liberals were unhappy, he turned to them, talking about market reforms. It was hard to avoid the feeling that the energies of the president and his team were being wasted on following the fluctuations in his ratings. As a result, there was no time or energy to set a general course.

Moreover, the president had become a hostage to his team, which had manipulated his rise. The team helped him win the elections. But keeping the election experts on at the Kremlin turned the president's administration into an endless election campaign.

After a year in power, Putin still had not answered the question about who he was. The question, posed by the journalists at the global summit of capitalist elites in Davos in the winter of 2000—"Who is Mr. Putin?"—had not lost its bite. Putin was still an amorphous political leader who constantly changed his contours, trying to appeal to all forces simultaneously. Artists who painted portraits of him complained that they couldn't "capture" him—he slipped away, he seemed inscrutable, and they could not find the defining features that former leaders had had. Paradoxically, on one hand, Russian society already knew a lot about its president and his goals. On the other, he was still a work in progress, and he often seemed to behave like a professional intelligence officer covering his tracks and hiding his true intentions. As a result, the president's image remained a blur.

Thus the most varied political forces continued to hope that Putin would end up on their side. The liberals hoped he would join them, and the left and statists felt he was much closer to them. "Who Mr. Putin is and how he pictures the future of Russia is still unknown," a reporter wrote in the December 26, 2000, *Kommersant-Vlast'*. "Just as much is known now as a year ago. And whether it is conscious or unconscious, Putin is not letting people find out."[19] That is to say, even as president, Putin behaved like an agent in enemy territory, letting no one learn his true intentions—if in fact he had any. Because of his unformed image and his political bartering with the main political forces—something for some, other things for others—he managed to preserve his power positions and social stability. At least for now.

Chapter 6

RUSSIA
TRANQUILIZED

─────────── ✦ ───────────

Back to the kitchen. Society seeks calm. Russian Gaullism.
Who loves Russia more? Pogrom at NTV. Wax dummies.

The first year of Putin's presidency ended in the spring of 2001. Instead of the animation and chaos characteristic of Yeltsin's tenure, we saw a wintry political and intellectual landscape. Now there was not even a single influential political force independent of the Kremlin, or a single public group with a strong independent voice. Almost everyone left on the scene was playing—voluntarily or reluctantly—by rules set by the authorities. People who still tried to say what they thought, especially if it was to attack the Kremlin, had no guarantee of political survival, not because they were threatened but because nobody listened to them any longer; what they said or how they acted did not matter anymore—they did not have any impact on the political process.

Political actors had become nondescript and difficult to remember. The political and intellectual personalities who just recently had raised the tone and vitality of society—liberals, oligarchs, prominent journalists, former dissidents whose public appearances were impatiently anticipated—had vanished from the open scene or spoke only in hushed voices; they were faded versions of themselves. The last of the Mohicans, famous Soviet dissident writer Alexander Solzhenitsyn, was living in seclusion outside Moscow. When he made a rare appearance in the capital, he was regarded as if he were a museum exhibit. Politics and public discourse had grown shallow and petty, reduced to the level of kitchen chitchat. No one in sight could or dared think big.

Under Yeltsin, even in the final stage of his administration and despite his personal decline, life was on at full blast, albeit not always with an influence on politics and the regime. But now even the purely external fairgrounds bustle was gone. Russians seemed less interested in both politics and the future. Weariness and indifference dominated. The outward calm often hid emptiness or lack of ambition. People's aim was simply to survive and limp along, with no claim to anything more.

In other societies, this relaxation comes as a result of satiety and material security. In Russia, the descent from activity to indifference, the giving up on hopes and slide into living day to day, was the product of disillusionment and weariness. Russians now regarded further reforms as not necessarily a good thing, because they were afraid that any reform could only make things worse.

The shift from the struggle and striving of the Yeltsin period to apathy did not occur instantaneously with the beginning of the new presidency. Putin would never have been elected in an era of vibrancy and desire to renew life. He would never have appeared as a public figure when Russian politics called for charismatic personalities, vivid leaders with electrifying powers—when the search for a goal was on. Putin in the Kremlin now was the reflection of the exhaustion of revolutionary ardor and, for many, the loss of courage and perhaps a feeling of being at a dead end. Russia seemed to want nothing but peace and quiet, and Putin seemed to be the man who could produce it. The new president became the embodiment of muddling along. Or rather, he was forced to assume that role, which he definitely did not like, for he seemed to have had much higher aspirations for himself and Russia.

The language of power and of the elites changed. Just a few years earlier, everyone had spoken of reform, progress, renewal, modernization, and democracy. It had been impossible to talk in any other way. Those words, symbolic of a new life, had become popular in Gorbachev's day. In Yeltsin's, they were the entrée into the ranks of the elites, and the passwords to power. Now completely different words filled the air—stability, statehood, order, sovereignty, greatness, power, patriotism. The change in symbolic words and rhetoric in general signified the new content of politics.

Politicians who were remnants of the past still cluttered the stage, but for the most part they were political ghosts. Some were afraid of being reprimanded by the Kremlin. Others tried to appear independent, but did not know what issues to take a stand on, what position to choose, or how to protect their independence, their freedom of expression and action. They had not decided on what issues they could disagree or were allowed to disagree with the Kremlin.

The irony was that the ruling team did not have the strength to force its wishes on Russians. The president, contrary to expectations, soon appeared to be not an ironhanded man who was ready to force people to accept his policy. Society and the political class, ready to obey the authorities, met them halfway. Politicians lined up voluntarily, without even being told. Witness the people from Unity, the propresidential party, united by one impulse: a readiness to do whatever the Kremlin said. They surrounded Putin, looking into his eyes as if begging, "Tell us what to do and we'll do it, Master." Bold, decisive, thinking people were leaving the stage. The ones who remained and who continued to disobey, like human rights activist Sergei Kovalyov, were perceived as eccentric and quixotic; no one paid attention to them. They fell by the wayside of the new life, where subordination and servility were seen as confirmation of pragmatism and rationality. Anything else was idealism and stupidity.

What was going on was a consolidation of the last echelon of the Soviet *nomenklatura*. Time and political struggles had swept away the early echelons, and power now belonged to the backbenchers of the Soviet ruling class. These were men in their forties. During the Gorbachev thaw and the Yeltsin chaos, they had neither the enterprise nor the aggression to rise to the top. Perhaps they did not have the talent either. They were young and inexperienced. This echelon had the strength only to be in proximity to power, playing secondary and tertiary roles. They bided their time, served, and worked as errand boys until their hour had come. Some of Putin's people had no ambition and ended up at the top by accident. Even for Vladimir Vladimirovich and most of his colleagues at the very highest levels, being catapulted to power came as a surprise, I think.

Most of the team came from Saint Petersburg, continuing the venerable Soviet and Russian tradition in which the leader brings people with him from his hometown. There were jokes about it in Moscow. For example: The Saint Petersburg train arrives in Moscow. Every disembarking passenger is approached by official-looking people and asked, "Would you

like to work in the Kremlin?" It was true that virtually all Putin's remotely close former colleagues and even some mere acquaintances from Saint
Petersburg had moved to Moscow and been given important posts. This
showed that the new president trusted only his own people. An infusion
of fresh blood into the Kremlin was vitally necessary to help the new president get out from under the influence of the circle that had ruled in the
latter Yeltsin era. But Russia needed an influx of professionals—not shallow, locally experienced bureaucrats.

The change of personnel and personality types was palpable. In Yeltsin's
day, you could come across anyone in the Kremlin, from democrats and
Westernizers to nationalists and supporters of autocracy. It was a motley
crew, the product of the sudden elevation of completely unexpected people. Putin's team may have vaulted to the top as well, but its members were
all alike, and quite different from Yeltsin's group. They were individuals
with unremarkable faces, buttoned up and not at all interested in joking.
Most were statists who felt nostalgia for Russia's vanished grandeur. They
must have hated the anarchy and degradation of the Yeltsin era. They could
not have approved of the winners of that era—those pushy oligarchs and
court favorites. The bureaucrat apparatchiks had come to power with
Putin, making Yeltsin's favorites seem lively and even extraordinary. Periods
of stabilization always call for average types—people who are unlikely to
harbor individualism and the desire to stand out.

Putin's people belonged to a single generation and were bound by a
common psychology and similar behavior patterns. Many had connections
to the power structures—*siloviki*—or at least shared a worldview with the
army and security services. They allowed people of another mentality—
the liberals German Gref and Alexei Kudrin, for example—into their
midst to achieve specific goals, but they did not give them freedom of
movement. They did not, could not, trust the liberals—they were people
of another blood.

Most of the new people at the top had their own principles and brand
of honesty. They were pragmatic, grounded, cautious, patient, and did not
set themselves unrealistic goals. But there was something in their pragmatism that undermined it. The majority of Putin's subordinates still lived in
the great-power paradigm—they were unlikely to picture Russia as a state
that thought about its people, not about power and greatness. It was not

yet clear whether the new team could escape that paradigm and treat the state as a means of serving the people. If that were to happen, we could safely conclude that Russia had overcome its past. At that time, Putin's team worked within the model they knew.

But the larger point is that not all the newcomers were capable. They brought provincialism and a lack of sophistication, for Saint Petersburg had long since become a fairly bleak city—politically and intellectually. To some degree, this provincialism was beneficial, because it brought the Kremlin closer to the greater part of Russia. But it also made it difficult for the new team to understand current complex strategic problems, to practice the art of governance in a huge and enormously controversial society that called for daring vision, experience, and knowledge.

The most important fact of life about the new ruling team was not even its conservatism or lack of expertise but something that was not really new. Ten years of Yeltsin's reforms had not produced alternative, non-Soviet elites in Russia. Yet again, the people in power had been brought up by the old system and had the old ties. Yes, they had breathed the new air and had developed new habits. But it was not clear to what degree they were oriented toward the future and whether they could give Russia a new strategy. In all successful transformations, society can move forward only after the appearance of new elites.

The revolutionary stage is inevitably followed by a period of stabilization, many pundits said by way of consolation. One had only to look at the former communist countries of Eastern Europe after their social and political upheavals. Stabilization in Russia, however, differed from stabilization in Poland and Hungary, for instance. There, the choice had been made of a new form and manner of life, and society had agreed in principle with that choice. In Russia, stabilization meant that people were tired of pursuing a new agenda, of seeking a new future, and had agreed to a halt in the search. At least for now.

During the turbulent Yeltsin years, the motto was "We must change to survive." Now many Russians, seeking calm, subscribed to another principle: "Change is dangerous and risky." Because only a minority benefited from Yeltsin's reforms, the great majority did not want any more experiments. And it seemed that the winning minority was not very interested in changes either, afraid of a new redistribution of power and property. Many opted to settle with what they had.

Stabilization came at a time when the problems of renewal and restructuring of society had not been completely solved. In its ten years of transformation, Russia had not fully transformed its system. Russian society still was a hybrid that combined contradictory elements: bureaucratic pressure and chaotic striving, market relations and the government's desire to control everything, habituation to personal independence and a readiness to limit one's personal freedoms, servility toward the authorities and distrust and suspicion of them. Russians simultaneously wanted to be free and were afraid of freedom, not knowing how to handle it.

The outward manifestations of democracy in Russia did not interfere with the spinning of the bureaucratic spider web that was stifling the country once again. To survive, to get things done, society had to retreat once again into the sphere of shadow relations, where ties, money, power, and manipulation, rather than the fair, transparent rule of law, decided everything. Even people who considered themselves liberals felt quite comfortable in the gray zone.

Could that hybrid society based on opposing principles be sustained? If so, for how long? If not, was Russia prepared to continue reform in an atmosphere of weariness and disappointment? A breather was needed. But that meant losing time, and history does not tolerate breaks. And could Russia allow itself time off when the infrastructure built in Soviet times was falling apart—with airplanes crashing more frequently, buildings collapsing, roads falling into disrepair, and the education and health systems crumbling? Russia seemed stuck without answers. Pundits were going around and around trying to decide whether Putin was still pondering, whether he was waiting, vacillating, or perhaps preparing for a new breakthrough. There was no visible evidence of consideration and searching in the Kremlin, but the former intelligence agent knew how to be inscrutable and take unexpected turns. Meanwhile, precious time was running out.

An important index for assessing the changes taking place in the country and people's minds with Putin's ascendancy was the attitude of Russia toward the West. During the Yeltsin period, a lot of Russians wanted to be like people in the West and strove to be part of Europe. At the end of the 1990s, however, many Russians became disillusioned with the West and distrustful of its intentions toward their country. Most of their hopes for serious capital investment in the Russian economy had not been fulfilled. Institutional forms borrowed from the West did not work in Russia; to be accurate, they worked, but in the interests of the minority. Democratization had turned into chaos. Privatization had ended up enriching the few.

More and more Russians were coming to the conclusion that the Western pattern of civilization did not fit the Russian framework of development. According to the early 2001 VTsIOM polls, 58 percent of Russians had become convinced that Russia and Western culture were incompatible. This reflected not hostility toward the West but rather a lack of hope that Russia would ever catch up with Western society.

At the same time, Russians continued to borrow the Western lifestyle—and elites the most actively of any social group. The more successfully the ruling class followed Western standards in their lives, the more it turned to supporting superpower status for Russia, as if looking for a cover for its foreign ways. It was amusing to listen to people who drove the most expensive foreign cars, owned villas on the Côte d'Azur, sent their children to school in Switzerland and England, and kept their money in Western banks weigh in with typically Soviet opinions on the decline of the West and the need to "rebuff" it.

Suddenly, both in the ruling class and in the rest of society, the desire to return to traditional Russian values and seek tranquility and healing in them was manifesting itself. More and more frustrated Russians began to think that Russia was doomed to follow its "special path" of development.[1] And the characteristics of this special path are a strong, centralized government, power concentrated in the hands of the leader, and a superpower ideology.

The beginning of Putin's presidency saw an increase in the number of people in Russia who believed that their country was different from the other states and that Russians were different from other people. Although

54 percent of respondents in 1994 said that Russians had become different from people in Western countries during the years of Soviet rule, 68 percent felt that way in 2000. Seventy percent believed that Russia "was distinguished by a unique way of life and spiritual culture," and 71 percent said that Russia "is a great country that can be understood only through belief in its great predestination."[2] Such beliefs were an antidote to Russia's vulnerability and the continuing disenchantment of its people. They also help to explain Russians' attempts to compensate for domestic problems with an appearance of strength in the international arena.

These data speak of disillusionment with the notions of easy integration with the West that had come with warmer relations in the late 1980s and early 1990s. By the late 1990s, hopelessness had spread, and many Russians doubted that their country could ever become "normal." One antidote to Russia's seeming helplessness is the belief that it has been marked out for a special destiny—Russians are not like other people and should not try to be, because they are meant for something greater and the goal itself demands suffering, pain, and coping with difficulties. Russia's special path has never brought a normal life, but belief in it confers a justification of hopelessness and an illusion of strength.

Poll results must always be treated with extreme caution. If Russians were asked even at that moment of disconsolate fatalism, for instance, "Would you like to continue on the special path, if that meant continuing poverty, excessive power for the bureaucracy, corruption, and embezzlement in Russia?" the great majority would undoubtedly support normality, that is, joining Western civilization. If Russians were asked, "What is the greatest threat for society—the West, Islamic terrorism, China, or domestic problems?" the majority most likely would say the greatest challenges for Russia lie in Russia.

At the same time, it is fair to conclude that during the first years of Putin's presidency, Russia's political class and some social groups were losing their hope that Russia would ever catch up with the West and be incorporated into the Western community. Putin's own ascendancy to power was a reflection and outcome of this shift. People looking at a president with a KGB background assumed he had to be a nationalist and a strong proponent of great-power status for Russia, as were the majority of the Russian *siloviki*. With characteristic servility, they were prepared to be "more Catholic than the pope," although Putin himself was still vague about his real inclinations. Soon, however, it would become evident that the longing for uniqueness in Russia was not—thank God—a stable and dominant trend and that President Vladimir Putin would prove that appearances were deceptive.

An essential element of the new retro mentality was the attitude toward the leader. He was forgiven all weakness and failures, out of a sense of self-preservation, because no one saw any benefit in criticizing the authorities, for criticism would not lead to anything positive soon. Faith in the leader was more emotional than rational, because the public still did not know Putin's plans and program. Trust in the leader and a return to a traditional rule were for many the ultimate guarantee of relative calm. Seventy-nine percent of citizens had decided by 2001 that "Russians can't manage without a strong hand."

The desire to have someone at the helm who inspired hope led people to lay blame for failure not on the president but on everyone else—the cabinet, the oligarchs, the Duma, the governors, the West. And that was yet another paradox, for the other institutions in Russia were an extension of the presidency. All this ensured that Putin's approval ratings remained high while those for Russia's other institutions (cabinet, parliament, courts) fell beginning in 2001. Putin was protected, spared, and preserved as a symbol of faith. People were prepared to forgive him many things out of fear of him failing.

In other words, conservatism became entrenched in Putin's Russia. Russian conservatives placed the individual's subordination to the state and the regime, which was identical to the president, at the top of their pyramid. The psychological subtext of Russian conservatism was fear, accumulated over the "time of troubles" of the previous fifteen years, beginning with Gorbachev's perestroika. It was fear of the unknown and unexpected—fear of the mob, of the permanent disasters, of the collapse of Russia, of entry into a new world for which a very large part of society was not prepared.

A new joke posited that a conservative was a badly frightened liberal. And in fact, quite a few active conservatives had recently hailed the demise of the Soviet empire and communism and had supported liberal reforms and taken part in them. Today they were afraid of what the reforms had wrought. They now wanted the status quo, which could be bolstered by an increase in the role of the secret services and power agencies. They hailed the presidency of a man who seemingly valued power above almost anything else and who could guarantee them security. Putin was the creation of the fears of society, especially of its elites, because he wouldn't have come to power without them, and at the same time he presented himself as the answer to these fears.

Looking for analogies in history, some Russian conservatives compared themselves with French Gaullists and Putin, naturally, with General Charles de Gaulle. There were some apparent parallels. De Gaulle's France and Putin's Russia both made use of anti-American rhetoric and tried to preserve the imperial grandeur of their nations. Both experienced stabilization through the strengthening of presidential power. Both presidents considered loyal cadres extremely important and used administrative pressure to achieve their ends. Because of the style of his rule, the French general with good reason was known as the "republican monarch." And the Russian colonel who became a leader demonstrated the ambition to build a strong presidency as well.

But this exhausts the similarities between current Russian conservatism and French conservatism. De Gaulle stabilized a completely different political reality, which included a structured society and counterbalances. And he did not stop at stabilization but pushed forward ambitious transformation, shaping the Fifth Republic. De Gaulle had a strong prime minister and could not have functioned without a vibrant multiparty system and an effective parliament. But he did not create a system, as Putin was doing, by replacing institutions with loyalists. For Russia to have Gaullism, it would need not only a de Gaulle but traditions, like France's, of fighting for liberty and the people's dignity.

It would be a mistake, however, to view the rise of conservatism in 2000–2001 in Russia as exclusively the consequence of Putin's policies and his pressure on society. Putin was not a politician who would use force to form public moods. At first, it had seemed that he was an authoritarian who wanted to break Russia by coercion. But it soon became clear that in many ways the president just followed events. And he definitely did not want schisms and tried to avoid blatant conflicts whenever possible. He had fallen into a stream of expectations and went with the flow. He may still have been considering his future course. In any case, he was waiting—or rather, drifting—and often yielded when faced with resistance.

Judging by his actions—or better, inaction—Putin's vision of the future at the moment might have fitted into the conservative model. But most of the time he followed the lead of those of his voters who demanded strong rule from him. Even though he must have understood the realities of the postindustrial world, inside the country he consciously used a language that all understood, the language of great-powerhood. Thus, by his behavior and rhetoric, the president reinforced the charged atmosphere roiling with frustrations and doctored memories of past glories and became the hostage of the mood he had helped create.

The new revival of the Russian conservatism was supported not only by the political elites close to the Kremlin and the bureaucracy but also by the intellectual community that sided with the president. While Putin contemplated which agenda to choose for Russia, as he doubted and tried to keep in the centrist niche while starting slowly to build bridges to the West, the Russian intellectual establishment began discussions on who loved Russia more and who was Russia's best patriot.

The spring of 2001 was the climax of the "Love Russia" campaign. I doubt such a discussion would have taken place in a Russia where society and its elites had reached agreement on which pattern of development they wanted to follow and saw that this pattern would lead to Russia's integration into the Western community. The fierce discussion on patriotism and Russian uniqueness, replete with mutual recriminations, confirmed that Russia had not resolved the basic issue of its future and had not yet settled on its perceptions of the world.

The division of Russians into Westerners and great-power advocates was not a new one for Russian political life. It continued the arguments between Westernizers and Slavophiles begun in the nineteenth century. That these arguments were renewed after the Yeltsin reforms showed yet again that the ruling class and intellectuals in Russia were unsure how to think about Russian needs and aspirations, how to understand Russia's new identity, how to define a new future and so sought refuge in the past.

Those who considered themselves "patriots of Russia" attacked the "patriots of NATO" or "patriots of the United States." Russian patriots wanted Russia to be a great nation, supported a military solution to the Chechnya problem, and severely disapproved of any criticism of Kremlin policies on freedom of the press or the Chechen war. The patriots demanded a symmetrical retaliatory response to the United States and the West in case of new NATO enlargement or abrogation by the United States of the Anti–Ballistic Missile Treaty, which Russia regarded as the cornerstone of its own and world security. They dismissed all criticism of Putin and his policies as the desire "to discredit a president of Russia who is inconvenient for the United States and who wants to restore the country's great-power status."[3]

Intellectuals who opposed Russia's great-power ambitions were classed among the patriots of the West. It was interesting to watch new adherents joining the camp of the Russian patriots—it's always safer inside the regime's camp than outside it. All the new patriots were convinced that Putin had made his choice and that it was anti-Western. It would be a blow for them when the president went in an opposite direction.

The division of the political scene into patriots of Russia and patriots of the West signaled a return to the Soviet days, when enemies of the homeland were sought and that search was an important way to consolidate autocratic rule. Specialists on "real" patriotism tried to deny others the right to their vision of what was good for Russia. There were signs that even the Kremlin people felt embarrassed by the unexpected ultrapatriotic surge within the political and intellectual community.

The patriots shrugged off questions they couldn't answer, especially about where Russia would find the financial means to confront NATO and the United States. Why did Russia need a powerful nuclear arsenal when people were living on paltry wages? Why did Russia require military might and influence on the countries around it when it could not solve elementary problems of its own national life? Patriots of Russia could not answer these questions because they had not thought along these lines.

Who were these new "patriots"? Quite often, they were successful "new Russians," who drove Mercedeses and wore Versace-designed clothes. For them, an anti-Western stance was a form of camouflage, especially if their wealth came from ill-gotten gains. No one knew which way the authorities would turn. What if they started nationalizing? What if Putin started looking for the source of their wealth? It was better to be more patriotic (anyway, it couldn't hurt).

For others, anti-Western feeling stemmed from ordinary envy and the realization that Russia would not achieve Western levels of material well-being in their lifetime. It would lessen the sting to simply wall off the West and call it a hostile force. The hopelessness and dreariness of life, the lack of success and inadequacy when faced with new challenges, made some people see an insistence on Russia's uniqueness and a refusal to join Europe as something that could assuage their sense of inferiority and restore their self-esteem.

It was true that Putin sometimes played on these sentiments, continu ing to appeal to his base, which included a lot of traditional great-power supporters. He even said once: "Either Russia will be great or it will not be at all." In fact, he placed a dilemma before society: either Russia remains a superpower or it vanishes completely. At that point, some groups within society understood greatness as first of all military might, not as wealth or economic power. The formulation of the issue excluded the evolution of Russia in the direction of a normal state that is concerned with the needs of its people.

As a pragmatist, Putin did not push this theme too much, and to count er it he spoke about the need for Russia to move "into Europe." He must not have wanted—and perhaps even feared—a return to the past. But, at least in early 2001, he also was not ready for a more determined move-ment into the future. All his turns and zigzags prevented people from drawing any firm conclusions about his true views, or at least his mindset. He remained a political sphinx; it was hard to read anything in his inscrutable face; it was difficult to decide which of his actions was a strategic one. Perhaps he was simply changing his position as circumstances dictated.

The anti-Western appeals and searches for an enemy in the West did not find mass support among ordinary Russian people. Despite the nationalis-tic rhetoric of the elites, 8 percent of those polled at the end of 2000 had very good feelings about the United States, 62 percent had basically good feelings, 16 percent had basically bad ones, and 6 percent had very bad ones (8 percent had no opinion).[4] The people could not be roused to seek an external enemy. Average Russians were much more tolerant and more pragmatic, and also less hysterical, than intellectuals and politicians. Artificial provocations by some forces around the Kremlin attempting to return to "uniqueness" did not last long. But the vacillating mood among certain political and social groups in Russia proved how unstable people's sentiments still were and how easily they could be manipulated.

This was the climate in which the final round of the struggle for NTV—the well-known and well-respected television station owned by Vladimir Gusinsky—took place. The state-owned monopoly Gazprom, which had obtained 46 percent of NTV's shares, took control of the station on April 3, 2001. Putin must have decided to put an end to the affair. At this point, I admit, he could not stop his persecution of NTV and Gusinsky, for that would have been seen as weakness. The fate of weak leaders in Russia is bleak: They are inevitably failures. And their fate is to be quickly replaced.

The only political party that openly supported NTV was Yabloko. Two rallies to protest the takeover of the station, organized by Yabloko and the Union of Independent Journalists, were held in Moscow. Most of those attending were young people.[5] A new generation in Russia had independent views and no longer feared the regime. Despite the rallies, however, NTV passed into the hands of Gazprom. Thus ended Russia's history of independent television.[6]

The intentional destruction of one of the best broadcasting companies in Russia and the cynicism with which it was done elicited a sharp reaction in the West. The *Washington Post*, in an April 1 editorial, called on Western governments to respond strongly to Putin's attack on freedom of the press. "The Bush administration and the government of the European Union, Canada and Japan now face an important challenge: to ensure that Mr. Putin suffers some consequence from his grossly anti-democratic behavior. To avoid action after so many warnings to Moscow would be a serious blow to Western credibility." The newspaper called for expelling Russia from the Group of Eight. But the disapproval of the West no longer worked on Moscow.

The conflict between the authorities and NTV showed that the regime could switch to authoritarian methods to achieve its goals. But another thing was made clear as well: Society's general support of the authorities at this moment was limited. Those who supported the journalists showed that there was opposition in Russia, albeit divided and unorganized. For the first time after a long hiatus, people rallied to a cause, and it was a sign that the new Russia had survived the surge of conservatism and was still breathing.

The NTV story had a sequel. The remainder of Gusinsky's media empire—the magazine *Itogi* and the newspaper *Segodnya*—were also liquidated (and then in June Gazprom tried to take over the popular radio station Ekho Moskvy). The same pattern was followed: One of the owners of each publication shut it down and purged the unacceptable journalists. Journalists who refused to follow the new rules found themselves on the street.[7] Just as in the case of NTV, part of the former team was rehired, and they began publishing a new *Itogi*, but with content that had not a hint of criticism of the president. On the surface, everything was fine—property rights prevailed, and the notorious oligarch had been punished. But in fact this was the final liquidation of a group that dared to resist the Kremlin.

The unsophisticated viewer or reader might even think that nothing special had occurred. NTV continued to exist, albeit without its former stars. *Itogi* was still published, without the old writers and editors, however. "Why make such a fuss?" the naïve might ask. Apparently, the authorities were counting on such naïveté—that people would assume the contents were the same as long as the sign was still hanging over the door. The construction of wax dummies speeded up. Russia has a long history of Potemkin villages.

As he destroyed irritants, Putin continued building his superpresidential regime. In early 2001, he decided to renew the power bloc. Secretary of the Security Council Sergei Ivanov, Putin's closest ally, was named minister of defense. Boris Gryzlov, the leader of the Unity faction and also Putin's man, became the new minister of the interior.

With these appointments, Putin attempted to create his own base in the power ministries—an important step in freeing himself from the embrace of Yeltsin's political Family. The new leader continued strengthening his position by bringing in loyalists. But he was unable to find trustworthy people to place as political commissars at the head of the other agencies. The problem was not that there were no good human resources in Russia; there just weren't enough people the president trusted. But even in this round of replacements, Putin could not rid himself completely of the old ruling group. He was forced to move former minister of the interior Petr Rushailo, who in his day had had close ties to the Yeltsin court and pretensions to the role of successor, to the post of secretary of the Security Council. In other words, the still-cautious Putin could not fully break with the past, which he very clearly wanted to do.

Once a political stage that was comfortable for the president had been constructed, it would seem there was nothing to distract the Kremlin from resuming reforms. Putin's team instead got involved in intrigues. Some members of his entourage decided that despite its loyalty the Duma must be disbanded so that a totally obedient parliament with a constitutional majority faithful to the Kremlin could be installed. With this majority, the Constitution could be amended—in particular, to extend the presidential term to seven years. With the liquidation of the current Duma, the Kremlin could also get rid of parties it did not need, including Yabloko and the Luzhkov–Primakov Fatherland, and weaken the Communists.

To execute the plan, early in 2001 the Kremlin forced its parliamentary faction, Unity, into an absurd action: supporting the Communist-initiated vote of no confidence in its own cabinet. However, the scheme was never carried out. Even the tractable members of the propresidential movement were not willing to give up their prestigious positions and the comforts of Moscow life voluntarily and return to their homes in the provinces. It also became clear that preterm elections to replace them would damage Putin's image, because he was associated in the public mind with stability. Thus the Kremlin team created a crisis and then lost face extricating itself from it.

The threat to disband the Duma, however, could be used again at any point. An axe hung over the deputies that could be brought into action if the Duma started acting up. This story was a repeat of the tempests of the Yeltsin years. But in Yeltsin's time, when Berezovsky was doing the plotting, the intrigues were much subtler.

———— ✇ ————

The Kremlin's political "technologists" did not stop with the notion of disbanding the Duma, for they had acquired a taste for political engineering. Their success in creating Putin's presidency and a loyal political cadre was pushing them toward more ambitious schemes; their few failures had not put them off. Judging by the actions that soon followed, the ruling team decided to create from above everything that existed in Western society—parties, trade unions, youth movements, the press, and clubs for intellectuals. What was important for them was that nothing arise spontaneously and without the Kremlin's knowledge or permission. Anything that had the slightest connection to politics had to have Kremlin approval. And everything that did not pass inspection was shunted off to the periphery.

The new team's invention was that the shutting down was done not by force or pressure but often through the courts. The Russian judiciary continued to be amazingly flexible and understanding—that is to say, it understood what the executive branch wanted. Judges received their salaries and apartments from the authorities, and being dependent on the executive branch, they became the instruments for purging politicians and businesspeople the authorities did not want around. That the rules of the game continued undefined in Russia made it possible to turn almost anyone into a defendant, rendering him tractable and free of excessive ambition or criticism.

In other words, Russia was undergoing the full-scale formation of a managerial system in which all social groups and political forces must take the place the Kremlin intended for them. Apparently, the Kremlin technologists had an image of Russia as a gigantic corporation made up of well-managed divisions, headed by a manager-president. The question was whether this outwardly docile but at its core unruly and even anarchic society could be disciplined without blatant force. Was Russia ready to become an obedient corporation? Even if the idea was put into action, could a corporation that was managed from the top break through into the future—which required freedom, enterprise, and personal liberty?

In the meantime, the construction of the new system went full speed ahead and with apparent success for the time being—the remaining political actors occupied the niches earmarked for them. Thus, under pressure from the Kremlin, the oligarchs joined the Russian Union of Entrepreneurs and Industrialists (RUEI). Arkady Volsky, an old apparatchik who survived under every regime, headed the union. The RUEI had been the lobby of a very dogmatic part of the Soviet directors of the state-owned enterprises that had not learned to become accommodated to the market and instead hoped for state, or "regulated," capitalism. The oligarchs joining that kind of union was an unexpected step—crossing the former "red" directors with the oligarchs was tantamount to crossing eels with hedgehogs. But the Kremlin managed to create a hybrid: Arkady Volsky, Anatoly Chubais, Vladimir Potanin, and Mikhail Khodorkovsky, pretending to be happy, sat together at the RUEI. The regime achieved its goal of getting all the industrialists and oligarchs in one place and under its control.

Putin's supporters insisted that the liquidation of Gusinsky's empire and Berezovsky's forced expulsion from Russia meant that the regime was cleansed of oligarchy. But life showed that all oligarchs had not been "equally distanced," as advertised. The oligarchic groups obedient to the Kremlin began growing stronger. New empires formed, such as that of the young and energetic Oleg Deripaska, who first established a monopoly in aluminum production and then started taking over enterprises producing other metals and energy, crowding out the old oligarchs. Deripaska enjoyed Putin's special favor. The president even visited the young businessman's properties to ski—a sign of particular closeness.

The Deripaska phenomenon highlighted a new tendency in Russia's economic development. Until recently, all the major financial-industrial groups had formed on the vertical principle within one branch of industry. But now groups were becoming horizontally integrated, reaching to different economic areas and giving rise to Russian versions of giant South Korean *chaebols*. There was a positive element here. Whereas the former oligarchs had taken money abroad, the new ones began investing in production.

But the new consolidation of regime and capital set off alarms. The new oligarchs all had to be personally loyal to the president; Putin's accent on "equally distancing" all the oligarchs from power was nothing but a myth. The Kremlin continued its deal making with big business. Representatives of the secret services, *siloviki*, played a substantive role in some of the new economic groups of influence. Besides, as the South Korean experience showed, sooner or later the existence of gigantic corporations under state patronage leads to the monopolization of the economy by the few clans and to the degradation of the state itself, with the regime subordinated to the interests of the oligarchic elites.

The next step in the regime's plans was the construction of a new party system. The creation of a ruling coalition was announced, to be made up of yesterday's rivals—Putin's Unity (Edinstvo) on one side and the Luzhkov–Primakov Fatherland (Otechestvo) on the other. One of the puns at the time was that the new acronym for Edinstvo and Otechestvo would be "Ediot." Newspapers joked that "the bear has put on a cap," a reference to the emblem of Unity and Mayor Luzhkov's favorite headgear.

In their day, Yeltsin and his people had tried to create pet party systems. They failed because they were not persistent and because life in Russia was on the boil then and not everyone cared to be subordinated to the center. The docile parties of the Yeltsin era tended to lose elections. Under Putin, the Kremlin parties had every chance of winning. That was another index of how the situation had seemingly changed.

The movers behind the party merger did not hide that they were doing the Kremlin's bidding. The Russian state apparatus wanted to end the schism in its ranks. Neither Luzhkov nor Primakov nor their followers wanted to be perceived as the opposition. The Russian bureaucracy was never in opposition to the center of power. Moreover, many Russians could not even imagine the ruling class breaking into two parts that would take turns in power. The bureaucracy was used to living in a society where the opposition never gained power and the regime was monolithic. Nor were ordinary people accustomed to the idea of the opposition taking power.

That Luzhkov gave up his independence and joined the presidential coalition meant that the last opponents of the federal center had realized that it was pointless to fight Putin and remain outside the Kremlin fold. "The new era has begun. Better stop dueling with the Kremlin," many people thought, watching authorities from the distance.

With the merger of the progovernment factions, Putin got a stable, powerful majority in the Duma that could pass whatever legislation he wanted. This simplified the management of politics. Instead of numerous parties that he had to support and to negotiate with, the president could give orders to a single structure. At first, Unity and Fatherland did not seem eager to unite. It was no wonder, for many functionaries lost their positions in the merger. But in the end the Kremlin won, and after lengthy deal making, the new Edinaya Rossiya (United Russia) movement was formed. Actually, this merger did not enlarge the Kremlin's electoral base, because some of the opposition-minded members of Fatherland stayed out of the new movement.

At the same time, the Kremlin-controlled faction was formed in the Federation Council, and senators rushed to join it. It could have been no other way, for without membership in the Kremlin bloc there could be no possibility of entrée into the offices of executive power. And without that access, no problems in the regions could be solved.

With solid majorities in the Duma and the Federation Council, the Kremlin had the obedient parliament that had existed only in Yeltsin's dreams. Amazingly, after almost fifteen years of parliamentary struggle, the country found itself back in a previous historical period, when the executive branch considered the parliament an extension of itself; the Soviet tradition of unanimity had been restored.

However, neither Putin nor Kasyanov or the other members of the government joined the Kremlin party. Because it lacked representation in the executive branch, the new party majority could not be detrimental. That majority could be disbanded or traded for another, also created by the Kremlin.

The movers behind the tame ruling bloc maintained that Russia was following the same path as Japan with its Liberal Democratic Party, which spent dozens of years in power. The Japanese Liberal Democrats, however, formed a cabinet, whereas the Russian "parties of power" were never even asked for advice on that matter.[8]

The party field was being put in order. The Union of Right Forces (SPS), which consisted of numerous small parties and groups, decided to transform itself into a party with a membership. The transformation was mandatory, according to the new law on parties, if the umbrella group wanted to compete in the next election. The process of forming a new liberal party created mixed emotions. The pressure from Chubais was too evident, because he tried to control the critical impetus and create an organization that would not slide into opposing the Kremlin. Boris Nemtsov's candidacy for leader of the new party was approved by the presidential team, which had to tie Nemtsov's hands. In other words, the authorities were openly supporting one of the elements of the future party system that, as was assumed, would then support the authorities. Those who were too oppositionist did not join the new party of officially supported chosen liberals.[9] Observers philosophized: "The Russian liberal likes power, being near power. Opposition behavior, which cuts you off from receptions at the Kremlin and dooms you to riding the trolley-bus to see your voters, was natural for the left, the human rights activists, but not at all for the right, which considers poverty a greater sin than cooperation with the Kremlin."[10] Besides, both sides needed the collaboration; the liberals needed the Kremlin to protect them from the hostile populist majority, and the Kremlin needed the liberals to give it a reformist image.

The construction of a "managed democracy" continued unabated. Although the Kremlin's struggle for control over television had had its flare-ups and conflicts, the taming of the press was done without particular fuss. Almost of their own accord, all the sizable general-interest publications (with the exception of two or three national papers) swore fealty to the new ruling team and created no problems for it.

With the active participation of the Ministry of the Press and personal help from Minister Mikhail Lesen, notorious for taking part in the attack on NTV, the Media Union was founded—led, naturally, by people close to the Kremlin. Now it could be said that the Union of Independent Journalists, which permitted itself critical remarks about the authorities and even organized protest rallies, no longer had the right to represent Russian journalists.

Next came pressure on the analyst and expert community. Kremlin advisers wanted a change in the intellectual elites. The analysts who were known for their critical attitude toward the regime and who did not show the appropriate respect for the president were not allowed on the air. Their articles were rarely published. They were not invited to official conferences and receptions and were not given access to information. The rebels had a choice: change their tone or their profession.

The representatives of the Kremlin administration thought about the new generation and created a youth movement called Walking Together. The movement had no program except to support Putin. Participants were rewarded with tickets to clubs, theaters, and sports events, and with trips to the capital. This was a hired youth regiment required to do nothing but obey and be present at events—at least for the time being. On May 7, 2001, the young Putinists were dressed in T-shirts with Putin's picture on the front and brought to a rally in Moscow. Muscovites gawked at the thousands of young people filling up Vasilyevsky Spusk, the square around the Kremlin. Walking Together members applauded and shouted in delight when their organizers asked them to turn to the West—with their rear ends. Some ordinary people out for a stroll found this unnerving.

The creation of tame political and public organizations was one of the favorite pastimes of the Russian state. Sometimes it reached absurd levels. In the summer of 2001, Gazprom, the most zealous liquidator of the independent media, including NTV, tried to organize a conference on freedom in the mass media. As a screen, prominent liberals were invited, Nemtsov in particular. That the attempt to convene the conference failed was a promising sign, warning the regime that imitation games can meet resistance both in the West and in Russia. But generally, the president's lieutenants had reason to be extremely pleased—they had created their own mechanism of power.

The Kremlin, satisfied with its shaping of the political scene, moved on to a more complex undertaking: Putin decided to create his own civil society with all its concomitant structures. The irony is that the idea for creating civil society came to the Kremlin politicians only after oligarch Boris Berezovsky, now Putin's chief antagonist, began financing and supporting the creation of independent organizations in Russia.

If anyone in 2001 rebuked the regime for not caring about the people, the authorities could respond: Of course we care, we are actively in dialogue with society—the one we ourselves have created. On June 12, representatives of public organizations were invited to the Kremlin. Some had been completely unknown before that. There were bookkeeping societies;

associations of cosmonauts, gardeners, and settlers; sports unions; Kremlin political technologists; and of course, young members of Walking Together. There were no guests who could spoil the president's mood with questions about Chechnya, human rights, or freedom of the press. Putin spoke at length with the chosen, and the gathering resembled nothing so much as the socializing of former communist leaders with select tame organizations.

The authorities decided to create a civil chamber under the president that would represent the new society. A grand congress of public and social organizations—the Civil Forum—was planned to inaugurate the chamber. The ideologues of the new "civil society" under the aegis of Putin explained their brainchild this way: For "Russia to enter world structures," society had to be formed the way British lawns are grown—"water and mow, mow and water." The Kremlin, of course, had to do the watering and mowing. The presidential staff even came up with a slogan: "For a great country, a great society." Quite a few politicians supported the creation of this civil society under the president—especially because the Kremlin was footing the bill.

Now it could confidently be said that at least outwardly the new Russian reality differed from Yeltsin's Russia. Back then, there were all kinds of parties, clubs, and movements. Anyone could create and register something without approval from on high. Of course, at some point the regime stopped reacting to all those spontaneous movements. Now the wild plants were being weeded out and replaced by hothouse plants tended by official gardeners. The removal of public organizations proceeded with outward civility.

In any case, it would be hard to accuse the Kremlin of authoritarian designs—after all, the president was meeting with representatives of civil society. People who did not know Russian reality would applaud. Not everyone asked the questions: Why was the Kremlin avoiding dialogue with human rights activists and organizations that had already earned their reputation in society? On what basis was acceptance into the Kremlin-approved "civil society" determined? Why did people and groups hurry to join these artificial unions?

The same questions applied to the new Media Union, which all the Russian newspapers and television channels hurried to join. Here the answer was simple: Those who joined the journalism group received benefits and financing from the state. But members of the Media Union could no longer freely criticize the regime. You paid for the benefits with your freedom.

The face of Russian "modernity" was gradually coming into focus. Outwardly, the same personalities continued walking down the scene: KGB officers, oligarchs, liberals, Communists, great-power advocates, and members of the intelligentsia. But this bland crowd was obediently moving along the outline of a carefully drawn circle. Of course, at any moment they might reverse movement. That could happen if the circling actors felt a weakening in centrifugal force from the authorities. This "pluralism" was based not on convictions or principles but on instincts and fears, and being amorphous and blurred, it was therefore unstable and unpredictable.

Chapter 7

THE LONG-AWAITED
BREAKTHROUGH

Putin renews market reforms. Fighting bulldogs under the carpet.
Moscow and Washington work it out. The Russian president
chooses the West. Disturbing signs.

At last the moment had come when Vladimir Putin felt confident. It was obvious in his manner, his gait, and his gaze, which had lost their former strain. The president no longer seemed stiff and reserved; he began speaking off the cuff. He stopped avoiding public appearances. The time had come for Russia's leader to show why he wanted a concentration of power. He was ready to respond to the accusations of hesitation and vacillation as well.

On April 3, 2001, the president addressed the Federation Assembly. Society had been waiting for this speech, hoping it would clarify his future policies. Putin spoke like a dynamic senior manager rather than a monarch. He would address the parliament many more times, and his annual speech would eventually become routine, as it had with Yeltsin. But his 2001 address will be remembered, because in it he spoke as an energetic advocate of the market and declared his determination to renew economic reforms that had stalled under Yeltsin. He promised for the first time to put an end to "status rent"—the bureaucracy taking bribes for the opportunity to lobby—and to reform the state apparatus. The liberals could finally heave a sigh of relief—after sitting on the fence and wavering for so long, Putin had turned his face toward them. The only disconcerting thing was that he said nothing about rights and freedoms, as if there were no problems in that area in Russia.

Putin's speech, ground-breaking as it was, needed action to make it live. And here the Russian leader stunned the skeptics, me included. He gave the Duma a package of draft laws that encompassed judicial reform, a land code, pension reform, changes in tax legislation and the regulation of business, and a new labor code. What he did in the spring of 2001 looked like a revolution. Even the democrats felt that passage of the liberal legislation could neutralize the negative impression that Putin's avid construction of his pragmatically authoritarian regime had created.

The president scored another breakthrough as well—he dismissed the head of Russia's most powerful "natural monopoly," Gazprom, and put in his own man. The state-owned giant Gazprom kept the country afloat with its exports of natural gas, earning almost a quarter of budget revenues. The chairman of its board, Rem Vyakhirev (who replaced Victor Chernomyrdin in 1992 when the latter became prime minister), had been all powerful; he could kick open any door in the cabinet offices, and not only in Russia. But Vyakhirev was forced to leave without a struggle. The Kremlin let him know that if he did not, interest would be taken in his son, other relatives, and friends, who were getting rich in Gazprom subsidiaries.

Putin installed his own man from Saint Petersburg, Alexei Miller, at Gazprom. The president needed a loyalist at the head of the gas empire to enable him to control its enormous resources. Putin's power was incomplete without Gazprom. It was unclear at the moment whether the president would limit his intervention to naming the new top administrator or whether he would begin a reform of the monopoly and its secretive and dubious business practices. Sooner or later, he would have to realize that the way to raise the value of Gazprom stock, attract Western capital, and pay off the company's $10 billion foreign debt was to restructure the gas empire and ensure its transparency.

In the spring of 2001, the president also decided to reform another "natural monopoly," RAO UES, the Russian electric utility, which was headed by one of the leading liberals, Anatoly Chubais. There were fears, however, that the energetic and determined Chubais would simply privatize the lucrative pieces of the energy system and give the rest back to the state—exactly as his comrades in arms had done, and not just once, during Yeltsin-era privatization in the 1990s. The moment Chubais and his team produced the reform plan, it immediately provoked sharp criticism from a variety of quarters, including Putin economic adviser Andrei Illarionov and Yabloko Party leader Grigory Yavlinsky.

Chubais, however, was accustomed to clashes and it only increased his adrenaline; he was an experienced and tough fighter. The struggle that was beginning around RAO UES restructuring proved that even Russian liberals had conflicting views on a new stage of market reform. The president had to take sides in this struggle, and with his longing for consensus, he obviously did not like the idea.

The important news was that the ruling team had declared its direction and the use Putin planned to make of his omnipotence: He would modernize the economy. After bowing left and right at the same time, he had made up his mind by the spring of 2001. People close to the Kremlin were talking about a combination of mild authoritarianism and market liberalism as a remedy for Russian problems. Yeltsin had not managed to succeed with that mix. Putin was going to repeat the experiment. We would find out where Yeltsin had gone wrong; was it just that his authoritarianism turned into chaotic rule, or did the combination of authoritarianism and the market no longer work in Russia? Russia would have to pay yet again if the new experiment failed.

When the deputies began studying the president's draft laws, the optimism of the democrats and liberals dimmed. Putin's drafts hedged on transformation. The judicial reform revealed the spirit of the whole package. On one hand, it took the positive step of weakening the role of the prosecutor general's office and distributing some of its powers to the courts. But on the other it increased the dependence of the courts on the executive branch, which fit the basic tendency of Russian politics: the strengthening of the autocratic presidency.[1]

The same could be said of the measures intended to make the life of Russian businesspeople easier, the laws on "deregulation of the economy." They significantly reduced the number of licenses that businesses had been required to obtain, and therefore the opportunity for bureaucrats to extract bribes and interfere with the market. The proposed legislation, however, seemed to deal mostly with corruption among minor clerks; as observers joked, bribery was put under the control of higher administrators. Such measures increased the dependency of the lower echelons of the bureaucracy on the higher ones. And the top was given immeasurable power.

Russia had about 400,000 federal bureaucrats and more than 1 million regional ones. All of them occupied themselves somehow, whether doing useful work, make-work, or downright criminal work. Limiting the number of business licenses was unlikely to change the rule of the bureaucracy. What Russia needed was a wide-ranging reform of the state apparatus, including a staff reduction, strict definition of new responsibilities, a long-overdue pay increase to lessen the temptation of bribery, ideas for changing bureaucrats' motivations, and efforts to attract better personnel. But the Kremlin was not yet prepared to go that far. That kind of administrative reform would undermine the foundation of the traditional Russian state and the "Russian System" of power given primacy by Putin. He couldn't saw off the limb he was sitting on.

After reading the president's proposed reform legislation, one could feel that it was designed not only to preserve the political weight of the higher echelon of the state apparatus but also to help oligarchic businesses—and not all big businesses, but primarily those involving natural resources, first of all oil, gas, and aluminum. There were no visible efforts to expand Russian high technology. Small businesses did not sense any particular concern on the part of the Kremlin for their plight. As Putin himself admitted, the number of small and medium-sized enterprises in Russia had fallen—every fourth business was on the verge of bankruptcy or liquidation. Many small businesspeople could not take the pressure from bureaucrats, demands for bribes, unreasonable requirements, and harassment by police and security services or the criminal underworld, so they chose to close their business and work for hire.[2]

Despite the incompleteness of Putin's initiatives, they meant movement after several years of stagnation. And there was no guarantee that the president would have succeeded with more radical reforms. The first obstacle would have been placed in the way by his own base: the bureaucrats and people from the power agencies on whom he still depended, as well as by the tycoons, bent on preserving preferential treatment for their holdings and avoiding competition. At the moment, he was not ready to rock the boat.

Putin's policy seemed to be successful. In the summer of 2001, presidential authority was continuing to gain in power and clout. It looked as if this would be the year of triumph for the leader and his team. He had managed to move simultaneously in two directions: on one hand strengthening his position and consolidating his social support, and on the other hand restarting economic reform. His stabilizer role allowed him to keep moderate and conservative groups in his orbit. His activity as a reformer gave him the chance to regain the wavering trust of the liberally oriented portion of society.

The more experienced Yeltsin had managed to unite these disparate social groups only in extreme situations, and then not for long: when the question of Russia's independence and its break with the Gorbachev center was being decided in 1991, and when Yeltsin became the symbol of parting with the communist past in 1996. Putin had managed to maintain his influence and popularity for two years, a record for mercurial Russia. In October 2001, 75 percent of those polled supported the Russian president, at the same time, only 19 percent trusted him. People still supported the president simply because they did not see any worthy leader around.

But suddenly the smooth course of events was interrupted again. That was always the case in postcommunist Russia, where—unlike in the USSR, known for its staid, closed, and nontransparent nature—stability was continually disrupted by clashes of interests that exploded in public scandals or vicious political fights. Thus, in October 2001, minister of transportation Victor Aksyonenko—one of the highest state officials, a man who had recently had pretensions to the role of Yeltsin's heir—was called in to the prosecutor general's office.

At the same time, the prosecutor's office began investigating the Ministry of Emergency Situations, headed by Putin's friend Sergei Shoigu. These events shook the elites; the prosecutor's office was going after the sacred cows. The prosecutors could not risk doing that without approval from the Kremlin. It was perceived as a sign that the president himself was looking for a way to get rid of the most corrupted members of the old ruling group and at the same time demonstrate his unbiased, impersonal position.

The subsequent desperate struggle among the factions in the Putin entourage showed that the "apparatchik wars," which had temporarily stilled after Putin's election, had resumed. This was a struggle not only for control over the president but for dominance in economics and politics. The battle involved many interest groups. But in numerous squabbles, the conflict between the Putinists (called the Praetorians)[3] and the old Yeltsin "Family"[4] was gradually coming to the fore. Both sides had been waiting too long before deciding on an open clash.

The Putinists were grouped under the banner of cleansing Russia and its politics of oligarchs and corruption and strengthening the state. Their message found support among the millions of Russians who were disoriented, humiliated by poverty, and worried about their future and, most important, who regarded the small band of Russian millionaires with envy and hatred. It was these very feelings that had once moved impoverished Russia to follow the Bolsheviks. Many Russians were unworried by the fact that, under the aegis of a crusade against the oligarchs, they were also gradually being stripped of freedoms they had been accorded under Yeltsin and were being told what to do and what not to do. Many did not even know that Putin's people from the security services and other power ministries, having tasted power, now wanted total control of the Kremlin, not for the sake of battling evil and rot but for the sake of absolute power.

The second group—the Yeltsinites—had achieved everything they could beyond their wildest imaginings. During the Yeltsin era, when there were no limitations on them, they were their own law. They privatized the state and the president along with it. They did much to discredit democracy and the concept of liberalism. They were the ones who kindled social envy and a desire for revenge in the Russian people.

Now, in their struggle with the power ministries and security services, the Yeltsin-era elites raised the banner of freedom and defense of democracy. They really did try to preserve a certain pluralism, realizing that if the siloviki destroyed a free press, political parties, and the parliament, eventually the tycoons' turn would come, whether loyal to the president or not. Or Praetorians might come for them even sooner. Yeltsin's circle had to fight. But they couldn't fight only for their saved or stolen millions—they had to fight for democracy. Neither side was angelic. It just so happened that at that historical moment in Russia, the political interests of the Yeltsin political entourage and the old oligarchs coincided with the interests of the democrats.

In the meantime, Putin's Praetorians were trying to put their own people in the posts of chief of presidential staff and prime minister. The attacks on Aksyonenko and Shoigu were tests to see how hard the members of the Yeltsin circle would resist.

Putin calmly observed the resumption of court squabbling but tried to avoid interfering openly. He was in no hurry to throw Yeltsinites to his Praetorians to be dismembered. In the end, he forced Aksyonenko to resign—there was too much compromising information on him. Besides, he had to nab a few bad guys to show that he was fixing problems, first of all fighting corruption, and he had to deliver something to his people who wanted scalps. But he left the other Yeltsinites, including chief of the presidential staff Alexander Voloshin, in their positions. It was true that they were foreign bodies among the Putin loyalists. It's unlikely that the president, with his acute dislike and distrust of oligarchs and other people who were responsible for Russia's decay, was impressed by the members of the Yeltsin group. And there was another reason why he would loathe these people: Who would like to have around the people who created one's political personality and who might anticipate reciprocity, and still want to have clout?

The president allowed the conflict among the two coteries to continue because he did not want to become hostage to whichever faction triumphed, driving the others out. He realized that the presence of several clans in the Kremlin allowed him to remain above the fray. Besides, he knew that his people, however loyal to him they might be, were still inexperienced. "Who will do the job?" he would exclaim whenever one of the Praetorians was too adamant about freeing him from the old ruling group.

The president's tolerance of the old guard also might have had one further explanation. The Yeltsinites represented economic liberalism, which also was Putin's ideology. Thus Putin again took up the survival tactics practiced by his predecessor. It said a lot about the system both had operated, which began to dictate its own laws, and one of them was this: The survival of personified leadership depended on the nonstop clan infighting that enabled a leader to play arbiter.

———————— ᏋᎧᏋ ————————

In due time, there was a new twist to the Kremlin struggle: The prosecutor's office began an investigation of Gazprom's subsidiaries, in particular Sibur, whose managers were subsequently put behind bars. That turn of events shocked both the successful bureaucrats of the Yeltsin era and the oligarchs. The president sent a message that he would continue his attack on the dubious winners of the previous era, even if they were politically neutral. It was hardly his own initiative—he was inclined to wait and observe calmly—but apparently he yielded to his entourage, which insisted on giving a lesson or two to the arrogant businesspeople.

The prosecutor's office was once more a major player, resembling a loose cannon firing at everything in its path. But the seeming independence of prosecutor general Vladimir Ustinov, who had become a hero in the Russian media, was deceptive. The prosecutor's motive for starting its investigations of the big shots was blatantly political. Ustinov's office investigated people who either were disloyal to the Kremlin in some way or could threaten the president in the future, or who were not ready to cooperate with the new ruling team—who, in other words, had not fit into Putin's regime framework, or who had forgotten to share with the state. Meanwhile, the oligarchs who came to Moscow with the Praetorians were above suspicion—for instance, Saint Petersburg banker Sergei Pugachev, who appeared out of nowhere and whose sources of wealth were murky.

The new stage of the "fighting bulldogs under the carpet" at the Kremlin was inevitable given the logic of the Russian System, even though it was rationalized by Putin. In the absence of independent institutions, the vacuum was filled by groups of influence, and the struggle among them for political clout and property was the major substance of politics in Russia. The victory of one side in the tug-of-war meant only a brief respite, for the next round would start with the birth of a new group of influence. The clan struggle was not something unnatural—it takes place in all societies. The problem in Russia was that neither the rule of law nor independent institutions constrained the clan wars.

Another circumstance that increased the tension was the Kremlin's attack in the fall of 2001 on the non-state-owned TV-6, where journalists from NTV had found refuge after their company was shut down in the spring, and which had begun turning a profit. There was a sense of déjà vu, of watching the sequel in the battle between the Kremlin and independent television. Once again, a legal pretext (annulled a few months later) was used to go after the company. The assault on TV-6 confirmed once more the Russian justice system's lack of independence. The executive branch easily manipulated the courts, and on a larger scale than in Yeltsin's day. One judge after another made decisions that suited the executive departments.

The servility of the court system was clear to see in the fall 2001 presidential election in Yakutia, which presented a picture of open manipulation. The Kremlin wanted to be rid of compromised former Yakutia president Mikhail Nikolayev and to install its own man as head of the diamond-rich republic. It would have been hard to accomplish that democratically, because Nikolayev had created a sultanistic regime, co-opting and bribing all major forces in the republic. The Kremlin put into motion the proven practice of pressure, with the courts as an integral element.

Getting rid of Nikolayev could have gone smoothly, but the judges in Yakutia got so confused that they couldn't understand whose side they were supposed to be on—that of their republican boss or the Kremlin. The legal proceedings turned into theater of the absurd, with the court changing its decisions several times, alternately permitting Nikolayev to run and banning him from running. The Yakutian elections were a sorry sight, revealing the cynicism of the emboldened bureaucracy that did not even try, as in the past, to create the appearance of legality.

Regional elections in Russia descended during Putin's presidency into blatant deal making and arm twisting without any democratic camouflage. It was now difficult to call a new regime an "elected democracy" when many regional elections turned into poorly disguised appointments from above. The drama of the situation was that occasionally—as in the case of Yakutia—free elections, without the Kremlin's intervention, would have secured the feudal rule of regional elites or families of the regional barons. The choice was between the regional autocrats and the federal bureaucrats. The latter were usually more civilized and pragmatic than the local princelings. Thus, one has to admit that in some cases following democratic rules might have preserved fraudulent and crooked administrations, or strengthened traditional forces resisting any change or reform effort.

But manipulations in getting rid of them hardly could help to promote "clean hands" rules of the game and liberal principles.

The events of 2001, with their fistfights and shaky balance of forces within the Kremlin, proved that the new reality in Russia was not stable— it continued vibrating, transmuting from one state to another. That was good, because if the regime and its base solidified completely, there would be no opportunity for change in the near future. As it was, volatility meant hope for evolution, which could mean either a harshening or a softening of the regime, movement toward either more defined authoritarianism or democracy. In any case, movement was better than stagnation and rot.

The zigzags of domestic politics were accompanied by twists in foreign policy. In early 2001, Russia's relations with creditor nations—especially with its main creditor, Germany—worsened after Moscow's announcement that Russia would not pay its debts to the Paris Club. That statement was followed instantly by a warning from German first deputy finance minister Caio Koch-Weser, who demanded that Russia be expelled from the prestigious Group of Eight.

Berlin's harsh tone had an immediate effect: Moscow promised to pay its debts. The confusion over debt payments demonstrated not only the inexperience of the Russian team but also an irresponsibility on the part of the prime minister and liberals responsible for economic policy. Russia's president also had to learn how to deal with foreign policy issues, and especially with the issue of Russian debt.

Very serious problems soon emerged in Russia–United States relations.[5] The Kremlin's hopes that the Bush administration would be a more congenial partner than the Clinton administration were not justified. More than once, Moscow would wax nostalgic about the Clinton era and former deputy secretary of state Strobe Talbott, the architect of U.S. policy toward Russia during the 1990s, for whom Russia was a foreign policy priority and Russia's transformation a key goal. Under Bush, Washington's course had changed in a fundamental way. Without fully formulating its foreign policy doctrine, the new Republican administration led Moscow to understand that Russia was no longer a major issue for the

United States and that Washington would maintain a policy of "selective engagement" with it. The new administration intentionally held itself aloof, as if to say, "Don't call us, we'll call you when we need you."

In short, President Bush offered Moscow a cold shoulder by ignoring it. The Republican team was not going to ingratiate itself with the Kremlin or indulge Russian imperial nostalgia. Washington apparently did not have time for political philanthropy and could not understand how Russia could be important without having something substantial to deliver. Russia was brushed off. During the administration's first months, the White House ordered a review of previous assistance programs for Russia and all other aspects of Russian policy. It seemed that U.S. assistance to Russia and American cooperation with Russia would be dramatically cut back.

Moscow was caught off-guard by Washington's shock-therapy-style policy. The sharp turn from engagement to disengagement produced first consternation, then dismay, especially among Russian elites who had hitched their star to the Republican administration. Clearly, the Russian political class needed to assess more realistically the country's position in the world and its agenda for relations with the United States—but a cold shower from Washington could hardly bring that about. Besides, a condescending attitude and even open ignoring of Moscow by some members of the U.S. administration only activated bitter feelings among the Russian political class. The Russia–United States bilateral relationship had frozen.

On May 1, 2001, in a speech at the National Defense University, President Bush declared that the Cold War was over and "today's Russia is not our enemy." Therefore, the security regime of mutual nuclear deterrence based on the threat of nuclear retaliation was outmoded. Bush called for moving beyond the 1972 Anti–Ballistic Missile (ABM) agreements, which Russia regarded as the major element of the system of its own and world security.

Bush's logic made sense. The Cold War *was* over, and a security system based on a bipolar view of the world—that is, on distrust and the idea of mutually assured destruction—definitely needed to be reviewed. One of the poles of that order, the Soviet Union, no longer existed, and former rivals—the United States and Russia—were no longer locked in a hostile rivalry. New threats had emerged, and Cold War deterrence was not enough to deal with them. The U.S. leader was right; a new framework of security was needed to counter the challenges of the new world. Bush proposed that the United States and Russia should work together "to develop a new foundation for world peace and security." Americans wanted a clear break with the past, and they wanted to move beyond the constraints of the old security system.

However, the way Washington was dealing with the security issue was not reassuring for Russians. First, Moscow was not ready for such a sharp rejection of the old security order. Second, Moscow had doubts that Washington considered Russia a genuine partner for a new security framework. The White House was planning to withdraw from the old security architecture without waiting for a new cooperative security system to be built. And even more important, in Moscow's eyes, the United States was dismantling the basis of Russia's global role. The Russian political class was not yet ready for that surgery. Even Russian liberals and pro-Western political forces seemed to be confused and to view Washington's security agenda with suspicion.

Washington's logic was not without flaws. If the Cold War was over, the reasoning went in Moscow, why keep its other symbols, like NATO, or the Jackson-Vanik amendment, which made United States–Russia trade dependent on levels of Jewish emigration?

No doubt, U.S. allies in Europe would eventually accept, albeit grudgingly, the American way of solving the problem, but it was trickier for Russia. Moscow was not prepared to abandon the nuclear agreements that were the last evidence and proof of its status as a great power. Along with hurt pride and other emotions that count in politics, Russians had concerns that the U.S. withdrawal from the ABM agreements would start a new nuclear weapons race that they had no chance to win.

The Kremlin began desperately looking for an adequate response. It was not so much a question of guaranteeing Russia's strategic interests (few in Moscow thought that the proposed U.S. missile defense was a real threat to their country's security) as of saving face. Making a tough answer to the United States was out of the question; Putin did not want to seriously exacerbate friction between the two countries. That fact was already a new phenomenon in the Kremlin's stance. Yeltsin would have gone ballistic under the circumstances, breaking the china and resorting to harsh rhetoric or even a demonstration of Russian might. Putin remained calm.

But once Washington began formulating new rules without paying attention to Russia's complexes and anxieties, the Russian president was cornered: He knew too well the sentiments of his country's political class, and he did not want to be accused of weakness.

There was an ironic angle to the story as well: It appeared that Russia could have been important for the United States only if it had been dangerous. Having drawn this conclusion, some Russian elites escalated their scare-mongering, militant rhetoric—trying, if not to intimidate Washington, at least to attract its attention and force it to return to its cautious approach to Russia. As for Americans, they decided to go ahead without paying attention to the political neuroses and obsessions of Russian elites.

In an effort to maintain its international stature, the Kremlin played on every possible field simultaneously. Russian diplomacy attempted to fashion a new, energetic European strategy. Russia turned to China and reactivated contacts with former allies such as Cuba and Vietnam. Finally, the Kremlin rediscovered its neighbors—the new independent states established after the breakup of the Soviet Union, and the countries of Central and Eastern Europe.

One could get the impression that Putin launched hectic diplomatic activity to reclaim Russia's world influence as a counterbalance to U.S. hegemony. At least, most members of the Russian ruling team understood Putin's campaign as the means to constrain American primacy. Apparently, at first it was one of the Russian president's goals as well—but not the only one.

Soon Moscow's decision to broaden its foreign policy agenda and to revive its previous contacts and ties acquired new and constructive dimension. The Kremlin team understood that Russia's immediate interests lay first of all in its neighborhood and in Europe. Thus Russia's growing engagement with the world was to a greater degree dictated by the growing pragmatism and commercialization of its foreign policy—that is, by the attempt to base foreign policy on economic interests rather than on nostalgia for the lost imperium or a desire to counterbalance U.S. hegemony.

Continuing to move in all directions at once, Putin invited President

Mohammad Khatami of Iran to Moscow. Russia signed a wide-ranging agreement with Iran on arms shipments and for Russian help in completing the construction of a nuclear power plant in Bushehr. Many read the pact as an open message to Washington: If you ignore Russia, we will be friends with Iran and other rogue nations. However, there was much more of an economic subtext in relations between Russia and Iran—Iran was one of the few countries that still bought Russian arms and nuclear technology, which helped keep the Russian military-industrial complex and atomic energy branch alive and created jobs for thousands of people. But the timing of the Khatami visit and the nature of the deal between Moscow and Iran gave ground to the conclusion that at least partially it was viewed by the Kremlin's team as retaliation for the U.S. decision to abrogate the ABM agreements and growing U.S. neglect of Russia.

Naturally, Washington considered the new agreements between Moscow and Iran a threat. "It is not wise to invest in regimes that do not follow international standards of behavior," U.S. secretary of state Colin Powell declared.[6] Washington's scolding was hardly the right reaction to Russian policy. By behaving like a stern teacher, the United States only increased resentment and even hostility within the Russian political establishment, which did not want to be taught how to behave and where its real interests lay. As some American pundits advised, economic incentives offered by the United States to compensate Russia for the economic losses it would suffer from ending its military cooperation with Iran would be a more constructive way of dealing with the issue. In any case, it was clear that even after Putin's pro-Western shift, the Russian foreign policy agenda could not be brought into conformity with U.S. plans and aspirations.

The majority of Russian analysts concluded that Moscow was doing the right thing by intensifying its relations with Iran. Representatives of various schools of political opinion, such as Andranik Migranyan in the March 5 *Nezavisimaya gazeta*, counseled Putin to answer Washington sharply and maintain an independent policy. Because the United States respects only strength, they said, if Russia bows to pressure from the White House and accepts Bush's rules of the game, no one will take Russia into account anymore.

But could Russia really resist U.S. pressure? How wise was it for

Moscow to support countries of dubious reputation and to create a belt filled with arms around Russia? Where were the guarantees that Iran, and any other country to which Moscow sold arms, including China, would not turn its back on Russia? And might not Tehran or Beijing use cooperation with Russia as a card in a complicated game of their own with the United States? The Russian political class avoided these questions—it was used to living day by day and it was still thinking in emotional terms. It was also true that in pressuring and ignoring Moscow, the new team in Washington did not facilitate Russia's search for new answers, and this policy only strengthened the position of Russian hawks.

Quite a few Russian politicians and observers suspected that the Republicans were intentionally trying to cool relations with Moscow to open up space for maneuvering on issues of national missile defense and NATO enlargement and to gain a free hand with their global goals—sour moods in Moscow were the best pretext for going ahead alone. Russians got the impression that Bush decided to withdraw from all treaties with Russia and build a new world order independently without wasting time on deals and bargains. Dismissive gestures by some of the members of the Bush team, such as defense secretary Donald Rumsfeld, were fuel on the fire to Russian nationalists and a source of dismay for pro-Western liberal groups.

Meanwhile, President Putin appeared to be more level-headed than the majority of Russian elites. Even if he did not feel comfortable with the U.S. decision to alter the post–Cold War security environment without listening to Moscow's objections, he must have reconciled himself to a new role for Russia. Though he had been uncertain at the beginning, when he was playing with different foreign policy goals, he was now more intent on shaping foreign policy priorities on the basis of Russia's limited resources.

In fact, he was the first Russian leader to think about Russia's ambitions in the context of capabilities. But he was operating in the same security and foreign policy community, with the traditional horizons and mentality. Moreover, he obviously was using outbursts of bitterness among his political class when he was buying time or hesitating as to his next step, or trying to get concessions from his U.S. partners. But he never allowed himself to fall into a hostile mood; he was always calm, poised, and patiently waiting for an occasion to begin mending fences with the Americans.

The Kremlin kept trying to set up a meeting of the two leaders. Not a trace was left of recent attempts to show strength in relations with Washington. In the spring of 2001, the ruling team in Russia was more and more energetically looking for ways to defrost the dialogue with the White House. But relations with Washington were a psychological trap for Moscow. On one hand, the United States–Russia relationship was the only thing that gave Moscow a sense of its significance. On the other, this relationship made the Kremlin feel even more acutely that Russia could no longer claim the status of an equal partner.

Bush, who had met with leaders of much smaller countries, seemingly avoided a meeting with Putin. It looked like Washington really had no intention of returning to the politics of bilateral summits. Besides, the U.S. leader had a concrete reason not to rush into a meeting with Putin. On February 18, 2001, a spy scandal had broken that involved a highly placed FBI agent, Robert Hanssen, who had been working for Russia and before that the Soviet Union for fifteen years (and who would plead guilty in July to fifteen counts of espionage and conspiracy).

As revenge, on March 22, the U.S. Department of State expelled 50 Russian diplomats suspected of espionage. Moscow as a reciprocal gesture announced a "symmetrical" expulsion of 50 American diplomats. A cold wind again blew through both capitals. High officials on both sides of the ocean began rehearsing aggressive rhetoric that had not been heard since the early 1980s. "Spying?" asked Robert Kaiser, a leading *Washington Post* columnist, commenting on the spy scandal in the March 24 issue. "We caught the FBI agent working for them because a Russian agent apparently working for us turned him in. . . . We are still in the grip of Cold War reflexes and assumptions. Who's to blame for this nuttiness? That's probably a futile question. This tango requires the usual number of dancers." The tango continued.

The Kremlin leader, however, showed no emotion even during the spy scandal, as if it had no connection with Moscow. He avoided anything that would make it impossible to normalize relations with Washington—he never got near the point of no return. And Washington finally (apparently not without pressure from its European allies) realized that it was time to stop ignoring Moscow. Bush agreed to a meeting with Putin in Ljubljana on June 16, 2001, during a European trip. The Kremlin team sighed in relief.

Despite the chill between the two capitals, the meeting of the two leaders was unexpectedly warm. Bush went much further in expressing friendliness toward Putin than either the Americans or Russians had expected. "I looked into that man's eyes and saw that he is direct and trustworthy. We had a very good dialogue. And I saw his soul," Bush said at a press conference after meeting the Russian president. Bush even invited Putin to his Texas ranch.

Ljubljana was a turning point. The Russian president's approach to relations with the United States was visibly different from that of many European politicians—instead of criticizing, Putin played down differences and the irritant issues, always keeping in mind his goal of normalizing relations with Washington, which he considered crucial for Russia and its dialogue with the West. Bush clearly appreciated that. The first meeting of the two leaders was the beginning of their personal rapport. Condoleezza Rice, Bush's national security adviser and one of his most trusted consultants, helped to build trust between the two, and she became the major force behind shaping a new Republican policy toward Moscow.

By the summer of 2001, the Republican administration had begun to promote the same kind of personal relations and close ties with the Russian president for which Clinton's opponents had roundly criticized him. That change in the wind only proved that without personal rapport and understanding between the leaders it would hardly be possible to build a constructive relationship between the nations, especially when one of the leaders accumulates all powers in his country and there are no other players to speak with. In any case, the personal chemistry of Bush and Putin helped their countries get out of the post–Cold War freeze.

In the meantime, Moscow continued its policy of playing on every field, and in July it signed a friendship agreement with China. Putin wanted to relegate Russia's and China's mutual suspicion to the past. He needed good relations with Russia's most powerful neighbor. Many observers, though, saw Moscow's treaty with Beijing as another response to U.S. hegemony. "Now Russia and China seem to be trying . . . to curb American power," an article in the July 16 *Economist* suggested. It was hardly so. Both Moscow and Beijing tried to use their rapprochement as an extra card in pursuing their relations with the West and the United States. But Putin did not see his dialogue with Beijing as an instrument with which to promote multipolarity, as Primakov had just two years before. Putin's dialogue with China was more pragmatically oriented toward achievable goals and economic priorities. For Putin, Beijing was neither a major partner nor a potential ally in the anti-Western game.

In August, Russia received a visit from North Korean dictator Kim Jong Il. Kim crossed the country in an armored train and was embraced by Putin in a warm welcome at the Kremlin (these train trips of Kim's would become a tradition—in 2002 he would come to Russia again). Outwardly, Moscow seemed to be returning to its old allies, which made Russian liberals uneasy. But in fact the negotiations with Kim had another purpose; Putin wanted to restore Russian influence over North Korea and become the intermediary between it and the rest of the world.

This was a fundamentally important shift. Russia, far from trying to form anti-Western fronts, now was trying to create the basis for a more profitable dialogue with the West, striving to be a partner that had something substantial to offer. Putin was suggesting a new role for Russia in the world: The imperial bully would become a mediator between the West and the states that created problems for the West. Thus Russia's diplomacy under its new leader had undergone serious evolution. At the beginning of Putin's rule, it was aiming at constraining the West and first of all U.S. dominance. But it gradually became an instrument in building a more constructive partnership with the West. How durable the change was remained to be seen.

On September 11, 2001, a trial for the West became a test of Russia's ability to determine its new international identity. Putin's reaction to the terrorist attacks on the United States was unambiguous: He was the first foreign leader to call Bush with words of sympathy and support. The hotline between the two capitals established during the Cold War now appeared to be handy when all telephone connections with Washington had been broken.

For the first time, Putin did not hesitate. He took an absolutely correct step from the human and the political points of view. It does not matter what prompted him: intuition, calculation, or emotion. His now-famous phrase "Americans, we are with you!" coming from this outwardly cold man, broke the barrier he had erected between himself and liberal-minded Russians. With his telephone call, he took a forthright stand as a pro-Western leader.

With those words and his readiness to become the United States's ally with no strings attached, Putin brought about a new phase in relations between Russia and the United States. Moreover, at that moment, he as a leader made his existential choice in favor of the West. Russia (and the USSR) had made a pro-Western choice during World War II, but that did not prevent them from entering a Cold War era. In 2001, in joining an alliance against terrorism formed by the United States, Russia for the first time in its history recognized the hegemony of another state and voluntarily chose to play junior partner. True, nobody, even Putin, at the moment would say whether this change in Russia's role was final and whether it would be accepted by the Russian ruling class—what was happening was too extraordinary, too breathtaking to believe!

What was no less significant was that Putin did not ask for any payoff. Unlike previous Soviet and Russian rulers, who engaged in horse-trading over every compromise they struck with the West, there was no request for a quid pro quo. Moscow did not bargain this time. Putin understood that being with the West at that moment of truth was in Russia's national interest. Irrespective of what would happen in the future, this pro-Western shift would acquire a logic of its own and its own momentum.

Putin's pro-Western turn was not a game, or a tactical maneuver; it was conscious and deliberate. His measured and calculated behavior during the cooling of relations with Washington argues the case. He must have understood that any hesitation, or wait-and-see tactics, would have strengthened mistrust between Russia and the West or even put Russia into the camp of outcast states.

Putin's reaction to the September 11 attacks was also the result of changes in the Russian mentality. Russia—despite the frequently arrogant rhetoric of its ruling class and its unhappiness with Moscow's new role during the 1990s—had been coming to grips with the new global reality and had not once made a serious effort to reverse the pendulum's movement. What is ironic is that it was a former KGB officer who officially acknowledged what Russian society and its elites had known for some time but would not admit even to themselves: that Russia's lingering hegemonic aspirations and global ambitions were an untenable fantasy.

It was true that, when it came to actions, the mood of the Russian political class was still ambivalent. Putin's close entourage showed no particular desire to join the antiterrorist campaign and the war in Afghanistan. Nor were his lieutenants ready to endorse a U.S. presence in Central Asia in preparation for military actions against the Taliban. The reaction of President Putin's comrades in arms just after September 11 was blunt: "[Commonwealth of Independent States] territory will never become a field for Western military operations, and no NATO soldier will ever set foot on Central Asian soil." So said defense minister Sergei Ivanov, one of Putin's closest friends.

Some Russian politicians even blamed the United States and its hegemony as the reason for the terrorist retaliation. The subtext with them was a gloating "Serves you right!" Russian society was shocked by the terrorist attacks, but the majority of Russians were reluctant to endorse Russia's direct participation in the military operations in Afghanistan. Russians—having experienced defeat in Afghanistan in the 1970s and still fighting without success in Chechnya—were not ready to get involved in one more battle.[7]

Putin had real difficulties overcoming the disagreements within Russia's political class—this was the first time he had gone against their advice and taken an independent position. Russia's role in the antiterrorist coalition was decided on at a meeting of the power ministries that Putin called for September 22. The session lasted six hours, interrupted only by a telephone call from Bush. During those hours, President Putin broke the resistance of his generals. It needed a lot of courage and will. In a national television appearance on September 24, Putin with a determined face clarified Moscow's position and, punctuating his words, declared Russia's readiness "to make its contribution to the war on terrorism."

This time Russian cooperation was not just rhetoric. Russia began sharing its intelligence information with the United States; it helped to build bridges between the U.S. military and the Northern Alliance, the main opposition in Afghanistan to the Taliban that Moscow had been supporting for a long time; and it agreed to U.S. use of military airports and bases in Russian allies Kyrgyzstan, Tajikistan, and Uzbekistan. Moscow also continued massive arms shipments to the Northern Alliance, announced other aid for its fighters, and offered Russian airspace for humanitarian relief flights.

A serious test for United States–Russia relations came when the Americans began moving into Central Asia preparatory to their attack on Afghanistan. For the first time in recent history, another great power was in Russia's backyard. Putin's response to the new challenge was calm. It was clear that Washington had informed the Kremlin beforehand and gotten a green light. Outwardly, even the Russian military was restrained in its reaction. The Russian deputy chief of the General Staff, Yuri Baluevsky, commented, "We haven't been enemies in a long time with America. But we are not yet full partners." He added that the presence of the United States in Central Asia was solving problems related to the security of Russia's southern borders. Either the military decided not to oppose the president or they felt that U.S. troops really would help Russia to secure its southern flank.

U.S. secretary of state Colin Powell had high praise for the Russian contribution to the military operation in Afghanistan, stating that Russia had been "a key member" of the international antiterrorist coalition and had played "a crucial role" in the coalition's success "by providing intelligence, bolstering the Northern Alliance, and assisting our entry into Central Asia." That praise was not sheer politeness; the magnitude of Russian assistance surprised even the staunchest skeptics.

There are times when leaders make history. There are also times when history makes leaders. That is what happened in the fall of 2001 in Russia, when the terrorist attacks on the United States forced the Russian president to make a choice that turned a mediocre politician into a leader who amazed the world by proposing a completely new role for Russia. Vladimir Vladimirovich had been moving toward the West for some time. But he needed a catalyst to make him take an open stand.

Putin's speech on September 24 had a second part—on Chechnya. Putin tied the world situation to the situation in Chechnya and delivered an ultimatum to all members of Chechen rebel groups: They had 72 hours to disarm. But if the separatists had been resisting for years, why would they give up the struggle voluntarily now? There was an implication that the president might be prepared to negotiate with moderate separatists. Putin also recognized in his speech that the war had "its prehistory," which implied that he was beginning to reexamine his understanding of the Chechen drama. But even if the Russian leader began to hesitate and try to find a peaceful solution to Chechnya, he did not pursue that option; he was not ready for one more breakthrough.

In the meantime, the Russian president continued his movement toward the West. When he arrived in Germany on September 25, he gave an hour-long speech at the Bundestag, in impeccable German, receiving ovations from the deputies. In essence, he proposed fighting together against Cold War remnants in thinking and politics. "We are still living with the old value system—we speak of partnership, but in fact we have not yet learned to trust one another," he said. "Despite the many sweet words, we continue secretly to oppose one another." He spoke like a European in terms the West could understand, and he said the right things. He also indirectly responded to Bush's call to "go beyond" Cold War arrangements, hinting that the West needed to do its part of the job as well.

It was true that ten years after the collapse of the USSR and the formal conclusion of the Cold War, world leaders continued to use concepts out of the past. The very existence of a NATO without Russia was confirmation of that. Russian observers pointed out that if Western leaders were sincere about closing the Cold War chapter, they should not stop at the abrogation of the old security arrangements with Russia but go further and liquidate NATO—or invite Russia to join the alliance. Otherwise, Russian suspicions about the anti-Russian orientation of the Western security institutions were justified. Russian observers were ignoring the fact that Russian elites and their behavior, not only Western prejudices, often served as the justification for the West to keep its old security framework.

Moscow seemed to have been unexpectedly prodded into a new foreign policy as Putin unfolded his latest round of activity in Brussels at the European Union–Russia summit and in negotiations with NATO leaders in the fall of 2001. Putin announced his desire to form a single economic space with E.U. countries and to take a more active part in European security structures. There was an increasing awareness in Moscow that Europe, long neglected by Yeltsin, was its primary resource for capital and trade.

Russia and Europe had already forged multiple links. Cooperation in the energy field had been the most productive. The European Union continued to be the main destination for Russian energy exports, its countries buying 53 percent of oil exports and 62 percent of natural gas exports. The volume of trade with the Union constituted 48 percent of all Russian trade. The Europeans' growing interest in their own security agenda made Russia a major partner of theirs in the security sphere. In fact, relations between Russia and Europe had a much broader base than those between Russia and the United States. Moreover, Brussels possibly had more leverage than Washington when it came to applying steady pressure on Moscow to implement European standards of democracy, the rule of law, and human rights. It was Brussels that forced the Russian military to at least try to behave in a more civilized way in Chechnya.

Cooperation between Russia and the European Union, however, was not smooth and easy. Russian politicians were increasingly disappointed by the sluggishness and bureaucratization of decision-making processes in Brussels. Russia itself was too slow in bringing its legislation into line with E.U. criteria and has yet to fully realize the potential of its Partnership and Cooperation Agreement with the European Union, which was signed in 1997. As for the E.U. leaders, they had too much on their plates, with Central and Eastern European countries being integrated into the Union, and with Turkey waiting in the wings, reforming its institutions and developing a design for further unity. Europeans had a justified fear of accommodating Russia with its enormous potential and no less enormous problems. At the same time, the E.U. leadership had to answer Russia's challenge, and if Russia was to become a full member of Europe, the

European Union had to consider how to proceed with that puzzle. It was high time to think about forming free trade zones with Russians and moving toward a customs union. Putin was pushing in that direction.

Pundits speculated that growing cooperation between Russia and Europe could lead to an alliance between Europe and Russia on a variety of international issues where their positions differed from that of the United States, for instance on missile defense. But the dreams of some Russian nationalists that this possible rapprochement might acquire an anti-American flavor were hardly grounded in reality, though they might worry Washington. Despite its frustration with Washington, Europe was not ready to freeze its relations with the United States. Putin at that time also did not show an interest in playing off the differences between the Western allies. Paradoxically, on some international issues, including terrorism, Moscow was much closer to Washington than Europe.

Moscow's next step was to restore cooperation with NATO, which had been broken off during the Kosovo crisis in 1999. Putin even risked noting that if NATO were to develop as a political rather than military union, Russia would not object to its new round of enlargement. He even hinted about a possible Russian interest in NATO membership. He hardly believed in such an option—rather, he wanted to see whether NATO was ready to cooperate with Russia and whether Russian elites were ready to relinquish their anti-NATO stance.

In any case, Russia was not prepared to join NATO and thereby give up its sovereignty. In fact, Russia's entry into NATO would mean the end of the alliance as it has been for half a century, and many in the West, especially in Eastern Europe, were not ready for that either. For them, NATO was still a means of "keeping Russia out." But Putin's testing the waters demonstrated how the moods in the Kremlin have changed.

In the eyes of Russians, NATO was losing its previous relevance, especially after it proved not very relevant during the war in Afghanistan. Future relations between NATO and Russia depended not only on Russia's new security thinking but on the ability of the alliance to transform itself. NATO was going through its identity crisis and was looking for a new mission. Russia was in the process of forming its new geopolitical role as well. Their ability to find new forms of dealing with each other might have been one of the ways of handling their identity problems.

There were a lot of questions to answer: Do we trust each other enough? Do we agree on threats the world is facing? Can Russia be directly plugged into NATO's activities, and does it want to be? One NATO insider put the dilemma this way: "Russia has an open door to NATO, but the train is moving!"

Meanwhile, Vladimir Vladimirovich decided that he should seize all opportunities. Hence, the Kremlin was dancing in all directions. The Russian leader might have felt that a Russia–NATO marriage would be a tricky business. That is why he was not very intent to pursue that option more vigorously. He understood the moods of the Russian military too well. There were more realistic and potentially promising goals for Russia. One was joining the World Trade Organization. Moscow began consulting on this issue with Brussels and Washington.

Amazingly, the Kremlin team, so awkward and inexperienced just yesterday, suspicious of all actions by the West, suddenly displayed both great readiness to cooperate and the energy to bring it off. Equally amazing was the change in the mood of the Russian political class. In 2001 and early 2002, almost everyone who was anyone among the Russian elites tried to outdo the rest in great-power sentiments and, especially, anti-Americanism. It had looked as if suspicious and ambitious Russia was returning to its "special path." And then—in a few short months—such an unexpected turn!

Now Russia not only announced that it wanted to be part of Europe and part of the West but made claims to a partnership with the United States, accepting its junior partner role. But the very unexpectedness of the mood shift created ambivalent feelings; if the country and its elites could turn in one direction so quickly, they could turn back just as easily. Russia had yet to learn the political consequences that emotions such as fear, humiliation, suspicion, hurt pride, and a desire for vengeance, even confined to elite circles, might have—and had yet to learn to control those emotions.

Sociologists hurried to test the nation's mood and discovered that a significant portion of ordinary Russians, despite surges of frustrating emotions, were essentially pro-Western. According to polls conducted by Tatyana Kutkovets and Igor Klyamkin at the end of 2001, the vast majority of Russians—87 percent—thought that Russia should orient itself toward Western nations, and only 8 percent (most of them Muslims) preferred an orientation toward Muslim countries. Recent longing to preserve "uniqueness" was forgotten—unexpectedly for observers. When asked, "Partnership with which countries best responds to the interests of people like you?" a strong majority (63 percent) named the countries of Western Europe, 45 percent Belarus, 42 percent the United States, and 40 percent Ukraine. Only 6 percent considered cooperation with Iraq, Iran, and other "states of concern" useful. Cooperation with China was considered desirable by 22 percent.[8]

Some social groups retained exaggerated expectations; 34 percent still considered Russia a superpower no less than the United States. But one saw a breakthrough in Russians' relinquishment of the superpower complex. Forty-three percent considered desirable for Russia the status of France, Germany, or Japan. The vast majority of Russians wanted a country that was not a military power but a "comfortable country, convenient for living, where top priority is given to the interests of people, their well-being, and opportunities."[9] The shift toward the West and its values in Russia was more widespread than many observers had thought. Russians were more ready than they themselves thought to live normal life in a normal country. It seemed that the great-power factor was no longer the only consolidating force in Russia.

Perceptions of Russia as a bastion of anti-Americanism turned out to be mistaken as well. According to polls that the Public Opinion Foundation conducted in October 2001, 35 percent of Russians had a good opinion of Americans, 44 percent were indifferent, 15 percent had a bad opinion, and 5 percent had no opinion. According to VTsIOM polls in November 2001, 65 percent of Russians wanted Russia and the United States to become allies, 13 percent did not care, 12 percent were against the idea, and 10 percent had no opinion.

But suspicions about America's intentions remained. In November, 37 percent of those polled thought the United States was a nation friendly to Russia, 44 percent thought it was not friendly, and 19 percent had no opinion. Yet when questions were posed about specific things, it became clear that Russians did not perceive Americans as the enemy. For instance, in answer to the question, "Would you give blood for Americans wounded in a terrorist act?" 63 percent said yes and only 10 percent said no (25 percent said they could not be blood donors, and 3 percent had no opinion).

There were things to give one pause, however. The majority of those who considered the United States a potential ally based their attitude toward America primarily on the existence of a common enemy of the two countries. That was typical Soviet Russian logic: Against whom will we be friends? If the common enemy were to vanish, what would the two countries have left in common? Russia and the United States could once again find themselves, if not in different camps, then at a distance, at which point mutual suspicions might flare up with renewed vigor. This happened sooner than anyone would have thought.[10]

On November 13, 2001, Putin flew to Washington for a summit meeting. As he was being received in Washington, Kabul was falling and the Taliban were beginning to disintegrate. Few in the Russian delegation understood that the swift collapse of the Taliban regime would undermine the partnership between Russia and the United States—Washington could act independently now. The ousting of the Taliban put a trump card in the hands of those in the U.S. administration who insisted that it waste no more time forming coalitions and cajoling its allies.

As for Putin, his mood was elevated at first. "I have great optimism," he said, beaming before his flight. "If anyone thinks that Russia could become an enemy of the United States again, I think that they don't understand what has happened in the world and what has happened in Russia." He apparently hoped that their personal chemistry would work on Bush and persuade him to retain the old security framework that the Russian leader wanted to preserve at any cost. Putin seemed to believe that his ability to preserve the ABM agreements would be a proof of his leadership strength for the Russian political establishment, and a failure to do this would be perceived as a blow for him personally. Washington, however, made it clear that its withdrawal from the old security concept was inevitable, and initially the Americans had no intention of signing a treaty on reducing offensive weapons, as Moscow insisted. The White House intended to make a clean break with the past without waiting for the Kremlin to become ready to join it in doing so.

It was difficult to get behind the inscrutable mask Putin always wore, but he was evidently frustrated—not because he felt Russia's security threatened but because he had to explain to his political class why he had failed to persuade Americans to preserve old rules of the game in the security area. To give such significance to the ABM agreements and to make Russia–United States relations dependent on them was Moscow's mistake. It was not prudent on the part of Russian diplomacy to waste so much time and energy on an unachievable goal and put the president in an embarrassing situation. But Putin soon demonstrated that he was learning from his mistakes.

Tony Blair sensed that his friend Vladimir needed urgent support, and on November 16, 2001, he sent a four-page letter to Lord George Robertson, NATO's secretary general, in which he proposed the creation of a Russia–NATO Council. The goal was to expand Russian influence on NATO decision making, albeit in strictly negotiated spheres. The proposal looked like moral compensation to the Kremlin for the liquidation of the old security structure. But the idea of raising the status of Russia's cooperation with NATO, even on a limited group of issues, elicited resistance from NATO's new members, Poland, Hungary, and the Czech Republic. That was understandable—they were seeking asylum under NATO's roof from possible Russian hostility, and here they were forced to sit at the same table again.

Most important, Donald Rumsfeld, the U.S. secretary of defense, openly resisted upgrading relations between NATO and Russia. According to the *New York Times*, "Mr. Rumsfeld in November made an eleventh-hour attempt to have the 'NATO at 20' reference removed from the draft communiqué that Secretary Colin Powell and the foreign ministers from NATO's 19 nations were to issue in Brussels." Only Bush's intervention helped preserve the idea of "NATO at Twenty."[11] There, apparently Powell and Rice's line for more active engagement with Russia won—at least for the time being.

In the meantime, on December 13, the United States announced its withdrawal from the ABM Treaty. Putin reacted with restraint and held to his position, characterizing the decision as "mistaken."[12] But at the same time, he acknowledged that the withdrawal did not threaten Russian security. He did not want Russia–United States relations at the mercy of irritants any longer.

Putin's second year in power was drawing to a close. After his initial hesitations and constant looking back, after his courting Russian conservatives, Vladimir Vladimirovich was finally feeling sure enough of himself to go ahead with a modernization agenda. He had proven that he had gotten and strengthened his power not for the sake of just keeping it—he had a mission. He could have been satisfied that he did not waste his time at least in two areas: the economy and foreign policy.

Beginning in 1999, Russia experienced high rates of economic growth; the economy expanded by 8.3 percent in 2000 and by 5.8 percent in 2001. The projected growth for 2002 was 3.6 percent. The Russian gross domestic product increased by 20 percent in 2001, to about 72 percent of the 1990 level. During those years, the problems of non-payment of salaries and pensions and barter were almost completely resolved, and the economy had truly become monetary. After the government introduced a flat 13 percent personal income tax in 2000, revenue collection jumped 50 percent. Putin balanced the budget and kept inflation in check.

For the first time since the Bolshevik Revolution, a new Land Code allowed individuals to buy and sell nonagricultural land. The Russian stock market became the world leader in 2001 with a 77 percent gain, and continued to steam ahead. "Since Putin came to power nearly everything has improved for investors," said Western investors. Barings's Eastern Fund, registered in Dublin, brought investors a return of 34 percent in 2001 and 50 percent over three years. The Credit Suisse First Boston bank was up 36 percent for 2001 and 45 percent in the first half of 2002. It looked as if the gold rush had returned to Russia, as Patrick Collinson suggested in the April 4, 2002, *Guardian*.

In mid-2001, growth rates somewhat declined, mainly because of the world economic recession. But observers predicted that even if oil prices fell to $15 a barrel, Russia would remain stable, losing only its financial reserves. In that case, it would have to turn to the International Monetary Fund in 2003 for help in paying its debts.

But there were other disturbing signs. Foreign investment in 2001 amounted to an insignificant $2.5 billion, somewhat lower than in 2000. Russia attracted less capital than Poland or the Czech Republic. Russian oil companies were not investing in other sectors of the economy. The markets remained risky. The bulk of Russian assets was in the hands of sharks—Russian oligarchs who were not ready for competition or to allow foreign players. There was no working banking system to enable the development of an effective and diversified economy. Above all, the legal system was in the pocket of either executive power or tycoons. "To become 'normal,' Russia must have entrepreneurs and an explosion of small- and medium-size businesses," affirmed an article in the May 13 *Newsweek*, and it was on the mark.

What was even more worrisome were new wage and pension arrears. At the beginning of 2002, wage arrears amounted to 2.7 billion rubles ($90 million). In ten regions, the average wage and pension arrears exceeded ten days. Meanwhile, social stability in Russia could be preserved only if wages and pensions were paid on time.

The Russian economy still was vulnerable. Three major factors contributed to economic stability in Russia: the energy and raw materials sector, the activity of major financial-industrial groups, and modernization "from above" using authoritarian methods. But these three factors also caused problems. The orientation toward raw materials created a lopsided economy heavily dependent on the export of oil and gas. The major conglomerates—the new Russian *chaebols*, which controlled the economy—did not allow medium-sized and small enterprises to develop. And modernization from above was producing immense bureaucratic pressure, which was an obstacle to private initiative and free enterprise, without which an effective market was impossible.

The Russian economist Yevgeny Yasin was right to call for the radical restructuring of the Russian economy; the steps taken by the president so far had not been enough. Yasin proposed several breakthrough areas, including banking reform, the creation of securities markets, reorganization of the "natural monopolies," reduction of state regulation, and expansion of private initiative. The question was whether the Kremlin felt the urgency of pushing for the next stage of reforms. As Yegor Gaidar said in the May 7, 2001, *Yezhenedelny zhurnal*, "The reforms are usually implemented when it is impossible not to initiate them anymore, not when they are needed." At the end of 2001 and beginning of 2002, the general feeling in Moscow was that the level of economic stability that had been achieved was sufficient and that Russia was not ready for more radical restructuring.

Beyond the economic obstacles that continued to hinder further economic recovery, there were more fundamental barriers to a modern market. They derived from the lack of definite separation of political and economic, and public and private, spheres—leading to the merger of business and power, which resulted in nontransparency, corruption, a distortion of economic behavior, and an administrative impact on the economic area. In fact, the key to further economic reforms was not dealing with economic obstacles per se but bringing about change in the political system.

It was not yet clear whether the president and his team were prepared to move from a policy of stabilization to one of structural reform that would radically transform relations between state and society, bureaucracy and business. After restarting economic reform, Putin again vacillated, alternately pressing different pedals. One of the most optimistic foreign observers of Russian market reform, Anders Åslund, said in early 2002 after visiting Russia: "The Soviet bureaucracy is creeping back, extending its multiple regulations. . . . The grand attempt at structural reform has come to an end."

First giving more oxygen to enterprise and private initiative, the Kremlin then pressed another pedal that increased bureaucratic control, blocking the forces of economic freedom and competition and turning the economy back toward arbitrariness. Examples of zigzagging over economic strategy were, on one hand, Russia's attempt to accelerate joining the World Trade Organization and, on the other hand, its turning to protectionist measures. That policy maintained a somewhat shaky equilibrium. But to respond to the new challenges facing Russia, the Kremlin had to turn for support to new social groups interested in more dynamic transformation and in defining a clear vision of the future.

———————— ✺ ————————

The only sphere in which Russia made a real breakthrough was international relations. In essence, in late 2001 the president started a revolution in Russian foreign policy, moving beyond the country's traditional geopolitical role. Putin made Russia an ally of Western states in the antiterrorist coalition, accepting the asymmetry of the alliance; he agreed to a U.S. presence in the post-Soviet space; and he demonstrated readiness to go beyond the traditional agenda in relations with the West. This was tantamount to rejecting Russia's great-power ambitions. This was a step that shocked even his comrades in arms.

Was the shift due to bewilderment in the Kremlin and lack of alternatives—that is, to forced pragmatism—or was it the product of certain calculations on a new agenda? If Putin's actions were forced, the Kremlin could return to its zigzagging at any moment, and perhaps even pull a U-turn.

The impression observers got was that the Russian president was influenced by a combination of the most contradictory circumstances. These included his understanding of Russia's weakness and its inability to resist pressure from the West and particularly from Washington, his desire to cooperate with the West and use Western resources, and at the same time a lack of understanding of how to promote Russian interests through cooperation with Western countries—of what could be negotiated, how, and when and where Russia could be a partner with the West and where only an ally. Let us add to that, perhaps, Putin's confusion. Events were unfolding too quickly, and he had too many things on the table, which even a much more experienced politician would have had difficulty handling. Often, he went with the flow, unresisting.

With all his concerns, doubts, and suspicions, however, the Russian president understood that his goal of a strong Russia could be achieved only through broader engagement with the West. He could have behaved differently on many occasions. He could have blocked the arrival of the U.S. military in Central Asia and especially in Georgia. But he did not. He could have watched from a distance how the war on terrorism was going in Afghanistan. But he got engaged more actively than some of the American allies. And overall, he could have behaved like the Chinese leaders, observing developments with a demonstratively cold air. But Putin met the Americans halfway. He went even further in his relations with Europe. He began to limit Russia's ambitions before September 11. Thus, despite the resistance of the military, he decided to give up two Russian military bases abroad—in Cuba (Lourdes) and Vietnam (Kamran)—that were symbols of Russia's geopolitical presence.

At the same time, Putin's foreign policy breakthrough still did not have a concrete agenda that would make clear how Moscow planned to cooperate with the West, and who among his entourage would be responsible for his new agenda. Putin started his revolution in foreign policy almost single-handedly, without the support of his team. It had been his personal initiative, his own project. He looked like the Lone Ranger pursuing it while his entourage stood off to the side looking as if they were making bets—would he win or fail? In this case, his authoritarianism allowed him to bring Russia closer to the West.

Unless he gained the support of the political class for that breakthrough, however, and unless he created a new team that included people free from the old mentality and Cold War stereotypes, Putin's new policy was unlikely to be durable and sustainable. Besides, he needed the support of society for such a breakthrough, and he was pulling this one off without explaining his goals to Russians, without trying to form a national consensus. Even liberals and democrats shrugged their shoulders as they watched his foreign policy chess game, wondering what it was that the president was doing: Was this tactics or strategy, a goal or a means?

The Russian turn to the West had caught the Western community unprepared as well. Europe was sincerely interested in a full partnership with Russia. But its inertia and habit of letting the United States lead the way took their toll. Meanwhile, America was preoccupied with its own concerns and obsessions. The West, busy with its problems, seemed not to have the strength or desire to think about how to include Russia in its orbit. People were tired of the constant hassles with Russia, and quite a few who had hailed Russian reform at the start were now thinking, "Maybe those Russians really are different. They'll never mature enough for Western values. Let them live in their Eurasia. At least they'll be useful, protecting the West from China."

Former British ambassador to Moscow Rodric Braithwaite, in his book

Across the Moscow River, wrote: "When the facile optimism was disappointed, Western euphoria faded, and Russophobia returned. . . . The new Russophobia was expressed not by the governments, but in the statements of out-of-office politicians, the publications of academic experts, the sensational writings of journalists, and the products of the entertainment industry. It was fueled by those who argued that the Russian orthodox civilization was doomed to remain apart from the civilization of the West."[13] Unfortunately, the Russian political class did a lot to feed Western criticism and Western suspicions of Russia.

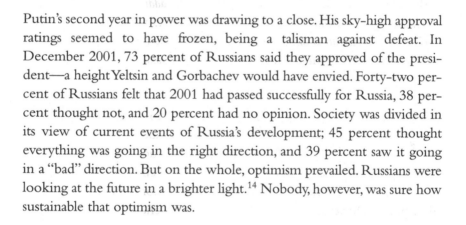

Putin's second year in power was drawing to a close. His sky-high approval ratings seemed to have frozen, being a talisman against defeat. In December 2001, 73 percent of Russians said they approved of the president—a height Yeltsin and Gorbachev would have envied. Forty-two percent of Russians felt that 2001 had passed successfully for Russia, 38 percent thought not, and 20 percent had no opinion. Society was divided in its view of current events of Russia's development; 45 percent thought everything was going in the right direction, and 39 percent saw it going in a "bad" direction. But on the whole, optimism prevailed. Russians were looking at the future in a brighter light.[14] Nobody, however, was sure how sustainable that optimism was.

Chapter 8

THE KREMLIN'S AMBIGUITY

—————————— ✺ ——————————

The nature of stability. The grudges continue. New address to the nation as the reflection of the Kremlin's disorientation. Putin moves to the West, leaving the elites behind. Yeltsin is dissatisfied with his heir. New uncertainties. Chechnya again reminds Moscow about itself. The traditional Russian choice: Freedom or order?

The year 2002 in Russia was supposed to be the last calm year before a new election fever, which was due in 2003–2004, when parliamentary and then presidential elections had to take place. Before getting an election fever, Russia still had a chance to ponder major trends and choices, and its president had time to continue his modernization policy. However, this country had always defied any plans and predictions. Russia could plunge into a new race and unruly political fistfight before it knew it.

The beginning of 2002 confirmed Vladimir Putin's political style and the nature of his rule. Having made a pro-Western shift in the foreign arena, on the domestic front he continued his policy of contradictory principles. He was liberal, statist, populist at the same time. He was a consensus guy and authoritarian politician, Russian patriot and pro-Western person simultaneously. Half of the Russian population did not know who their leader was. Everybody still saw what they wanted and imagined the face they would like. It was amazing that Putin had succeeded in playing Everybody's Man for so long—it clearly needed skill and luck.

Thus, contrary to prevailing opinion, Putin announced that capital punishment would be banned in Russia. This was a step toward the

European model. He also gave Russian citizens the right to have bank accounts abroad. He supported a new package of liberalization laws introduced by the reformist part of his cabinet. He continued his pro-Western foreign policy, moving further in institutionalizing Russia's relations with the West and building trust with its Western partners.

But at the same time, the Russian president made decisions that were aimed to cajole the traditionalists among the Russian population and elites. He endorsed the law on "counteracting extremism," in which the broad definition of extremism gave the law enforcement agencies the opportunity to view any opposition and even any dissent as a form of extremism. He supported the alternative military service bill pushed through by the General Staff that treated alternative military service as a punishment, and the migration law that toughened the rules for getting Russian citizenship.

Clearly not without the president's knowledge, trials continued in Russia of people accused of espionage for allegedly passing secret information to Western intelligence services. Particular notoriety attached to the case of journalist Grigory Pasko. Pasko made available to the Japanese press information about nuclear pollution from Russian atomic submarines in the Sea of Japan. The journalist was accused of revealing state secrets and was sentenced to four years in labor camps on charges of treason. Despite protests in Russia and abroad, the sentence has not been reviewed.

Putin apparently had not determined how far he could go with his market breakthrough. At that moment, he did not dare attack the foundations of oligarchic-bureaucratic capitalism. Under the table, sweet deals continued to dominate the playing field. The cabinet continued to spend much of its time and energy coordinating the interests of clans and moguls. The president personally decided the fate of economic laws and institutions. Even the new market legislation was constructed so as to give the leader the opportunity to make economic decisions independent of the parliament.

In some cases, the Kremlin accelerated economic reform. But overall, the market's exclusive dependence on executive power limited economic freedoms and preserved the domineering role of bureaucracy in managing the economy. In fact, the highest level of the executive branch increased its control over the market to an extent comparable to that during Yeltsin's rule.

On the political front, Putin's rule no longer resembled a rigid superpresidential regime, which according to the initial Kremlin plan had to function as a perfectly oiled conveyer belt. The authorities had already understood that such a regime was impossible to implement in Russia without harsh coercion. The Kremlin, however, was not ready to return to coercion and dictatorial ways. Russia, it seemed, would not tolerate that any more.

Thus the rule of the second Russian postcommunist president, irrespective of how he personally differed from his predecessor, more and more resembled Yeltsin's electoral monarchy. It also included the fusion of incompatible elements: an emphasis on subordination and an inability to cope with the inner resistance; attempts to strengthen a unitary state and acquiescence to feudal regional regimes; a desire to stop bargaining and permanent deal making. It was true that Putin's Kremlin so far had succeeded in implementing stricter rules and achieving more compliance. But under the surface the old spontaneity again was bubbling up. All this proved that if the leader were not ready to reject personified power, in the end unwittingly, even contrary to his plans, he would be forced to return to Yeltsin's methods of rule—that is, to political barter with vested interests and to an imitation of order.

A hybrid political regime guaranteed calm in Russia; it was the means to link past and present, conservatives and modernizers. It was an instrument to neutralize conflicts, a painkiller that softened the drastic outcomes of Russia's transformation. But there were serious doubts that a hybrid regime could help make the breakthrough to the future.

For the time being, the president seemed to be leaving his political portrait undone. Journalists who tried to determine the character of Putin's leadership wrote about "The Flight of the Two-Headed Eagle" and that "Putin's skis were going in different directions." This was a metaphorical way of showing that the president, while executing pro-Western policies and liberal economic reforms, remained an adherent of the semiauthoritarian model of power, which inevitably meant a suspicious attitude toward the institutions Western civilization had built.[1]

Putin's position was understandable; he was afraid of destroying the fragile balance. He was not prepared to take a risk and make a final decision, betting on one ideology and system of principles, which would mean if not confrontation in society, then at least a violation of the stability that had been created. Moreover, in 2002 the president was already in a rather risky position. His foreign policy had no support, even from his closest entourage. It was true that even the foes of his turn toward the West had quieted down. But any moment, sensing weakness, they could start an attack—and Putin realized this. There were signals that more determined economic reforms could lead to open dissatisfaction in Russian society. Thus, in the spring of 2002, the residents of Voronezh took to the streets to protest housing reforms that led to a sharp increase in rent. This was the first mass protest in Putin's term. It had to have made him think.

Despite the outward stability, there was no guarantee that the political establishment would continue to endorse everything the Kremlin was doing. The elites continued to express their obedience. But the bureaucracy, with the centuries-old habit of sabotage, could block Putin's reforms wherever they touched on its deepest interests.

Putin had already felt the strength of resistance. In early 2001, he tried to get rid of the corrupt governor of Primorye, Yevgeny Nazdratenko. Numerous attempts under Yeltsin to depose Nazdratenko had all come to naught. But after a winter of severe power shortages in Primorye, there were good reasons for removing him. Putin called the governor and persuaded him to resign. I can imagine their conversation: "You must leave, Yevgeny Ivanovich," Putin must have said. "Otherwise we will have to arrest you. And we don't want to create a scandal." Nazdratenko agreed with the reasoning but apparently found a way to blackmail the president. In any case, Putin removed him from Primorye but made him a minister in his cabinet. There were knots the president could not untie. But even after leaving Primorye, Nazdratenko remained its boss. All of Moscow's attempts to support its candidate for governor there failed, and the election was won by a man from Nazdratenko's clan (Sergei Dar'kin) with criminal ties. That defeat showed Putin he was not omnipotent; having all power resources, he still couldn't force events to go his way.

Another defeat for the Kremlin took place in the bastion of democratic reform, Nizhny Novgorod, where despite Moscow's direct engagement, a Communist won the elections for governor.

Later in 2002, by applying open pressure and manipulation, Moscow succeeded in getting its candidate elected as Nizhny Novgorod's mayor. But the angered electorate retaliated; nearly one-third of those who voted did so "against everybody." This was proof that Putin's tactics of pressure and deal making were not always successful and that people were getting more and more frustrated with the "imitative democracy."

Also in 2002, the governors began grumbling openly. They were unhappy with having their hands tied and with being required to report to their overseers, the presidential appointees. Quite a few of them were watching the Kremlin with hardly hidden hostility. But the governors knew they had to wait. Presidential elections were approaching. Putin would have to make a bargain with them, because they controlled the regions and the electorate. It was in their power to help him win or lose. They had lost a lot of their privileges, but they still were dangerous and they were no longer intimidated by the Kremlin.

Another pillar of the Putin regime—the security services and the prosecutor general's office—were probably not very pleased with their president either. Putin never did totally become their man. His former colleagues from the security services could not have been thrilled that he made them share influence with the other interest groups. He also had no reason to be happy with the former colleagues he had brought into the Kremlin with him: They appeared to be lousy administrators.

The military also was disillusioned. Its members were not confident about the future and could not understand the president's position on defense policy. The conservative members of the officer corps had trouble with Putin's "Gorbachevism" in foreign policy and what they saw as his constant retreat before the Americans. In the beginning, they kept their grudges to themselves. But gradually, some of them became more vocal, complaining, as did the former deputy chief of the General Staff, General Leonid Ivashov, about Russia's "geostrategic suicide." The retired generals, including former defense minister Igor Rodionov, began publishing open letters in the newspapers and speaking to the media, accusing Putin of betraying national security interests.

In their turn, the oligarchs did not feel very safe, because the prosecutor's office could send in people to examine their books at any moment. Some tycoons who usually tried to be reticent and keep their dissatisfaction to themselves suddenly came out in the open, showing criticism of the Kremlin. Powerful Russian businesspeople watched the president carefully, not trusting the ruling team and not sure of Putin's intentions.

The left had every reason to be unhappy with the president and his policies. Leftists began talking about Putin's "antipeople regime" in the same spirit that they had attacked Yeltsin's regime. The Communists, for their part, should not have been underestimated—they still influenced a third of the electorate, and because the other political forces were too weak, the Communist Party could become a shelter for other opposition groups.

The political center on which the Kremlin counted, the pro-Putin United Russia, remained amorphous and balanced on a single principle: servility to the leader. In a crisis, with the appearance of a powerful new personality, United Russia could switch to a new leader as easily as Luzhkov and Primakov's Fatherland Party had done. Or even likelier, it would become a burden around Putin's neck. The Kremlin managers understood this and began a game of promoting new rubber-stamp parties (among them the "Party of Life" headed by Federation Council speaker Sergei Mironov, and the left-wing social democratic party created by Duma speaker Gennady Seleznev), preparing for the moment when United Russia had to be scrapped.

The democrats, despite Putin's pro-Western choice, treated him gingerly. Anatoly Chubais, restrained before this, suddenly announced that the regime could evolve in a dangerous direction. In an interview with Robert Cottrell for the February 16, 2002, *Financial Times*, he replied to the interviewer's statement, "Russia is turning into a police state" with: "The fear is not only in the West, it is here, too. We can't just push it aside and say it is stupid. No, it is serious. There are political forces not far from Putin who would support exactly that style of development for Russia."

Chubais had reason to deliver this warning. In January 2002, the last all-national television channel, TV-6, owned by the exiled oligarch Boris Berezovsky, was closed.[2] It was one more victim of the Kremlin's decision to clear the scene of influential opposition instruments on the eve of the

2003 parliamentary elections. The Praetorians in the Kremlin's circle knew the power of television and did not want one of the most popular channels in the hands of their enemy. And from the beginning of the Putin team's tenancy in the Kremlin, the free media had given it indigestion.

Chubais, now realizing what the total victory of the power ministries—the *siloviki*—would bring, came to the aid of the journalists who were losing their station a second time. Chubais helped to organize a pool of oligarchs to raise money to buy the shares of a new private television station being created by Yevgeny Kiselev, the former director of TV-6, and his team. Among the shareholders were people from the Yeltsin entourage: Roman Abramovich, Alexander Mamut, Oleg Deripaska, and even Alfred Kokh, who had taken part in the destruction of NTV. Kokh's role in the TV-6 rescue campaign only proved how quickly people in Russia changed camps and loyalties. This action by these businessmen who were close to Yeltsin to save an independent television station was a challenge to Putin's *siloviki* and proof that the Yeltsin echelon had no intention of surrendering without a fight. This was one more vivid clash between two eras—the era of Yeltsin, and the era of Putin and the competing echelons of postcommunist *nomenklatura*.

After weighing the pros and cons, Putin endorsed the new broadcasting company with the participation of several oligarchs. He wanted no mutiny on the part of the old Yeltsin group, standing behind the scenes, though that would mean the failure of his own Praetorians who were trying to gain control of the nationwide television channel. But to make absolutely sure that the new channel would behave "reasonably," the Kremlin suggested that former prime minister Yevgeny Primakov and head of the Union of the Industrialists and Entrepreneurs Arkady Volsky, two old apparatchiks, join the board of the broadcasting company. It was a double censorship move by the president; journalists and the oligarchs both had to agree to several levels of subordination. Putin's response demonstrates that he had learned how to create an informal system of checks and balances and neutralize potential enemies. He was following in Yeltsin's footsteps.

In February 2002, the long-silent Yeltsin spoke out as well. Putin's political godfather, speaking of his successor's personnel policies, declared "that it is necessary to surround oneself not so much with loyal people as professional ones." And Yeltsin was much harsher about freedom of the press. "I tolerated all criticism, and today it is difficult to voice even justified criticism," the first Russian president said darkly. In his isolation, the old bear, buffeted by political and personal troubles, still retained his intuition and common sense. He felt that his successor was headed in the wrong direction.

Nor could Putin fully depend on society. His version of a soft Bonapartism guaranteed his power if his administration achieved good economic results and brought at least some normalcy into the lives of ordinary people. But if there were social problems, if corruption and degradation of the state continued, the fickle Russian electorate might begin looking for a new object of its affections. Besides, to have people's steady support the leader had to address them, talk to them, explain his policy to them, ask them to back him. Putin instead preferred a cold and distant style. He offered some of the populist gimmicks, including speaking to selected audiences, but he never really had a dialogue with the nation; he felt awkward, unable to talk to society, or afraid, or did not think it was necessary.

The renewed struggle among the court clans, the muted dissatisfaction among some social groups, the persistent corruption, and the Kremlin's failure to control the regions—all indicated that Russia's calm was an illusion. Moreover, in 2002, sometimes it was not clear whose hands held the power, who bore responsibility for certain decisions, or what the Kremlin's agenda was. Reality was again becoming blurred and hard to predict. The impression was that the presidential regime was being privatized by several groups and used without Putin's knowledge. "Power is making the rounds," skeptics said in Moscow.[3] For now, Russia supported the image of the "virtual Putin" making deals with all strata of society. But the impression persisted that this intentional ambiguity on the domestic front was the result of the Kremlin's weakness and disorientation.

Scholar Peter Reddaway was among the first to notice that the concentration of power resources in Putin's hands did not mean real consolidation of power. "Formally," wrote Reddaway in the January–March 2002 *Post-Soviet Affairs*, Putin had consolidated power "to a very considerable extent. But substantially, he has not. If one reason for this state of affairs were to be highlighted, . . . it would probably be the financial subversion by rich business, or magnates, . . . of key bureaucrats at all levels of government." There were other reasons for unconsolidated power as well: the unruly nature of Russian society, the decentralization of economic wealth, and the existence of patron–client relations.

Once again, the essence of Russia's postcommunist system revealed itself. Lacking independent institutions and definite principles, it could survive only with informal centers of influence to counter the omnipotence of the leader, with intentional ambiguity, constant bickering, and sweet deals. This system could not be consolidated; that is why its outward stability was deceptive, hiding underneath incompatible trends and permanent conflicts. But that forced the leader to constantly monitor the political scene, leaving him no time to think on a macro level; the more he was busy pressing the buttons, the more he was losing his general vision.

On April 18, 2002, the president made his annual address to the nation. This time, there was no response. "The prose of life," a "crisis of the genre," was the indifferent reaction of observers. Some began comparing Putin to Brezhnev, hinting that elements of stagnation had reappeared in Russian life. Such comparisons had to infuriate the leader, whose motto was to be dynamic and active.

Putin seemed to realize that the state machine was beginning to stall again. He grew nervous. He more frequently expressed dissatisfaction with his cabinet. He demanded that the government set "more ambitious goals"—instead of 4 percent economic growth in 2003, he demanded 9 to 11 percent from Prime Minister Kasyanov. He was clearly in a rush— he wanted to get out of the swamp as quickly as possible. But was this growth expectation realistic for Russia while it continued to rely on the former sources of growth, among which the main ones were, as in Soviet times, oil and gas? It was unlikely.

Kasyanov replied stubbornly that Russia did not need "big leaps." The prime minister was probably correct—you couldn't speed up the economy by fiat, as in former times. Putin demanded no more leaps from the cabinet, at least during this period.

People unexpectedly began to talk of Kasyanov as a potential rival in the next presidential election. Kasyanov had grown imperceptibly from a "technical prime minister" into a personality. He now had his own opinions. He began arguing with the president. It would be difficult to fire him without serious cause. The entire Yeltsin group stood behind Kasyanov; it seemed to be telling Putin: "If you misbehave, there are other candidates for president." But the structure of power in Russia is such that the prime minister is fully dependent on the president, who can end his political career with the stroke of a pen. Thus, Kasyanov or any other Russian premier could be dealt with. The fact that some elite groups began to look around in search of other potential leaders proved that the establishment was no longer mesmerized by Putin.

Meanwhile, Putin's political team—both parts, the Yeltsinites and the Praetorians—continued their intrigues, as if trying to show their boss that they were constantly busy, worrying about him and strengthening his presidency. One of the most memorable intrigues of that time was with the Communist Party. At the beginning of Putin's rule, the Kremlin had done a deal with the Communists and shared the most important posts in the Duma with them, which had been part of the policy to cajole all political forces. In the spring of 2002, the Kremlin decided to squeeze the Communists out of the parliament. Under Kremlin pressure, the Communists lost their leadership of influential Duma committees. At the same time, the Kremlin tried to create a schism in the Communist Party and initiate the formation of a loyal left-wing party under Duma speaker Seleznev.

Outwardly, this was a victory for liberalism. But only outwardly. The Duma remained managed (obedient to the Kremlin), and the president pushed through with ease all the decisions he needed. The Communists were no obstacle. Then why did the Kremlin want a fight with the Communist Party? At first, one might think that the Kremlin manipulators were trying to get rid of the left-wing opposition and make the political process fully manageable. But in fact, this intrigue had a false bottom— the Kremlin was trying to push Communist leader Gennady Zyuganov toward a more intractable opposition and thereby re-create the situation of previous presidential elections, when Yeltsin and then Putin won because their main opponent, Zyuganov, seemed like an implacable symbol of the past in the eyes of the vacillating electorate. The Kremlin began to prepare for the election battle of 2004. And the main electoral strategy was not a vision of the new Russia, but a repetition of the old election tricks.

What happened as a result? The Communist Party truly was radicalized and its opposition was strengthened, but the party was not weakened. In Russia, you could predict that it was collaboration with the regime, instead of opposition to it, that could have weakened the Communist Party. The country retained its left-wing and nationalist electorate that did not support the regime. The Communist Party was its only outlet. Its dissatisfaction grew, and a more oppositionist Communist Party could increase its positions. By the end of August, 34 percent of respondents to a poll stated that they would vote for the Communists if the Duma elections were held at that moment (only 29 percent would vote for the "party of power," United Russia). As for the split in the Communist Party, nothing influential came of the separatists loyal to the Kremlin forming their own party.

The Kremlin manipulators did not stop there. They continued squabbling, creating the appearance of activity and the appearance of their being needed. By creating bustle around the president, they forced him to continually be acting as peacemaker and referee. In other words, they were busy with the daily "technology of power," as it's called in Russia. Putin was getting mired in details, superficial and insignificant things. It was not just that his team was always fighting. It was the logic of personified power—it forced the leader to micromanage. The president seemed to realize—he could not be oblivious to this—that the intra-Kremlin squabbles were hampering his initiative and making him hostage to trifles. But he could not escape from the regime's trap, or did not wish to—in any case, not until the presidential elections. That was understandable—why rock the boat, when keeping the current situation would guarantee preservation of power and cautious modernization?

Putin's foreign policy in the first half of 2002 presented a contrast with domestic politics, which was becoming more and more bogged down in the court intrigues and attempts to keep stability. On the international scene, the Russian leader continued to demonstrate a strong desire to make Russia a systemic element of the Western community. The president, as if believing that he couldn't achieve much inside the country before the elections, began to pursue his international goals with redoubled energy. It was not any more meddle and muddle. His pro-Western orientation was now beyond doubt. The Kremlin was changing the very substance of Russian foreign policy, making it a projection not of military ambitions but of the country's economic interests.

Putin also proved that the relations with the United States were crucial for his agenda. This relationship underwent an amazing evolution after a rocky start in early 2001. A year later, the world was watching a level of personal chemistry between Bush and Putin that would have been unthinkable for earlier leaders of the former rival states.

Unexpectedly for many, in the spring and summer of 2002 the United States–Russia relationship looked much better than relations between Washington and Europe or between Moscow and any other nation, including Russia's former allies. The reason was not only the personal rapport between Bush and Putin but also that they had the same understanding of the major world challenge: Both considered terrorism the key threat for international security, and both were thinking in realpolitik terms.

In a *Wall Street Journal* interview on February 11, 2002, Putin confirmed that he and Bush were heading in the same direction. "In what President Bush said and what I said there is something in common, which is the following: we all recognize that terrorism has taken on an international character." Bush's idea of the "axis of evil" apparently impressed the Russian president. He even mentioned that he was the one who had first, before Bush, spoken of the "arc of instability," meaning hotspots of world terrorism. However, the roots of their unanimity were different; the "arc" was Putin's excuse for a military decision in Chechnya that he was sure was an important piece in the global terrorist chain.

It was true that the Russian president seemed not to like two things in the U.S. leader's conception of the problem: that the "axis of evil" included former Soviet allies, and that the United States was trying to solve the problem of the axis in a unilateral way. But the impression at that moment was that Putin endorsed the idea of the terrorist axis.

The Russian reaction was in sharp contrast to European criticism of the U.S. foreign policy agenda. French prime minister Lionel Jospin couldn't hide his emotions: "The problems of the world cannot be reduced simply to the struggle against terrorism, however vital that struggle may be."[4] The rest of Europe was adopting the same line; on the issue of terrorism, Europeans and Americans were drifting apart. And that emphasized even more suddenly the United States–Russia consensus.

When American journalists asked Putin directly whether Russia would support the United States if Washington began military action in Iraq, he first expressed his desire that the problem be resolved within the framework of the United Nations, and then added: "But that does not mean that Russia in the future would not, under certain conditions, work together with the U.S. and solve the problem of terrorism in a framework of the coalition." Translation: Putin wanted to avoid a repetition of the Yugoslav syndrome, which led Russia to support Yugoslav president Slobodan Milosevic almost up to the moment of his abdication, and after suffering defeat jump onto the Western bandwagon just as it was pulling out. Moscow did not want to endure a new humiliating failure.

At the beginning of 2002, the Russian leader seemed to be giving a message that next time Moscow was prepared to go along with the United States—especially if Russian economic interests were taken care of. One might assume that at that moment Putin could have supported U.S. action in Iraq even without waiting for Europeans. This was really a breathtaking change in Russia–United States relations. It was true, though, that observers soon would understand that Putin might backtrack if he felt he had gone forward too far and his position were not endorsed by Russian elites or his stance were not met with the reciprocity he had hoped for.

The ambiguity of the Kremlin's position, which would have quite unexpected outcomes, would become apparent later. But in the spring of 2002, Bush and Putin were the only two world leaders who openly and without hesitation endorsed the war on terrorism as the top priority in the field of international relations. These leaders of two completely different countries, these politicians with different principles and backgrounds, unexpectedly found themselves thinking alike. It was astounding, puzzling, . . . and worrisome. Cooperation based on a common enemy never survives the enemy. Will it be different this time? Will the United States and Russia find other areas of cooperation as well?

Relations between the United States and Russia continued to improve. The Bush administration, contrary to its initial inclinations, preserved all of the Clinton-era security and economic assistance programs and even increased some. It promoted a dialogue between the United States and Russia to encourage private investment in the Russian economy. It also asked Congress to graduate Russia permanently from the Jackson-Vanik amendment, thus removing a Cold War–era obstacle to normal trade relations.

At the beginning of 2002, U.S. officials viewed United States–Russia relations as the best in history. The White House continued to praise Russia as "a key member" of the international antiterrorist coalition. Moreover, Washington, working on the security agenda with Russia, made it possible to perceive Russia as a great power—which massaged the complexes of the Russian establishment.

In Russia, however, the initial euphoria of mutual rapprochement gradually began to vanish, and voices of disappointment became louder. Even pro-Western Russians were complaining that Russia had agreed to all the concessions to the United States that it had regarded as unthinkable several years ago: endorsement of a U.S. military presence in Central Asia and, later, a U.S. presence in Georgia; acquiescence to NATO enlargement and Anti–Ballistic Missile Treaty abrogation; and contributions to the antiterrorist campaign, for which it so far had received no substantial "deliverables" from the United States. The incredible happened: Putin was openly criticized in Russia and accused of acting like Gorbachev—giving a lot and getting little or nothing back. The fact that Russian elites were waiting for U.S. "deliverables" proved that they still viewed their endorsement of U.S. policy and their partnership with the United States as some kind of deviation or as a concession to the United States, but not as a strategic course for Russia.

For its acquiescence to the U.S. security measures, Moscow hoped for compensation in the economic field and upgraded cooperation in the security area—first of all, those in joint defense and relations with NATO. Unlike Yeltsin, who could be satisfied with symbolic gestures, Putin wanted more substance in ties with the West, above all with the United States.[5] It appeared, however, that such compensation was hard to come by. Even the repeal of the notorious Jackson-Vanik amendment seemed to be a difficult process. Moreover, the spring of 2002 saw the steel–poultry war, which cast a shadow over United States–Russia relations.[6]

"Long-term marriage between Moscow and Washington is impossible," was the verdict of Russian analysts. What the White House called a coalition, most Russian observers called "just light flirting."[7] The overwhelming elite skepticism concerning perspectives of the Russian–American dialogue was rooted in both—suspicion of the U.S. intentions concerning Russia and doubt about Russia's fast revival. Some American observers, especially in the Democratic Party, also were rather pessimistic, criticizing Bush's approach to relations with Russia. "We wanted full Russian cooperation in the war against terror and we have received it," wrote Leon Fuerth, a former adviser to Al Gore. But in return "we wanted to take such nuclear reductions as suited us, we offered a reinvented version of what already exists (the NATO–Russia Council), we imposed tariffs on Russian steel." "Solid partnerships are not built on winner-take-all rules, they require a search for win–win outcomes," was Fuerth's conclusion.[8]

Americans who wanted to justify limited engagement argued that Russia does not have the capacity at this point to engage in a truly mutually beneficial partnership with the United States. There are several responses to such a view. As the one remaining superpower, the United States has asymmetrical relations with all its closest allies; reciprocity is impossible when one side has such enormous weight. In addition, Russia had already shown that it can hold up its end of the bargain in the antiterrorist campaign—and at that moment one had the impression that Russia was learning, albeit, somewhat grudgingly, a new part: that of a responsible partner.

However, concerns about the nature and sustainability of the United States–Russia relationship had their point. The relationship was constrained not only by the vestiges of the past and the asymmetry of American and Russian capabilities. With the exception of the antiterrorist struggle, there was nothing substantial on the plate. Elites in both countries still could not go beyond discussing irritants—arms reduction, Iran and Iraq, nuclear proliferation. And relations were hampered by a lack of a new concept of international relations and tainted by remaining mistrust between both elites. Influential forces within the Bush administration viewed Russia as a nuisance that should be shrugged off.

Robert Legvold, analyzing U.S. policy toward Russia, wrote at the end of 2001: "Nothing suggests that Washington or the American public is in a mood to embrace an ambitious policy toward Russia. The inertia leading the United States to disengage from the Russia problem in the last years of the Clinton administration, therefore, seems likely to continue. The Bush administration inherited a policy of benign neglect: Russia is acknowledged, the lines of communication are opened, and various cooperative projects are proffered as a sign of good intentions, but little effort is made to address the hard problems at the core of the relations."[9] This conclusion continued to be true in 2002.

As for Russian politicians, they still watched Washington with suspicion and often hostility, anticipating double standards and unilateralism. The policy community in Moscow continued to have problems translating rapprochement policy into a practical agenda. Most Russian politicians were trying to channel the Russian–American relationship into the nonstop nuclear arms control talks that would allow Moscow to imitate a superpower and would secure a niche for its foreign policy and security establishment, which was totally unable to function in the new environment.

The Bush–Putin summit in Moscow on May 24, 2002, had to prove to what extent both sides were ready to turn their tactical alliance into a more meaningful partnership. Putin had delivered everything he could at the moment. The ball was on the American field. Putin badly needed from Bush the nuclear reduction treaty. Moscow considered this treaty as a compensatory gesture for abrogation of the Anti–Ballistic Missile Treaty. Putin also expected Washington to repeal the Jackson-Vanik amendment and give Russia market-economy status. In this case, he could prove to the Russian political class that he was not a Gorbachev II who was only weakening Russia's positions without reciprocity.

Bush had to overcome his aversion to treaties and his pledge to stop making symbolic gestures and help his new buddy Putin. The Americans proved that they understood Putin's difficulties at home; they met him halfway. Bush agreed to sign a legally binding document on the reduction of offensive nuclear weapons. In the clash in Washington between those who regarded Russia as too weak to matter and those who favored cooperation, the latter won—at least at that time.

On May 24, the Strategic Offensive Reduction Treaty was signed. It was the shortest nuclear treaty in history and the most far-reaching. It stipulated that both countries would cut their strategic arsenal from 6,000 to between 1,700 and 2,200 warheads by December 2012—the steepest nuclear reduction so far. There was no real verification procedure, no legal enforcement, and no performance mechanism. "The Treaty of Moscow," as it was called, was based on trust, and it had to both manage the Russian–American relationship in a period of the likely introduction by the United States of ballistic missile defenses and also prevent the proliferation of nuclear weapons. Both the U.S. Congress and Russian Duma had to ratify the treaty. The Russian parliament, controlled by the Kremlin, did not present a problem. But nobody was sure how Congress would react.

Ironically, each side viewed this treaty in a different way. Americans considered it the confirmation of the end of the Cold War era based on bipolarity, while Russians continued to look at it as proof that nuclear parity still mattered. And this difference in approaches could become a source of future frustrations.

The Treaty of Moscow was not the only outcome of the May summit: The leaders signed a joint declaration on the new strategic relations that was setting a basis for joint dealing with new challenges and created a framework for new cooperation on security. This was an attempt to build a new concept of the relationship, laying out common interests.

But Moscow was thinking along practical terms, and from that point of view the Bush–Putin summit did not justify Russian hopes. Bush did not bring any resolution on doing away with the Jackson-Vanik amendment, nor recognition of Russia's market-economy status. Putin was disappointed, even upset, and that was clear in his behavior. But he restrained himself and did not stress his unhappiness with the Americans. "We are not thrilled that this did not happen," he noted in passing on May 26.

Even though not all the Kremlin hopes for the Moscow summit came to pass, ordinary Russians' attitude toward the United States was again amazingly warm. In May 2002, according to a VTsIOM poll, 69 percent spoke of the importance of the Bush–Putin summit (24 percent doubted its importance). Thirty-five percent felt that Russia had to try to join NATO (47 percent thought otherwise).

Personal relations between Bush and Putin—at least outwardly—were so friendly that some observers began speaking of the "Bush–Putin axis." *Le Monde* wrote on May 18: "Europeans, caught between two fires during the Cold War, should be happy for the new climate between America and Russia. However, we must think—will we be given the role of extras in view of the appearance of the Bush–Putin axis?"

But relations between Russia and the United States looked so good and cloudless only in comparison with the noticeable cooling of relations between the United States and Europe. So far, this was a relationship of allies against a common enemy, not a partnership based on recognition of the same values. This meant that new distancing, and even freezing, between Moscow and Washington was quite possible. The question was whether this cooling would be caused by different visions of national interests of the respective states within a single ideology, as in the relationship between the United States and Europe, or by a retention of conflicting views of society and the world order.

There was a feeling among realistically thinking circles on both sides of the ocean that not only the May 2002 summit but the whole pattern of the United States–Russia relationship was "less a form of power politics than of psychotherapy," as Charles Krauthammer put it in the *Washington Post* on May 31. But sometimes sessions of psychotherapy are useful before world politics can acquire new form and new substance, and most important, before political elites find new roles for their respective states.

In analyzing the new U.S. policy toward Russia, James Goldgeier and Michael McFaul wrote in the October 2002 issue of *Current History*: "Bush's policy represents continuation of Clinton's strategy. . . . The approaches of Bill Clinton and George W. Bush differ in one important way. Bush does not believe that Russia's internal transformation must precede Russia's external integration into the Western clubs."[10] Goldgeier and McFaul called the new policy "integration without transformation." The fact that the Bush administration—at least outwardly—did not try to teach Moscow democracy really can explain why the Russian leader so easily formed a personal bond with Bush. In his turn, the U.S. president, rejecting previous "romanticism"—the attempt to promote democracy in Russia—was quite successful in achieving his major security goals. But the question remained: To what extent were these security gains durable without Russia's further transformation?

Whatever the future development of Russian–American relations, one positive aspect was without doubt: Both sides during the previous decade had gained mutual experience of ungrounded expectations and exaggerated frustrations that forced them this time to be more realistic. "In sharp contrast to the earlier period, however, there was now little euphoria. The sense of possibilities was now tempered by knowledge of the failed hopes of the early 1990s, of the rough road the two countries had traveled later in that decade, and of the challenges that lay ahead," Thomas Graham wrote in his book *Russia's Decline and Uncertain Recovery*, describing new stages of the United States–Russia relationship.[11] That experience could help both Moscow and Washington—to avoid old bumps on the road and to deal with new bumps.

Further events followed with kaleidoscopic speed. On May 29, 2002, the E.U. delegation headed by Romano Prodi arrived in Moscow and brought Putin a long-awaited present: The European Union recognized Russia's market-economy status. This step speeded up Washington's decision to do the same. Bush called Putin in the Kremlin and gave him the good news himself. Recognition of Russia as a market economy created a better climate for Russian trade. Russia lost about $1.5 billion annually because of restrictions on its products on international markets. Now Russian companies would have wider access to Western markets.

The E.U. and U.S. recognition of Russia's status improved its chances of joining the World Trade Organization, which the Kremlin wanted badly. As Mike Moore, the organization's director general, said, "I believe there are in Washington, Brussels, and Moscow people, the horsepower, firepower, and will power to make this accession possible." Encouraged, Putin began talking of the creation of a "single economic space" with the European Union. However, the European reaction to the Russian president's initiative was reserved. The European Union set numerous conditions:

first of all, bringing Russian legislation into correspondence with international standards; and second, raising tariffs on energy to correspond to world prices (low domestic prices were an annual energy subsidy for Russian enterprises, estimated to be $5 billion). Russia also had to open its markets.

The last two demands were hard to meet for Moscow. Both Russian and foreign economists warned that Russia's noncompetitive industry could not stand a wide opening of the market, and its collapse could provoke uncontrolled social consequences. "It might be that forcing the pace of change ultimately proved counterproductive," warned economist Padma Desai in the *Financial Times* on July 11. The Kremlin had to walk a tightrope, on the one hand gradually opening markets, and on the other, preventing negative consequences of these steps for stability. This task required not only thoughtful leadership but also a broad social dialogue.

There remained, however, a deep divide in the relations between Moscow and the European Union—the problem of Kaliningrad, the Russian city in the Baltic Sea, the former capital of East Prussia. Kaliningrad had to be cut off from Russia by the pending entry of Poland and Lithuania into the European Union and to be turned into a Russian "exclave" within the union. Putin tried to get a visa-free regime between Kaliningrad and Russia. But the European Union was not ready to change its Schengen rules, which have formed a visa-free zone for E.U. members, citing concerns about illegal Russian migrants to Lithuania and, from there, further to the west. Negotiations were at an impasse, creating a strain in relations between Brussels and Moscow. The Kremlin, however, could not afford to endanger its European policy and had to reach a compromise with the European Union on Kaliningrad.

The next development came on May 28, when the first NATO summit with the participation of Russia was held at the military barracks outside Rome, where the NATO–Russia Council was formed. Putin sat between the leaders of Spain and Portugal, ordered alphabetically by country. In his opening remarks at the inaugural meeting of the council, the NATO secretary general, Lord George Robertson, said: "The leaders of twenty of the word's most powerful nations assembled, not to carve up the world, but to unite it." Putin was also positive, saying: "We've come a long way from confrontation to dialogue and from confrontation to cooperation." But at the same time, Putin suggested that Russian cooperation did not represent unconditional support for any action NATO might choose to take.

The new council provided opportunities for NATO–Russia consultation, joint decision making, and even joint action. The list of issues for cooperation included assessment of the terrorist threat, arms control, nonproliferation, theatre missile defense, military-to-military cooperation, and civil emergencies. Russia did not get a veto right on NATO actions. The new Russian responsibility within the council also was far from defined. But the whole structure represented a step forward from the previous arrangement—the Permanent Joint Council, where Russia had a much narrower role. The NATO–Russia Council could become a platform for dialogue between the former foes; everything depended on the political will from both sides. NATO and Russia were making a second try to forge a partnership. A new failure might raise a question: To what extent was it a result of the leadership problem, the tactics issue, and to what extent was it the outcome of the systemic incompatibility of NATO and Russia?

Then came the June Group of Eight meeting in Kananaskis, Canada. Here Putin was completely self-confident. He felt he was an equal. Russia was already in the front seat and not asking for help. The Kremlin had proven its desire to become a member of the Western community. In response, the group decided to make Russia a full-fledged member, even though the Russian economy did not warrant such status; it was an acknowledgment of Putin's pro-Western policy. The industrial countries also promised Moscow $20 billion to safeguard and dismantle Russian weapons of mass destruction; this aid was linked to Russia's fulfilling its obligations regarding nonproliferation. As if to endorse a new role for Russia, the Group of Eight leaders agreed that in 2006, Russia would assume the presidency and host the group's annual summit.

In solidifying his pro-Western turn, the Russian president made an attempt to show that his politics remained multivectored. He tried to demonstrate Moscow's interest in relations with other nations as well. In May, after the summit with Bush and the creation of the Russia–NATO Council, defense minister Sergei Ivanov went to China to assure Beijing that Russia's turn to the West was not aimed against China. Besides security considerations, Moscow had material interests in good relations with China. In the past decade alone, the trade turnover with China had grown to about $10 billion. China bought modern jets and the famous S-300 missile complex from Russia. In 2001, trade between China and Russia grew by $1 billion. Moscow was definitely interested in a dialogue with Beijing.

In the summer, Moscow initiated meetings within the Shanghai Cooperation Organization. Putin had consultations with members of the Euro-Asiatic Economic Union and the members of the Treaty of Collective Security of the Commonwealth of Independent States, and individual meetings with the presidents of Ukraine and Belarus. The Kremlin seemed to be trying to prove that its Western orientation did not mean forgetting Russia's previous ties.

All these steps evinced the formation of a Putin Doctrine for foreign policy. The essence of the doctrine was a pro-Western orientation, a priority for economic interests in foreign policy, and a normalization of relations between Moscow and its neighbors, especially former allies of the USSR. Putin's multivectored approach, however, differed sharply from Primakov's multipolarity—Putin demonstrated that the West is the priority for him.

But these are just the contours of the doctrine. Putin's foreign policy remained insufficiently structured and vulnerable. Most seriously, a significant group of elites continued to resist the president's orientation toward the West. The Ministry of Foreign Affairs and the Ministry of Defense remained bastions of conservatism. The weakly defined distinctions between these institutions and other foreign policy players, along with their lack of clear areas of responsibility, did not make implementing the Kremlin's new foreign doctrine any easier. It was still unclear who made certain foreign policy decisions, how much political support they had, and how the president could guarantee their irreversibility. If the Russian political class was not sure that a decisive pro-Western orientation was necessary, would Putin's successor turn in the other direction? asked Western observers. Their concerns were not without foundation.

The realization of the Putin Doctrine required an understanding of Russia's new role and defining new identity in the world both from elites and from society as a whole. A new philosophy of foreign policy was urgently needed, and new able people were needed to execute it. "Relations between Russia and the West have rarely been better. But what does it mean in practice? And can it last?" wrote the *Economist* on May 16, 2002, and it answered, "The real danger is not that Russia's march to the West goes into reverse, but that it bogs down for lack of ideas and people."

Meanwhile, the Kremlin had not been making any efforts to prove the rightness of its policy before its own society. This was a problem not of weak propaganda, but insufficient democracy. The Kremlin seemed to be saying to the country, "We will have whatever policies we deem necessary. We have no intention of explaining our goals to you."

It was not only very sad but also destructive that Russia's turn toward the West was made in the same old undemocratic way— without any attention to society, without any effort at explanation. The authorities did not believe that people would understand the reasons for the new policy, and they did not trust Russia. The absence of a constructive dialogue between the regime and the nation on foreign policy issues created a niche for critics of the new policy in the ruling class. Until the Putin Doctrine was supported by the public, it could not be considered the final Kremlin line in foreign policy.

In contrast to foreign policy and new international developments, the shallowness of domestic policy was surprising. The major events were over; there was no open confrontation, no political drama. The struggle continued, but it was reduced to rope-pulling among a few interest groups and clans.

Only one event shook up Russian political life in mid-2002: the reappearance of Boris Yeltsin. He had begun showing signs of life, meeting with politicians and making comments through intermediaries. On Russian Independence Day, June 12, he appeared live, giving an expansive interview on Russian television. Amazingly, he looked energetic, physically stronger, much thinner, and clear-minded. It could have been a double. Tsar Boris admitted that he had had five heart attacks during his presidency. "Yes, five," he confirmed with a sneaky look. "But I remain active, mentally, physically, and emotionally." He said that he had lost 20 kilograms (44 pounds) in recent months. He had not only shed weight, but about ten years. Yeltsin said he had begun studying English. "To train the brain," he explained.

Then Yeltsin headed to Minsk for vacation, untiringly giving interviews and making comments on Russian politics. "I meet every day with ministers, with Prime Minister Kasyanov, Putin—all the time. It is like being a guarantor of stability," Yeltsin said with a sly squint. Everyone noticed that he mentioned Putin in passing. Moreover, he was clearly critical of his successor, whom he had recently praised, including in his memoirs. Russians began to joke: The Guarantor of Stability, as he called himself, was trying to lecture the Guarantor of the Constitution, that is, Putin. And Yeltsin was frankly promoting Kasyanov as a presidential candidate. This was a clear challenge to Putin. Yeltsin's return meant one thing—his political Family had no intention of giving up. Bringing out the heavy artillery—Grandpa himself—it decided to prove that it still had influence.

Putin responded to his godfather and predecessor. He was brief, but harsh. At his press conference on June 24, which was supposed to sum up his two years as president, he announced, "Yeltsin is a free individual who can move about, meet with anyone, and express his opinion. We respect his opinion. However, I have my own opinion, and I will do what I think is best for Russia now and in the future." Putin's words meant, "I will not be scared off. I no longer need advisers and guides."

This open dialogue showed that the relationship between Tsar Boris and his heir was not great. Putin was gradually coming out of the shadow of the Yeltsin entourage, and naturally the old ruling team did not like it. Vladimir Vladimirovich was diverging from Yeltsin's line on some cardinal political issues. He went further than Yeltsin in his movement toward the West. He began reviewing the Yeltsin model of relations with the former Soviet republics, rejecting the former paternalism. At the same time, he rejected Yeltsin's attitude toward the press and freedoms. But much more important for the Yeltsin group was something else—Putin was building his own political regime, which presupposed no godfathers and no gratitude for the predecessor. It looked as if Putin were ready to cut the strings that tied him to Yeltsin.

What was amazing, however, was the fact that even as he stood on the threshold of open polemic with the man who had given him power, the new master of the Kremlin still had to put up with a number of appointees and members of the Yeltsin group. Outwardly, it was incomprehensible and illogical. But the explanation was simple: His own people, the ones he had brought from Saint Petersburg, were blatantly weak. And he had not yet managed to form a new team in the two years of his administration.

So far, Putin preferred burning no bridges, avoiding conflict with powerful forces and with the old political Family. He was not a political gladiator. He did not like open political struggle or even polemic. Was he a fighter at all? Was he prepared to fight for his power or his principles? And what were his principles? Only a real threat or crisis would give the answers. And the new regime had not yet faced such an ordeal. The clash with Yeltsin could have been one more step for Putin toward independent leadership, and it was a litmus test for his ability to stand his ground. But it did not say how he would behave in the moment of truth.

Besides the clearing of the air between the old and new leaders of Russia, besides the tension among several clans in Putin's entourage, the summer of 2002 was far from hectic. Russia tried to get a respite from politics. How long can you live in a state of squabbles and conflicts? The country had been under stress since Gorbachev's *perestroika*, in the mid-1980s. For the past seventeen years, Russians had sought answers to existential questions: Where was Russia going? How should it define its identity? What system should be built?

In 2002, the discussion wound down to almost nothing, not because everything had become clear, but because apathy and indifference had overtaken society—the desire for a Grand Design and a definition of life's goal had been lost. And the Putin regime, with its ideology of pragmatism—its focus on details—did not stimulate interest in Russia's strategic problems and in its continuing soul searching. The policy of pragmatism itself looked like a rejection of any far-reaching strategy.

The summer of 2002 was devoted to private life. The exhausting heat, the worst in years, enervated the country and paralyzed the megalopolises, especially Moscow, slowing down traffic and humans. Putin left Moscow and switched to a summer work regimen—he was in his residence in

Sochi, by the sea. There he saw his subordinates and received international guests. French president Jacques Chirac made his official visit to Russia in Sochi. Without Putin in Moscow, there was no politics, for only the president was the main political event.

And yet the absence of political movement and a clear agenda was upsetting: Because in Russia a lull was always followed by a new wave of political intrigue or a series of other upsets. Because outward calm hid the vagueness of the future. Because this was the last calm summer before the next elections and new fistfights. And because in Russia a political lull could always be illusory.

Soon events, not at all connected with politics, confirmed that Russia could not yet be considered a quiet and balanced country. First, the southern regions were swallowed up in floods, which literally washed away dozens of towns, killing dozens of people and taking heavy financial tolls. But while similar flooding in Europe made world headlines and elicited support for the victims, in Russia, yet another disaster was merely reported in daily news roundups. Russian society was so used to catastrophes that it seemed to be immune and no longer reacted to them. In any case, Russian television devoted more coverage to the streets of Germany underwater than to the suffering of Russia's own citizens, left without shelter.

Then came August, which Russians have learned to fear. Too many dramatic events of the past decade had taken place in August: the putsch in 1991; apartment building explosions and the separatist invasion of Dagestan in 1999, which began the second Chechen war; the *Kursk* submarine disaster in 2000. And once again, catastrophe struck. On August 19, a military helicopter crashed in Chechnya with 140 people on board. The next day a residential building in Moscow blew up, killing several people and leaving dozens wounded.

In the next few days, more helicopter and plane crashes and another apartment building explosion followed, as if to strengthen in Russians a feeling of foreboding. Russians no longer believed in accidents and technological causes—they saw conspiracy and criminal intent behind every disaster. But even dramatic mistakes, technological failures, evil fate, and tragic coincidence were proof of the fragility of Russian stability and how defenseless ordinary people were there. Putin's power, just like Yeltsin's, could not stop the never-ending flow of disasters that were in part the

consequence and echo of the collapse of the Soviet empire, the continuing decay of outdated infrastructure, but mostly the result of the sloppiness
and inefficiency of the new system and of the irresponsible bureaucracy.[12]

The fall of 2002 brought signs that despite the political lull and absence of
visible political threats to Russia's stability, hidden trends and unresolved
conflicts could pose a challenge for the Kremlin. Russia's postcommunist
history had proven that its transformation still could take quite a few
unexpected turns. The kaleidoscope of myriad perspectives on events continued to turn as Russia's policy positions continued to evolve.

In the foreign policy arena, skeptics seemed to be proven right as
Moscow's long romance with the West turned icy. Moscow continued to
be offended by the European community's constant criticism of its
Chechen war. Soon Russia would get involved in a real clash with
Denmark—after Copenhagen refused to extradite Akhmad Zakayev, one
of Chechen president Aslan Maskhadov's associates, in October 2002 and
became furious with the United Kingdom for doing the same.

The emotional discussion of the Kaliningrad visa regime clouded
Russia's otherwise warm relations with the European Union. Finally, after
a long-standing dispute with Russia, the union offered special transit
arrangements for Kaliningrad residents—"the Kaliningrad pass," a simplified transit document that would be issued free or for a small fee by the
consulates of Lithuania and Poland after these countries joined the union.
Brussels also promised to look into the feasibility of nonstop, high-speed
trains between Kaliningrad and Russia proper. This ended the dispute and
simultaneously proved that the union was not ready to accommodate all
of Russia's demands. Moscow would have to make an effort to formulate
its European policy so as to avoid future conflicts that could emerge as a
result of its desire for special treatment by the union.

Russian relations with the United States also came under strain. The
Kremlin riled U.S. leaders by resuming trade negotiations with Baghdad
and declaring its intention to expand its nuclear assistance to Iran. Putin
made the decision to push forward with a project to link the Trans-
Siberian railroad with North Korean rail lines. During his fall visit to

Beijing, Prime Minister Kasyanov signed new arms-sales agreements with China worth billions of dollars. Russia sold China not only Sukhoi fighter jets and Kilo-class submarines but also assisted in building a helicopter manufacturing plant and delivered a wide array of nuclear technology.

U.S. dismay was thinly veiled at best. "Lately, Russia isn't just continuing its tradition of schmoozing with rogue states around the world. It's actually stepping up relations with several of them," wrote *Newsweek* on September 2, accusing Moscow of forging its "own axis of friendship" with Iraq, Iran, and North Korea. Russians in return argued that they had gained too little from their pro-Western orientation and were simply pursuing—as was the United States—their own economic interests.

As if to add more fuel to an already fiery atmosphere, in September tension deepened between Russia and Georgia. Putin accused Georgian leader Eduard Shevardnadze of lacking the political will to root out Chechen rebels from Georgia's Pankisi Gorge. On September 11, the anniversary of the terrorist attacks in the United States the year before, Putin delivered an ultimatum to Tbilisi—essentially, "We are preparing to strike established Chechen terrorist bases on your territory whether you like it or not." In justifying his position, Putin quoted Bush's words about the legitimate need for "preventive measures" against countries harboring terrorists. Both the United States and the Council of Europe spoke out against Russia's desire for such aggressive action. For the first time during their honeymoon, Russia and the West seemed to be on a collision course.

This is not the end of the story. In late September, Washington imposed sanctions on three Russian enterprises for allegedly selling military equipment to countries it believes sponsor terrorism. Pundits predicted a new schism between Russia and the West, as well as Moscow's return to nationalistic anti-Americanism. This was hasty and ungrounded, however. The reality was much more complicated. Putin wanted no rupture with the West; clearly, he continued to consider Moscow's relationship with Washington a top priority and its relationship with the West the major prerequisite for Russia's modernization. But by the end of 2002, his pro-Western movement had encountered not only situational, strictly political obstacles, but—more important—structural difficulties. Besides, some global events did not help Russia strengthen its pro-Western orientation.

U.S. plans for military action and regime change in Iraq at the end of 2002 became a new test for Russian–American realignment. For the first time after September 11, 2001, the foreign policy agendas and economic interests of the United States and Russia openly diverged. The Kremlin feared that a war in Iraq would destabilize the already volatile situation in the region close to Russian borders. In view of the unfinished story in Afghanistan, it was a justified worry. The Russian political establishment and Russian tycoons were even more concerned that a successor regime in Iraq would not honor Iraq's $8 billion debt to Russia, and that the war would imperil Russia's investments in the country, including multi-billion-dollar contracts. The apprehension in Moscow was that future Iraqi oil would bring falling world oil prices, while oil revenues continued to be the major source of Russian economic development.

At first, Russia (together with France and China) did not support the U.S. draft resolution on Iraq suggesting the automatic use of force, and it opposed military action against Saddam Hussein. Moreover, other European states also expressed their concerns over U.S. policy toward Iraq. This European disagreement with Washington allowed Russia to express its unhappiness with the U.S. policy even more strongly. It was true that President Putin, in his usual reticent manner, said that he would not make negotiations over Iraq into the "Eastern bazaar"—he still did not want to engage in horse trading with Washington. But the Russian establishment tried to get guarantees from the United States that, in return for not obstructing U.S. policy, Russian economic interests would be taken care of. In the Iraqi case, Russia's economic interests prevailed over geopolitical aspirations.

In the end, Moscow—despite "some concerns"—supported a new resolution on Iraq demanding that Baghdad make a full declaration of any weapons of mass destruction and allow weapons inspections. This time, Russia stopped trying to save Saddam's regime and chose to stand together with the Western community while at the same time trying to take advantage of disagreements among Western allies.

It was apparent that in the end Moscow and Washington would eventually cooperate in dealing with Iraq and in a post-Saddam situation. But the controversy over Iraq demonstrated that the emergence of new conflicts of interest between Russia and the United States is possible, and that these conflicts could become quite severe if Moscow failed to solve the structural problems of Russia's further development.

Russia seemed to have problems reconciling its economic interests with the new vector of its foreign policy. Moscow had yet to draw the line between tenable and untenable levels of disagreement with Western powers over policy. The criteria were amorphous. Among the Western powers, minor conflicts were normal and did not provoke serious breaches within the Western community. With Russia, it was a more complicated matter. Russia's political class has yet to understand that sometimes short-term financial incentives and benefits obscure longer range political danger. For example, massive amounts of weaponry and even nuclear technology sold by Moscow to its old allies could increase instability on Russian borders and create situations with which Moscow is not prepared to deal. Besides, cozy relations with these states can endanger partnership with the West. But a different argument should be mentioned as well: Staying friendly with traditional allies can help Russia to become a mediator that one day can help the renegades join the modern nations. The problem: How should a line be drawn between pragmatism and adherence to the past?

The discrepancy between a pro-Western foreign policy and a nondemocratic regime in power in Russia has slowly taken on greater prominence. Putin, relying upon support from conservative circles that were the basis of that regime, realized he could not afford to ignore their interests entirely. Hence, in the fall of 2002, he drove a hard line on Georgia to massage the military and the security community. The irony was that the Kremlin hawks skillfully appropriated Bush's "preemption" strategy to justify action in Georgia. The argument that if Americans can attack potential terrorists in Iraq, Russia can do the same in Georgia became popular, even among Russian liberals.

Putin faced an inescapable dilemma: to retreat from his pro-Western course and strengthen the authoritarian nature of his rule, giving his Praetorians more influence, or to consolidate momentum along the pro-Western vector, which would require the adoption of more democratic rules of the game at home and would be appreciated by an entirely different—and democratic—audience. Moscow could not sit forever astride two horses running in opposite directions. Operating on two incompatible principles, Russia could never become a true member of the Western club, Putin's ultimate goal. In this situation, every adversarial line Russia took against the West could be perceived as a red flag, warning of hidden anti-Western sentiment among Russia's policy makers.

In the meantime, Russia moved inexorably toward new parliamentary and presidential elections. And that meant that the political break was coming to an end and the public was beginning to think about the successes and failures of Putin's first term and what lay ahead. A new period of animation and political struggle was coming for the country.

Those who have already tried to take a snapshot of the Putin presidency got a slippery and contradictory image that had no less conflict and half shadows than in the Yeltsin years. The seemingly clear, schematic, logical Vladimir Vladimirovich consistently ended up the hostage of group interests, the Yeltsin legacy, Russian history, the daily grind, and his own prejudices and fears. In the two years of his administration, he desperately tried to stop the momentum of Russia's decay. He succeeded in achieving a great degree of stability: The state began functioning; the bureaucracy started, albeit halfheartedly, working; and people were overcoming their helplessness.

But Vladimir Putin also failed on several accounts. The most dramatic for Russia and its president was the problem of Chechnya. The situation appeared to be stabilizing. Large-scale military actions had ended. An administration of Chechens loyal to the Kremlin had been formed with Akhmad Kadyrov at the head. Money was flowing into the region, and restoration work had begun. But in essence, the guerilla war in Chechnya continued. Casualties on both sides continued to grow.

Former minister of the interior Anatoly Kulikov, who knows the situation well, announced that in the course of the two wars in Chechnya Russia had lost as many men as in the war in Afghanistan in 1979–1989, that is, about 15,000. According to official sources in Moscow, in the second Chechen war—from 1999 until August 2002—4,249 Russians were killed and 12,285 were wounded (and military data gave the number of separatists killed at about 13,000). But human rights activists maintained that the losses on the Russian side were much higher. "The number for the military death toll should be multiplied by three or four," said the representative of the Committee of Soldiers' Mothers, campaigning for service members' rights. Moscow did not even try to establish the civilian casualties in the Northern Caucasus.

In the fall of 2002, the Russian public no longer believed in a military solution to the Chechen problem. Only 17 percent of those polled by VTsIOM supported a military variant for Chechnya. More than two-thirds supported a peaceful solution. For the president who had entered the Kremlin on the wave of the "antiterrorist operation" in the Northern Caucasus, this was evidence of a fiasco. Besides, this was also a trap. For now, the Kremlin had to think not only about what to do with Chechnya but also about how to preserve the legitimacy of the team that had come to power endorsing antiterrorist operations. The Kremlin was now in a situation where the problem of saving face was turning into a question of survival.

What could be the way out of this seeming dead end? By October 2002, more and more politicians and pundits in Russia—among them even the always-cautious former prime minister Primakov—were coming to the conclusion that the only answer was negotiations with the leaders of the Chechen opposition, particularly Maskhadov, to end military action and reach a peaceful resolution. In rejecting negotiations with Maskhadov, Moscow could lose a chance to come to terms with the generation of Chechen leaders still willing to talk to Moscow. The new generation of separatists, who grew up during the war with Russia and who think only of the holy jihad against Russians, wants only bloody revenge. These thoughts gradually began to dominate public disputes in Russia.

Viable peaceful options for Chechnya discussed that fall in Russia stipulated Russia's recognition of broad Chechen autonomy or the division of Chechnya into two parts—one part loyal to Russia, which would be part of the Russian Federation as one of its subjects and where the Chechens who wished to remain in Russia would move; and the other part an independent Chechnya. In this case, enormous international assistance would be needed to help the Chechens pursue their own statehood. Was this statehood possible in principle? The previous attempts to do this in 1991–1994 and 1994–1999 had ended in disaster—in the emergence on the territory of Chechnya of lawless lands ruled by warlords who had been engaged in criminal activity, drug trafficking, and kidnapping. How to prevent it from happening again when the peace was restored was a task not only for Russia but for the international community as well.

The Russian president needed all his courage to admit that his war in Chechnya was lost and now his goal was not to win but to achieve peace. A peaceful resolution in Chechnya would have meant a new approach from the Kremlin toward Russian statehood and power—a new policy in Chechnya might become a step in finally overcoming the old Russian System. But the Kremlin was not yet ready for that step. And soon the possibility of a peaceful solution for Chechnya became even less possible.

On October 23, 2002, a group of Chechen fighters seized a theater in downtown Moscow and took more than 800 people hostage. The fighters placed explosives around the building, promising to blow up themselves together with their captives. They had only one demand: an end to the war in the Northern Caucasus. Thus brutal war came to the Russian capital.

President Putin rejected any negotiations with the terrorists. For the Kremlin to start negotiations would mean acknowledging that the war with the Chechens was lost, and this war was an important legitimization of Putin's ascendancy to power. No, Vladimir Putin was not ready for defeat—especially when he was facing the elections. Instead, he ordered special services to storm the theater building. This ruthless rescue operation, in which an unknown gas was used, killed about 120 hostages. Many more—about 600 hostages—found themselves in hospitals suffering from the mysterious gas cocktail.

Initial relief at the success of the special forces in freeing the captives soon gave way to frustration and apprehension. No doubt, the leader and the government had to make a difficult decision, and they had little choice. But the rescue operation was done in a typically Soviet style, reminiscent of the old days. The attack had been launched without making sure that there was enough antidote to treat the hostages for gas poisoning. The rescued people were dying from poisoning, and the state was refusing to say what type of gas it had used—in fact, all the hostages who had died, with the exception of two who had been shot, had died from the poisoning. And relatives were not given immediate access to the victims, who were virtually imprisoned.

"This is a disgrace, a throwback to the worst of Soviet military secrecy and disregard for human life. The greatest failure is the old Russian nemesis: the failure to be honest," wrote the *Times* of London on October 28, 2002. Meanwhile, the authorities—just as in the days of the Chernobyl nuclear power plant explosion and the *Kursk* submarine disaster—were lying and trying to deliberately hide the truth and escape any responsibility.

The disastrous handling of this hostage crisis—it was as if the government had learned nothing from the previous numerous tragedies—proved that the authorities were much more concerned with their own image and prestige than with the lives of ordinary Russians. Protecting the president's reputation and demonstrating the strength of the state were the imperatives—as if a state that can't guarantee people's security can be considered viable. It was true that Putin, in his brief television address to the nation after the crisis was over, apologized for the loss of life. Yet in his speech, he could not avoid emphasizing the most important aspects for him and for the authorities: "We proved that you can't bring Russia to her knees." That was what really worried the Kremlin.

The Kremlin was not ready to think about the domestic roots of the terrorist problem. Instead, it equated the struggle with the Chechen separatists with the U.S. struggle against Osama bin Laden and interpreted the hostage crisis as the activity of an international terrorism network. Nobody wanted to acknowledge that the Chechnya problem had not been solved. Besides, President Putin, apparently following Bush's preemptive strategy, said in his speech that he would grant the military broader power to deal with what he called "suspected terrorists," and "would take appropriate measures against these terrorists, wherever they may be."

After vacillating for some time as to what to do about Chechnya, the Kremlin's hawks apparently tried to persuade Putin to start a tough offensive—as if several years of war had not been enough to demonstrate that military measures were futile. This step could only have played into the hands of the terrorists and further radicalized the Chechen population. This meant that Russia had to prepare for more hostage taking and suffering by ordinary citizens.

Negotiations with the Chechens now really looked well-nigh impossible because the hostage crisis discredited the only potential Russian partner for negotiations: Maskhadov, who had failed to distance himself from the terrorists. His legitimacy in the eyes of both Russians and the West had suffered a devastating blow. Even the democrats were skeptical as to the possibility of peace talks with the Chechen president. The fragile hope for talks had been destroyed.

Opinion polls conducted by VTsIOM from October 25 to 28, 2002, showed that the public mood had changed with regard to Chechnya. Now 46 percent of respondents were in favor of a "military solution," and only 44 percent supported the idea of negotiations (in July, 61 percent were for holding talks). The Russian president's actions during the hostage crisis were supported by 85 percent of those polled. Half of those who did not usually approve of his actions had in this case supported him. The president could be satisfied: The crisis and high death toll had not damaged his popularity. He was definitely a lucky politician. The tragedy had breathed new life into the myth of his strong and effective presidency.

In the aftermath of the hostage crisis, Moscow declared its intention of toughening its policy in the Northern Caucasus. It was, however, difficult to toughen it further; all types of weapons and scorched-earth tactics had been used already, without much result. How could this policy become even harsher?

What was clear was that the Praetorians around Putin had decided to use the crisis to make the regime more authoritarian. Manipulated from above, military hysteria and xenophobia had created the ground for an increased role for the security services and more macho rule. Frightened Duma deputies immediately endorsed restrictions concerning media activity, and they were apparently ready to endorse anything to please the president.

Putin let his hawks go public with hard-line rhetoric and with attempts to bring the media under total control, which corresponded to his way of thinking. But he was not ready—yet—to allow his colleagues in the security services to change the existing balance of power and take the dominant upper hand. Besides, society—having supported the president during this new test of his leadership—has been anticipating more than simply tough talk.

After some vacillation and evidently painful deliberation, Putin decided to reject the idea of a harsh campaign in Chechnya—he did not want
a new bloodbath; he was not ready for criticism from democrats; and more
important, he was eager to preserve good relations with the West. Besides,
he should have understood by then that a new offensive would lead him
into a new dead end. Instead, he chose another solution: "Chechenization"
of the conflict. That meant that all responsibility for further developments
would be shared by Chechens loyal to the Kremlin, who would get not
only an endorsement from Moscow but also democratic legitimacy. On
December 12, 2002, the anniversary of the Russian Constitution, the president signed a decree calling for a referendum on a constitution and presidential and parliamentary elections in Chechnya. He did not set a time
frame, but it was assumed in Moscow that the referendum would be held
in March 2003 and that elections would follow in December 2003, at the
time of Russia's parliamentary elections. This plan had to be a political
solution for Chechnya.

Critics of the plan argued that the referendum and elections would be
meaningless given the situation—with fighting continuing and half the
Chechen population having fled the republic. Besides, these steps could
hardly put an end to the hostilities, and in any case, everybody understood
that the results of the elections would be falsified. During the first
Chechen war (1994–1996), the same pattern of pacifying Chechnya had
been followed, without much success. But at the moment, the Kremlin
was not ready for a different option. All other options seemed hardly
viable—so Chechen limbo continued.

Moscow faced many domestic problems on the eve of the elections due in
2003–2004. There was the need to digest and start implementing the laws
passed in the first term. The ruling team had to find the time and means to
secure social services that had been left unattended to. Health, education,
culture, science, pensioners, invalids, the homeless and orphans, neglected
small towns—all these issues waited patiently for the Kremlin's attention.
Even ten terms in office would not be enough for President Putin to solve
all the problems of the land—especially if Moscow continued behaving the

way it had in his first term, through a system of micromanaging and constant pushing of buttons, of manual drive. For example, after the building explosion in Moscow in August 2002, the firefighters, police, and rescue workers who arrived on the scene had to wait two hours for the arrival of minister of emergency situations Sergei Shoigu and only then set to work clearing rubble and looking for victims. Waiting for orders from above has been the major organizing principle of the Putin regime.

The president and his team may not have liked manual drive much, either—it's the most reliable way to have a heart attack. But this is the style of management dictated by the logic of a superpresidency, whereby the leader is the only full-fledged political actor. Everyone else is part of the crowd of extras. Putin's ministers, representatives, officials, and he himself were constantly on the road around the country, fighting fires and floods, turning electricity back on, paying salaries, finding housing, organizing the elections of needed people, settling local conflicts. They were exhausting themselves, but the number of problems kept growing. Local authorities, deprived of powers and money, cowed and cautious, or cynical and gloating, waited for instructions from the center that they were not necessarily planning to obey.

The authorities faced a dilemma: Should they continue working like a squad of firefighters and first-aid workers, putting out the hottest conflicts and dealing with the avalanches most dangerous for general stability, leaving the rest for later? Or should they try to find solutions that would let Russia know that a truly new era was coming, that is, give society confidence and possibilities to decide its own future? This decision demanded that the authorities reexamine the still-reigning vision in the Kremlin *of freedom and order*.

The Yeltsin period gave Russia quite a few freedoms. Never had Russia been so free. But freedom in the absence of orderly habits, with a weak legal culture and egotistical elites, led to chaos and illegality, a disregard for all taboos and restrictions. Russia—frightened by the unfamiliar freedoms and not knowing how to deal with them—swung the pendulum back toward order in 1999. Putin came to power with that idea, and that idea was supported by the country.

But order can be legal or it can be bureaucratic.[13] Putin's Russia followed the path toward bureaucratic order—through reliance on the apparat, administrative methods, subordination, loyalty, and instructions from above. This order could be yet another illusion: Everything seems to work, commands are given, and subordinates report. But the problems are merely pushed more deeply away and with time become explosive. Igor Klyamkin, the Russian researcher, was right when he said that "the problem of transition of the state and society toward the rule of law (overcoming the dominance of the regime over the law) is fundamental."[14] A transition to the rule of law meant that the regime trusted society, giving it the chance to truly participate in government, and was relying not on behind-the-scene pacts, force, and fear, but on the law and on independent institutions. Without a strategy of participation for society, millions of people could not consciously participate in the restoration of Russia, and the modernization of which the president spoke could not take place.

Chapter 9

RUSSIA GOES THROUGH
NEW ELECTIONS

———————— ⚕ ————————

Putin considers his course. Why does Russia choose "old Europe" and disappoint America? The Kremlin's "anti-oligarch revolution." The December Duma elections—certain results in uncertain circumstances. The optimism of youth.

If we look back at 2002 and try to sum up the tendencies of that year in Russia's life, we will see that after a rather energetic start in 2000–2001—when Putin had demonstrated his readiness to define vectors in his policy by centralizing his power, renewing economic reforms, and choosing a pro-Western vector in foreign policy—the Russian president began to show signs of confusion, as if he had lost his sense of direction. By the end of 2002, he was vacillating, apparently trying to decide on whom he could depend, which priority to pursue, what to do in economic policy, and what his dialogue with the West should be about. Apparently, he was under the pressure of mounting constraints on his leadership that he had not been aware of at the beginning of his term. He had to feel discomfort that people from the Yeltsin team remained in key positions: Mikhail Kasyanov was the head of the government, and Alexander Voloshin continued to run the presidential administration. Anatoly Chubais, the godfather of Russian capitalism, who in his time had opposed making Putin Yeltsin's successor, was in charge of the Russian power grid and remained an influential figure who might take politically risky action.[1]

This situation meant that the Yeltsin team continued to act in its corporate and personal interests, and Putin had to accept it. And no one knew whether the old and ailing bear Boris Nikolayevich Yeltsin was still giving advice to his former comrades from his den in a dacha outside Moscow. It was known that he occasionally called Putin to express disapproval of his heir's actions and to remind the new Kremlin boss about the origins of his power. At the same time, Mikhail Kasyanov—impressive, handsome, confident—was turning into a visible political figure. Many people looked at him and said, "And why shouldn't he be the next president of Russia?" Behind Putin's back, his "technical" prime minister was being transformed into a potential rival.[2]

The president could not feel confident and calm as long as the key positions in his administration were held by people from the old team who did not owe their careers and wealth to him. On the contrary, he was beholden to them. But he put up with them. Why? Obviously, because his own team had not learned how to steer confidently and he was definitely afraid of conflict. What if the Yeltsinites decided to resist Putin's attempt to squeeze them out of the Kremlin? Putin did not like conflict. He preferred to untie knots calmly and gradually. It's possible that he kept the spider's web of several clans around him because he was not ready to elevate his *siloviki*, and the technocrats he brought from Saint Petersburg, too high. He undoubtedly could see their weaknesses, inexperience, provinciality, and lack of scope. He needed professional managers, and he needed experienced intriguers and manipulators. But as it happened, they all belonged to the Yeltsin team. Yeltsin knew how to pick people who could survive in Russia's piranha-infested political waters. But the time was nearing when Putin would have to break his dependence on the past and on the people from the past.

The president could no longer postpone picking the package of new economic reforms. In 2000–2002 he had put off the more painful ones, in particular the reform of Gazprom, bank reform, a new stage in tax reform, and the reform of the state apparatus, something he had long discussed but was afraid to start. The president did not touch the social infrastructure, which had not changed much since Soviet times and was in a downward spiral as a result of chronic funding shortages. This included health care, education, and the decrepit housing system. Of course, he would not embark on these difficult reforms. Before the elections, he tried to avoid stirring trouble in society and in the bureaucracy. But he had to set his priorities, at least for himself. He naturally understood that if modernization were to continue, he would have to take on the reorganization of the executive branch—this was crucial for Russia's reform, because it was the key to all other restructuring projects.

And, finally, Putin had to decide on the direction in which Russia would move in the international space. He did not intend to distance the country from the West, much less be hostile to it; he still considered the Western community as the most important resource for Russia's modernization and as an ally in guaranteeing the country's strategic security. But he already sensed that the former rosy dreams of Russia's swift integration into the Western space would remain just that: Neither he nor the political class had any intention of giving up their principles and views on Russia's political system and the way Russia has been ruled, and the West was not prepared to integrate Russia on Russia's terms. Consequently, he had to think about a new formula for the interaction of Russia and the West.

In the meantime, the Russian president, disappointed by the weak partnership between Russia and Europe and America, began paying greater attention to the post-Soviet space. What pushed him in this direction was not only the timeless desire of every Russian leader to expand influence in Eurasia. Russian business, which was feeling cramped in Russia, was demanding guarantees for activity in the post-Soviet economic space. Even liberal technocrats like Anatoly Chubais called on the Kremlin to build an empire, albeit a liberal one, which implied that the government would create conditions for the expansion of Russian business onto the territory of the former USSR. Russian security interests also forced the Kremlin to consider reenergizing relations with the former Soviet republics, particularly on the perimeter of the southern boundaries between Russia and Central Asia and the Caucasus.

Statists in the Kremlin team thought that reactivating the Russian presence on the territory of the former Soviet Union would be a barrier to American and European influence and would help Russia to strengthen the role of regional power. That was natural and not surprising—all former empires jealously regard the regions of their former influence. The new Russian expansionism and motivations behind it had to worry the West, which had not yet determined its own attitude toward Russia—

whether it was to be treated as a partner or as a rival and opponent. Paradoxically, though the West seemed to be ready to acquiesce to Russian authoritarian moods within the country, it found a revival of Moscow's influence in Eurasia unacceptable.

Putin continued pondering and vacillating throughout 2003. He clearly was not ready to clarify his policies, which would have meant making tough choices, and creating winners and losers. He wanted to preserve his image as "president of all Russians." And so the Russian leader kept returning to the Yeltsin tactic of getting support from all sides and continuing the old Yeltsin dance of "one step forward, one step back, one step left, and one step right." Putin was simultaneously a stabilizer, the guardian of the traditional pillars of the state, and a reformer. He was a statist and a Westernizer. He appealed to all strata in the society, but at the same time he tried to avoid taking anyone's position. He doubled and tripled himself, creating amorphous, diffused leadership. This ambiguousness created an impression of indecisiveness—as if Putin and his people did not know which way to turn or what to undertake. This could not continue indefinitely. The elections were coming up, and the president had to determine his new agenda and choose a clearer course: to renew the stalled economic reforms, or to settle for the status quo; or to make a total break with the Yeltsin past, and rid his entourage of Yeltsin's men, or to stay in the shadow of his predecessor; or to embark on a broader collaboration with the West, and limit himself to a cautious selective engagement; or to head toward a harsher authoritarianism; or to maintain the field for political struggle.

It has become customary in Russia to expect the President's Address to the Federal Assembly to reveal the Kremlin's plans. However, Vladimir Putin kept postponing his annual address, apparently still trying to decide on his priorities. When he did give it, on May 16, 2003, he announced: "We are facing serious threats."[3] He spoke of a weak economy, an undeveloped political system, an ineffective bureaucracy, and a complex international situation. Therefore, he concluded, Russia needed to consolidate. That could mean only one thing: Consolidate around the president. It became clear that the Kremlin had decided to build an election platform without the risk of recommending reform, fusing the country around the leader on the basis of threats and search for the scapegoats. But one couldn't avoid one question: What had Putin been doing for three years in the Kremlin if Russia again faced the same old threats?

Putin advanced three primary goals for his future policy: doubling the gross domestic product, overcoming poverty, and modernizing the army. Knowing that these problems could not be solved before the end of his presidential term, he proposed achieving them by 2010, which was beyond his likely second term. The choice of goals showed that the Kremlin was unable to set realistic goals for Putin's election platform and had to settle for utopian ones instead. There was one more idea in Putin's 2003 address—the reform of the Russian bureaucracy. But he had spoken of that in 2002 as well, and nothing had changed. I doubt that before the elections the president was prepared to begin a restructuring that could have made him enemies in the bureaucracy. So the ruling team was going into the elections with only the president as a unifying factor.

Domestic challenges at the moment were not the most urgent. In the early months of 2003, Putin had to concentrate on foreign policy and to respond to events that threatened to change the whole international political situation. The turbulent discussion on Iraq and the search for weapons of mass destruction or guarantees of their dismantling was coming to a head—Washington had decided that Saddam Hussein had not destroyed the weapons, that he had ties to international terrorism, and that he was the main danger. War by the world's sole superpower against the Iraqi regime seemed inevitable, and the military outcome was obvious. Quite a few observers thought that sooner or later, even without the tragedy of September 11, 2001, George W. Bush would have made Iraq his main enemy target: His intransigence toward Saddam was well known.

After lengthy negotiations and pressure on the part of the United States, two main American allies—France and Germany—failed to support Washington's plans. France and Russia declared in the U.N. Security Council that they would veto the second resolution on Iraq, which would have given Washington carte blanche for its military operation. Putin hesitated on his position on Iraq, and at one point it seemed that he would support his friend Bush. Thus, in early February 2003, during his visit to Kiev, the Russian president announced that if Iraq continued to disobey the Security Council's resolutions, it might be worth considering methods harsher than purely diplomatic ones. Obviously, the Russian president had no sympathy for Saddam; he did not trust him and did not share the sense of obligation toward Iraq felt by former Kremlin leaders.

Putin thought long and hard, trying to weigh all the components—the character of the political struggle in Russia on the eve of the elections, the degree of realism of the American goals in Iraq and the Middle East, Russia's position in the triangle with America and Europe, and Russian geopolitical ambitions. This may have been the first occasion in a long time when Moscow did not follow events blindly but chose, deliberated, calculated, and played diplomatic poker. Putin had several choices: One, he could offer his own model for settling the Iraq crisis; two, he could actively support or even join the Americans; three, he could support "old Europe"; and four, he could stay uninvolved and watch events unfold, following the example of China. Moscow had a wide field for maneuvering, and for the first time Russia was needed, and seriously so—both by Washington and the new Paris–Berlin axis. The possibility that Moscow could devise a compromise solution to the Iraq quagmire was very small. That would require not only sophisticated diplomacy for an exit scenario that would satisfy parties with very different desires but also—most important—the irreproachable political weight of Putin in international issues.

Moscow was not prepared for that turn of events. Besides which, stopping Bush, who seemed to have decided to destroy Saddam, would be very difficult. Moscow could choose among the remaining three courses. After long hesitation and under constant pressure and persuasion on the part of Paris and Berlin, Putin chose the European position, speaking out against a violent solution of Saddam's fate. Putin unequivocally supported the U.S. campaign in Afghanistan, considering the war against the Taliban, which constantly threatened Russia's Central Asian borders, in his country's interest; the popular line in Moscow at the time of the Afghan war was that the United States was defending Russian national interests in Afghanistan! But in the case of Iraq, the Russian president apparently did not think the military option was in Russia's interests.

I believe that Moscow—and not Paris, as many felt—played the determining role in deepening the schism in NATO by its choice in early 2003. I am convinced that if Putin had behaved like the Chinese leaders on the Iraq question—that is, taking a wait-and-see position—Jacques Chirac would not have been so active in his opposition. And Gerhard Schröder, without the urging of the French, would have remained neutral. That meant that America could have gotten the Security Council's approval for its war in Iraq, or at least, not received complete criticism for its actions, which is important. Perhaps if the Security Council had approved military action in Iraq, Saddam might have retreated, accepting the U.N. resolutions, and there would have been no reason for going to war.

It was Putin's position against military action in Iraq that made possible the formation of the "coalition of the unwilling," thereby increasing the contradictions throughout the Atlantic community, which finally moved events the way they did. Paris and Berlin understood Russia's potential role, which is why the French president and the Germans devoted so much time to persuading and pleasing Russian minister of foreign affairs Igor Ivanov and Putin himself. I remember Chirac meeting Putin on the tarmac in Paris on February 10, 2003, with a huge bouquet of flowers, as if he were an opera diva, which seemed to surprise the Russian leader, who unexpectedly found himself the object of the French president's ardor, when previously Chirac had treated Putin rather coolly. We can imagine the persuasiveness of Chirac's entreaties for Putin to join the opposition. The arguments were no less convincing in Berlin. Irrespective of the arguments offered by the leaders of "old Europe," Putin's entourage, particularly Igor Ivanov, saw benefit in joining the French–German axis not because they liked Europe but because they disliked America.

In the meantime, Bush was certain that his warm relations with Putin meant that Moscow would not dare speak out against the United States and would in fact support it. That is how the White House understood the strategic partnership between the two countries, which both presidents endorsed. And that is how President Bush apparently understood the nature of his personal relations with Putin. Perhaps the American felt that Putin's strong position on Chechnya guaranteed that he would make a direct analogy with Iraq and support the military variant in the Iraq issue or at least remain neutral. Before Iraq, Putin had agreed with his friend George on all important issues, even if reluctantly. Russian opposition to the military scenario in Iraq was a shock to Washington. This time, Putin showed that Russia could not be taken for granted as a silent and obedient partner. Russia could kick over its traces now and then.

The question thus arises: Why did Putin not support America, when he obviously wanted to preserve his partnership with it? Was Europe's view of the world order and its soft, compromising approach to international problems more acceptable to Moscow than the American use of force? Russia had always preferred military might and force. There was no doubt that in its foreign policy mentality and in its approach to the solution of international problems, the Bush administration was much more understandable for the Russian political class, even on Iraq, than the "soft-bodied" Europeans with their constant calls for dialogue and negotiation.

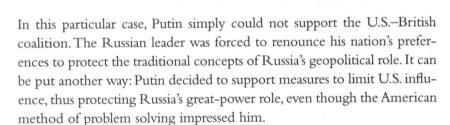

In this particular case, Putin simply could not support the U.S.–British coalition. The Russian leader was forced to renounce his nation's preferences to protect the traditional concepts of Russia's geopolitical role. It can be put another way: Putin decided to support measures to limit U.S. influence, thus protecting Russia's great-power role, even though the American method of problem solving impressed him.

Several factors determined Putin's position in the period of the Iraq events, foremost among them the worry that his open support of America would not only create a hostile belt of Muslim states around Russia but would also upset the Muslim population in Russia. The Russian president had to take into account the growing dissatisfaction of the Russian establishment with what it considered "a payoff" in Russian–American relations, which meant that the Russian political class, in reciprocation for its acquiescence to the U.S. policy, anticipated "deliverables" from Washington, either in the form of investments or other concessions— which according to their view did not come. Finally, Russian elites continued to reject American hegemony, which they still considered a threat to Russia's core interests. The last was one of the most significant considerations; it would be hard to expect the Russian political class, still smarting from the loss of its international status, to give altruistic support to its former rival. Besides, Putin apparently felt, based on information from Russian intelligence, that there were no weapons of mass destruction in Iraq or such a small number as to be no threat to the region's stability. It is obvious that the Kremlin also feared unexpected consequences in its region from war in Iraq.[4] As events later showed, Putin's doubts regarding the consequences of the American scenario in Iraq were justified.

The Russian president also had to take the country's mood into account, especially on the eve of the election. Russians were not prepared to support America's war in Iraq, both because they knew from personal experience (in Afghanistan and Chechnya) that such wars are hopeless and because they did not want to support the United States in the role of world police force. They were not ready to support anyone as a global police force, in fact. In January 2003, 52 percent of Russians were against a possible U.S.–British operation in Iraq and only 3 percent supported it.[5]

A large role was also played by a seemingly insignificant but actually extremely important fact: America took Russia for granted. Chirac and Schröder consistently and demonstratively displayed attention and respect for Moscow, while Washington was silent, as if to say: You're bound to support us without any courting or pleading. I am almost certain that a timely visit to Moscow by Colin Powell or Condoleezza Rice could have changed Putin's position or at least the form in which he presented it. He would not have joined the U.S.–British coalition, but he would not have taken such an active part in the anti-American campaign of "old Europe." The White House did not send its ambassadors to Moscow when it would have influenced the Russian position—before the discussion of the second Security Council resolution on Iraq.

On the basis of Russian interests, Putin was right not to support the military attack on Baghdad. But he could have expressed his disagreement and removed himself from further discussion, thereby not endangering Russia's relations with the United States. That is what the wise Chinese leadership did, calmly stating its disapproval of military action in Iraq one time and never threatening to use its veto in the Security Council against the United States. This would have been the optimal position for Russia. It would have helped Moscow retain equally smooth relations with

Europe and America. Putin's instincts betrayed him, and he allowed himself to be dragged into the "coalition of the unwilling." This was a mistake, diplomatically and politically.

Naturally, Russia's support of "old Europe" was a blow to its partnership with America. The Iraq problem showed that this partnership was built on very fragile underpinnings, if the partners could have such different understanding of the basic strategic challenge worrying the United States. The much closer and systemic partnership of the Atlantic allies was also put to a test, and found wanting. However, the crisis between America and Europe had a chance of being overcome sooner or later, because it was a crisis between states of the same political structure with the same values. In the view of many analysts, the cooling of relations between Russia and America could have repercussions more difficult to overcome due to their different value systems. This is what worried the realistically thinking Russian analysts, who were against Russia's being drawn too far into the French–German axis and who believed that America was much more ready to help Russia to respond at least to its security concerns than was Europe.[6]

And in the meantime, the Russian political class saw Moscow's disagreement with Washington as the Kremlin's sanction for anti-American hysteria and returned to its favorite pastime: attacks on the United States. The old troubadour of the Cold War, General Leonid Ivashov, who was deputy chief of the General Staff under Yeltsin, called for the "formation of an alliance of states against the violent policies of the Americans."[7] I remember the popular television talk show hosted by Svetlana Sorokina on the state-run Channel One. The great majority of participants, with heated emotion, spoke of American aggression against Iraq and how to stop it. "The Americans are bombing unarmed women and children," they said in horror, even though they showed no pity for the Chechens being bombed by the Russian army. Anti-Americanism seemingly had been injected into the mentality of the Russian political class! But this time, the growing negative attitude toward America was universal—all of Europe felt the same way. Even observers who were friendly to the United States could not understand how Americans could have started the invasion of Iraq without thinking through all the possible consequences.

Russian analysts of the great-power orientation sang an even louder chorus of their old song about Russia's getting nothing from cooperation with America. Alexei Pushkov, the host of the television program *Postscriptum*, maintained that "The U.S. . . . is constantly selling us air, clearly thinking that we are supposed to buy that emptiness and pay for it with real, tangible support of America." It's very clear, Pushkov went on, that "Iraq is just a testing ground for America to test its ability to impose violent solutions and to overthrow regimes that don't suit it in other countries." His conclusion was that America's swift victory in Iraq is dangerous, because "inspired by such a victory, the American hawks will definitely take on Iran, Syria, and other countries in the region, paying no attention to the UN or us."[8] Many observers outside Russia thought the same way as Pushkov. Unfortunately, the actions of the American administration throughout 2003 made it possible to conclude that America might continue its attempts at preventive regime change, forgetting that almost all its previous attempts to democratize regimes had failed.

The surge in anti-American feeling among the Moscow elites led some European observers to conclude that the period of cooperation between Washington and Moscow was over. "The Russian–American partnership, proclaimed under the slogan of fighting terrorism, no longer exists. It is dead and buried. Having extended its hand to Washington and received no dividends, Moscow today is distancing itself from America, without any spiritual upset," wrote the French newspaper *Le Figaro*.[9] That was a hasty conclusion. Russian–American relations had been through similar chills before and had returned to a warmer temperature.

After some confusion, the Bush team developed a differentiated approach to the members of the anti-American axis: "Punish France, ignore Germany, and forgive Russia." It has been said that this principle was formulated by Condoleezza Rice. In any case, Bush did decide not to push away Russia. Stephen Sestanovich confirmed that after the anti-Iraq campaign's early success, Washington decided to "forgive Russia and rebuild relations."[10] How can Washington's amazing mildness toward its unfaithful partner be explained? Apparently, Russia—with its geographical position near new sources of world tension, a certain influence in the Arab world, and an ability to play against the West—was needed by America as an ally in the war on terrorism. One could guess that the Bush team thought that it was easier to repair relations with NATO allies than to keep things friendly with Russia, which was unbalanced and did not have a Western system. That consideration might have been instrumental when Washington decided to seek a new rapprochement with Russia. Besides, "It's the psychology, Stupid!" I believe that both Bush and Putin had developed some warm feelings toward each other and it also helped to build bridges, whereas Bush's antipathy toward Chirac and Schröder was more difficult to overcome.

In its turn, Moscow also realized that it had to smooth over relations with Washington before the chill became irreversible. Russia supported the U.N. resolution that legitimized the presence of the U.S.–British coalition in Iraq and decided at that moment not to demand full payment of Iraq's debt to Russia or preference for Russian oil companies in post-Saddam Iraq. In the summer and fall of 2003, Moscow was unusually forthcoming toward the United States. Putin's steps toward Washington irritated not only the Russian oil companies, which had hoped to keep their positions in the new Iraq, but also his loyalists. Yet again, Putin in his relations with America went against the mood of the Russian elite, which demanded militancy and harshness from the president.

The now-habitual spring downturn in United States–Russia relations soon improved. On May 20, 2003, Bush came to the festivities for the 300th anniversary of Saint Petersburg, Putin's hometown, demonstrating that despite their disagreements on Iraq he still treated Putin with trust as before. In group events involving all the world leaders, the aloofness verging on coldness between Bush and Chirac and Schröder was glaring. The American president pointedly ignored his Atlantic allies and demonstrated his friendliness toward Putin. But emotions have no place in politics; or rather, they always reflect conscious interests, and this time Washington's interest was in bringing Putin closer and through dialogue with Moscow breaking up the "coalition of the unwilling." Now, it looked as if Putin's role in holding together an anti-American axis was understood by Washington.

Let me make a brief digression about the Saint Petersburg summit. This May–June 2003 summit was a gift for Putin. All the Western leaders came to Saint Petersburg. They did not come to be tourists but out of respect for Putin, who had managed to become an equal in the club of world leaders—quite an achievement for a street kid from a simple family, who had recently been a modest, unnoticed man, always playing supporting roles. The respectful treatment from Bush, Blair, Chirac, and Schröder was not for show but seemed to be sincere. They must have been comparing Putin with Yeltsin, and Putin profited from the comparison. This Russian leader, perhaps not the most charismatic, in fact rather unremarkable and unimpressive, turned out to be more goal oriented and successful than could be expected from a man with no political experience or even political ambitions. In any case, it was he who stabilized the enormous and incomprehensible country, still dangerous in the eyes of the Western community, and it was he who took the side of the West in the fight against the new global threat.

Saint Petersburg did look renewed and improved. But the facades of the palaces could not hide the dilapidated apartment buildings and courtyards. The government spent tens of millions of dollars on reconstructing architectural monuments, and it created fantastic window dressing. Behind it continued the gray impoverished life of ordinary people who could barely make ends meet. Once again, as it had been for hundreds of years, the need to maintain a proud state grandeur proved more important to Russia's ruling class than meeting the basic needs of ordinary Russians. Of course, Putin, who came from that milieu and had lived on a landing that smelled of rats, understood those needs. But once in the Kremlin, he became a functionary and symbol of the state, and tradition required him to think in other categories. Otherwise, he would be in danger of losing that role.

The new Iraq war once again confirmed the superficial character of the Russian–American partnership, which seemed to be shaken by the first serious challenge. At the same time, the Iraq events showed that Putin and Bush did not want to deepen the contradictions. Angela Stent wrote perceptively, "The U.S.–Russian relationship has returned to its prewar equilibrium since the St. Petersburg and G-8 Evian summits. . . . Nevertheless, the relationship, although strong rhetorically and endorsed enthusiastically by both leaders, lacks substance."[11] Leon Aron also concluded that the Russian opposition to the American operation in Iraq "makes us ask serious questions regarding the essence and future prospects of the U.S.–Russian partnership after September 11."[12] Russian analysts were even more skeptical about the Russian–American relationship.[13]

And in fact, the relations between America and Russia throughout 2003 showed that both countries had problems in finding areas and issues that would not divide them but bring them together. Both capitals sensed the need to develop constructive dialogue on issues of security and energy. But it required quite a bit of effort to turn that need into a concrete agenda tied to domestic interests. One of the most potentially fruitful ideas for the Russian–American partnership—dialogue on energy—was in reality the strongest example of the conundrum facing U.S.–Russian relations. Russia unsuccessfully awaited capital investment from the United States in the infrastructure for transporting oil to America. And American business was waiting for a more reliable investment climate and permission from the Kremlin to build private oil pipelines, which was delayed by the resistance of Russian state monopolies. And then came worrisome signals that caused American business to set aside its plans for direct investment in the Russian economy: the Khodorkovsky case (more about this below) and the complications with Sakhalin-3, which involved Exxon Mobil and Chevron Texaco.[14]

Everything suggested that America and Russia could manage without each other, because their collaboration was not decisive in guaranteeing their domestic development. The Russian–American partnership was turning in to a facade created by the powerful and efficient diplomatic and political machines in both countries, convenient for both sides, but neither side would ever admit that they were largely pretending to be partners. There was only one area that really demanded mutual understanding and close cooperation and defied imitation: security. The long tradition of Russian–American security dialogue has produced groups of professionals in both capitals who could manage the security agenda and damage control without much political interference. These people knew each other, in most cases trusted each other, and understood the dangers they had to cope with and limit. But they could manage only the old mutual deterrence paradigm of relations; they could not exchange it for a more effective formula that was adequate to new needs. That would demand not only the political will of their leaders but, more importantly, shared values.

It was difficult to avoid the impression that Putin started to follow the dominant beliefs among the Russian political class, which suspected that partnership with America was unlikely to help with Russia's modernization, and he might have begun to have doubts about the sincerity of the U.S. political establishment's interest in Russia's regaining a weighty geopolitical role. Bush apparently also saw that Russia was unlikely to be a consistent ally in American strategic goals. Angela Stent was very much to the point describing the moods on both sides: "Many Russians question whether the Putin administration has benefited concretely from its support for the war on terror. Russians are to some extent justified in citing the lack of initial economic support after the fall of the Soviet Union and the enlargement of NATO as sources of disappointment or anger over broken promises. However, Russia itself has not delivered on promises it made to the United States, especially with respect to the proliferation of weapons of mass destruction to 'rogue' states and troops withdrawal from Moldova and Georgia, as mandated by [the Organization for Cooperation and Security in Europe]." Besides, as Stent pointed out, American officials "were disinclined to believe that Russia should be richly rewarded economically or that it should be treated as a great power, given its weakened situation."[15] Thus, a litany of disappointed expectations and hopes on both sides went on and on, sometimes reflecting an attempt to justify either lack of desire to pursue the partnership's course or an attempt to explain policy mistakes or a lack of vision.

In this regard, Sestanovich wrote: "American demands for more supportive policies are growing. Confidence that Putin will offer such support is not."[16] As Russian observers saw it, Putin had given Bush more than enough support without any reciprocity. We can't rule out the fact that Putin worried that closer proximity between Moscow and Washington could complicate his position with the Russian elite, which was suspicious of America. After Russia failed to support him on Iraq, Bush maintained cordial relations with Putin but was unlikely to feel his former goodwill toward the Russian president. He must have known that he could not count on Moscow. In other words, both sides had to be dissatisfied with each other, and both sides had reason for their dissatisfaction.

What did the Russian people think of America these days? According to the data of the Foundation for Public Opinion, in late 2002, 30 percent of those polled considered the United States friendly toward Russia, 51 percent hostile, and 18 percent had no opinion. In March 2003, at the height of the Iraq events, 27 percent considered America friendly, 59 percent hostile, and 13 percent had no opinion. The Iraq war and the position of the Kremlin influenced the attitude of Russians toward America. The warming of relations between the leaders had an immediate impact on public opinion. In August 2003, 37 percent of Russians considered America friendly, 48 percent hostile, and 19 percent had no opinion. Interestingly, 29 percent of respondents characterized the relations between the two countries as a "forced partnership," 17 percent felt that Russia and America were more equal partners, and 16 percent thought they were more rivals than partners.[17] But in any case, 46 percent of Russians spoke of partnership with the United States, and this showed that anti-Americanism was not the dominant feeling in the public—despite the consistent effort of the statist- and nationalist-oriented ideologues and politicians to strengthen anti-American moods in Russian society.

The events in Iraq in 2003 gave a clearer picture of how Russia's foreign policy evolved. First of all, Iraq showed that this time Moscow no longer attempted to save Saddam, as it had during the first Iraq war in 1991.[18] Second, Russia tried to avoid deepening of the conflict with Washington, even when it disagreed with U.S. policy. Moscow's critical attitude was much softer than that of America's most vocal critic, Jacques Chirac. Third, the Iraq debacle showed the limits of the United States–Russia partnership. Though Russia was unable to be an equal partner, it was not prepared—out of great-power considerations, among others—to become America's junior partner, even though it had acted as one several times. Consequently, the contradictions and instability of that partnership were congenital. Fourth, unable to implement its position independently, Russia turned to international institutions, primarily the United Nations and its Security Council, where Russia's membership was one of the few remaining guarantees of its great-power status. Fifth, the Iraq events confirmed both Russia's fear of America's excessive strengthening and its role as world arbiter and also Moscow's attempts to find ways to limit that role, as long as it did not involve confrontation with the

United States. Russia's concerns about American hegemony and unilateralism were shared by America's Atlantic allies, which incidentally tried even more actively to constrain U.S. predominance.

The schism inside NATO over Iraq and the issues of the new world order, which revealed the differences in the political thinking, mentality, and even strategic agenda of the United States and Europe, theoretically expanded the field of action for Russian diplomacy and raised Russia's role in the international arena, because its collaboration was needed by both Europe and America. However, that same division in the West simultaneously disoriented the Russian political establishment and the public about the possible partners and framework for Russia's international role. The elites said, with growing frequency, "The West doesn't know where it's going. Let them figure it out first, we'll just wait. Or take our own path again." The tensions and loss of direction in the Western community complicated Russia's movement toward the West.

And yet another event was drawing near that would catch the attention of Russia and the world. In June 2003, Alexei Pichugin, the unknown chief of security for YUKOS, the largest oil company in Russia, was arrested on charges of organizing a contract murder. At that moment, few people could have predicted that this was only the beginning. On July 3, Platon Lebedev, one of the major shareholders and managers of YUKOS, was arrested on charges of embezzling shares of a company called Apatit. People who understood the inner workings of Russian politics could sense that a storm was brewing. The next day, Mikhail Khodorkovsky, the head of YUKOS, and his friend Leonid Nevzlin, the largest shareholder, were called in by the general prosecutor for questioning.

Now it was clear to everyone: The Kremlin had opened the hunt on YUKOS. There was only one question: Why YUKOS? None of the Russian oligarchs were angels, and they all had skeletons in the closet. Why was YUKOS being attacked just when it was trying to come out of the shadow economy and be accepted as a civilized, transparent, law-abiding company both in Russia and the West? After all, this was the fourth-largest producer of oil in the world, and a number of regional budgets in Russia and the state of the Russian market as a whole depended on it. Not long before this story began, YUKOS and Sibneft had agreed on a merger (one approved by the Kremlin), which would have created a global giant that could easily compete with the largest Western corporations. And suddenly, this blew!

Events unfolded rapidly. The YUKOS offices were searched. Khodorkovsky, trying to stay unruffled, told reporters, "If I am given the choice of leaving the country or going to jail, I'll go to jail." But at the time, few people, including Khodorkovsky himself, believed that it would get that far. Still, on October 25, 2003, Khodorkovsky was arrested. The arrest looked like something out of a potboiler action film: Masked special forces soldiers blocked Khodorkovsky's plane with trucks at the Novosibirsk Airport, and with shouts of "Down on the floor!" burst into the cabin. The head of YUKOS was brought under guard to the general prosecutor's office in Moscow for questioning, as if he were a particularly dangerous prisoner. He was accused of hiding his profits, not paying taxes, and embezzling, and new charges were starting to pile up. Apparently, the authorities needed to make a point, and they did: The Russian elites shuddered, seeing Russia's most influential and wealthy businessman in handcuffs—still an unusual sight for Russia.

Khodorkovsky had been warned more than once that the Kremlin was unhappy with him and that he could have problems. But he must have believed in his luck and thought it enough to have the protection of Alexander Voloshin and the Yeltsin group and good ties to the West. The arrest of the head of YUKOS showed that no one was untouchable as far as the Kremlin was concerned. Soon after Khodorkovsky's arrest, Voloshin, the chief of the presidential administration, resigned. He was the gray cardinal of the Kremlin, who held all the ropes and symbolized the succession of power. A chapter in Russian development was coming to an end: the history of the Russian oligarchy and the history of the Yeltsin political Family.

The YUKOS story should not have been a surprise to the attentive observer of the Russian political scene. The oligarchs with political ambitions and the Yeltsin cronies in key positions did not fit the new architecture of Putin's political regime. Imagine what Putin felt, having to deal every day with Voloshin, who saw the president as being in another position and another weight class. There is no doubt that Putin, due to his upbringing, could not stand the oligarchs either, suspecting them evidently of economic crimes and political ambitions. The president was bound to run out of patience sooner or later and begin his farewell to the final symbols of the passing era.[19]

But why was it Khodorkovsky who fell victim to the Kremlin's attack on the oligarchs? journalists wondered. Why not Roman Abramovich, the Yeltsin Family's "moneybag," who openly transferred his funds abroad, outraging Russians with his extravagant purchases, most egregiously of the British Chelsea soccer team? Why not other billionaires Potanin, or Aven, or Fridman? Were their reputations so much better?

Khodorkovsky, one of the most aggressive Russian businessmen, had undoubtedly made enemies. He might have had many more personal enemies than his colleagues in the oligarch club, simply because he was more successful. True, he was more successful mainly because he was both clever and ruthless in achieving his goals. His competitors, the state-owned oil companies Rosneft and Transneft and the private LukOil, were interested in his annihilation. There were quite a few people eager to snatch a piece of the property of powerful YUKOS in the circles close to the Saint Petersburg team, who had come too late for the privatization feast, when all the good chunks of property were taken by the lucky members of the Yeltsin group. But these reasons were not enough to put Russia's richest man behind bars. Khodorkovsky was doing what all businessmen were doing; that is, he tried to minimize his taxes by using offshore companies and loopholes in the law.

The reasons for the attack on YUKOS were initially mostly political, and they would have come into play no matter what President Putin's personal feelings were about Khodorkovsky and YUKOS. That Putin could barely conceal his antipathy for the head of YUKOS merely sealed the inevitability of what happened.[20] Systemic developments were more important than emotions and feelings. The new regime formed under Putin rejected all the potentially independent political actors who could violate the logic of absolute rule. It was not Khodorkovsky's wealth but the fact that he had

begun thinking politically that was making him a threat to the regime—
he was independently making contacts with Western governments, especially with the American administration, without working through the
Kremlin, and he was opening up his company and reducing its dependence on the state. He was a threat not on a personal level but as the
embodiment of a new tendency in the state–business paradigm, which
meant that the oligarchy openly challenged not only the leader but also
the way Russia was ruled. Khodorkovsky was seemingly thinking about
an alternative strategy, about a different regime and system, or creating the
impression that he was contemplating movement in this direction. The
YUKOS owners had openly discussed the variant for transforming a presidential republic into a parliamentary one and the ways of increasing their
influence on the Duma and the government.[21] All these discussions
undoubtedly were made known to the Kremlin.

What had accelerated the events was the fact that YUKOS, in the most
cynical and aggressive way, torpedoed government decisions in parliament
if they limited its interests. Khodorkovsky's people did it by openly buying off deputies en masse and blocking the adoption of the cabinet's decisions. The company's managers did not particularly hide their goal of
forming a powerful lobby in the new Duma, trying to bring in their own
people through the lists of various parties, including communists and liberals. Putin regarded this political activity as a threat to his power, and it
was a threat to his ability to control the legislature.

The blow against Khodorkovsky came first because he was trying to
escape the control of the state; and second, because he was the potential
founder of a new political tendency that might—if it took hold—threat-
en the existing regime. As a businessman trying to play by the open rules,
the head of YUKOS represented a perfectly positive trend. But it is not clear
how he would have used his political influence—to promote his corporate interests or for the common good. So far, with his activity, he had
demonstrated that he could move in any direction. We will never learn
which way Khodorkovsky would have gone once he had formed his
political base. But Khodorkovsky's evolution in 2002–2003 allows us to
suppose that he might have started thinking about a new formula for tri-
angular business–power–society relations, and it is not unlikely that he
would have found it, if he had not been imprisoned.

What links the case of the fallen oligarch with the departure of Voloshin, Yeltsin's main player? Simply this: Voloshin was the last protection for the oligarchs left in Putin's camp. He apparently had tried to help Khodorkovsky and failed. And Voloshin, a subtle politician, understood that the time was up for the Yeltsinites and that he had overstayed his welcome in the Kremlin. He had done his work and had to leave before he was thrown out.[22] In other words, by taking Khodorkovsky out of play, the authorities were solving two problems simultaneously—striking a devastating blow against the oligarchy and the Yeltsin loyalists. Only by cutting the leash to Yeltsin's ruling corporation and by destroying autonomous actors could the regime of personified power consolidate itself—if its leader did not dare to start "de-hermeticizing" it. Putin did not show such an intention, and his turn toward familiar means of survival could be understood: Restructuring the political regime would have taken some time and its consequences would have been unpredictable, and he had to deal with obstruction to his power now.

Why did the anti-oligarch revolution begin in the summer of 2003? That is also understandable—the elections that were supposed to legitimize the Putin regime were approaching, and the Putin team could not countenance any opposition to its own scenario. Khodorkovsky's attempt to privatize the parliament was in the way of the Kremlin plan and also set a bad example for the business community.

Of course, along with the political aims in the campaign against YUKOS, some administration officials also had economic aims—a desire to redistribute the oil giant's assets in their own favor or to change its management so as to gain control. The events of 2004 showed that this goal was also part of the campaign against YUKOS and Khodorkovsky, and after YUKOS was politically finished, the economic aim became the dominant one in dealing with it.

For liberals and democrats, the YUKOS story was yet another warning of the direction the authorities were taking. For many, of course, Khodorkovsky was not an attractive figure, just like the other oligarchs, because they discredited not only privatization but also political freedoms, which they were using to promote their own interests. But the attack on Khodorkovsky and its means proved that the executive branch had begun setting limits on the most powerful group that could counterbalance it. Once it had neutralized the political ambitions of big business, the ruling team could easily control the Russian political arena, which already resembled a desert landscape. But still there was some bubble beneath the surface, and one could imagine that the logic of centralization would force the Kremlin to continue its cutting of the political grass unless all signs of uncontrolled political ambition were gone. At that moment, there remained some spots if not of resistance then of spontaneity: grudging regional elites, media people, and of course intellectuals, who have always been difficult to deal with.

The attack on the biggest oil company outraged some—but not all—Russian liberals. "If YUKOS doesn't pay everything it should into the budget, its leader should not be taken hostage and then be blackmailed for ransom, the way professional kidnappers act. It is not appropriate for a state. The law prescribes civilized methods of action in these cases," wrote the journalist Otto Latsis.[23] Yevgeny Yasin, the godfather of Russian reformers, said that the attack on Khodorkovsky would inevitably lead to a weakening of big business and an increase in its loyalty to the state, as well as to a strengthening of the agencies of law and order. But these pluses, as the regime saw them, were far outweighed by the minuses: violation of justice, the inculcation of shadow rules of the game, the loss of the regime's reputation, and the reduction in investment in Russia. "Forget economic growth and development! Forget rights and liberties! The country is moving backward, toward the early 1980s," warned Yasin.[24] But these were lone voices of indignation. Quite a few liberals and democrats preferred to keep silent or approved the action of the authorities. Even representatives of Yabloko, which received financial support from YUKOS, tried to distance themselves from the Khodorkovsky case, not only because oligarchs were not liked even among democratic circles but also because the Yabloko people were disgusted by the YUKOS attempts to make them instruments of its lobbying efforts in the Duma.

What was the public reaction to the YUKOS case? Seventy-four percent supported the Kremlin's "anti-oligarchic revolution," which was to be expected, for the oligarchs and their lifestyle and irresponsibility had long become a source of irritation. The political class, with the exception of a few weak voices of protest, refrained from commentary. The Kremlin had become so strong that no one wanted to get into a fight over Khodorkovsky. However, at first there were contradictory opinions at the very top about how to deal with YUKOS. At least Prime Minister Mikhail Kasyanov was not afraid to say on July 24, 2003, that violent methods of dealing with the company were detrimental to the economy. As for business, at the first the oligarchs tried sending Putin letters and demanding meetings with him, to help YUKOS.[25] But Putin did not respond. Then big business understood the message and lay low trying to survive individually.[26]

Although the majority of Russians supported the government attack on YUKOS, only one-fourth (26 percent) felt that it was brought about by the company's financial misdeeds and had nothing to do with politics; 18 percent thought that it was a power struggle; 9 percent thought that the attack was related to the coming elections; 10 percent thought that this was the start of a war on all the oligarchs; and 3 percent had no opinion. Curiously, 54 percent felt that the prosecutor was doing Putin's bidding.[27] Obviously, ordinary citizens had a rather good understanding of what was going on and saw the political underpinnings.

The government's attack on YUKOS and the primarily positive public response indicated more than the fact that the struggle for power and resources continued in Russia. It also meant that the Kremlin still could not give up direct control of business, and that the Russian state had not fully accepted the results of privatization. The whole story and perception of it among Russians also meant that Russian business failed to develop a sense of social responsibility and create a dialogue with society, which still perceived business as robbery.

If society accepted calmly the destruction of one of the most effective companies, it meant that privatization was still considered illegitimate in Russia. It was understandable; the criminal takeover of state property by a bunch of entrepreneurial people was too fresh and blatant, and big business was too disdainful of the people.[28] And the people felt frustration and indignation watching as a few upstarts grew fantastically rich just because they were in the right place to pick up state property for a song.

However, the public view of corruption was oversimplified. Quite a few people in Russia did not understand that corruption was an even more important problem than privatization, and that corruption was not the consequence of the existence of big business but of the state acting as a parasite on the economy and of the bureaucracy keeping tight controls over business. People did not see that most of the Russian oligarchs had been appointed by the bureaucracy to take property out of state control, and that they were privatizing property primarily in the interests of the bureaucracy. As Igor Klyamkin said, "It will not be easy to explain that a reexamination of the results of privatization does not change things per se. Or that the businesses under fire are the very ones getting out of the situation created by dirty privatization and trying to overcome its negative consequences."[29] A paradoxical situation was created, with the state attacking a company that was trying to become transparent, which in the end had to reduce corruption. The motives behind the attack on YUKOS were evident: Bureaucracy did not want to lose control over it. However, these motives were not always understood by Russian society, partially because Khodorkovsky's people had actively participated in the corruption of the state and power, and few believed in Russia that oligarchs all of a sudden could change their ways.

The events surrounding YUKOS and the discussion of legitimacy of the privatization increased the illusion among some social groups that a redistribution of part of the riches of the oligarchs would solve Russia's problems and help the war on poverty. The idea of taking away "natural rent" from big business, that is, taking part of its profits, became popular in Russia.[30] In fact, taxation on big business in Russia was not very effective, and more taxes had to be collected, particularly from the oil companies. But an endless raising of taxes and the absence of stable rules of the game could kill the goose that laid the golden egg. The growth of redistribution sentiments among some layers of Russian society threatened to stop (and for a long time) the expansion of the Russian market. And some people did not understand that taking capital from business and giving it to the state was unlikely to solve the poverty issue. On the contrary, there would be even more corruption. The history of redistribution, including the 1917

Russian Revolution, tells us that confiscated wealth never trickles down to the people but is taken by groups close to the regime.[31]

The already tense atmosphere around big business was intensified by the publication of a special edition of *Forbes Russia* in May 2004, with a list of the 100 richest people in the country. It included well-known names, such as the recent directors of state companies like Rem Vyakhirev of Gazprom and his deputy, Vyacheslav Sheremet. Also in the list of Russian billionaires was Elena Baturina, wife of Moscow mayor Yuri Luzhkov. Tycoons on the list immediately started a hysterical campaign denying that they were as rich as the *Forbes* reporters had calculated. They knew that in the new political environment, a list like that would be studied closely by the prosecutor's office. In any case, Putin must have examined the information on Russian billionaires closely. The publication soon showed practical consequences. The Kremlin began working on weakening the position of Luzhkov and his group, which had long been an irritant for the federal authorities. Luzhkov's billionaire wife complicated his struggle for survival.[32]

The prologue to the Russian elections was the presidential election in Chechnya on October 5, 2003, which demonstrated the Kremlin's ability to get the results it wants. Moscow brilliantly ran its operation to get its candidate elected. Akhmad Kadyrov had demonstrated for several years both his loyalty to Putin and his ability to hold his power with an iron fist in Chechnya. The Kremlin spin doctors quickly and without any finesse or pretext got all the other candidates for the Chechen presidency to withdraw. One of them, Aslanbek Aslakhanov, was offered a position as adviser to Putin (an offer he couldn't refuse). Another one, Malik Saidulaev, was removed long-distance by the courts over technical errors in his candidacy. Moscow got rid of everyone who didn't quit on his own. The Kremlin did not want any opposition to Kadyrov. Moscow needed his total victory, and Moscow assured it. To the amazement of observers, Chechnya voted for Kadyrov, giving him 82.55 percent of the vote.

The result of the Chechen election was a return to the old Soviet method of total affirmation, which meant that the number of votes was not important but who was counting the votes did matter. The Moscow authorities got Kadyrov legitimacy for his almost-dictatorial rule. It's possible that a few people did vote for the new Chechen president; after all, the Chechens were tired of war. They wanted peace and elementary order. Kadyrov was the only alternative offer. At least it was a Chechen alternative, and part of the Chechen population took it, however reluctantly. But such a large majority for Kadyrov appeared to prove that the election had been rigged.

Thus, the Putin scenario for the Chechenization of the regime—that is, the gradual transfer of power in the republic to loyal Chechens—was under way. At that moment, it seemed the only way to solve the problem, and it looked successful. But in reality this puppet show inherently had a legitimacy problem and undermined Putin's scenario of Chechenization: Chechens wanted to chose their leader themselves, even if they were doomed to live in Russia's shadow.

Putin seemed to trust Kadyrov as much as he could trust anyone. Despite the objections of his generals, Putin was betting on a former Chechen mufti who only recently had declared a jihad against Russia. The Russian military hated the dictatorial Kadyrov, who brushed them aside and preferred to push his plans through Putin personally. Amazingly, Kadyrov managed to get more and more autonomy out of Moscow. He was becoming a more independent leader than Aslan Maskhadov had been in his time. Many simply shrugged, looking at Moscow's new satrap in Chechnya: Why had the center initiated the second Chechen war, if the result was still the same?—Chechnya was moving away from Russia. But this time, the head of Chechnya was not a former Soviet colonel with whom one could talk but a warlord with dictatorial ambitions to build his own regime.

The omnipotence of any clan and any warlord in Chechnya was an illusion, however. Everyone knew that Kadyrov was a doomed man. He knew it, too, as if he were walking a tightrope. He was threatened fighting Moscow, and he was threatened even more fighting his old comrades-in-arms. Attempts were regularly made on his life. His closest loyalists and relatives, who acted as his bodyguards, died by the dozens. The separatists could not forgive his betrayal. Before switching sides to join Moscow in 1999, he had been one of them. He had been lucky, for he had managed to survive and even constrain the activity of the Chechen rebels. He neutralized them in a simple way: Those rebels who came out of the woods and promised not to fight were taken into the ranks of his personal guards. This regiment had grown to several thousand people (varying estimates of 3,000–5,000) and it was a force to be reckoned with. The Kadyrov men had begun behaving in ways that angered the civilian population. In time, they could have become a new problem for the federal authorities.

Stability in Chechnya, being dependent on a single leader and the authoritarian regime built under him using his own clan, was not secure. The partisan war in Chechnya continued, albeit at a lower intensity. Land mines blew up federal troops and pro-Moscow Chechen officials. Terrorist acts in Russia by the Chechen rebels became routine. Maskhadov and Shamil Basayev, the separatist leaders, remained elusive, and this raised many questions regarding Moscow's political will to neutralize them or regarding the corruption that prevented federal services from eliminating them. The populace hated the Russian troops, who were considered an occupier force. The demoralized soldiers continued their rampages against civilians, feeding the spiral of mutual hatred.

Russia had grown accustomed to life with the suppurating Chechen wound. Chechnya kept flaring up with bloody terrorist acts, even in Moscow.

While the attack on YUKOS unfurled, the election campaign for the Duma began. In fact, clamping down on YUKOS was part of the campaign. At the beginning of 2003, polls showed that 14 percent were planning to vote for the Kremlin party of power, United Russia, and that the Communists could expect 24 percent. The Kremlin would lose, and that was not acceptable to it. The parliamentary elections are the Russian New Hampshire, an indicator of how the presidential election will go. The picture in the spring of 2004 was not a pretty one for the authorities. The Kremlin's campaign against the oligarchs became a very effective means for raising the ratings of United Russia. YUKOS had supported the

Communists and the democratic parties—Yabloko and the Union of Right Forces (SPS). The blow against Khodorkovsky made it possible to also discredit in the public eye the political parties he had sponsored. For SPS voters, most of whom belonged to the new middle class, the connection with the oligarchs was not devastating, but the Khodorkovsky connection with the Communists and Yabloko elicited a severely negative reaction among voters.

The new parliamentary campaign, unlike previous ones in Russia, influenced the character of the Putin victory. But it could not change the general vector of Russia's development. The 1993 Duma elections determined the process of public support for the new regime created by Yeltsin after the existing parliament had been disbanded. Those elections took place at the same time as the referendum on the new Constitution and became a system-forming factor. The 1995 parliamentary elections were a form of confrontation between the Kremlin and the Communist Party, which won and thereby gave parliament an opposition character. The 1999 Duma elections were a power struggle between two ruling clans—Yeltsin and the Luzhkov-Primakov group. Those elections created the preconditions for Putin's rise to power. The loss of the United Russia Party, which Putin supported, could have meant that Yeltsin would have picked a different successor.

The 2003 elections no longer determined the fate of the regime and the system. But they could weaken Putin's legitimacy in his second term, if United Russia lost. No one doubted that Putin would win a second term. But he could win in the first round, beating all the other candidates, or he could get a modest win in the second round. The Kremlin, naturally, wanted a landslide victory for United Russia, which would demonstrate Russia's total support for its president.

What were the issues of the new election campaign? The first was over who would win the biggest percentage, United Russia or the Communist Party. The "party of power" had never come first in the Duma elections.[33] The second question was which of the liberal parties would get into the Duma, if any. The third issue was whether the Kremlin would try to change the party system and whether it would succeed.

The Kremlin decided not to reinvent the wheel and repeat the formula used in 1999. In those elections, the power party used the popularity of

Putin, who refused to give his own program. United Russia did the same thing in 2003. But this time, the party used its so-called administrative resources more actively and openly. That is, it enjoyed the support of the authorities on all levels, as well as access to the national state-run television channels, which had become the most powerful method in Russia for forming public opinion. But United Russia was no longer new and fresh, so a new gimmick was needed to guarantee its success. An enemy was needed to agitate the electorate and unify it. If you don't have your own platform and your own slogans, you need to consolidate people against something else. In the 1999 elections, the journalists who worked to promote the regime attacked the Communist Party and Luzhkov and Primakov. In 2003, the enemy was once again the Communist Party, for it was still the biggest opposition party. Therefore, the fewer votes the left won, the more convincing the victory of United Russia.[34] Journalists close to the regime, politicians, and bureaucrats began denouncing the Communists, once again the Kremlin's enemy number one.

It almost seemed as if the Communist Party existed only to become the whipping boy during elections and guarantee victory for the authorities. Not many people wondered why thirteen years after the fall of the USSR and the defeat of communism, the Communist Party remained the only real political party and why the Communists had the support of a rather significant segment of the people. This fact was a judgment on the efficacy of the regime, because the opposition is always a reflection of it; therefore, the regime was unable to solve society's social ills, and the most needy saw the Communists as their protectors. Yet there were signs that the administration was creating an artificial field of activity for the Communist Party, whose leaders, particularly Zyuganov, showed their spinelessness and fear of confrontation with the regime. That is why the Kremlin at the moment did not want full and devastating collapse of the communists, who have turned into a permanent sparring partner of the authorities.

This time it must be admitted the Communists set themselves up for attack by including YUKOS representatives on their party lists. This was a gift for the Kremlin; it gave its political television programming a wonderful topic: how the Communists sold out.

Another direction for the Kremlin was the formation of the left-wing patriotic bloc Rodina (Motherland), whose goal was to take away leftist and nationalist votes from the Communist Party. Two ambitious politicians were put at the head of Rodina—Sergei Glazyev and Dmitri Rogozin. The former appealed to the left-wing voters. The latter began to play the role of a new Zhirinovsky, and with obvious success.[35]

The Duma election on December 7 brought a resounding victory for the regime. For the first time, the Kremlin managed to assure the victory of the pro-Kremlin party.[36] The voter turnout was 55.75 percent. These parties crossed the 5 percent barrier: United Russia, 37.57 percent; Communist Party, 12.61 percent; Liberal Democratic Party (LDPR), 11.45 percent; and Rodina, 9.02 percent. "None of the above" got 4.70 percent. This was the first time that the liberals and democrats did not get into the Duma: Yabloko got 4.30 percent; and SPS, 3.97 percent.[37] Including the single-mandate regions, the Duma's seats were distributed as follows: United Russia had 305 mandates, the Communist Party, 51, LDPR, 36, Rodina, 39, and independent deputies, 15.

The PACE delegation of election observers came to a sad conclusion: "The elections were free but unfair, and the Russian movement toward democracy has significantly slowed."[38] This conclusion may sound contradictory, but it reflects Russian reality. The point is that in the 2003 Duma elections the authorities no longer had to expend excessive effort to assure the victory of the pro-Kremlin party. Yes, they used pressure and the "administrative resources." But on the whole, there was probably less manipulation and cheating during the elections and ballot counting than before. The elections were relatively free. They were not fair because for the last several years the arena for independent self-expression had been narrowed. Under those conditions, parties and movements in opposition to the regime could not get equal time with United Russia, which monopolized television and the other media. The most unfair aspect of the election (as had been the case in 1999, as well) was that United Russia was supported by the most influential politician in Russia, who for many people was the personification of the state and its symbol: President Putin. His support changed the odds greatly in favor of United Russia, practically guaranteeing its success.

United Russia clung to the president's ratings from the start of the campaign. The party did not fight, it did not participate in televised debates, it did not present its platform—it did nothing. The party's message was, "If you're for Putin, you have to vote for us!" Russians equated the president with stability and the hope for an improved life. A significant portion of the public that pinned its hopes only on Putin switched its support to the party that he supported.

To be fair, other factors also worked for United Russia, particularly the weakness of the rest of the participants in the election and their inability to present new leaders and slogans to attract voters. The Kremlin was also helped with the "anti-oligarch revolution," which let both United Russia and the new Kremlin clone Rodina, as well as numerous small pro-Kremlin parties created on the eve of the elections, play up the war on the oligarchs and populism. True, the small parties were not successful in the election, nor were they expected to be. They were meant to take away some votes from the Communists and Yabloko and to create the semblance of political pluralism.

The most dramatic result of the elections was the defeat of the liberal parties, which failed to cross the 5 percent barrier and therefore found themselves out of the Duma and out of public politics, because public politics in Russia involves work with the institutions of power. To some degree, that result was predictable. But the liberals and democrats and their allies had hoped that at least one of the parties would get into the Duma. Neither did.

I remember participating in a live television analysis of the election on December 7 on Channel One. After the early results were announced, the two eternal enemies, Yavlinsky and Chubais, leaders respectively of Yabloko and the SPS, came to the studio. Yavlinsky, unlike Chubais (who was glum and had lost his usual arrogance), was amazingly gleeful: Putin had called him and congratulated him on his victory. Apparently, the president had been sure that Yabloko would get enough votes for the Duma. Moreover, it's quite likely that Putin even wanted to have a small liberal party in the Duma and preferred that it be Yabloko. Otherwise, why would he have met with Yavlinsky right before the elections, thereby demonstrating his support for Yabloko?

Obviously, the president felt that a democratic opposition that was no threat to the regime would be useful. Yabloko's politicians, and especially Yavlinsky himself, had refrained from attacking Putin during the campaign, which suggested that they were prepared to enter into a constructive dialogue with the Kremlin. On the contrary, Boris Nemtsov, an SPS leader, had taken the risk of making open attacks on the president. The situation was different from the elections of 1999. Back then, Yabloko had attacked the regime and the SPS had acted as part of Putin's base; this time, part of the SPS criticized the regime, and Yabloko tried not to antagonize Putin. But the miracle did not happen, and even though Putin had extended a helpful hand to Yavlinsky, Yabloko did not enter the new Duma lineup.

Even if both or one of the liberal parties had been in the parliament, what would have changed? It's unlikely that in the new situation the liberals and democrats would have been able to block the overwhelming Kremlin majority in the Duma. But most unpleasant was the fact that the liberals and democrats had been unable to consolidate their electorate. The SPS and Yabloko jointly had 8 percent of the vote at a time when the number of voters with liberal leanings in Russia was 15 to 29 percent, that is, a significant group of people. Thus a large number of democratically inclined people either voted for other parties or did not vote at all. They were disillusioned by the liberal-democratic parties and by the liberalism of the 1990s, and with good reason.

Both liberal parties not only could not find a way to cooperate but actually began fighting among themselves. That fight disoriented the liberal-democratic sector of the populace. The SPS started it, trying to steal away Yabloko's voters, and the desire among SPS leaders to discredit and get rid of Yabloko often took on dirty and cynical form. So, instead of expanding the democratic field, the SPS consciously started taking away votes from a party that was close ideologically.[39]

Neither party managed to define a new role for itself in the new political situation. They were torn between opposition to the regime and the need to cooperate with it. Going too far into the opposition would have made it impossible to continue a dialogue with society, because it would have deprived them of financing and access to television coverage. And without that, people would simply forget about their existence. In Russia, politics exists only as much as it is shown on TV. As soon as a politician or party vanishes from the screen, it vanishes from real life as well.

But sitting on two stools—opposition and dialogue with the regime—made survival for the liberals and democrats much harder, leading to a split in their voter base and confusing their supporters. This split was unusual for the SPS. Being loyal to the regime, its supporters could not understand, or approve of, Nemtsov's harsh stance in opposition. For the always oppositionist Yabloko, the ambiguity of position and vacillation of its leaders was even more destructive. It would not be an exaggeration to say that Yabloko paid for its attempt to enter into a dialogue with Putin. But if there had been no dialogue, Yavlinsky and his team would not have been able to bring their message to the people. Besides, there was some support among the voters of the liberal parties for Putin, who was seen as the only politician who could make positive changes. In other words, the liberal parties were caught in a trap from which they could not escape. Perhaps at that moment there was no escaping.

At the time of the elections, there was also an increase in populism with overtones of nationalism or great-power chauvinism, which led to more votes for the LDPR and Rodina. This increase was due in great part to the anti-oligarch campaign by the Kremlin. In that context, the unexpected success of Rodina, created by the Kremlin, should be mentioned. The regime started playing the populist card, awakening sentiments that had been dormant in society. But once the populism emerged, the Kremlin was unpleasantly surprised and tried to localize it once again.[40] It was obvious that it feared that one of the Rodina leaders, Sergei Glazyev, would use populism to become a serious contender in the presidential election. Even if it did not happen in 2004, some observers did not rule out that the new party under certain conditions could become a magnet for populism in the future, in the elections in 2007–2008. Whether it was possible remained to be seen.

In any case, Rodina could have been an unpleasant surprise for the administration. The people who voted for that newly hatched party, perhaps without realizing it, were opponents of the Kremlin and Putin. They considered the official policy too soft and not authoritarian enough, and they were displeased by the president's pro-Western orientation. It's a paradox, but true, that Rodina, created by the Kremlin, could in its essence and the sentiments it exploited become an opposition party; this was history in the Frankenstein mode—creating a monster that destroys you.

Although expanded, the field of nationalist, great-power, and populist feelings in Russian society was still rather limited. The number of voters for the parties espousing these views grew by 4 percent from 1999 to 2003 (in 1999, the Communists together with the LDPR got about 30 percent; and in 2003, the Communist Party, LDPR, and Rodina together got about 34 percent).[41] So Russia had not yet become a land of nationalism, chauvinism, or populism. But playing with these sentiments could end badly in a country where part of the populace and a majority of the ruling class dreamed of reviving former glory and power.

The 2003 Duma elections created a new party system in Russia, with United Russia as the axis, framed on one side by the Communist Party and on the other by the national-populist parties, LDPR and Rodina. The new system could be tentatively called the "dominant party system." It was a strange mix, which included a state apparatus organized under the aegis of United Russia, a Communist Party that has been a residue of the old system, and national-populist parties sponsored by the Kremlin. Such a mix would distort society's moods rather than structure them. The question was: What will be the result of this distortion?

The new Duma, naturally, was much more pro-Kremlin than before. United Russia took on the distribution of committees and the organization of parliamentary work. Now the Putin team did not need to worry, because it had full guarantees that the new parliamentarians would approve all its legislative initiatives. However, there was a danger of another sort—the absence of considered, conscious control over the executive branch, which no longer had any limitations upon it.

What was 2003 like? Personally, I remember it as the year of getting used to feeling personally vulnerable at all times. I'm referring first of all to terrorist acts, which became a constant element in the Russian political landscape and the lives of ordinary citizens. February was the bomb in the Moscow metro—39 dead, hundreds wounded. May—a bomb in the state house in Grozny—54 dead, 300 wounded. July—a bomb at Tushino Airport in Moscow at a rock festival—15 dead, 40 wounded. July—a bomb in Dagestan—3 dead, 40 wounded. September—two bombs on the

Kislovodsk–Mineralnye Vody commuter train—5 dead, 33 wounded. December—a bomb on the commuter train in Essentuki—42 dead, more than 100 wounded. December—a bomb near the National Hotel in Moscow—6 dead. This meant that ordinary Russians could not feel safe in the metro, or commuter trains, or stadiums, or the street. Let me add to this sad list the paid assassination of the famous democrat Sergei Yushenkov and the loss of the submarine in the Barents Sea. These events could not have made 2003 memorable as a peaceful and happy year.

And nevertheless, the sociologist Yuri Levada concluded that most people polled considered this year better than the previous one. Young people under 30 in particular found it better. For people 30 to 40 years old, it was the same as the previous year. But for the elderly, 2003 was harder. And all age groups felt tired and indifferent. Only the young people were optimistic and expected even better things in 2004.[42] Well, optimism is characteristic of youth. But the young generation reacts more strongly when its hopes do not come to pass. Hardy Russians trying to regain their hope for a better and stable future felt that even more severe experiences were awaiting the nation in 2004.

Chapter 10

RUSSIA HAS A NEW PRESIDENT—AGAIN PUTIN

———————— ✿ ————————

How to win an election by ignoring it. Firing the unsinkable Kasyanov. The liberals are paralyzed. Putin gets his new legitimacy, which again looks vulnerable. Moscow ponders its relations with the West. Russia and the European Union: dating without hope of marriage.

Mixed feelings of weariness and hope were the background for the presidential election campaign in 2004. Vladimir Putin had no reason to worry: Russia, if not quite satisfied, was at least not looking for new leaders. The most important thing for Russia was to avoid deterioration and keep going. The Duma elections had shown that the nation trusted the president and agreed to a continuation of his administration. There were no doubts that Putin would win in the first round. As in 2000, Putin decided not to campaign; he simply ignored the elections. He behaved not like a candidate but as the sitting president who was confident of a second term and who had no (and could have no) opponents.

The Kremlin, in holding a referendum on extending the acting president's term, was acting rather wisely. The Russian authorities had acquired experience in holding events that were able to legitimize power using democratic instruments while simultaneously excluding any alternatives or threats to it. On the one hand, the Kremlin presented Putin as a leader who guaranteed stability, repeating the 2000 scenario. On the other hand, Putin's team skillfully retained a certain incompleteness in Putin's image, leaving things unsaid so that he could also be "the president of hope."[1] The

Kremlin continued playing several instruments at once, appealing to both those who feared change and those who wanted it.

It was, in fact, a schizophrenic game leading to a split national identity, to conflicting moods and incompatible trends in the society, to the simultaneous pursuit of opposite goals without guarantee to reach any of them. Putin's campaign staff tried to make people feel a sense of confidence in the future if Putin were to remain in the Kremlin. But they also reminded people of the problems that were hard to control, suggesting that the leader could not foresee everything and could not be held responsible for negative processes or unrealized longings and dreams. This policy, which was oriented toward achieving tactical results, in the end triggered among people both optimism and pessimism, self-assuredness and feelings of vulnerability, and this could produce unpredictable repercussions in the future. But who cared about the future, and who thought beyond the election year in Moscow?

Putin could behave any way he wished. He had such a supply of goodwill and support that he could do anything. He had turned into a Teflon president who could resist all blows.[2] According to the Levada Center (known as VTsIOM until 2003), polls in February 2003 showed that 95 percent of United Russia voters, 60 percent of Yabloko voters, 66 percent of Liberal Democratic Party (LDPR) voters, 64 percent of Union of Right Forces (SPS) voters, 63 percent of Rodina Party voters, and 63 percent of Russians who had not voted in the parliamentary elections were prepared to vote for Putin in the presidential elections. This showed that it was pointless to fight the acting president.

Political life was not, however, totally predictable. On February 24, before the elections, Putin did what no one then expected: He removed the Kasyanov government, appointing Viktor Khristenko acting prime minister. Rumors of Kasyanov's departure had circulated regularly. But logically, everyone expected him to remain until after the election, when Putin would form his new cabinet. Putin's decision created shock waves in the political milieu. To calm the disturbed beehive that was the political establishment, the president appeared on television and with a grim look announced not very convincingly that the removal of the prime minister was intended to save time in forming the new cabinet and facilitating the continuity of the reforms. There was something discouraging about the announcement, for Putin was telling people that he had no doubts about his reelection and that he wanted to take a new course with a new government even before the election. The Russian audience sensed something else, however; it did not believe the president and his explanations. Experienced politically, Russians said to themselves: "Something's fishy here."

Their suspicions were confirmed. It turned out that Putin had no candidate for prime minister. Therefore, the decision to get rid of Kasyanov had been prompted by completely different reasons. After tense consultations and several days of uncertainty, Putin proposed Mikhail Fradkov, then the Russian representative to the European Union, a typical bureaucrat about whom little was known, except that he knew how to survive in various posts and positions.[3] Everyone was stunned yet again. Only one thing was certain: Putin needed a prime minister who could never be a threat to the president and who was a good executive. Fradkov was not known as a reformer, which was the alleged reason for his selection. Fradkov was known for other qualities—he never rushed in with initiatives and therefore stayed afloat. The appointment of Fradkov as the new Russian premier could mean that Putin was looking more toward stability than modernization. But even if this were not a systemic move but a decision forced by murky circumstances, it definitely would influence the future agenda of the presidency.

Instead of Putin's promised swift shift to reforms, the political class was plunged into endless discussions of the hidden springs of the nomination. The apparent pointlessness of the step was astonishing; the Duma would have to approve Fradkov temporarily, until the elections, and then Putin would have to nominate him again and the Duma would have to approve him yet again. That was, of course, if Putin intended to keep Fradkov. Why all that hassle? The only explanation was that Putin was afraid of something and had to get rid of Kasyanov fast.[4] Only then did the turnabout à la Yeltsin, and totally not in Putin's style, make sense.

But what could have threatened Putin in the presidential election? Had he received information that keeping Kasyanov during the election could be dangerous to him? Bewildered pundits in Moscow looking for an explanation started to make guesses that the removal of the prime minister was the result of the Kremlin's fears of a low voter turnout that could lead to new elections. In that case, the prime minister could become a central figure, some thought. But there was no serious basis for that worry, turnout was expected to be high, and Putin would win the election both because he had popular support and because he controlled the political class. But I can't rule out that Putin had been warned about the possibility and had decided to remove Kasyanov from the political scene—just in case. That told volumes about the Kremlin's insecurity and rather awkward tactics.

Mikhail Kasyanov's unexpected retirement remains a mystery, for unlike in the Yeltsin years, there have been no leaks about the real reasons behind it. Kasyanov himself made very few comments, and very restrained ones, but it was still clear that he was holding back his irritation. He only let it be understood that his firing had been contrary to his previous arrangement with the president. Soon after his departure, he disappeared from the public eye. It was yet another confirmation of how easy it is in Russian politics to lose your political future.

Whatever the reasons for Kasyanov's removal, it meant that Putin was rejecting the past even before the elections. He had put up with the Yeltsin people too long, and he had decided to cut them loose. But he did it in a way that had almost plunged Russia into a political crisis. This unusual behavior of a very cautious person who usually hated any reshuffles allows us to make two suppositions: Either Putin was in fact an emotional person and could not control his long-growing annoyance with the prime minister; or he had had serious reasons for parting with Kasyanov related to a threat, probably exaggerated, to his power.

In the meantime, Mikhail Fradkov's new government was born slowly, not without pain. The president decided to use the occasion of forming the new cabinet to restructure the government, something that had been long postponed because of Kasyanov's resistance. In place of the traditional cabinet divided into branch ministries, a new three-tier structure was created:

ministry–federal service–agency. A strictly centralized cabinet structure was put in place. Thus, Fradkov now had only one first deputy, Alexander Zhukov. The number of deputy ministers for each minister was reduced to two. But it was clear that neither the prime minister nor the ministers in charge of the now-gigantic ministries could possibly handle the day-to-day operations and that certain prerogatives would have to be delegated to other levels of government. Analysts watched the government reform skeptically, knowing that enlarging the ministries and reducing the number of deputy ministers, who ordinarily handled the workflow, would lead to a slowdown and even deadlock in decision making. Moreover, the reform resulted into a clumsier structure, with 73 institutions replacing the former 52 ministries.

In the makeup of the new cabinet, the Yeltsin forces lost heavily. Only two members remained—Sergei Shoigu, the minister of emergency situations, and Mikhail Zurabov, who now headed the Ministry of Health and Social Development. The Saint Petersburg liberals (German Gref and Alexei Kudrin) kept their posts in the new government (but Gref lost his two reformer deputies, Dvorkovich and Dmitriev). The Saint Petersburg *siloviki* kept their positions, too. But, contrary to expectations, they did not get to expand their influence.

It was too soon to judge the viability and effectiveness of the new government. But there was a built-in source of conflict between Prime Minister Fradkov and the chief of administration, Dmitri Kozak, who was close to Putin and was supposed to control the cabinet and restrain the prime minister's power. The incompatibility of mentality and views between the old regime's representative, Fradkov, with his cautious approach and antiliberal views, and the liberal technocrats Gref and Kudrin was another inevitable source of tension within the cabinet. Mutual hostility among the top members of the cabinet—for instance, between Kudrin and Zhukov—and the ongoing competing interests ensured that the new government would soon become another battleground for fierce infighting. Whether Putin could succeed in moderating the new conflicts and soothing the new tensions was unclear.

The parliamentary defeat of the Communist Party and Yabloko meant that their leaders, Zyuganov and Yavlinsky, could not be Putin's rivals for president. Putin and his campaign managers found themselves in an unexpected situation that they had not considered when they cleared away the political stage and weakened the other parties. The leaders of the destroyed parties were no masochists and had no desire to suffer humiliation a second time by entering the presidential race and acting as sparring partners for Putin. After brief consideration, both Yavlinsky and Zyuganov refused to participate. Soon afterward, Zhirinovsky, the perennial candidate, also decided to bow out and nominated in his stead, as if intentionally making the election a laughingstock, as the candidate from the LDPR his bodyguard Oleg Malyshkin, a taciturn hulk with huge biceps and slow-witted looks. Another candidate appeared on the scene—someone named Sterligov who owned funeral parlors. A farce was unfolding that could undermine the seriousness of the electoral process and the legitimacy of Putin's second term.

There was another at least theoretical problem, too: the threat of boycott of the elections by the communist and democratic electorate, which could severely reduce the turnout. If fewer than 50 percent showed up, according to the Constitution, the presidential elections had to be held again.

The farce continued with the self-nomination of one of Putin's closest allies, the speaker of the Federation Council, Sergei Mironov, who admittedly became a candidate not to compete with Putin but to support him! Some members of the ruling team had a strange concept of the election process.

Realizing that they were in big trouble, the Kremlin spin doctors tried to persuade Yavlinsky and Zyuganov to run. Rumor had it that they were offered $25 million each for their presidential campaigns. Both refused. Yavlinsky was the more stubborn, categorically boycotting the elections. Zyuganov gave in (not the first time, he made compromises with the regime) and instead of boycotting, as the Communist leaders had promised, the Communist Party nominated a second-string candidate, Nikolai Kharitonov. The nomination alone should have brought a sigh of relief in the Kremlin: Kharitonov's participation gave the enterprise at least some gravity.

But on the whole, the campaign of 2004 could not have pleased the Kremlin. The desire to secure victory for the current president, who would have won in any case, forced the regime to discredit the elections through excessive manipulation and dirty tricks. The other presidential candidates also behaved in a way that raised questions about the sources of their financing and the goal of their participation. The campaign was filled with scandals and strange stories: the disappearance of Ivan Rybkin, one of the candidates, who was suddenly found in Ukraine;[5] the murkiness of the financing of Irina Khakamada's campaign (there were suspicions that she was being sponsored simultaneously by the Kremlin, Berezovsky, and Leonid Nevzlin, one of the directors of YUKOS); and problems with signature gathering for the candidacy of Sergei Glazyev. Of course, this election had been destined from the start to be pointless and scandalous, because Putin was not participating in the campaign and its result was predetermined.

The presidential campaign had started, and the liberal parties appeared to be in total disarray, having had no time to recover from the defeat in the parliamentary elections. What was to be done? This eternal Russian question was debated at innumerable meetings of the democrats and liberals. Opinion split: some wanted a total boycott of the election, hoping that this would make Putin's election illegitimate. Others proposed voting for "none of the above" in protest. Still others called for identifying and rallying around a single candidate from all the democratic forces to preserve a niche for the democratic flank. I remember a group of liberals at the Liberal Mission Foundation, headed by Yevgeny Yasin, proposing to the two losing parties—the SPS and Yabloko—to take as their candidate Vladimir Ryzhkov, who represented the young generation of politicians and had shown in recent years a clear democratic position. It was in Ryzhkov's favor that he was not a member of either Yabloko or the SPS, and because the parties were at odds with each other, a new person could become the rallying point for democratic forces. Other nonparty candidates were also mentioned, in particular, Nikolai Fedorov, the president of Chuvashia. But none of the suggested candidacies was approved by the liberal parties. And the impression was that Yabloko was more resistant to having a joint candidate, for the only candidate who suited them was Yavlinsky.

When the idea of a single candidate fell through, Irina Khakamada, one of the leaders of the SPS, presented herself as a candidate, to the surprise of many. She was not supported by either Yabloko or, even more important, her own party. Nevertheless, she entered the fray. Her self-nomination elicited mixed feelings in the democratic community. Some saw it as a Kremlin ploy. And in fact, the participation of a democratic candidate suited the administration, because it gave the elections the veneer of competition. Others saw it as a desperate attempt to stay in the political game. But a small part of the democratic community supported her, considering her participation as a way of bringing the democratic platform to the public and of consolidating the fragmented and confused liberal electorate. Khakamada ran her campaign courageously and energetically. But she did not manage to unite the democratic end of the spectrum. No one and nothing at that moment was able to consolidate liberals and democrats, even the looming threat of being forced into a political ghetto.

The final list in March 2004 had six registered candidates: Putin, Malyshkin, Mironov, Glazyev, Khakamada, and Kharitonov. The participation of the last three gave the elections an appearance of competition. But in fact, each candidate except Putin was pursuing other goals, because the election uncertainty in Russia by that time had successfully been eliminated and the nation knew the name of the winner. And the winner knew that he would stay in the Kremlin for at least four more years.

Putin made a point of not campaigning—he did not debate and did not stoop to explanations or discussions. He paid no attention to his rivals. In fact, he paid no attention to the election itself and continued his normal activities. He said, "I believe it is inappropriate for an incumbent head of state to be advertising himself." (!) Russia introduced a few innovations into democratic procedures: party leaders proposed their bodyguards as candidates in their stead; the president's own supporters ran so that he would not be lonely and bored; the democratic candidate did not have support from the democratic parties; and the president ran for reelection by not campaigning. But the public was so sick of elections that changed nothing and elections that it did not control, that it remained indifferent.

Because none of the candidates presented an alternative to Putin, Russia was prepared to entrust the Kremlin to the incumbent.

However, Putin should have outlined his second-term program, if only out of sense of decency. He could not automatically continue his first term. At least a few people in the Kremlin understood the need for an idea of the second term. After lengthy consideration, on February 12, 2004, the president gave a program speech to his representatives, which was supposed to outline his major priorities for the second term. To the surprise of many observers, his speech was openly liberal. It was hard to believe that after building his authoritarian regime and getting rid of public politics, the president was suddenly speaking out as a convinced liberal. Here is what Putin said: "I am certain that only a developed civil society can ensure the stability of democratic freedoms and the guarantees of human and civil rights. In the final analysis, only a free person can secure economic growth and a flourishing state. In brief, this is the alpha and omega of economic success and economic growth."[6]

Apparently, Putin's campaign speech was intended for the liberal audience, with whom Putin was at odds, and also oriented toward the West, which was beginning to have more suspicions about the Russian leader. Putin told those two audiences: "I am a civilized man. What I had done before was a necessary consolidation of power. Now I intend to develop freedom and pay attention to society." Of course, the question arose: Because Russia no longer had any independent television, independent parliament, or viable liberal parties, with whom was Putin planning to develop political freedoms?

Putin won the election on March 14, 2004, as expected. This was the most predictable election in modern Russian history: A total of 64.3 percent of the voters participated, and 71.2 percent voted for Putin (48,900,000 people).[7] But Putin had not much reason for euphoria, because only 34.06 percent of the population voted for him. He thus had far from overwhelming support from the Russian public, but he had enough of a basis for any independent policy.

Election day was marred for the victor by the fire in the Manege, an architectural monument near the Kremlin wall. It was an apocalyptic sight on television. Flames filled the sky and seemed to be reaching for the Kremlin's towers. Many viewers took the horrible scene as an evil omen. Someone in authority quickly banned showing the fire with the Kremlin in the background. But the huge fire that roared all night in the middle of Moscow and could not be controlled by all the firefighters in the capital added a bitter note to the victorious mood in the Kremlin.

The presidential and parliamentary elections and the way they had been conducted only added to frustration with Russian developments among Western and liberal observers. "The trajectory of the last decade has been clear—a growing role for the state and declining role for society in determining electoral outcomes," wrote Michael McFaul and Nikolai Petrov. "More than a decade after the collapse of the Soviet Union, the state's dominance over society is still overwhelming."[8] The elections in Russia had turned into a rather effective mechanism for legitimating the self-perpetuation of power and had succeeded in nearly totally eliminating the element of unpredictability. But all those who thought that elections even in this guise would remain as the only possible mechanism of giving the authorities legitimacy would soon discover that they were wrong. The further evolution of the political regime and the logic of centralization would demand erasing the other remaining weak signs of uncertainty.

For Putin, the elections were really important, even with a guaranteed result. This time, he acquired his new legitimacy, which was now real and not borrowed from anyone, and he was no longer the successor of the former tsar, brought to the throne by Yeltsin's dubious entourage. Putin began his new term without any obligations to the old ruling group. Russian observers loyal to the regime, including Andranik Migranyan and Vyacheslav Nikonov, came to this conclusion: "Now Putin controls all the levers of power and he has the opportunity to move into broad modernization."

Western observers were skeptical. "Things are not that simple," warned Gernot Erler, who had been appointed by the German government to coordinate German–Russian cooperation. "The social atmosphere in Russia has deteriorated, and that is the result of this and other elections."[9] In explaining why things were not so simple, Erler mentioned the same package of issues: Chechnya, human rights, Khodorkovsky. Western politicians were telling the Russian president: "We feel no euphoria over your election." But while some Western politicians were openly critical of Putin, his colleagues in the presidents' club, in the Group of Eight (G-8), appeared to feel relief over Putin's victory because they knew him and could work with him.

It remained to be seen how far Putin was willing to go in his second term. It did not take long to find out.

The events of the first half of 2004 forced Moscow to start rethinking its relationship with the West. After a brilliant military operation, the Americans were mired in Iraq, and their continuing presence there was meeting growing local resistance. These American problems brought on gleeful gloating from the Russian nationalists and statists: "We told you so!" To be fair, the same feelings were prevalent in Paris and Berlin. The Russian mass media gave detailed and vivid information about the scandals at the Abu-Ghraib prison and the abuse of Iraqi prisoners by U.S. military personnel. But the critical tone of the reports in the news reeked of hypocrisy, because maltreatment, usually much more brutal, of inmates had always been the norm in Russia. It is unlikely that the treatment of Chechens, and especially Chechen rebel prisoners, by Russian soldiers fell within civilized parameters.

American failures in Iraq, and more important evidence of their ungentlemanly attitude toward the local population, were a blow to the pro-American sentiments some Russians still had and also to Russian perceptions of Western democracy. Photographs of smiling soldiers, apparently satisfied with their inventiveness, in front of piles of naked Iraqis did what the old Soviet propaganda and today's anti-American rhetoric of Zhirinovsky and Rogozin could not do. "How are these abuses better than our Chechnya?" asked simple Russians as they looked at the photographs published in Russian newspapers. "Many people all over the world believed that American leadership would bring the world freedom and well-being, respect for human rights and satisfaction of people's needs," wrote the pro-American analyst Viktor Kremenuk. "Now there are doubts about their ability to handle that leadership. . . . Perhaps the problem lies only in Bush and his team? But what if the self-adoration of Americans and their blind faith in their predestination has gone so far that America must be treated first and only then the rest of the sinful world?"[10]

The unfolding Iraqi drama and American difficulties there became one of the most popular arguments of Russian traditionalists who were trying to prove that Western civilization can't bring a happier and more benevolent world order. Further events, however, would demonstrate that Americans found ways to deal with their scandals through transparency, public inquiry into the behavior of the military, and public dispute over reasons and repercussions of the Iraqi war. The Russian leadership and political class still preferred to hide the truth about the brutality and crimes of their troops in the Northern Caucasus, in a typically Soviet way trying to save the prestige of the state.[11]

The events in Iraq deepened Russian disillusionment with America. In May, only 10 percent of respondents to a poll thought that the United States was a positive factor in international relations, and 61 percent thought that America was trying to force its will upon the world.[12] Such survey results could be expected when all Russian television channels made the U.S. brutality and failures their everyday major news topic. One could get an impression that the Russian media were intentionally trying to point their finger at Americans to force Russian society to forget Russian human rights violations and the quagmire in Chechnya. The vector of Russian official propaganda demonstrated that the Kremlin was using anti-Americanism to distract attention from its Caucasus war.

The pendulum was swinging toward a new chill in Russian–American relations, and not for the first time. However, another fact is worth noting: The Kremlin tried to avoid creating problems for the United States in the international arena and in Iraq as well. That meant that Moscow did not miss the opportunity to use anti-American slogans for domestic purposes but was not interested in the United States' being defeated in Iraq or even in the weakening of the U.S. global role, fearing destabilization of the international scene.

In any case, America's growing problems in Iraq did not evoke only gloating and revulsion. Pragmatists, including those in Putin's entourage, were worried, and with good reason; if the Americans could not hold Iraq and left, there was fear that instability in Iraq might spread to Afghanistan and Pakistan, which would sooner or later threaten the Caucasus and Central Asia. That was just a stone's throw from Russia. Putin understood the threat. Perhaps it was to quell the joy of Russian statists over America's failures that he told reporters in Tambov on April 2, 2004, that Russia has no interest politically or economically in a U.S. defeat in Iraq. Moscow let it be known that it was prepared to support the U.S.–British coalition in Iraq, but only within the international mandate under the aegis of the United Nations. Putin and his team, though ambivalent in their attitude toward the United States at that juncture, did not want either to undermine the American effort in Iraq or an American military withdrawal from Iraq.

Yet another factor for worry appeared. Russian and Western observers for quite a long time had been warning of the inevitability of tensions and even rivalry between the United States and Russia in the post-Soviet space, which Russia considered its sphere of influence. Now prophecy seemed to have become reality. Moscow had tolerated, barely, the presence of Americans in the post-Soviet space. But with growing strength and confidence, Russia began to see its return to that area as a natural and necessary condition for restoring its international role. Russia's increased interest in Eurasia was at least in part due to Moscow's disappointment in its partnership with the West and the schism in the West, which prompted a reanimation of Russian diplomacy. But even more important was the fact that Putin's effort to reconstitute the traditional state and the centralized system inevitably brought the revival of superpower, traditionalist instincts in the foreign policy field; in Russia, the centralization of power and expansion of international influence always went together.

Contrary to some expectations and prognosis, this time Moscow did not try to resurrect the Commonwealth of Independent States (CIS), long a political corpse, but attempted to find more flexible ways to restore its presence on the territory of the former USSR. This meant both economic expansion and an assurance of military and strategic interests, but through softer approaches, in the former Soviet republics. Moscow was reviving its presence in Belarus, Ukraine, Moldova, the Central Asian states, and the Caucasus. The Baltic republics have been successfully hiding from Russia under the umbrella of the European Union and NATO, and this fact provoked bitter feelings among Russian elites and especially the military.

Sooner or later, Russia would have turned its gaze on its neighbors, with whom it shared a common past, economic interests, and security interests. Moreover, as many as 25 million Russians lived in these neighboring states. So far, Moscow had been using this fact only for its superpower rhetoric without really caring for Russians abroad. But now the Kremlin started to show a growing interest in the surrounding Eurasian space. Whether Moscow's policies stabilized the post-Soviet space or undermined it was another question. Could Moscow help the economic and democratic development of the new independent states, or was it hindering the process? Was Moscow able to help other new independent states while it was having so many problems with its own transformation? The answers would show how much Russia had changed and how much it had remained the same.

The building of a Russian air base in the Kyrgyz Republic near the American base; the conflict with Ukraine in the Kerchensky Strait over control of the controversial Tuzla Peninsula; the attempt to offer its formula for regulating the Dniester region; pressure on Belarus on the issue of Russian natural gas transport; and demonstrative support of the separatist leaders of Abkhazia and Adjaria—these are just a few examples of Russia's attempts to guarantee its presence in the former Soviet space. The results and repercussions of these attempts were ambiguous. In Belarus, the Kremlin's pressure on the Belorusian leader Aleksandr Lukashenko was justified because it helped to solve the issues of how to transport Russian gas toward Europe without having to continue the policy of appeasing Minsk. In other cases, Russia's beefing up of its presence and intentional demonstration of its muscles only complicated the situation. For instance, Russia's attempt to circumvent international bodies and push through its own solution in dealing with the Transdnistria conflict was a rather heavy-handed policy.[13]

The test for Moscow politics in the post-Soviet space was its line regarding the conflicts in Abkhazia, South Ossetia, Nagorny Karabakh, and Transdnistria that were legacy of the Soviet Union collapse. So far, Russia had succeeded in freezing these conflicts. To solve these conflicts meant that Moscow had to stop supporting the regimes that had emerged in these "twilight zones," to reconsider previous loyalties, and to think how to help constructively solve the territorial integrity problems of Armenia, Moldova, Georgia, and Azerbaijan. At any moment, those separatist "time bombs" could implode, triggering regional military conflicts, which would constitute a security threat both for Russia and the outside world. But moving toward a solution meant for Moscow that it had to recognize that the status quo in these hot spots in the former Soviet Union couldn't be preserved for ever. I would agree with Michael McFaul and other analysts who advocate in this case internationalization of the approach and possibly involvement of the international peacekeeping forces as one of the first steps under the aegis of the United Nations.[14]

But this line of thought still is wishful thinking. During 2004, Moscow was not ready for any kind of internationalization effort in the former Soviet space. On the contrary, the Kremlin began to show open dissatisfaction with the desire of the United States and European Union to have a presence on the territory of the former USSR. The Russian Ministry of Foreign Affairs regularly asked Washington when the United States intended to bring its troops out of the CIS countries. Moscow's greatest irritant was growing American influence in Georgia, with which the Kremlin continued to have poor, sometimes even hostile relations. The appointment of a special E.U. representative to the South Caucasus also received a chilly reception from the Kremlin. The increase in the new Russian parliament of supporters of the great-power course—who demanded an expansion of Russian influence in the CIS—meant that there might be even more tensions in the relationship between Russia and the West.[15] The Russian political class still was living in the world of realpolitik, dividing the globe into spheres of influence. What was lacking were the economic and military resources to secure Russian interests in the areas that Moscow continued to view as its legitimate sphere of influence and the ability to ensure these areas' stability and development.

America perceived Russia's attempt to beef up its presence in the former Soviet territory as a return to Russia's former expansionist traditions. State Department officials on more than one occasion stated that the former USSR was not a zone of exclusive Russian interest. For instance, the

U.S. ambassador to Russia, Alexander Vershbow, defined the American position quite unequivocally in January 2004: "We recognize Russia's interests in these regions [Moldova, Central Asia, and the Caucasus], and we feel that its good relations with its neighbors will have a positive influence on the situation. The United States also has its interests in these regions, but they do not develop at the cost of Russia's interests and, we hope, they bring benefit to all interested parties."[16] Moscow did not think so, and its representatives reciprocated, asking how Washington would feel if Moscow were to expand its presence in Mexico. One could only guess what dominated the Russian approach: real strategic interests, albeit not always properly defined; or an irresistible desire to be equal to the United States and to follow the same pattern of policy that Washington was implementing. There were, however, two problems with the Russian desire to replicate American-style geopolitical power in Eurasia: first, not all countries welcomed the Russian presence and Russia's domineering power; and second, this new expansionism did not help the Russian domestic transformation—on the contrary, it pushed toward a more traditional state and provoked antimodernist moods.

Russian observers once again sought more adequate definitions for the role of Russia, now speaking of "multivectorness" (not to be confused with Yevgeny Primakov's multipolarity), which would accommodate cooperation with the West; cooperation with other countries, especially China and India; and the formation of a single economic and strategic space inside the territory of the former USSR. This approach was a positive change from Primakov's idea of Russia as the center of an international system that was alien to the West. But the practical nature of the "multivector" framework was lacking clarity, and it could easily become another myth that would serve as compensation for a lack of well-defined national interests.

Analyzing the new directions in Russia's foreign policy, Dmitri Trenin offered his vision of a new formula for Russia's behavior on the international scene, which he called "new isolationism.""Russia's leaders perceive the Western community less as a 'common home' and more as a source, on the one hand, of resources for modernization and on the other, of geopolitical challenges. Contradictions and friction in the post-Soviet space can serve as a forerunner and trigger of Moscow's new Western policy," wrote Trenin.[17] The U.S. ambassador to Russia at the time, Alexander Vershbow, also was thinking along these lines. "There are very many dots on radar screens, as the air controllers would have said. We do not know, however, if it is possible to draw lines between them. Still, we do fear that this is some tendency towards neo-isolationism," he said in an interview by *Novaya gazeta*, looking at the trend as a negative one.[18] Andrei Zagorsky and his colleagues addressed this same tendency in Russia's foreign policy, concluding, "The Russian foreign policy establishment has an entrenched illusion of 'self-sufficiency,' the renaissance of the country's status as a great state which with the strengthening of its economic power will no longer have to fall in with the Western states."[19] How the "new isolationism" was related to the "multivector" approach was not clear at the moment.

As if to prove its distancing from the West, Russia seemed to become more and more frustrated and irritated by its Western partners: by American dominance and at the same time by America's ignoring Russia, by the European desire to teach Russia democracy and good behavior in Chechnya. The Russian political class, driven both by its ghosts from the times of past glory and by new phobias, was becoming increasingly suspicious of the West's intentions toward Russia, constantly anticipating double standards or hidden attempts to undermine, weaken, and encircle Russia.

At the same time, while watching Russian developments, quite a few people in the West did fear Russia's becoming a rival. But that was understandable; after all, Russia, despite huge changes in its values and attitudes, despite its amazing adaptive instincts, still remained alien to the West. The rise of statist nationalist groups in Russia had to increase Western concerns and forebodings about the intentions of this huge country that had historically survived and consolidated itself through expansion and aggression. Russia frightened Westerners both with its dynamics and its controversies, with its past and its turbulent present and its still unpredictable future, especially when they couldn't grasp the drama of this alien Russia's fight with itself and its past.

Of course, one could understand why Western politicians who tried to constantly accommodate and massage Russia, and to think about Russian complexes, couldn't conceal their resentment and distrust of Russia. Quite a few Western analysts and observers openly demonstrated their fear of Russia's revival, which they perceived as a direct threat to the West, and called for deterring Russia. And such resuscitated Western Cold War attitudes inevitably bred Russian anti-Western responses.

The distrust of Russia's political class for the West was to be expected after decades of the humiliating loss of internal gravitas and international influence. At a new juncture, they were reinforced by frustration with the previous stage of cooperation with the West, which was considered by the Russian elites as hardly effective and even fruitless. The new Russian assertiveness and the return of confidence born of stability and economic success only increased Moscow's disenchantment with the Western capitals. Now the Russian elites were thinking: "We can develop without waiting for assistance. We are ready to swim independently." Even representatives of liberal-democratic circles, Yavlinsky and Khakamada, for example, began to speak of the need for a more independent course for Russia, allowing for its disagreement with the West. Some previously pro-Western liberals openly criticized the West: America for its intervention policy, Europe for not understanding Russian problems.

Summing up, the appearance of this new disaffected attitude toward the West even in the pro-West audience was the result of several circumstances: contradictions within the Western community; disillusionment with the West's ability to help the Russian transformation; the American war in Iraq; and the belief that influential Western circles do not wish to see a stronger Russia, preferring to keep it stagnant. There was a genuine misunderstanding among Russian political elites of the new American fears with regard to Russia—that is, the American concern, both among Republicans and Democrats, that Russia's weakness could destabilize the post-Soviet space and beyond. As James Goldgeier and Michael McFaul wrote: "In contrast to thinking about the Soviet Union a decade earlier, a weaker Russia—that is Russia not able to exercise sovereignty within its borders—was considered a problem for and threat to the Unites States."[20] The Russian political establishment did not believe this set of arguments. Whatever the reasons for its suspicion and irritation toward the West, the Russian political class by the end of the first Putin presidency had given up hopes for altruism in international politics and for hothouse conditions for the restoration of Russia.

Vladimir Putin himself in 2003 and early 2004 tried to choose a median course between the statism of the Russian political class and the readiness of a significant part of Russian society to move closer to the West. Apparently, he no longer hoped to integrate Russia into the structures of the Western community. But my guess is that he could not have been seriously thinking of isolationism with regard to the West. First, he was too pragmatic and understood the consequences of isolation for Russia. And second, his pro-Western stance was part of his legitimacy—many Russians had voted for him as a pro-Western leader. I think that at that stage the Kremlin was seeking a formula for Russia's "selective partnership" or even vaguer "selective engagement" with the West. But we have to see just how interested Putin was in that formula, how far he was ready to expand it and on what it was based. Too many attendant factors influenced the process of Russia's self-determination in the world. So far at least, Russia—despite the anti-Western and superpower rhetoric of its political class—had been amazingly fast in adapting to its new capabilities and starting a dialogue with Westerners. In fact, the "Pristina dash" during the 1999 Kosovo crisis was the only deviation from this formula for adaptation. But new domestic developments could push Russia toward a new isolationism, irrespective of Putin's intentions.

Controversy over Iraq and the threat of possible conflicts of interest in the post-Soviet space were undermining the partnership of Moscow and Washington, which looked more and more fragile, despite the continually warm personal relations between the leaders of the two countries. This was proof that sooner or later the relations based on personal chemistry would start to unravel if they are not substantiated by a more solid basis and agenda.[21] And a new reason had appeared for intensifying the mutual distrust between the two capitals: the Khodorkovsky case. Apparently, Putin had not expected the oligarch's arrest to affect his relationships with his colleagues in the presidents' club. Yet the attack on YUKOS was perceived in Washington and other Western capitals as a blow against not only Russian business but the institution of private property in Russia.

For the sake of its international goals, the White House was prepared to turn a blind eye toward Chechnya and the limitations on human rights in Russia. But there were certain things that American leaders could not ignore—especially the violation of property rights, a sacred institution in the West. The YUKOS case was seen as just that, and once the Russian leader lost his image as a market liberal, it would be harder to deal with him. American politicians who said, "Well, even if Putin's no democrat, he is our partner in the coalition and he is for the market," found themselves in a quandary. It looked as if Putin were not much of a partner and not quite a market liberal, either.[22] "Putin remains secretive, as befits a former KGB agent. But events such as the brutal arrest of Russian oil billionaire Khodorkovsky and the impounding of a portion of the shares of his YUKOS–Sibneft company help fill in a revealing portrait of the man who succeeded Yeltsin nearly four years ago," wrote Jim Hoagland in the *Washington Post*, expressing the feelings of Washington's influential circles.[23]

In the fall of 2003, Senator John McCain and Representative Tom Lantos denounced Russia as a "despotic regime" and called for its expulsion from the G-8. Soon after that, Lantos came to Moscow and, when he tried to visit the Duma for a discussion, was not allowed in. The Russian deputies had no desire to argue with their critics. This hardly could improve relations between the Duma and the U.S. Congress. If Russia still held out hopes for the repeal of the Jackson-Vanik amendment, it could now forget about it, at least in the near future.

On January 26, 2004, Colin Powell came to Moscow. On the eve of his visit, *Izvestiya*, one of the national newspapers, ran an article in which the U.S. secretary of state for the first time harshly criticized Russian domestic policy. "Certain developments in Russian politics and foreign policy in recent months have given us pause. The democratic system of Russia, it seems to us, has not yet found a necessary balance between executive, legislative, and judicial branches of power. Political power is still not completely tied to legal norms. Key aspects of civil society, such as free media and developed political parties are not yet stable and independent. We are concerned about several aspects of Russia's domestic policies in Chechnya as well as toward neighbors once part of the USSR," wrote Powell.[24] Never before during the Bush presidency had a high-ranking official delivered such strong criticism of Russian domestic policy—which, by the way, took the Kremlin by surprise. The Kremlin responded with unveiled annoyance to Powell's statement, apparently hoping that it was just an election maneuver on the part of the White House.

It's not out of the question that the secretary of state's criticism of the Kremlin really was predicated on the U.S. election campaign and George W. Bush's desire not to give the Democrats the Russia card against him. Bush and his team apparently remembered the "Who lost Russia" campaign started by the Republicans during their election struggle with Al Gore; at that time, the Republicans rather skillfully made use of Bill Clinton's closeness to Yeltsin to undermine the Democrats' position during the election campaign. Bush did not want to fall in the same trap. By criticizing the authoritarian tendencies of Putin, the Bush team could say, "See, we see Putin with all his flaws and we tell him what we think."

But even without the usual election-year political logic, it was becoming difficult to avoid the conclusion that the relationship between Russia and the United States—despite the best efforts of Moscow and Washington to give the impression of a successful partnership—looked like an empty shell. Neither the mutual sympathy of the leaders nor the imitation technique of their teams and the nonstop work of the huge diplomatic machines on both sides of the ocean that had been supporting the bilateral relationship since the Cold War epoch could conceal the fact that there was not much to talk about. The partnership had turned out to be a costly, time-consuming effort that did not lead to much. The elephant gave birth to a mouse, as Russians say about a powerful effort that produces few results.

Analysts started again for the hundredth time their ongoing mantra about a crisis in Russian–American relations. To say something positive about these relations was not popular either in Moscow or in Washington, and in fact sounded like a sign of poor analytical ability. The talk of this crisis had become a common refrain for everyone who wrote about America and Russia. What interested me was something different: Why does the relationship spring back up after every downturn, like the *van'-ka-vstan'ka* dolls with weighted bottoms? Here is my explanation of the *van'ka-vstan'ka* phenomenon: There is a recognition on both sides of common threats and a realistic understanding of the consequences of a scenario of confrontation with each other. And there is an understanding of differences in normative, value approaches between both countries. The fear of crisis and of its implications have a very strong moderating and soothing effect on the political establishments of both countries. At the same time, the relations between Russia and the United States have not been an important factor in the resolution of the countries' internal problems. This means that Russia and the United States do not desperately need closer cooperation for their domestic development, and that there is no strong interdependency between them that eases pressure on their foreign policy agenda.

Therefore, theoretically there is no real necessity felt among the elites and the public both in Russia and the United States to build an enduring and strong Russian–American partnership, and now there are no more excessive expectations. I have to admit that this lack of serious domestic need in broader relations may lead to more estrangement in U.S.–Russian relations. But as was just noted above, this threat is mitigated by a fear of crisis. Thus, in the end, we may conclude, to put it crudely, that no substance means that nothing would collapse or disintegrate, which really narrows the threat for crisis. The much more serious tension between the United States and Europe, at least at recent junctures, was provoked by the high American expectations of its transatlantic allies.

The same could be said about the constant disillusionment in the relationship among the broad social and political circles in Russia and the United States—it has been caused by excessive and not always justified hopes.[25] If we look realistically at the relations between the two former enemies, Moscow and Washington have managed rather successfully to avoid pitfalls and maintain a completely successful dialogue even in the face of irritants and mutual distrust. This is particularly true if we remember that they are dealing with a relationship between different systems that is maintained by the political will of their leaders.

By early 2004, the relations between Russia and the European Union had become even more complex than the Russian partnership with the United States. Curiously, just in 2001–2002, Russia's relations with NATO were much more strained than those with the European Union. But soon the situation had changed, and the relationship between Russia and the once-hated NATO was almost idyllic, while Russia's relations with the European Union on the eve of the E.U. expansion in 2004 looked almost tense. Russia and the European Union have started to have inevitable problems as they pursue contrary aims: Russia is trying to fortify a traditional state with the commensurate attributes (accenting territory, military power, and sovereignty), and the European Union is developing a new form of integration, doing away with elements of the traditional state. As Dov Lynch wrote, "Russia is a sovereign state, with a unified political, economic and military system," and "the EU is nothing of the sort." Besides, according to Lynch, "Russia has become a staunch conservative in some areas of international affairs," whereas the EU "stands at the forefront of the elaboration of new customs of international relations, including the notions of 'humanitarian intervention' and 'limited sovereignty.'" Finally, "while simultaneous pursuit of values and interests may not seem contradictory for Brussels, it does from the Russia perspective." These differences "have rendered the development of genuine strategic partnership difficult."[26]

Their different developmental vectors had to have influenced the different approach of Russia and a united Europe to basic values and world-order principles. So, despite common economic and security interests, contradictions and dissatisfaction with each other triggered by systemic disparities have become inevitable.

Such an apparent change of moods contrasts with the situation just a few years ago, when the Europe–Russia Summit agreed to develop the concept of a Common European Economic Space. In 2003, the summits in Rome and Saint Petersburg elaborated the idea of forming "four spaces"—a common economic space; a common foreign security space; a common space for freedom, security, and jurisprudence; and a common space for science and education, as well as culture.

But by the spring of 2004, relations between Moscow and Brussels had clearly worsened. The European community was becoming disillusioned with Russia's inability or lack of political will to implement the Agreement on Partnership and Cooperation signed in 1994. The basic integration projects with Russia, including the energy dialogue, were at a standstill. Europe was increasingly concerned with the authoritarian tendencies in Russia, the continuing civil war in Chechnya, and the reduction of civil rights. Moscow's intransigence on the ratification of the Kyoto protocol was also a factor.

In its turn, Moscow was upset by the human rights rhetoric and constant lecturing from Europe. A stumbling block for the Russian government was the bureaucracy in Brussels, which stubbornly insisted on criteria of cooperation with Russia that were unacceptable to Moscow. Thus, Brussels continued demanding immediate increases in energy tariffs from Russia, which might in the view of Russian experts destroy the Russian economy. The European Union refused to budge on Russia's entry into the World Trade Organization. The administrative nitpicking brought on an outburst from the usually restrained Putin, who spoke in unflattering terms about the bureaucrats in Brussels.

Then Moscow unexpectedly discovered that the expansion of the European Union brought it new challenges, for which it was unprepared. One challenge was the question of extending the Agreement on Partnership and Cooperation with the European Union to its new members in Central and Eastern Europe. That expansion could cost Russia up to $150 million a year, according to some analysts. Moscow made a show of delivering an ultimatum to Brussels of fourteen points, basically demanding a review of the conditions of its agreement with the European Union. The list demanded trade concessions and an easing of the visa regime.[27] Brussels responded no less harshly, and understandably; its plans did not include changing its rules in response to the demands of a nation that was not an E.U. member state.

The accumulated mutual claims and rebukes made Russia regard the European Union with consternation, expecting nothing good from it. In turn, the authorities in Brussels changed their formerly polite tone with Russia and seemed to change their policy of acquiescence for a tougher line. The European Commission froze the implementation of the ideas of the resolution it had published in early 2003 under the title Wider Europe, in which Russia, along with the other countries on the perimeter of the European Union, was defined as a nation in the E.U. "circle of friends." On February 9, 2004, the European Commission approved the resolution titled Relations with the Russian Federation, which demonstrated the community's disappointment in its relations with Russia. The European Union insisted that before negotiating with Russia, E.U. member nations must agree among themselves about "red lines" that cannot be crossed in talks with Moscow; that is, a recommendation was made to Western capitals not to make concessions to Russia. Yet at the same time, other documents prepared by official E.U. agencies called for continuing the course for Russia's integration, primarily through the creation of the four spaces described just above.

The contradictions in the European Union's positions evince the existence of various approaches to Russia in Brussels; the desire to continue the integration project despite all obstacles remains, along with a different approach that is beginning to dominate, at least at this stage. Its adherents feel that Russia has no intention of making changes that would allow it to think about integrating into the E.U. structures. For the first time, there appeared within European institutions an open call to build relations with Russia on interests and not on the basis of integration, and a readiness was shown to make relations with Russia a lower-level priority.

Apparent frustration with Russia on the part of the E.U. community was the inevitable result of the failure of the concept of Russian integration into the Western institutions that had been elaborated in the West in the 1990s. According to this concept, Russia could become a member of these institutions (for instance, of the G-8) despite the facts that it did not quite qualify and that its participation in the Western club would gradually change its behavior and even domestic principles. To some extent, Russia's membership in the Council of Europe and in the G-8, along with the activity of the NATO–Russia Council, really did have an impact on Russian domestic developments. Abuses of human rights in Chechnya and the crackdown on media in Russia would have been much harsher if not for Putin's desire to become a member of the Western community and its institutions. But it is also true that the Russian ruling elites started to believe that Russia should be accorded special treatment and could be integrated into the Western community while still preserving its traditional state and its own rules and domestic principles. That has really changed the Western attitude toward further integration of Russia into its organizational networks. Now the dominant mood in the West is that Russia must meet first the standards of international institutions and then be offered membership. And if Russia stops meeting the criteria, then expulsion must be considered.[28]

Examining the reasons for the mutual disillusionment of the European Union and Russia, the Russian analysts Timofei Bordachev and Arkady Moshes found that the systemic differences in these international subjects had taken their toll on the relationship. Europe no longer believed that "Russia could become part of the community of nations sharing similar values." The European Community was increasingly thinking "that Russia basically was incapable of being integrated and will remain a partner-rival outside the European space," concluded Bordachev and Moshes.[29]

Russia itself fed the European pessimism regarding Russia's integration by constantly referring to its own special interests and needs and demanding total freedom in foreign and domestic policy. In short, Moscow paid lip service to the idea of integration but was not prepared to give up its sovereignty for it, and so it continued its realpolitik based on its interests.

In this regard, I also agree with Andrei Zagorsky, who has said that one of the main reasons for the deceleration of cooperation with Europe was "Moscow's overestimation of its role and influence on the international arena" and its demands "to build relations with Western countries and their multilateral organizations on the basis of total equality."[30] Pekka Sutela has noted Russia's "tendency to demand the impossible." "Russia may well think that demanding the impossible will at least bring another concession elsewhere," continued Sutela.[31]

Demanding the "impossible" meant, for instance, that Moscow insisted on the right to participate in the E.U. decision-making process without being a member, which the union could not permit, naturally. It was a vicious circle: Russia's further integration into the European space called for the concordance of Russian legislation with the normative base in Brussels; that is, Russia would have to accept the rules of the game of the European Community. But for Moscow, this would mean unequal relations and Russia was not prepared to play junior partner. Besides which, the acceptance of certain E.U. principles could be destructive for Russia, which was still on a different level of development. Nor was the European Union prepared to allow a country that had different standards for law and order take part in decision making. This situation frequently made the union and Russia opponents, and severe ones, rather than partners. There did not seem to be a way out of this contradiction. That did not mean, of course, that diplomatic relations between Moscow and major European capitals became strained. Not at all! European leaders, among them Schröder, Berlusconi, Chirac, and Blair, individually cultivated special friendships with Putin, often leaving the European Union and Brussels to play the role of a "bad cop." The existence of two levels of relations between Moscow and Europe—more warm on the bilateral level and more difficult on the multinational level—left Russia a broad field for maneuvering. Indeed, Moscow would prefer to deal with the first level.

Interestingly, Russians continued to think that Russia should persist in its movement toward Europe. But fewer hoped for membership in E.U. structures; in January 2003, 57 percent of respondents hoped Russia would join the European Union, but in November 2003 only 35 percent felt that Russia should work toward becoming an equal member, and 30 percent thought Russia should strive for equal relations with the union without becoming a member. Only 16 percent felt that there was no point in Russia's wanting to be part of Europe.[32] So despite the problems on the political level, the majority of Russians still thought that Russia should move closer to Europe, and this was a heartening fact.

Vladimir Putin's inauguration as the president of Russia took place on May 7, 2004. He looked like a new man. At his inauguration in 2000, he walked through the Kremlin halls and went up the long staircase in obvious discomfort and embarrassment, trying to hide his nervousness. This time, he strode confidently, looking around, making eye contact with people in the crowds on both sides of the aisle. His expression was calm and aloof, and appropriately perhaps, even mocking. Or did I just imagine that? President Vladimir Putin was the master of the situation. He exuded self-confidence.

The ceremony was brief and impressive. The president made a speech and went out onto the royal balcony to review the parade. This time, horse guards were part of the parade. I can imagine how worried the organizers were. The horses came from the herd at the Mosfilm Studios menagerie. When they began to rehearse the parade, something unexpected occurred. As soon as the band played, the horses bowed down. They had been trained for some historical film. Up to the last moment, the parade organizers could not be sure that the horses would not kneel before the president. Putin would not have liked those excesses—he preferred a simple ceremony without pomp and had rejected a number of monarchic symbols introduced by Yeltsin. Fortunately, at the crucial moment, the horses did not insist on genuflecting.

Vladimir Vladimirovich reviewed the parade and began his second term.

Chapter 11

FROM OLIGARCHIC AUTHORITARIANISM TO BUREAUCRATIC AUTHORITARIANISM

———————— ✤ ————————

Putinism as a continuation and rejection of Yeltsinism. The economics of growth without development. The social sphere: Degradation continues. Russia and the West in search of selective partnership. Did the president have an alternative? The dangers of oversimplification. An evaluation of political leadership.

Those who thought that Vladimir Vladimirovich Putin would be no more than Yeltsin's successor, defending Yeltsin's legacy and especially the positions of his political "Family," were wrong. Putin in his first term became a dialectician, and an elemental one at that. On the one hand, he demonstrated a continuity with the past, not only Yeltsin's but the pre-Yeltsin era as well. He preserved the paradigm of the rule that even Gorbachev and Yeltsin, who dared to destroy the state and the empire, did not have the nerve to do away with—personified and undivided power. On the other hand, Putin rejected Yeltsinism as a style and method of rule. He created a new political regime and started a new cycle in Russia's development.

What did the second Russian president do during the period 1999–2003? Putin brought the country out of its revolutionary stage by ending Yeltsin's chaotic experiment with democracy and freedoms. In economics, Putin strengthened the market vector, but in the end he began to lean toward an interventionist policy that undermined his own reforms. In the social sphere, Putin retained a degraded social system that became the source for social tension. On the international scene, Putin retained Russia's pro-Western vector, but zigzagged and failed to integrate Russia into the Western community, although that was not his fault alone.

Putin tried to do the impossible: to stabilize an incomplete transformation. No one has ever been able to make an unfinished building sturdy and
long-lasting, no matter how it is bolstered. Basically, Yeltsin's successor
embarked on two incompatible projects simultaneously, evidently not realizing their incompatibility: trying to keep traditional rule while building a
modern economy. This incompatibility triggered new contradictions,
which were not only situational but also systemic—between the conservative political class, fixated on its own interests, and the more dynamic
society; between a pro-Western course and statist feelings; between liberal economics and statist bureaucrats; between a desire for freedom and
attempts to stifle it; and between stability and the need for dynamism, and
therefore for the overhaul of mechanisms developed under Putin. The second Russian president thus created contradictions that will have to be
resolved by someone else. If he does try to resolve them, he will have to
destroy much of what he created in the course of his first term.

But let's not try to guess the future now. Let's think about the recent
past. I realize that not all the consequences of Vladimir Putin's rule are yet
evident. Not all the tendencies that have emerged will remain; some will,
and others will be transient. Nevertheless, I think that at the moment I am
writing, in the fall of 2004, there is enough evidence to deduce the logic
and dilemmas of Putin's first term.

So let's follow fresh tracks, beginning, of course, with politics, which
remains the driving force in Russian development, even though there was
very little politics left by the end of Putin's first term. The very fact that
politics (if by that we mean a combination of independent institutions and
mechanisms for communication between the regime and society) had
dried up is also an important result of Putin's rule.

Vladimir Putin, a complete novice on the Russian political scene, cautiously and gradually, without entering into confrontation with the former
ruling group, managed to restructure Yeltsin's political regime, without
particular tension or struggle. The Yeltsin regime in the final stages of its
evolution could be called *oligarchic authoritarianism*, that is, personified
power oriented toward first implementing the interests of the big business

group close to the Kremlin. The remaining groups of influence within the ruling elite—in particular, the technocrats and bureaucrats—were also oriented toward serving the interests of the oligarchy.[1]

Putin created a political regime in which the main resource for personified power is the bureaucracy. It is trying to subordinate the technocrats and big business (and it succeeded in great part by the end of Putin's first term). Tentatively, Putin's rule can be described as a bureaucratic-authoritarian regime.[2] This concept is not new and was used by several scholars, including Guillermo O'Donnell for Latin American regimes of the 1960s and 1970s that were instrumental in modernizing economies based on natural resources. The direct parallels between Russian and Latin American political regimes should not be overemphasized, however, for they function in different historical contexts. I am borrowing the concept, which I hope permits us to identify two elements in today's Russian regime: authoritarianism and the leader's use of the bureaucracy. It is the combination of those two elements that distinguishes Putin's regime from Yeltsin's.

Russian authoritarianism has a reformist, modernist component, as evinced by Putin's foreign policy and his economic liberalism. But at the same time, its modernization potential is much narrower than the potential of other authoritarian regimes, such as those of Chile and South Korea. The latter limited democracy and the access to power of independent political forces, but it also created legal principles that extended to the state with its bureaucracy, which thus had to follow the law. This eased the transition to a law-based society.

In Russia, we see something to the contrary: the strengthening of a state that prefers to extend informal rules that constantly change, rather than follow the law. These are under-the-counter deals, which the regime covers up by using the courts and the prosecutor's office, which participate in the formation of a non-law-based system. Russian bureaucratic authoritarianism thus is totally devoid of any signs of Weber's rational bureaucracy and cannot create an institutional framework.[3]

Among the numerous factors influencing the emergence of the new political regime in Russia, I would mention the following: the role that Yeltsin assigned to Putin; the systemic logic formed under Yeltsin; Putin's own vision; the character of the team he put together; and the reigning sentiments among the elites and the public.

Yeltsin and his ruling corporation appointed Putin to the role of stabilizer, whereby he was supposed to solidify their positions after Yeltsin left office. But once in the Kremlin, Putin had to obey a logic that contradicted the interests of the Yeltsin clan. Ironically, to maintain power, Putin in the end had to sacrifice the interests of the ruling stratum to which he owed his rise to power. He did it cautiously and gradually, pushing Yeltsin's loyalists out of the circle and reshuffling the basis of his rule.

Putin's leadership was influenced by his worldview as a statist, a former member of power structures, and simultaneously a market supporter. So far, *market authoritarianism* has been Putin's basic philosophy. He renewed the market reforms stalled under Yeltsin while centralizing his power. Putin's choice of regime can be explained by his distrust of democracy. He must believe that democratic institutions undermine the Russian state and cannot guarantee economic reform—not a rare sentiment among technocratically oriented leaders.

There is another motive behind Putin's authoritarian ways: Putin needed to shape his own basis of support. He could not count indefinitely on Yeltsin's people, who formed his entourage at first. The fastest and simplest way to hold on to power is to place your own people in key state posts. With Putin's background and mentality, he began resurrecting the administrative carcass by bringing in people from the security services.[4]

To be fair, Putin did not rely solely on the *siloviki*—he included technocrats and pragmatic bureaucrats, who became part of the complex web he created as a counterweight to the *siloviki*. The people Putin brought with him were unable to form a tight team, but they mastered the ABCs of officialdom, and at the end of the day, they pushed out Yeltsin's comrades-in-arms and co-opted a few of the remaining ones (such as Vladislav Surkov). They created a much more opaque and immovable bureaucratic machine, resembling the Soviet state, which could not respond flexibly to external stimuli and crisis situations. The only island of improvisation around Putin in his first term was the economic bloc of the government, with German Gref and his people. But they were soon forced to accept the bureaucratic rules trying to survive in the Kremlin's corridors.

The Putin regime was formed in a period of popular exhaustion with Yeltsin's vacillations and shenanigans, which to some degree explains its trajectory. Both the political class and a large portion of the public in 1999–2000 wanted order and a strong leader. Even some of the liberals were prepared to sacrifice the chaotic and unregulated democratization that was being exploited by the ruling clans as a cover for their corporate interests.

All these factors pushed Putin in a more authoritarian direction compared with Yeltsin's rule. Putin's first term suggests that it is impossible to secure nascent democratic institutions and political freedoms that have not been formalized by the rule of law. As long as society and the regime do not come to terms with restructuring power on the basis of the law, the monopolist-corporate tendency inevitably deforms or subsumes the weak democratic impulse. Putin, by strengthening this tendency, thereby gave the impetus to create a new authoritarianism.

At the same time, it would be naïve to consider authoritarianism as the main tendency of Russia's development in its post–Yeltsin stage. The curbing of political freedoms under Putin took place simultaneously with the growth of the bureaucracy. Disoriented and fragmented in the 1990s, the officials who had seemed pushed out of the power circle under Yeltsin by big business (even though the "oligarchy" was created by apparatchiks) started to consolidate around the new leader. By the end of Putin's first term, the matrix that existed until the fall of communism had been gradually reinstated: The leader is at the top, and under him is his support, the bureaucracy, which simultaneously tries to be a key player.

Yet here, too, it is difficult to capture a single tendency. For even under Putin, big business, now out of the inner circle, retained its ability to influence the regime. But it had to switch from direct pressure to spending money on lobbying for its interests. Instead of going to the offices of ministers and kicking open the door, instead of openly and blatantly bribing Duma deputies, the "oligarchs" now had to move more circumspectly, through intermediaries. The old Russian tradition, in which the Desk is more important than Money, had returned—which only strengthened the tradition of intertwining power and capital.

Besides, the new bureaucracy that arose around the president began to develop its own business structures. It was a repetition of what had occurred in the Yeltsin years, when bureaucrats appointed representatives to privatize state property who were also empowered to implement the interests of the bureaucracy. Now, after the choicest pieces of state property had already been privatized, the appetites of the new bureaucracy and the new "oligarchs" could be satisfied mainly by redistributing private property. The YUKOS affair was an important test, which had to show whether the authorities were ready for a massive redistribution or were dealing with an isolated case of "crime and punishment." In any case, one thing was certain: Older and wiser, the new "oligarchy" would sooner or later try to escape the control of the apparatchiks, as had happened under Yeltsin. The next boss of the Kremlin would once again have to decide how to control big business—through a new anti-oligarchic revolution or through legislative regulation of business and its relationship with the regime.

The revanche of the bureaucracy under Putin has become also a brake on his personal power. There are other constraints on his power, including the influential regional interests and the interests of the *siloviki*, the increase in society's independence from the state, the remaining spontaneity of development, and the weakness of mechanisms of enforcement and their corruption. The existence of the business community with its still powerful interests also narrows the president's maneuverability. During his first term, Putin looked like a strong leader, but this strength and even omnipotence were limited by too many drivers. In some cases and areas, Putin was even more limited in his movements than Yeltsin, who had been considered a really weak leader.

There is a temptation to explain the authoritarian swing under Putin as a deformation of the Russian system that emerged under Yeltsin. Meanwhile, we are dealing with a logical result of Yeltsinism and the inevitable consequence of the degradation of undeveloped democratic mechanisms. And because the new regime had to break with the past in order to assert itself, Putinism began rejecting Yeltsinism as a mentality, a form of rule, and a balance of forces. Stephen Kotkin was right when he wrote about "a misinterpretation of the 1990s, when disarray rather than institutionalized rule of law prevailed" and that the authoritarian offensive in Russia could not be credited solely to Putin.[5] Let me stress this: The Putin regime was not only the embodiment of Putin's ideas of power but also a reaction to the Yeltsin past that Russia was trying to escape. That the Russian elites sought an exit by returning to the past says volumes about their inability to face new challenges.

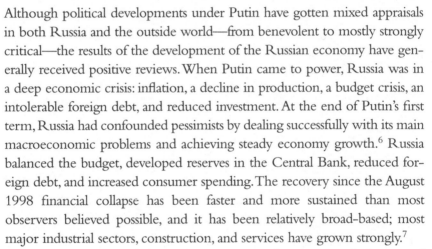

Although political developments under Putin have gotten mixed appraisals in both Russia and the outside world—from benevolent to mostly strongly critical—the results of the development of the Russian economy have generally received positive reviews. When Putin came to power, Russia was in a deep economic crisis: inflation, a decline in production, a budget crisis, an intolerable foreign debt, and reduced investment. At the end of Putin's first term, Russia had confounded pessimists by dealing successfully with its main macroeconomic problems and achieving steady economy growth.[6] Russia balanced the budget, developed reserves in the Central Bank, reduced foreign debt, and increased consumer spending. The recovery since the August 1998 financial collapse has been faster and more sustained than most observers believed possible, and it has been relatively broad-based; most major industrial sectors, construction, and services have grown strongly.[7]

For the first time, Russian economic growth was not only motivated by oil prices. According to a survey by the Organization for Economic Cooperation and Development (OECD), the Russian economy would have grown very robustly even at average oil prices.[8] Hope emerged that Russia had started to get rid of its oil "addiction." But the same OECD survey and other sources (World Bank and Russian Goskomstat) demonstrated that the Russian economy was still not diversified.[9] That meant that despite positive economic trends, Russian economic performance in the long run would continue to depend to a great extent on resource-exporting sectors. And that in turn meant that Russia was vulnerable to external shocks, the risk of "Dutch disease," and institutional pathologies, particularly rent seeking and corruption.

Spectacular economic growth was mainly restorative growth. "Restorative growth is at first always a pleasant surprise for the elite. And then it turns into a problem: The rate cannot be maintained and begins to fall," warned Yegor Gaidar.[10] The reforms that would have guaranteed the economic growth on the basis of high-technology industries were not completed, and some (for instance, bank reform) were not even begun. By 2004, the reform wave in economics begun by Putin in 2000–2001 had receded. "The economic upswing of the last four years that replaced decades of crisis has not led to the modernization of the economy but to a consumer boom of a population tired of the difficulties of the preceding decades," wrote Leonid Grigoryev.[11] The situation at the end of Putin's first term started to resemble the consumer well-being created by high oil prices in the 1970s under Brezhnev. The resemblance stirred up bad forebodings, because too many people still remembered what had happened after oil prices fell—a deep economic crisis and the collapse of the Soviet Union.

In the course of Putin's first term, the obstacles on the path to further economic transformation became visible. The first obstacle was psychological—it is difficult to undertake painful reforms in a situation of stability and beneficial foreign trade. This "leads to the temptation of entering the sphere of populist decisions," warned Vladimir Mau.[12] High oil prices led to a higher rate of exchange for the ruble, the concentration of capital in the natural resources sector, and the eating away of the revenues from oil and gas export. The flow of petrodollars induced the lulling effect that the wealth would continue indefinitely, especially because the situation in the Middle East and in Iraq remained tense and the world needed Russian oil. But the bonanza could dry up unexpectedly, and Russia was not prepared for that sobering period.

The second obstacle to the economic reforms is rooted in the peculiar structural characteristics of the Russian economy. They include the sweet deals in much of the economy, insecure property rights, a still insufficient level of monetization of the economy, economic inequality among the regions, and the confused situation in the budget relations between the center and the regions.[13] Yevgeny Yasin mentioned that one of the structural causes of the economy's inefficiency is the preservation of the nonmarket sector, which includes education, healthcare, culture, the armed forces, and housing. Unless that sector is reformed, he believes, the economy will not be able to develop efficiently.[14]

Oleg Vyugin, the head of the Federal Service on Financial Markets, identified another constraint: the fact that the Russian economy is structured on the principle of group monopolies, which excluded constructive competition.[15] The state continued to support this structure, which is evidence of the cozy relationship between the government and the monopolies (both private and state-owned ones, for instance, Gazprom). This fusion of business and regime was the third obstacle on the path to economic reforms.

The fourth and most formidable obstacle was political: the very centralized system of power that worked to satisfy the interests of the bureaucracy, which wanted to preserve the natural resources economy and the revenues it brings.[16] Though he is usually upbeat about Russian economic performance, Anders Åslund argued that Putin's centralization of power would incapacitate the engine of new economic growth. "Now that the balance of power between the *siloviki* and big businessmen has been replaced by centralized power exerted by an alliance between the same *siloviki* and big state companies, it is difficult to postulate that such securely entrenched vested interests would support reforms that might precipitate their weakening," wrote Åslund.[17]

And fifth, the economic reforms were complicated by the absence of a consensus in the Russian political class regarding the model for economic development. Russian society recognized the market as the optimal form for organizing the economy. But the discussion continued on the kind of market Russia needed. The arguments centered on three models: the left-wing-populist (dirigiste) model, based on a statist ideology and industrial sectors' priorities; the oligarchic model, that is, dominance by large financial-industrial groups; and the liberal (institutional) model, based on stimulating entrepreneurial activity. The absence of agreement on the economic model also led to a lack of clarity about the strategic vector of economic development. The debate over where to invest money has not stopped. Some have insisted that it should continue to go into the natural resources sector. Others have countered, "No, we must invest in processing industries and machine building." Still others have maintained that high-technology development, especially in aviation and telecommunications, is the right choice.

The beginning of 2004 showed that neither the Russian government nor Russian business had come to an agreement about the volume of state regulation or what the relationship between the state and the entrepreneurial community should be. There were two opposing sides within the government. One tried, with ever-weakening efforts, to create institutional foundations for macroeconomic stability; the other displayed the desire to speed up the redistribution of revenues and property by populist means (by using revenues from export-oriented fields) and to return once again to industrial policy.[18]

Even the liberally oriented economists were not united on the basic priorities for economic development. Some economists wanted economic growth, supporting the government policies on this.[19] Thus, Victor Polterovich said, "As reforms are implemented, the rent becomes available, and the fight over it . . . makes everyone forget about production." Thus, he felt, Russia had to focus on economic growth, which could create the conditions for the development of new economic institutions in the future.[20] Polterovich and his supporters also felt that the state must not leave the economy, because it alone could reform it. Yasin and his adherents, on the contrary, maintained that the nonmarket sector had to be freed from state control immediately, even if that led to a temporary fall in economic growth, and that the state's interference in economic growth had to be curtailed.[21]

This contradiction was present in Putin's initiatives. Thus, the president embarked on administrative reforms, one of which was intended to debureaucratize the economy—that is, liberalize it further, freeing business from the oversight of the bureaucracy. But at the same time, the YUKOS case evinced something else: the state's desire to increase control over big business. As Philip Hanson wrote, deliberating on the repercussions of the YUKOS story for the Russian economy, "Events since mid-2003 indicate that the economic policy is 'liberal to a point.' The leadership apparently wishes to maintain the power to intervene ad hoc in at least some sectors of the economy. It seeks to do this, in part, by preserving a large gap between formal and informal rules, so that state action is not constrained by an independent legal system. . . . Many analysts, including the present author, find this new (or newly revealed) character of Putin's economic policies disappointing."[22]

Grigory Yavlinsky, analyzing the economy at the end of Putin's first term, concluded, "If the situation is not changed radically, we will be doomed to growth without development, without social transformation, and without long-term prospects. And that is the best case, because in the worst case, we can expect economic stagnation and new crises."[23]

Thanks to economic growth, the authorities managed to soften the profound social crisis of the 1990s. The government started regularly paying salaries and pensions, which was a positive change compared with Yeltsin's period of chronic wage and pensions arrears. By 2004, real wages and real disposable incomes in Russia were well above their precrisis peaks. Real wages grew by 25 percent, with the average wage reaching about $210 per month in early 2004, and real disposable incomes grew by 12 percent.[24] The unemployment rate had fallen from 13 percent in 1998 to about 8 percent in 2004 (to 5.7 million people). For the first time during the postcommunist transformation, the living standards of the Russian population as a whole, not merely the better off, have improved significantly.

Nevertheless, enormous disparities among regions and localities remained, with respect to both real incomes and unemployment. The gap between the haves and have-nots was growing, and the average incomes of the 10 percent richest exceeded those of the 10 percent poorest by a multiple of 15.2 in June 2004. Recent years have witnessed the emergence of a large group of people—including mainly young adults, families with children, and single parents—living below the poverty line with no hope of improvement in their living standards.[25]

During Putin's first term, because the government was bogged down in addressing political issues, strengthening the state, and dealing with macroeconomic stability, it openly neglected social policy.[26] Overall, there were no tangible shifts in the state's social policy or even an intention to conceptualize social policy. The president and his administration apparently wanted to reduce the poverty rate, but by a sporadic effort of plugging holes and the old mechanisms of redistribution. Yevgeny Gontmakher, a government official responsible for social development, admitted, "The state has simply refused to perform many elementary obligations for the social security of the population."[27] Declaring the idea of a "social state" in the Constitution, the regime did not support it with resources. To maintain social and political stability, the authorities continued to use the Soviet mechanisms of social security. But without resources, those mechanisms were doomed sooner or later to give rise to social tensions.[28] The administration failed to allocate social responsibility among separate levels of power. And the distribution of social benefits continued to be done in ways that were not always just and did not direct aid to those who really needed it.[29]

The inability to implement more efficient social policies, keeping the population dependent on the state, was related to the bureaucrats' desire to retain the social system, which promoted corruption and theft. The state was the only actor in the social sphere. The nongovernmental organization sector was not brought into social aid. Moreover, the recentralization of power did not permit increasing the role of local self-government in solving social issues (such as housing). No tax or other incentives were created to bring business into social development. Russian business limited its role to basic charity, which was not enough to change the woeful state of social services.

As a result, the state lost control over the processes in some areas of human welfare, mainly in demographic and health areas, in which degradation seemed on the brink of irreversibility. It appeared that economic growth had no impact on major demographic and health indicators. A few facts reveal the dramatic problems facing Russia. The population continued to shrink (from 149 million in 1991 to 144 million in 2003), which raised the question of whether Russia would be able to control its geographical space fifty years hence. In 2003, for every 100 newborns, 173 people died.[30] Between 1997 and 2002, life expectancy for males fell by three years; the rate for females fell by one year. Mortality rates continued to increase. Optimistic forecasts indicated that by 2050 the population of Russia would be down to 102 million, while pessimistic ones estimated 77 million.

The health care situation was no less troubling. In 2004, only a third of Russians considered themselves healthy, with 40 percent being sick frequently and 30 percent chronically. Two-thirds of Russian children were sick, and that was a threat of reproduction of an unhealthy population. Diseases thought to have been eradicated in the USSR, such as tuberculosis, are spreading again. And Russia is on the brink of a uncontrollable epidemic of HIV/AIDS.[31] True, health and mortality trends were puzzling, given that Russia is experiencing economic growth and that poverty rates have fallen sharply. Continuing problems with health and mortality indicate, first of all, a continuing absence of government policy with respect to human welfare. Another reason behind the deterioration of health was the low living standards of the most vulnerable part of the population. Public spending on health during Yeltsin's term was about 4 percent of the gross domestic product, and during Putin's first term it remained at the level of 6.5 percent—too low to solve the existing problems and restructure the health care system.

There are also other serious problems affecting Russia's human welfare situation in the short term, for instance, children without parents or with parents who are not taking care of them. By 2004, the country had about 3 million orphans—more than the Soviet Union had after World War II. This is the price society is paying for years of disorientation, the collapse of the state, and the decline of family values. Hundreds of thousands of homeless children live in the streets, where they are fodder for growing crime and drug abuse. Hundreds of thousands of crippled children who have lived in state-run homes and were given no education or training will end up on the dole, for which the state is not prepared. Yet another problem is forced migration, with no jobs for millions of the newcomers.[32] This painful list can be continued almost indefinitely.

The few positive changes that occurred during Putin's first term do not alter the general picture of the deterioration of society's pillars. The new authorities once again demonstrated their indifference, apparently thinking that the patience of the Russian people was unlimited. It was not so much that the state refused to increase spending on health and welfare, preferring to increase the budgets for the apparatchiks, defense, and special services.[33] More important was the fact that the state was not creating incentives for people to help themselves, particularly by starting small and medium-sized business. The state was not giving people any fish, nor was it supplying the fishing poles with which they could catch their own.

In comparison with the pitiful picture in the social sphere, Russian foreign policy in Putin's first term can be considered a success. The second Russian president increased Russia's international stature and reinvigorated its presence on the international scene. And he did it not with militant saber rattling but restraint and pragmatism. Putin tried to do what Yeltsin failed to: He tried to turn foreign policy into an instrument for realizing domestic goals and to bring Russia's foreign policy ambitions in line with its capabilities. And he scored several successes.

Putin clarified Russia's priorities in foreign policy. He stressed Russia's relations with the Commonwealth of Independent States (CIS). Not only Russia's great-power state adherents but also its liberal-democratic circles supported Putin's vector toward the post-Soviet space, albeit for different reasons. However, the Kremlin never did solve the conceptual question: Is it trying to establish, on the territory of the former USSR, a new community of states headed by Russia as an alternative to the Western community; or is it trying to ease the movement of Russia and the other newly independent states toward the West? In other words, should Russia try to freeze the transitional condition of the CIS nations and try to use its alliances with them to reinforce its superpower role, or should it promote their transformation by bringing them closer to the West?

So far, integration within the former Soviet space has had no transformational potential; that is, the CIS has not pushed its members toward developing more effective rules of the game in politics and economics. In some areas—security and trade—an integrative effort could be instrumental for some states to achieve certain goals, but often at the expense of the interests of other members of the alliance. Integration in the post-Soviet space could acquire reformist substance only if it were seen by its participants, at least in the European part of the former Soviet space, as a framework for their collective integration with Europe. But so far, each of the participants has seemed to develop its own bilateral relations with the European Union and with the West as a whole, and this has made all the alliances within the post-Soviet space seem shallow—a kind of short-term dating, not even marriages of convenience.

At the concluding stage of Putin's first term, new aspects of the relations between Russia and Europe began to materialize. In 2001–2002, it was fashionable in Moscow to speak of integration into the European community. Quite a few Russian, European, and American observers started to build concepts of "Russia's transformation through integration" or "integration through transformation." For instance, the participants in the international project "Transformation and Integration in the Twenty-First Century," sponsored by the Carnegie Corporation of New York, stated that "Russia's transformation and integration is not just good only for Russia. We also believe that, despite the tensions affecting US–EU–Russian relations ... now is the time for Russia, Europe, and America to appreciate that their own self-interest entails cooperation. Indeed, we argue that just as Europe and America can help Russia with its democratic transformation, so too Russia can help Europe to overcome its growing division into east and west while both Russia and Europe can mitigate America's tendency to pursue go-it-alone policies."[34] I'm almost certain that Putin himself for some time seriously considered Russia's integration scenario, trying to sound out the probability of its accession to NATO and the European Union and getting, if not veto power, then at least influence on the decision making in those structures. But by the end of his first term, it was clear that Russia was not ready for direct integration into the European Union.

Neither was Europe prepared to embrace Russia. The Eurocrats in Brussels hardly were trying to think, and perhaps did not have the time to think, about more constructive forms of partnership with Russia. They had their hands full with embracing Central and Eastern Europe. Besides, the new E.U. members were not ready to support Russia's integration into the European Union, in which they have been trying to find escape and guarantees of security against the revival of the ambitions of the neighboring former Soviet empire.

The end of Putin's second term brought the need for a new conceptualization of the Russian–American relationship. The moods in Moscow showed that Russia was not prepared to be America's junior partner, following blindly in its wake. The early years of Putin's administration had created an impression that in practice Russia might grudgingly agree with U.S. initiatives or be forced to accept them, not having the resources or possibility of arguing. The first serious divide between Washington and Moscow was provoked by Russia's refusal to support the military operation in Iraq. But playing junior partner had its limits for Putin. He could do it until it threatened to cause open resistance among his political base and his comrades. And even his loyal followers were starting to grumble about Putin being a yes man for Washington.

The Russian president had at least four possible variants for a relationship with the United States. The first was to be more militant in rhetoric but without taking any action that could damage relations with Washington. The second was to take a tougher stand against American interests, especially in the post-Soviet space, even risking an open conflict with the United States. The third was to move to a more constructive dialogue with the United States, which because of the different weight classes of the two countries would mean accepting the junior partnership. And the fourth was to move to a policy of greater isolationism by distancing itself from the spheres where Russia did not have resources to cooperate with the United States as an equal and by having dialogue only where Moscow would be able to push through its interests. To some degree, this fourth option resembles China's policy.

Putin was not prepared to escalate relations with America. But he also apparently hardly saw a real basis for extending the partnership. The evolution of his policy was influenced by the remaining asymmetry in the capabilities of the two countries that still was bothering the Russian political class, by the presence of great-power feelings among the Russian elite, and by the hegemony of American policies and the way Washington was pursuing them. Russia, still expecting to have regional if not global influence, was unable to voluntarily accept America's leadership, especially the traditional type of leadership demonstrated by military might. At the same time, Russia was not yet ready for a dialogue as an equal with the United States. This situation prepared the way for the formula of selective partnership (or selective engagement) between Russia and the United States. But the formula needed refining and developing.

In the meantime, the political class in Russia began to feel self-confidence and started to believe that Russia, in dealing with the United

States, had to operate from a position of strength, because that was all America respected. Alas, the American administration, with its foreign policy assertiveness, often gave grounds for such a conclusion. Therefore, Russian politicians, even moderate ones, sought ways to equalize the asymmetry in Russia's relations with the United States.[35] U.S. neoconservatism strengthened Russian neoconservatism. The latter still dreamed that elements of the old bipolar system might return. Putin had a much more sober view of Russian–American relations than the home-grown neoconservatives, but he did not pour cold water on their dreams.

On the whole, if we look at how Russia was positioned in the course of Putin's first term in the international arena, we will see that Russia was simultaneously in the Western orbit—being tied to the West by a number of common interests—but remained outside the Western system and its decision-making processes. The relations between Russia and the West were based on partnership in some spheres, and in others on cooperation based on common interests but not common values. In some areas, the relations had signs of contradiction and confrontation, even if covert ones. In other words, Russia and the West were simultaneously allies and potential foes.

This unique situation gave rise to both hope and worry. The optimism stemmed from the fact that the system of relations between the West and Russia was mutable and their common interests could in the final analysis be an impetus for a more active integration of Russia into the Western system. The worry was that Russia's intermediate situation could continue indefinitely and even expand into its isolation or could move to greater assertiveness. In any case, the preservation of different values in its society and the absence of a consensus on questions of national interest within Russia made Putin's turn to the West inconsistent. The West's lack of a strategy for integrating Russia also complicated Putin's pro-Western course and Russia's future choice.

Putin was right to seek a way out of Yeltsin's oligarchic capitalism when he came to power. He had three theoretical paths. The first was to begin restructuring the old system and moving toward liberal democracy. The second was move to a harsh market authoritarianism with support from the people, bypassing the bureaucracy. And the third was to choose bureaucratic capitalism with support from the apparatchiks. The system that arose under Yeltsin was multivectored; that is, there was a possibility of movement in various directions. Putin chose the third path.

Could development under Putin have gone in the direction of liberal democracy? Let us imagine Putin beginning his term by cutting the threads tying him to the Yeltsin Family and starting to build independent institutions, distancing himself from the "oligarchs," and strengthening the independent mass media (independent from the "oligarchs," as well). Could that have been possible in a situation where the public was disillusioned with political freedoms and dreamed of stability, when the political class wanted only the status quo, and when the democrats were weak and bickering among themselves? Could Putin have begun his *perestroika* when he was all alone in the Kremlin among people who considered him their puppet?

For Vladimir Putin to even try to get out of the elected monarchy, the following had to be in place: the existence of influential liberal democrats who could have become a support for him; an active desire for institutionalized democratization among the people (that is, pressure from below); and an understanding by the political class of the need for systemic reform. Yet even the Russian liberals supported the "strong-hand" regime, apparently hoping that an authoritarian leader could be a guarantor of market transformation. Actually, these same hopes had moved the technocrats of the Yeltsin government when they began building a market system using Yeltsin's personal rule as their support.

So, when Putin came to power, there were no drivers to push him toward liberal democracy. At the start, when he ascended to power, it might have been suicidal for him to take that direction. But once he received public support, he could begin dismantling the traditional state, at least to remove its most archaic elements. It is unlikely that Putin could have overturned the entire old system. But he could have initiated a systemic breach, which would have facilitated the building of a new state. For instance, he could have chosen a government of parliamentary majority, responsible to the Duma, and therefore, to the voters. This would have been the start of a way out of Russia's regime, which is totally irresponsible; parties cannot influence policy, having no chance to form the government or even to control it; the parliament passes laws without being accountable for their quality, also because it does not form the government. The president forms the government, but he also avoids responsibility for it. The system breeds irresponsibility.

But political will was necessary to attempt such a change. If Putin had decided to dismantle his authoritarian "conveyor belt" regime, even his closest allies would not have understood him. It was easier for Gorbachev; he began destroying the leading role of the Communist Party at a time of growing public enthusiasm and the rise of a reform minority within the party. But more important, the planned economy had been exhausted even before Gorbachev's rule. Putin found himself in the Kremlin in a quantitatively different situation. Society was tired of restructuring, the majority of the elites wanted no more changes, and high oil prices let the country sit and do nothing. Nevertheless, I suggest that the people would have supported the creation of a more responsible system guaranteeing the rule of law rather than the rule of a single top leader. In late 2000 and early 2001, the president had the strength to try at least to change the logic of Russian traditional rule. Polls show that 45 to 47 percent of the public could have supported Putin's breakthrough if he had appealed to Russia directly, over the heads of the state apparatus, and called for independent institutions. The people would have supported the breakthrough, especially if it came from the president, who had their trust.

But Putin did not take the chance. He chose the simplest variant for himself—he picked the bureaucracy as his major ally. Moreover, he actually increased the traditionalism from which Yeltsin had moved away. Was he protecting his own neck? Perhaps. But I think his choice can be explained not by a lack of courage but a lack of faith. He must not have believed that Russia was ready for modernization without the tight hold of authoritarianism.

Skeptics may say that Putin could not even have sensed the existence of a choice. For a former KGB man, there could be only one scenario: Clamp down on political freedoms. However, I am trying to avoid being categorical in my judgments, and I believe that we must not underestimate Putin by denying him the capacity for reflection and doubt. Like his predecessors who began reform in Russia, he is not a linear personality lacking internal vacillations. There is ample proof of that; he has wavered and still does over foreign policy, his economic agenda, and the selection of people for his team. Most of his decisions are marked by inconsistency and, apparently, doubts. In this, he follows in Yeltsin's footsteps. I think that Putin understands the nature of the choices before him, and even after making his choice, he vacillates over its implementation.

The ruler of an exhausted, chaotic country that is continually torn between conflicting options and developing by trial-and-error has to be a complex person—who, in Russian historian Yuri Pivovarov's acute phrase, must be Pope and Luther in one: reactionary and reformer, Westernizer and traditionalist. This politician has to keep turning one face, then the other, to the public.[36] He must either be a multifaceted character or he must know how to play various roles, which requires a certain mastery. Running unstructured Russia calls for greater artistry than running a tranquil, measured, and law-abiding Western country, where a weak leader is always bolstered by independent institutions or an organized society.

I don't rule out that Putin, who is a politician on a smaller scale than Gorbachev or Yeltsin, has a more contradictory nature than his predecessors. Just think: He left the KGB to work for one of the most vivid liberals and destroyers of Soviet history, Anatoly Sobchak, at the same time breaking ties with his agency and refusing to spy on his new boss. What a transformation! I don't doubt that Putin has constant inner turmoil and even more urgent decisions to make than his predecessors, because he is clearly running out of time to successfully combine traditionalism and modernism—both in the society and personally. Gorbachev and Yeltsin had the luxury of wallowing in indecision, taking one step forward and two back. But Putin is in a situation where continuing ambiguously is harder and harder, because society wants to know at last which way it is going. Putin continues playing incompatible roles and endorsing change and the status quo simultaneously, which once helped him maintain stability, when the people now want more certainty and definition from him. This is a risky game for any political leader.

The question of what was possible and what was not in Russia in the period 1999–2004 is not only theoretical. The answer will give us greater accuracy in forecasting Russia's future trajectory. Some Russian and Western scholars believe that Russia is doomed to traditional authoritarianism. Take, for example, Richard Pipes, an old Russia hand, who sees nothing but dark colors there. In his article "Flight from Freedom," Pipes tried to show that Russia is not prepared to exist as a liberal democracy.[37] As evidence, he cited sociological polls that are supposed to confirm that Russians do not like private property, are suspicious of the West, and are trying to create a new identity combining tsarism, communism, and Stalinism.[38] Actually, not only polls but also real life seem to prove that after the emancipation of the 1990s, Russia at least politically is returning to the past.

Does that mean that the pessimist Pipes is right? Not at all. In reality, the picture of public sentiments in Russian society is much more complex, and many polls do not capture the dynamics of those moods. It all depends on how the questions are posed. If you ask a Russian audience "Do you want Russia to be a great power?" the majority will say yes, because Russians do not know what it is to live in a small country with limited influence. But if you ask, "Are you prepared to pay the price for Russia to be a superpower?" you will get a very different answer—only 10 to 24 percent would be willing to pay for the country's greatness with their standard of living. If you ask Russians about their attitude toward the USSR, for many the very mention of the Soviet Union will bring on nostalgia—if only because so many respondents spent their youth in the USSR. But the same 10 to 24 percent, or even fewer, would want to return to the USSR.

According to surveys done by Igor Klyamkin and Tatyana Kutkovets, only 7 percent of Russians continue to support the basic principles of the "Russian System"—dominance of the state over the individual, paternalism, and national isolation—and 22 percent support two of those earmarks of the old system. They are primarily the elderly and people with low educational levels. The adherents of the modernist and postmodernist alternative, who support the priority of the individualism, independence, and openness of the country, make up 33 percent of the population, and 37 percent are prepared to support the modernist project.[39]

I am not going to go to the other extreme and idealize Russian society. It has never been a real democracy, it does not have the habit of self-organization and self-control, and it has not yet learned to think of itself as a nation of citizens. It still is easy to disorient. But for people without a tradition of political freedom and independent institutions, Russians have picked up new values very quickly. The dominant modernist values in Russian society can be seen in its acceptance of private property, media freedom, opposition, and so on. On the whole, the total of respondents who chose the modernist answer to basic questions of society and its structure is 60 percent, while the percentage of conservatives is half that.

Thus, Russians have accepted and legitimized the principle of private property. Yet they are suspicious of privatization, which is natural, considering its actual robber aspect. But what is important is that the majority of Russians are opposed to forced nationalization. According to polls taken in 2004 as part of a Russian–German sociological project, 45.5 percent of Russians are simultaneously positive toward entrepreneurship (and private property) and negative toward "oligarchs." Consequently, a rejection of "oligarchs" in Russia does not presume a hostility toward private enterprise in general. Of those polled, 77.2 percent agreed that natural resource revenues should be redistributed in favor of society, but 75.3 percent believe that the state should strictly adhere to the law in conflicts with business.[40]

The majority of Russians have a very healthy view of the role of various elite groups in Russian development. Thus, Russians consider the "oligarchs" a lesser evil than the bureaucracy; the "oligarchs" are considered a stumbling block for Russia's escape from its crisis by 35 percent, and government officials by 62 percent, that is, by almost twice as many respondents.[41]

The Russian people as a whole, despite many statements to the contrary, are no longer citizens of an imperial nation seeking survival through subordinating other nations, and they are no longer prepared to support Russia's superpower status at any cost. Thus, only 24 percent of Russians want to see Russia as "a mighty military nation, where the interests of the state are most important," while 76 percent want to live in another country, one that is "comfortable, convenient for life, where most important are the interests of people and their well-being."[42]

Russians do not want confrontation with the West—fewer than 20 percent feel hostility toward Western society, and then often under the influence of the authorities. The majority are against the automatic extension of Putin's rule, even though they give him a good approval rating.[43] However, in trusting the president, Russians do not trust the regime, which has lost its sacredness for them.[44] Despite the mass sucking up and brown nosing of the political class and the official press, Russians en masse do not feel servility for their leader.[45]

Russians still do not know how to live in a liberal democracy. But today Russia is fundamentally different from what it was a hundred years ago, when the great majority was categorically against liberal values. Only people who are prepared to accept new rules of the game could in a 1993 referendum support Yeltsin's economic policy after a few years of transformation had plunged them into humiliating poverty and could, after the financial crisis of 1998 again ruined their lives, support Putin's economic reforms. Only people who hope for a civilized solution could remain calm and patient when confronted with authorities that are unable to meet their elementary needs. A traditionalist nation would start storming the palaces of the "oligarchs" and bureaucrats or elect Zhirinovsky, Lebed, or Zyuganov president. However, Russia has never elected an extremist, nationalist, general with dictatorial aspirations—or a Communist.

The growing national and even fascist moods among some social groups in Russia are worrying, as are the manifestations of extremism and xenophobia in certain strata, particularly among the young. But in view of the extremely difficult circumstances in which Russian society is developing, and of the complexity of transforming a superpower and empire simultaneously, we can only be amazed that extremism remains a marginal phenomenon in Russia, despite the fact that the authorities themselves feed it and flirt with it. For example, in March 2004, no more than 3 percent of the population at least rhetorically expressed understanding of the activity of fascistic thugs, so-called skinheads.[46]

But if there were fewer barriers of political mentality on the road toward liberal values in Russian society, why, you may ask, did Russian society not vote for the liberals and democrats in the last elections? The answer: Because they were disillusioned with the actual parties—the Union of

Right Forces and Yabloko—and did not believe in these parties' ability to offer Russia a convincing program of reforms. In the last elections, the people did not reject liberal democracy; they simply did not support particular liberals and democrats who did not inspire trust.[47]

The more conservative sentiments in Russian society during the Putin years are primarily a reaction to Yeltsin's administration—the chaos, indecisiveness, corruption, and decay of the political class that came to power under democratic banners. I wouldn't rule out the possibility that even a society accustomed to democracy might react to these phenomena in the same way—with a desire for stronger rule.

There are other reasons that Russians do not make more efforts to actively support the modernist project—in particular, the absence of a new democratic opposition and the fact that Putin, just like Yeltsin, pays lip service to liberal values. Of course, another explanation is the rise in prosperity for part of society, which creates the illusion that market authoritarianism will be able to bring order to postrevolutionary development. But once people realize that the solution to their problems will require changing the system, the picture of Russia's political swamp may change abruptly.

I admit that part of the population may possibly become active in left-wing patriotic parties faster than the society consolidates itself around the transformation project. The first coalescence could appear on an emotional protest wave, which could be brought on by certain forces in the ruling class. Unification on the reformist platform requires not emotions but more complex intellectual and organizational efforts.

Nevertheless, it is important to stress that Russia's basic problem is not in society but the ruling class. Here we encounter the particular problem of Russian development: that today's ruling class is much more archaic that society itself, which forces us to revisit the old axiom about every society getting the government it deserves. Yet there are exceptions to that rule, and Russia today is one of them. Before the 1917 Revolution, part of the Russian political and economic class was without a doubt more progressive than the populace, which was a backward, agrarian society. But over the course of communist modernization, the numerous purges and personnel changes led to the formation of a servile ruling class with no initiative and interested only in its own survival. At the same time, during the

Soviet period, society, or at least a significant portion of it, began to free itself from the habitual archetypes and became more receptive to change than the ruling elites. In Russia, society and the ruling class moved, and are still moving, in different directions. The majority of the people reject being treated as a passive object of state manipulation, like a stupid, unimaginative herd. They have outgrown the Russian System, even though they are not yet protesting it, not knowing how to organize themselves.

After the fall of communism, Russians were prepared for a big breakthrough to a new system. But the men at the top were not, alas.[48] The elites never did learn how to govern this society in a new way, and it is these elites who cling to the old myths about Russia's "special path" and about the people who have not matured for democracy and therefore are in the way of modernization. Unfortunately, these myths are believed by some scholars, who prefer to see Russian reality in cut-and-dried terms or are accustomed to seeing Russia as the eternal foe of Western civilization. It is hard for them to give up the comfortable, simplifying stereotype that spares them from dealing with the complex and puzzling Russian reality.

Russian society is still wavering. The society frequently does not know where to turn. But at the same time, it displays amazing steadfastness and even pragmatism. Despite all the ups and downs of the 1990s, Russian society avoided the apocalyptic scenarios predicted by observers. This fact speaks more to the common sense of the population than that of political and economic elites. But Russians individually managed to free themselves from the state, and a lot of them live now by depending on themselves and not on the state (45 percent of Russians today do not depend directly on the state). On the whole, the post-Soviet Russian is not the bearer of traditional consciousness or socialist collectivism. Usually, that person is an individualist counting on himself or herself and friends and relatives, though not completely free of the paternal-state complex.[49]

Of course, the formation of a new civic spirit in Russia is a difficult undertaking, especially when the intellectual strata are interfering rather than helping. The majority of today's Russian intelligentsia preferred to take the side of the ruling class and supported its course for achieving stability the old way. But let us not forget that Russian society during only the past decade has come to accept the principles of a way of life that other nations took much longer to reach. Therefore, if Russia slips further into authoritarianism, it will be despite the wishes of the majority and because the people were not offered (there was no one to offer) a convincing liberal-democratic alternative.[50]

Because leadership is the major—actually, the only—political institution in Russia, it is appropriate to discuss its effectiveness during Putin's first term. Various criteria can be used in an evaluation—how Putin accomplished the function for which he had been appointed by Yeltsin; whether he reached the goals he proclaimed and at what price; and how far Putin moved Russia toward a stable industrial society

If the criterion is his role as stabilizer, by 2004 Putin performed his part brilliantly. He really did bring order to Russia and got support for his policies from the great majority of the Russian population. If we look at Putin's own stated goal of modernizing Russia, there is reason for a positive evaluation here, too: Good macroeconomic indexes were achieved during his presidency.

The cost of Putin's policies? The president showed that he reaches his goals without expending excess energy and by trying to get the support of the political class and the public. Yeltsin fomented crises by bringing down governments and initiating conflicts. Putin, however, is a political minimalist. He does not like personnel changes and avoids confrontation. If he cannot get what he wants, he does not turn to mass pressure but rather creates the effect of a threat by issuing a warning. For instance, if the Kremlin decides to get rid of an inconvenient governor, the prosecutor's office starts investigating his activities, which is enough to make him give up trying to get reelected. In the YUKOS case, the prosecutor put Khodorkovsky in prison and thus solved the problem of political neutralization of big business as a whole, without having to resort to mass arrests. Under Putin, the regime mastered the art of threatening through the prosecutor's office, which turned out to be an effective management tool.

Putin has showed himself to be a tactician who can maneuver and not rock the boat. If we stick to this scale of criteria, then this Russian president deserves positive marks as a leader who keeps Russia stable at a moderate cost.

But how secure is this stability? A regime built on the principle of a leash can work only with a flawless system of subordination. And that comes through fear and violence. If the mechanism of coercion is weak, the leash works poorly. Even a small malfunction can create disequilibrium, because all the elements are vertically interdependent. The salvation of Russian authority is that, despite the appearance of subordination, it is diffuse. Thus, failed structures can be compensated for by others. The defects of the one-man rule are not apparent—for now. But at a moment of crisis, this form of governance is unlikely to be efficient.

The liquidation of the independent media and the annihilation of the opposition left the regime without feedback from society, which meant that it could not have a suitable understanding of events. Thus, the president was shocked when he flew over Grozny in the spring of 2004 and saw the destroyed city with his own eyes. He was stunned by the scale of the terrorist attack in Nazran in June 2004, when he noted in confusion, "It's not at all what I was told."[51] Obviously, he will be surprised more than once in the future, for without alternative sources of information, he may lose sight of the country's real life. The result of such interrupted feedback is mistaken decisions.

Russia's political serenity is also misleading because it is based in great part on imitation—imitation of order, of democracy, of power, and of responsibility. This imitation is a way of resolving the systemic contradictions between authoritarianism and democracy. So in the final analysis, an imitation of leadership, that basic regulating political institution of Russia, is inevitable.

There is no comfort in the fact that all the structures that organize society depend on the president' popularity polls. A fall in his rating threatens the stability of the entire system: The rating of United Russia will instantly fall, tied as it is to the president's rating; the presidential government begins to rock; the governors who are the president's yes men become vulnerable. Political and social stability are directly dependent on the leader's ratings. That is the answer to the question of whether Russia became more stable under President Putin. Bureaucratic authoritarianism that reproduces a natural resources economy, orienting society toward elementary survival, cannot ensure internal sources of development, without which Russia cannot respond to postindustrial challenges. This is the answer to the question of whether Russia is becoming a modern society.

The evolution of Vladimir Putin's regime shows us the limits of political engineering, which Russian rule has come to like, and its consequences. You would think that with immense administrative resources you could realize any plan: Create and destroy parties, build your own "civil" society, manage the parliament. These dangerous and obviously interesting experiments were begun by Boris Berezovsky, who created a new "power party"—Unity—in a few weeks in 1999. Pro-Kremlin Unity became the dominant force in the new parliament. A new generation of Kremlin technologists followed in his footsteps, and they began creating virtual reality without any thought to consequences.

But after the December 2003 Duma elections, it became evident that the Kremlin experimenters could not always control the results of their experiments. Where is the assurance that the Kremlin can handle "the pyramid of power" it has built? How long will the regime be able to keep the hushed and frightened business and regional elites on a leash? How much does the servility of today's elites reflect their agreement with Kremlin policies? In any case, it is always difficult to control imitation, for sooner or later the control can also turn into imitation. What will happen then, what forces will come into the political arena, and who will take advantage of the authoritarian construction erected by Putin?

By having secured his rule, Putin in his second term is less hampered by former commitments and theoretically should have more freedom to act. Yet I've come to the conclusion that it may actually be harder now for Putin to escape the system he created, as it is now living its own life. History has many examples of leaders who became captives of the rules they had set down.

The evolution of a new Russia—its transition from Yeltsin's oligarchic authoritarianism to Putin's bureaucratic authoritarianism—is often explained by the inevitable cyclical nature of development, in which every revolution is followed by a "restoration."[52] It is true that cycles always exist in transformational development, for every revolution runs out of steam and the need for a pause arises. The question is only on the nature of that pause: Is it for securing the transformation or for returning to the past? In the former communist states of Central and Eastern Europe, the stabilization took place on a liberal-democratic base, the result primarily of their inclusion in the European community. In most of the new independent states on the territory of the former USSR, the pendulum swung in the other direction, toward authoritarian regimes, some with feudal accents. Russia managed to avoid a Soviet or monarchist restoration. Here there is, in Leon Aron's felicitous definition, "an amalgam, a patchwork," a hybrid that includes personified power, liberalism in economics, and a Western vector in foreign policy.

Putin tried modernizing Russia in the manner of Peter the Great, that is, by subordination. But he has not yet realized that what his predecessors could do with an archaic Russian society is unlikely to happen with the new Russian nation, where most people are no longer traditionalists. The conflict between means (authoritarianism) and ends (modernization) was blurred in the period 1999–2004, because oil prices assured economic growth and stability. This created the impression that Putin's authoritarian modernization was working. The conflict between traditional power and new needs was not understood either by the society or the regime—the conflict was hazy. But it can resurface at any moment, especially if oil prices fall, and it will have to be solved. There are only two solutions: Give up bureaucratic authoritarianism or give up modernization.

This may cause a curious problem: To give up bureaucratic authoritarianism, the president may have to use his authoritarianism (his will and pressure) to put an end to it. In his day, Charles de Gaulle used his personal power to modernize France and to create better-working and democratic systems. Russia has not had politicians of that stature, who could use their personal power to set the limits on it. But I may be too skeptical; such master politicians are created by the times and public need.

The history of Putin's administration, as of the administrations of Gorbachev and Yeltsin, makes us think about the role the leader plays in Russia's political history. Why is my last point about the leader? Because in a society where the leader is the most important, and often the only, political institution, he determines the vector of society's movement. If I were to simplify, the conclusion is: *Gorbachev was a reformer who tried to reform an unreformable system. Yeltsin was a reformer who tried to build effective oligarchic capitalism that could not be anything but ineffective. Putin has become a stabilizer and modernizer of a system that cannot be stabilized or modernized.*

Does the very fact that the mission is impossible make the attempt to accomplish it only a failure or fatal error? No—I think we are dealing with a more complicated process. If a society has a weak or no reform potential, if the elites have no vision of progress, the experience of a dead-end road is also a form of development. Russia under Gorbachev and Yeltsin passed though the failures of *perestroika* and the post-*perestroika* revolution and came to understand that you cannot reform what should be dismantled and that you cannot guarantee freedom without order. Under Putin, Russia is undergoing another experiment, which should show whether a society can be modernized without freedom.

This path may bring forth new illusions. Thus, Putin's first term created the impression that bureaucratic authoritarianism can solve issues. If his second term dispels this illusion, that will be his contribution to the Russian transformation. Yes, Putin's failure at authoritarian modernization might even be more beneficial for Russia than his success. This failure might force the Kremlin to abandon personified power. Success will merely prolong the illusion, and it will still be only a temporary solution. Sooner or later, another leader will have to prove that Russia has taken a dead-end path and will need to find a way out.

The question remains: Can Vladimir Vladimirovich himself see that Russia needs to leave the dead-end system? His second term should provide the answer. We do not have long to wait.

Chapter 12

NEW AGENDA AND NEW DISAPPOINTMENTS

————————— ✣ —————————

Russia wants democracy. The social Darwinism of power. Khodorkovsky repents.
Liberalism versus neoconservatism. Chechnya: the ritual murder of Kadyrov.
Are there parties left in Russia? Putin's economic challenge. The banking crisis.
Russian foreign policy: trial by "new realism." The Beslan tragedy and its
aftermath.

With massive support in the second presidential elections, Vladimir Putin could formulate his priorities as he wanted, without disturbance. The Russian political establishment started guessing what the president would undertake in his second term. Some thought he would resuscitate market reforms. Others felt that Russia had reached the maximum in reform and needed time to digest what had been done in the previous decade. There was only one certainty in what was happening in the political area: Its vector was determined and set to reinforce bureaucratic authoritarianism.

The Kremlin no longer hid its plans to build a single-party state and was preparing to change the mixed electoral system to a proportional one, discussing the issue of cancelling gubernatorial elections. The regime continued to destroy the last vestiges of independence in the media.[1] The Kremlin's horticulturalists, armed with clippers, peered keenly at the political field before them, ready to pounce on any growth that threatened to destroy the political landscape they had created.

The authorities apparently believed that Russia expected an intensification of personified rule. But they were wrong. The mass sentiments at the start of Putin's second term had changed, and the proportion of people expecting an expansion of democracy from the president had risen sharply. In March 2000, 35 percent expected that from Putin, and in April 2004 it was 55 percent. In Putin's second term, democratization was the main demand from the public. In 2000, about half those polled felt the need for a political opposition—47 percent (24 percent were opposed). By 2004, the proportion of those who believed that opposition was necessary had grown to 61 percent, while those who did not think it was needed had declined to 17 percent.[2]

Everything points to the fact that the president's public support did not mean support for an authoritarian rule. The retention of support for Putin when the people wanted more democracy can be explained by two circumstances: Russians did not see any other leader who could protect them from dictatorship (people did not believe that Putin was capable of establishing a dictatorship—in 2000, 10 percent thought he would, and in 2004, 9 percent) and Russians hoped that Putin would revive democratic institutions.

Thus, the clampdown on democratic institutions took place despite the mood of the majority of the Russian public. The democratic strivings, however, did not take shape as a desire to change the rule. And that was understandable, too; there were no forces in the society to make a persuasive case for a political structure that could simultaneously guarantee freedom and order. But the increased longing for independent institutions and opposition meant that Russian society and the regime had acquired incompatible agendas and that their clash was becoming inevitable, sooner or later.

Putin's annual address to the Federal Assembly on May 27, 2004, indicated the priorities for his second term, which he had finally chosen after long deliberations. He repeated the line from his 2003 address on the war on poverty and doubling the gross domestic product (GDP) by 2010, which met with skeptical comments from the public. But by bringing the deadline outside his second term, he was relieving himself of the responsibility to achieve the goals. A more substantive point in the address was Putin's readiness to begin the painful reforms that he had been postponing.

Indeed, there was the sense that the president had decided to cut back social subsidies but did not want to say so openly.

There were also unpleasant surprises for liberals and Westernizers. Putin spoke harshly about nongovernmental organizations, especially those financed by foreign foundations, accusing them of "serving dubious groups and commercial interests." That was another whiff of the old Soviet attitudes toward human rights groups and Western foundations. The only thing missing was an accusation of espionage.

In May 2004, Mikhail Fradkov's appointment as prime minister was confirmed by parliament for a second time. The Kremlin clone, the Rodina Party, joined the Communists in voting against Fradkov's candidacy. Thus, a new opposition was born in the Duma, speaking out against the government yet supporting the president who had formed the government—according to the plan of the Kremlin manipulators who ran Rodina to create an impression of pluralism in Russia.

Dmitri Rogozin, the leader of Rodina, enthusiastically went about disparaging the government. "A big torpedo is ready for your ship," he threatened the government from the Duma podium. Rogozin had a platform of three "antis"—antiliberal, anti-West, and anti-oligarch—and he did not mind stooping to crude provocation. The professional nationalist-extremist Vladimir Zhirinovsky looked almost respectable next to the new left-wing patriot.

As people began to see that the Kremlin looked kindly on the left-wing patriots, everyone with the least bit of ambition who had not found a place in politics hurried to that corner. The Kremlin was calm about this upswing in kitchen patriotism and populism. "Everything's under control," the Kremlin spin doctors assured. But it was a risky game, especially on the eve of the social reforms planned by the president.

In the meantime, Putin hastened the stalled administrative reform. No other reform had elicited this much resistance among the ruling class, simply because it threatened to undermine their leadership positions in the bureaucracy by reorganizing the state. The reform's basic aim was to subject the command system of governance to the demands of the market and establish new criteria of effectiveness. Putin began the reform cautiously. At first, German Gref and his team started "debureaucratizing" the economy (1999–2002), limiting the control of the state over business. They did not get very far.

The second stage of administrative reform began in 2003–2004 and consisted of reevaluating the functions of the agencies of the executive branch and liquidating overlap and duplication. The commission in charge, headed by former vice prime minister Boris Aleshin, found 800 excess government functions and tried to reduce the administrative load by 30 percent. But this time, under pressure from corporate interests, the Kremlin had to compromise, turning over the excess functions of the state to "self-managed organizations," which in actuality meant business bureaucrats.

The reform's next step was dividing up areas of management among levels of power, correlating the expenditures with the revenue possibilities at each level of the administration ("the Kozak package," named for Dmitri Kozak, the deputy head of the presidential administration). A new structure of government was established: ministry–federal service–federal agency. Then the Kremlin passed the law "On State Civil Service," which was supposed to be the basis for forming a new Russian bureaucracy.[3]

The initiators of administrative reform hoped that the results would be a more transparent management process and a reduction in the pressure from branch and bureaucratic interests.[4] The new rules would make rational demands—in particular, to limit state control of the economy, to institute a competitive hiring process for positions in the executive branch, and to change the motivation of civil servants. But the reform did not resolve the issue of conflicts of interest in management structures, for instance, between the interests of an official and his business interests. An unexpected side effect was an increase in supervisory functions in all branches of the economy. The conflicts of interest among individual ministries were not resolved. In 2004, the reform's only tangible result was a salary increase for officials, which was presented as a method of fighting corruption.[5]

Even observers loyal to the Kremlin began to voice their skepticism about administrative reform. As Arkady Volsky, the head of the Russian Union of Industrialists and Entrepreneurs, put it vividly, "The madam of a brothel should be changing the girls, not the beds." But Volsky was wrong. The reforms should not be implemented by the madam—that is, the officials—but by an independent public agency. But the president gave the apparatus to reform itself.

Eventually, the Kremlin moved on to more sensitive reforms, which would change people's living conditions in the long run: budget reform and a package of social reforms that included dozens of new laws regulating all aspects of social life. President Putin, unexpectedly for many, started to make risky moves, doing what neither Gorbachev nor Yeltsin had dared try: He was hazarding a rejection of state paternalism and restructuring the state's social functions in response to market demand.

Putin thus was undertaking a revolution as significant as privatization had been in its time. In 2003, the Duma approved a law on local self-governance and a law on the organization of organs of power in the territories that changed the system of relations between the center and regions. In the summer of 2004, the Kremlin decided to pass a packet of laws that would redefine the state's social responsibility. The most painful decision for society was the replacement of benefits in kind with monetary compensation.[6] In practice, this decision meant the liquidation of about a third of the state's existing obligations, which it financed only by half. At the same time, part of the obligations were shifted to the regions (the federal authorities still took care of 14 million beneficiaries, and 19 million were moved to regional authorities).[7]

One of the factors speeding up the passage of the new package of laws was the growing legal literacy of the population. People were beginning to sue the authorities and win what they were entitled to by law—housing for retired military, children's aid, extra pay for combat duty, and so on. The government was up against the wall, having to pay all the damages won in these lawsuits, totaling tens of thousands of rubles.[8]

The time had long been ripe for establishing market relations in the social sphere. And it was high time for the state to end its hypocrisy of accepting responsibilities that it had no intention of fulfilling. The system of social benefits, a hangover from the Soviet period, was not always individualized or fair and needed to be reformed.[9] Besides, the rejection of benefits opened the way for reforming medical and social insurance and the housing sector.

However, the authorities tried to carry out these painful reforms quietly, hoping that the public would not understand what they were doing. The "social revolution" took place in the summer, when people were on vacation and not following politics. And pushing through legislation that would change the relationship between state and society without a dialogue with the society was setting a time bomb. Just a year later, when the new laws were to come into force, people would decide that they had been duped.

And it was not only the way social reform was done but also its content that was a problem. The regime was trying to rid itself of the social burden by shifting most of it to the regions. But at the same time, the regions' tax bases were being reduced and aid from the federal budget was being cut back. The regions were now expected to take care of the people entitled to benefits and to pay the salaries of 7 million people.[10] But the regions did not have the revenues to carry out these obligations. "The regions are given a series of new obligations, but they are not being given additional tax resources," wrote Mikhail Zadornov. "On the contrary, they are forced to pay to the federal budget 1.5 percent of the tax on income, payments for forest resources, and water tax. We can predict the social tension for residents in forty subsidized regions."[11] By the end of 2004, the government discovered that it was almost $57 million short in paying the monetary compensation for benefits in kind.

The beneficiaries in rural areas, who never used their benefits, won because they got a supplement to their pensions and salaries of $11 to $45 a month. But the beneficiaries in cities lost, and lost badly.[12] Thus, only a third of 10 million invalids, including war veterans and handicapped people, would get full compensation for their benefits. The state was also planning to cut support for education, no longer guaranteeing free enrollment in municipal colleges. The law on support for small business was repealed, and so were laws protecting citizens' housing. The only thing the Kremlin decided to keep paying were the subsidies toward housing costs. Not too many Russian citizens could pay their full rent.

While the Duma was passing the law on the "monetization" of social benefits in July and August 2004, the building was cordoned off by ranks of Omon special forces. This was the first occasion in a long time that the parliamentarians had needed protection from angry crowds. The crowd shouted anti-Putin slogans. The Federation of Independent Unions resisted the social reforms and began rallying people. Then the governors started speaking up. Even prominent members of United Russia rebelled; for example, Vice-Speaker Georgi Boss said, "The government's strategy is correct, but its implementation is wrong from start to finish."[13]

The reform was like a bucket of cold water for the public, which was used to the fact that its miserly wages and pensions were somewhat mitigated by benefits. For many people, benefits conferred status (for instance, free rides on city transport for war veterans). Of those polled, 61 percent felt that the state was replacing benefits with monetary compensation to save money at the expense of the poorest strata (only 29 percent thought it was to improve the lot of those strata, and 10 percent had no opinion).[14] As usual, the Russian authorities were "solving" a problem with a social reform without considering its impact on the living standard of the poorest citizens. "This is a new policy of cutting costs in the budget at the expense of the most poor," wrote Ivan Preobrazhensky.[15]

The government was shedding obligations that were remnants of socialism. But capitalism, whereby the government was pushing society, was built on the principle of "save yourself." The authorities were not creating appropriate conditions for the public to take care of itself through private initiative. Citizens began asking why it was the poorest who had to be sacrificed. Why not start with the flagrant abuses of the bureaucracy, the "black holes" in the federal budget, the massive theft of aid for Chechnya? Finally, the people could not avoid the question: Why has the government started to eliminate social benefits at the moment when Russia is enjoying an inflow of oil money?

At the same time, applying Darwinian principles toward society, the Kremlin was expanding social preferences for government officials. Each month, the average pensioner got 1,100 rubles in benefits (about $38), a federal minister got 85,000 rubles ($3,000), and an ordinary government bureaucrat got 42,640 rubles ($1,487).[16] The social reforms begun by the Kremlin would inevitably widen the already huge gap between rich and poor.

Observers were naturally interested by the question: What was the probability of social tension? The great majority of Russians were anxious about the reforms. People felt that these reforms did not meet their needs.[17] But people were not prepared to protest in June 2004: A total of 56 percent of respondents said that "life was hard, but possible," only 20 percent considered their situation catastrophic, and the remaining 20 percent thought it quite acceptable. The index of unwillingness to protest rose from 63 percent in 2003 to 67 percent in 2004. Only 21 or 22 percent of those polled were prepared to join protests, and only 19 percent thought mass protests likely.[18]

But the public's apathy was misleading. As the unpopular social reforms continued to unfold—in particular, once the housing services reforms began—we can assume that there would be an increase in protests. Those most open to protesting might be the groups not poor enough to get aid and financial compensation from the state, that is, the lower or middle middle class.[19] Protests of some social strata over the switch to market forces in the social sphere could then fuel the discontent of other strata with their unrealized hopes for democracy.

Did the ruling team sense the threat of growing social tension? Undoubtedly. And the team decided that the best way to handle unpopular reforms was to totally control society while creating channels for blowing off protesters' steam. Not for the first time, the authorities were in thrall to the illusion that protest could be managed and even be used for their own ends.

The Kremlin started to work hard to neutralize possible unrest—creating right and left wings within United Russia, discrediting the Communist Party, increasing Rodina's attraction of the left-wing electorate, forming domesticated parties to influence active voters, and controlling the unions are just a few examples of its efforts. And let us add the creation of the image of the enemy, first and foremost the "oligarchs," as a means of channeling discontent into areas that did not threaten the regime.

But management always has is limits. It has been impossible for the regime to exclude all the diffuse forms of social protest against its actions. New forms of disobedience have appeared—for instance, hunger strikes—that are difficult to handle. Extremist movements have appeared among young people, which could be the fuse for further unrest. The "new left" who came out onto Moscow's streets was a signal of the likelihood of that scenario. Another source of concern—has been the leaders created by the regime, who might escape its control and ride a possible new wave of protest, threatening the regime itself.

The system of governance built as a conveyor-belt mechanism, which is functional in stable situations, is unwieldy in moments of crisis and tends to respond with force to public protest, which will only increase it. At this point, however, the hotbeds of unrest in a fragmented society pose no serious threat to the Kremlin. The authorities can sleep peacefully. But the future is undefined, and something could happen at any moment to ruin that sleep. The ruling team has destroyed the old mechanisms of social stability without thinking of new ones. The regime has given the push for future tectonic shifts in the behavior of society.

While Russia was reelecting its leaders, Mikhail Khodorkovsky was still in prison. Many thought that the head of YUKOS would be released after the elections and that the YUKOS case would die quietly. But not at all. The Kremlin had decided to change course and to go after the mammoth oil asset, and that meant changing its owners and management. Thus, political interests, which had predominated at the start of the YUKOS case, were now complemented by economic motivations.

Khodorkovsky was tired of resisting and sought a compromise with the regime. This was reflected in his two letters addressed to the president, which were full of repentance. Russian prisoners liked to write letters to the highest authority; the Communist Party leaders Kamenev and Zinoviev wrote similar letters to Stalin after he had them imprisoned, and this parallel tinged the current situation with gloomy foreboding. Here are the basic points of Khodorkovsky's letters from prison: The liberals are responsible for the failures of the Russian transformation and if they do not exculpate their guilt before society, they must leave the political scene; the president is the only power and one must come to terms with him. "The president is the institution that guarantees the wholeness and stability of the nation.... The country's history dictates: bad power is worse than none," wrote the head of YUKOS in his servile cringing.[20] Apparently, prison made him "remember" to be flexible. There is nothing surprising in that—better men had been broken by Russian prisons.[21]

In his letters, Khodorkovsky was saying, "I am giving up my political ambitions. Let me out and forgive me."[22] But Putin did not react to the repenting letters, and the case against YUKOS picked up steam. The regime wanted more from Khodorkovsky than his repentance; it wanted the property of the biggest oil company.

The letters did not bring freedom to the head of YUKOS. But they stimulated a lively discussion about the fate of liberalism in Russia among the "old" liberals of the Yeltsin generation, including Gaidar, Chubais, and Nemtsov. The liberals announced that they had nothing to repent. Chubais gave an interview to the *Financial Times*, in which he said grimly, "Let Khodorkovsky repent for his sins, I'll deal with mine myself."[23]

Yegor Gaidar published his response to Khodorkovsky, stating that he did not agree that the liberals bore the responsibility for all the failures, even though he personally was not trying to evade responsibility for the development of the country. But the specific errors made by liberals in the government did not mean, according to Gaidar, a collapse of liberalism in Russia, with which I agree fully. Responding to those who concluded that liberalism was at an end, Gaidar proclaimed: "It won't happen!"[24]

Gaidar's optimism regarding the fate of liberalism seemed to be unfounded. The situation in Russia was developing in the opposite direction. All the people who hoped to survive on the political scene washed their hands of liberal ideas so that, God forbid, they would not be considered in the losers' camp. Being a liberal in Russia in 2004 meant being doomed to freezing in the political ghetto. The official press, loyal to the Kremlin, and parties and their leaders started badgering everyone who had not given up their ties to the liberals. Defending liberalism was deemed foolish and hopeless. Liberals were guilty of everything bad that had happened in Russia. Curiously, the attack on liberalism took place just as Putin was reviving his liberal reforms. This is more evidence of the complexity of the Russian landscape and how it does not fit cookie-cutter concepts.

However, Khodorkovsky was right on at least one thing: There was a crisis in Russian liberalism—for which there were good reasons. The liberals had been in the government for more than ten years and had not managed to bring about reforms that would have supported democracy in Russia and significantly improved the lives of ordinary people. Under the banner of liberalism promoted by "limousine liberals," as the press had dubbed them, oligarchic capitalism had become entrenched in the country and led to the degradation of society.

In that context, the next question is: Were the people who limited themselves to economic transformations and had forgotten about democratic institutions liberals at all? Were they liberals if, like Chubais, they counted on the authoritarianism of the Kremlin boss? Besides, let's not forget that the technocrats who came to the top with Yeltsin never did have full power. And Gaidar's government lasted only a year. After the fall of communism, Russia was still run by the Soviet *nomenklatura*, which had learned to mouth liberal slogans. Therefore, the conclusion seems to be that Russia had never had full-fledged liberalism as a state course, but instead a form of camouflaging the interests of the ruling class. Thus, it was natural that this "Russian liberalism" was rejected by society.

The intensified attacks on the liberals were accompanied by the formation of yet another Russian fad—this time, neoconservatism. There had been a conservative tendency in Russia. But it was nationalism or communism; in other words, the ideology of return to Soviet or pre-Soviet times. The ideologists of this new pro-Kremlin neoconservatism tried to explain the need to preserve the status quo.[25]

Here are their basic arguments. First, ideal democracy is impossible, the apologists said, and treated criticism of the regime is a naïve striving for perfection. Second, the development of democracy is always gradual, they maintained, pointing out that there was slavery for the first century of democracy in America. Third, there is and cannot be a liberal democratic alternative to the Russian regime. Russia is threatened by the communist or nationalist alternative, the neoconservatives asserted.

Russian neoconservatism was a form of loyalty to the regime for the political class. And Russian neocons were consistent in that they always said the same thing no matter who the leader was: The regime is right and all alternatives are worse. They said it under Yeltsin and repeated it under Putin.

Although outwardly pragmatic, Russian neoconservatism actually distorted reality and blocked innovation. It was neoconservatism that was the basis for modernization through a return to a traditional state. It could easily become the basis for a rollback to dictatorship, if "the regime was always right" and everything that existed was reasonable. Whether it was conscious or not is not really the issue, but the Kremlin neoconservatives were tabling the question of Russia's further transformation, focusing society and the political class on a meek acceptance of what was. It's possible that in their next incarnation, neoconservatives could become social democrats or liberals, depending on the rhetoric chosen by the regime. It was the old story of surviving in the tsar's court at any cost.

The next act of the play called YUKOS began. In June 2004, the tax ministry demanded that the company pay $3.4 billion in back taxes and fines for 2000. Another blow on the back of YUKOS came from Roman Abramovich, who dissolved his merger with YUKOS and tried to profit from the YUKOS drama. The Russian market shuddered. Putin, in an attempt to calm things down, broke his silence on YUKOS and in early June announced that "the government was not interested in bankrupting YUKOS." His announcement immediately raised YUKOS share prices and gave hope that the president intended to preserve the company. However, just a few days later, the attacks on YUKOS began again. The tax ministry sent another huge bill, this time for unpaid taxes in 2001—the amount was identical to the claim for 2000, also $3.4 billion. And then the ministry began talk of payments for 2002–2003. It looked like blatant mockery, for the company could not pay its debts because its assets were frozen. These kinds of ups and downs would happen several more times. And some people made a lot of money in the abrupt price fluctuations of YUKOS stock.

The board of YUKOS and Khodorkovsky still tried to come to an agreement with the Kremlin. They even asked a very experienced Hercules, Viktor Gerashchenko, former head of the Central Bank, to become chairman of the board. Then former Canadian prime minister Jean Chrétien was asked to negotiate. But YUKOS was mistaken in thinking that it could negotiate with the Kremlin. The Kremlin demanded total capitulation on its terms.

Searches of YUKOS offices continued, accompanied by the special forces, as powerful pressure on the company. The firm's capitalization, which had recently been more than $40 billion, was down to $16 billion by the summer of 2004. Along with YUKOS, the rest of the Russian market began experiencing a downturn; in the spring and summer of 2004, the Russian market lost about 30 percent, that is, billions of dollars. Investors started fleeing the country. The government was silent, as if nothing was wrong.

In July, at last, the trial of Khodorkovsky and his partner Platon Lebedev began.[26] Khodorkovsky made another step in the direction of the authorities and offered to give the 44 percent in shares that he owned to sell in order to pay the company's debts. But the state ignored Khodorkovsky's offer. Journalists joked that YUKOS would soon be so transparent as to disappear completely. Bruce Misamore, the company's financial officer, stated: "The actions of the Russian government have brought the best and most creditworthy Russian company to the point of being unable to pay and perhaps even possible bankruptcy."[27] The switch of owner and managers to state representatives seemed inevitable. The only question was how it would be done—by bankrupting the company or some other way. Potential buyers showed interest. Western investors began frequenting Moscow, waiting for a chance to get a piece of the YUKOS empire. And not all Western economic circles were discouraged by the drama of the Russian oil company. At least major

Western oil firms were ready to invest in a politically risky environment, and uncertainty did not frighten them.

At the end of July 2004, the government decided to sell Yuganskneftegaz—YUKOS's main company, which brought in 60 percent of the overall holding's oil—to settle the tax debts. Without that company, YUKOS was an empty shell. Now the question was, Who would get the remnants of Khodorkovsky's oil empire? There was no doubt that they would go to structures close to the Kremlin. It is true that in the end, the Russian authorities decided to create an impression of impartiality and hired a Western company, Dresdner Kleinwort Wasserstein, to estimate the price of the major assets of YUKOS. This was a clear sign that Putin wanted to keep up appearances, which had already become very difficult to do.

Judging by how events unfolded, however, there was no agreement on how to act either within YUKOS or within the government. After Khodorkovsky was taken off to prison, the company lost direction, because everything in YUKOS depended on its leader, who had built it with one-man rule. Arguments and contradictions broke out within the board and between the board and management about how to proceed.[28] The beheaded company developed several centers of influence and lost the ability to resist. But the regime lacked a plan of what to do with the holding company as well. The Kremlin, obviously, had given the order to attack Khodorkovsky, but the details of the campaign against YUKOS had not been coordinated. Some members of the government tried to use the tax problem to force Khodorkovsky to obey the Kremlin's rules. Others, along with their business associates, lusted after the property. Still others dreamed of nationalizing the company. The chaos inside YUKOS was echoed in the chaos inside the administration.[29] The absence of coordination and the presence of several positions on YUKOS in the Kremlin led observers to conclude that the president had lost control over his entourage.[30] That was not so. Putin had lost control over the process that he had initiated. And he wavered over which group in his entourage should get the prize—control over Khodorkovsky's former empire.

In the meantime, the appointment of Igor Sechin, Putin's closest ally, as chairman of the board of the state company Rosneft confirmed that Putin's comrades-in-arms were converting their political clout into economic influence. Putin's team was trying to get control over the "strategic assets," because in its perception only the state could control the natural resources that were the major source of the Russian budget. But apparently there was another motive as well: by overtaking the "strategic assets," to guarantee for themselves an advantageous position in the fight for power in the next elections.[31] Naturally, the goal was control of the natural resources that make up the base of the Russian economy. It seemed that the old rule of Russian development was still in place: Reshufflings of ruling elites in Russia have always been accompanied by redistribution of property. Putin's team had failed to follow this rule during his first term, and they apparently were in a hurry to fulfill their goal now. "They are all set to move into business," wrote a journalist, "and the most important question is whether Russia will see any new oligarchs arise by 2008."[32] There were other signs that preparations were under way for a new round of "privatization." The government approved the sale of a state-owned stake in LukOil, and a decision to privatize Aeroflot was finally endorsed. New officials were ready to become new oligarchs, and YUKOS was their main course.

The whole drama around Khodorkovsky's empire proved that the authorities had problems with their redistribution of property; they still were looking for ways to somehow justify it. In any case, in summer 2004 Putin had not yet determined how control over YUKOS would be implemented—as a new state oil and gas holding that Gazprom was intended to create; as quasi-state companies, like LukOil; or as loyal but private holdings? It was not certain which group in the ruling team would win the battle for strategic natural resources. There was no doubt, however, that the fight over YUKOS and the future redistribution of property had broken up Putin's entourage. The YUKOS saga was the battlefield on which the future balance of political forces and the relations between the regime and business were being determined.

Clearing away the Russian oligarch field did not mean that the federal authorities would treat foreign investors in the same way. Putin demonstrated an interest in foreign investment and appeared in certain cases to prefer dealing with foreign companies, which displayed no political ambitions. There was one condition for foreign companies to operate safely in Russia: They had to have the president's approval for the deal.[33]

Khodorkovsky himself, apparently, realized that he had lost YUKOS.

Now it was his personal fate at stake. In his statement to the court, he promised, "I will prove the groundlessness of the charges." But no one cared about his evidence anymore.

On July 4, 2004, after many postponements, Putin at last met with the representatives of big business. This meeting was strikingly different from previous ones between the president and Russian magnates. Earlier, the magnates had sat around an enormous round table in one of the most prestigious halls of the Kremlin and traded jokes. Putin had gone around the table and shaken hands with each of them, thus showing his respect. He had heard out his guests attentively and even permitted them to argue with him. But this time, after Khodorkovsky's public whipping, Putin took a different tack. The "oligarchs" were gathered in a modest room and made to wait. When the president entered, he did not look at anyone and sat in the center of one side of a rectangular table opposite the hushed businessmen lined up on the other side. Putin began the meeting politely but coldly, gazing upon his interlocutors. Under his unblinking stare, they wilted and stammered. Just yesterday, they had been the most powerful people in Russia, and now they looked like schoolboys permitted to enter the teacher's lounge.[34] The form and manner of the meeting were intended to show the "oligarchs" that the president had deigned to receive them in order to give them his proposals, which sounded like demands.

The meeting created doubts that the Kremlin was still interested in its policy of co-opting business, that is, treating business organizations as junior partners of the regime.[35] In the early stages of Putin's term, the government supported business organizations—in particular, the Russian Union of Industrialists and Entrepreneurs, which suited the regime as a means of controlling business and was good for business as a communications channel with the regime.[36] However, it soon became evident that the Kremlin was changing dialogue for diktat. And the business organizations, because of the variety of their interests and internal contradictions, were unable to play the role of junior partner of the regime very well.

At the same time, the ruling team clearly indicated that the principle of equidistance, which Putin had proposed earlier as a model for behavior of business, was no longer adequate. The chairman of the Audit Chamber, Sergei Stepashin, formulated a new method of behavior for Russian businessmen. The "good" magnate not only avoids politics and pays taxes but also participates in the state's social projects.[37] All the major businessmen rushed out to find "socially responsible projects" so that the authorities would leave them alone and the public like them more. The magnates came up with philanthropic ideas, from help for orphanages to the construction of sports complexes. These proposals were marked by one characteristic: The financing frequently came from the company coffers, not the oligarchs' personal assets.

Putin continued pondering. He had not yet completely formulated his attitude toward big business. It was clear that he did not like the "oligarchs," but he realized that they were the driving force of the Russian economy. However, he had not decided whether to make the YUKOS case the norm or the exception. If it were a beginning of the new normal practice, then who would be the next victim among the "oligarchs"? And would the new interventionist policy end in the natural resources area or expand to other economic spheres? In fairness, Putin continued his liberal vector. But the YUKOS debacle had introduced a certain kind of logic that would be difficult to stop.

Putin had not decided how to deal with privatization: whether to legitimize it completely, first making the magnates pay some tax for the property they obtained on the cheap, and revisiting the more dubious privatizations; or whether to retain the vagueness in attitude toward privatization, keeping the magnates in total dependence on the will of the regime. He wavered.

A confirmation of his vacillation was the June 2004 report of the Audit Chamber on 140 cases of privatization. The results of their investigation disappointed those who thirsted for blood. First of all, the auditors concluded that the state had lost only $1.6 billion on privatization, when Abramovich's Sibneft alone had been undervalued by $1.5 billion. The auditors were clearly underestimating the loss to the state from privatization. Second, in 89 percent of the cases, said the auditors, the guilty parties in criminal privatization were government officials and not businessmen. This conclusion undermined the Kremlin's anti-oligarchic revolution. Obviously, the president was not prepared for wide-scale action against big capital, at least in the summer of 2004. But he was in no hurry to draw a line across the turbulent past.

In the meantime, the chairman of the Audit Chamber, Stepashin, demanded decisive action against the "oligarchs," including repossession of their property. Stepashin attacked Roman Abramovich particularly energetically, and if Putin had approved the investigation of the closest comrade-in-arms of the Yeltsin family, the Audit Chamber would have found a hook. Putin did not give Stepashin free rein. Putin pondered—his modus operandi. But his indecisiveness widened the scope for the dealings of the shameless bureaucrats who flagrantly blackmailed business. Russian business, with no confidence in the future, fled the country and took its capital with it.[38]

The politics of the Kremlin toward big business throughout 2004 brought headaches to observers. On the one hand, the state increased its control over the economy. Thus, Gazprom was taking back the chunks of property that it had previously sold. The head of Gazprom, Alexei Miller, announced the creation of Gazpromneft, a state holding company that would manage strategic natural resources. Chubais's restructuring of RAO UES was put on hold. The state was openly trying to take control of YUKOS. But on the other hand, Putin personally approved the sale of part of its stake in LukOil to an American investor, ConocoPhillips. A list was published of the major state-owned enterprises that the government was offering for sale, including shares of Svyazinvest and Aeroflot, which evinced a continuation of the privatization process. This policy created the impression that there was no coordination in the administration on the rules of the game. The role of the state in the economy and the inviolable right to private property continued to be the subjects for debate.

How big business would react to the new situation was still not determined. For the time being, the "oligarchs" who were feeling insecure tried to make peace with the executive power and prove their loyalty to the regime and all its members. This only perpetuated the "oligarchs'" dependent relationship with power—with corruption being the inevitable outcome. One couldn't totally exclude the option that Russian business, looking for security, would turn to power structures for protection, striking a new and dangerous alliance of money and coercion. This alliance can be directed both ways—against populist sentiments in the society, yet also against a modernist leader who may try to implement more transparent rules of the game, rejecting old bargains between state apparatus and money. In this way, business would make itself even more dependent on force and bureaucracy and would become even more vulnerable. The other way would be to free itself from the original sin of its birth in the 1990s, to associate itself with a reformist agenda, to move toward civil society and try to promote a new relationship with power. Stephen Sestanovich was right when he pointed out that the future of Russian political pluralism will depend above all on choices made by Russian business. "Of all potential forces in Russian politics," he pointed out, "'money' has the strongest material base and the greatest doubts about its legitimacy. How it resolves this dilemma will tell us whether Russia's political system has assumed its 'final' post-Soviet form"—and I couldn't agree more.[39]

On May 9, 2004, Chechen president Akhmad Kadyrov was assassinated. It was preordained. There had been seventeen attempts on his life. This time it worked: A bomb went off under the seats in the stadium where he was watching a parade in honor of the USSR's victory in World War II. The separatists killed Moscow's protégé on the day of Russia's state holiday, a day of pride for the country. The separatists wanted to mark the day as one of humiliation for Russia.

This was no ordinary man who died. In 1995, he had proclaimed a jihad against Russia, calling on Muslims to kill Russians wherever they encountered them. It was Kadyrov who said, "There are a million Chechens, and 150 million Russians. If every Chechen kills 150 Russians, we will win." In 2004, the former *mujahid* was posthumously awarded the star of the Hero of Russia. It looked sometimes as if Putin trusted him more than his own generals. The president gave Kadyrov, rather his own entourage, control over the financial aid flowing into Chechnya. Kadyrov's assassination was a direct blow against Putin and his policy of the Chechenization of the republic.

Kadyrov was not liked; he was feared but respected. Chechen field commanders turned themselves in, trusting his word. He managed to get money from Moscow, defend Chechnya's independence, and keep the civil war from spreading. Now, without Kadyrov's harsh rule, there was a danger that the Chechen resistance could again grow into a mass movement.

Moscow needed to hold new elections and find a successor to Kadyrov who would be willing to play kamikaze. The death of Moscow's stern protégé destroyed any illusions that anyone might still have had about things settling down in Chechnya. I remember a television news story from the Kremlin, with Putin receiving Kadyrov's son Ramzan, chief of Kadyrov's personal bodyguards. Ramzan had come to the Kremlin so urgently that he had not had time to change his clothes. The sight of the clumsy young man, who looked like a street thug in his crumpled sweatsuit, and pale, bewildered Putin in the dark Kremlin rooms was more upsetting than any commentary: It was obvious that the ruling team did not know what to do with Chechnya and with the Kadyrov people.

The president was being pressured from all sides with various solutions to the Chechen problem. Most pressure came from the *siloviki,* who lobbied for the introduction of direct presidential rule in Chechnya. In that case, the power structures would have control over the financial aid coming from Moscow. But Putin withstood the pressure, and once again he bet on Chechenization, supporting Alu Alkhanov (then 41 years of age), the Chechen minister of the interior and part of the Kadyrov clan, as his candidate for president of Chechnya.

In the meantime, the separatists struck another blow, carrying out a raid on the territory of Ingushetia, repeating the scenario of the attack on Budyonovsk nine years before. On the night of June 21—another symbolic day for Russia, the anniversary of the Nazi invasion of the USSR—a large unit of soldiers entered Nazran and several other Ingush cities. The *mujahadeen* walked openly in the streets, shouting "Allah Akbar!" The raid was headed by Shamil Basayev, who found time for a taping of his television interview in a weapons warehouse they captured. The law enforcement officers drove themselves into the trap; when they heard shooting, they hurried to the scene and were shot at by the rebels, many wearing the Russian military uniform. Once the operation was finished, the guerrillas slipped away into the woods. Some of them went back to their identities as peaceful civilians. As a result of the night raid, 80 law enforcement officers and quite a few civilians were killed. The federal troops had been caught unawares yet again.

In a cruel twist of fate, at the time of the raid, Russian defense minister Sergei Ivanov was in the Far East of Russia, observing training on how to fight terrorists. The maneuvers were a success. But the real fight with the terrorists was not. The president flew out to Nazran immediately and walked through the areas of recent slaughter. He knew that the latest Basayev raid was a defeat for him personally, but he did not seem able to change the logic of his Chechen policy—for the time being.

Yet Putin had to react to the failure, and he reacted in the traditional Kremlin way: He fired the military commanders responsible for Chechnya, including the unsinkable chief of staff, General Anatoly Kvashnin.[40] The president took the path laid by Yeltsin, who changed the people in charge of Chechnya over and over instead of changing the policy.

Chechnya was not letting Russia forget its existence. Yet the Russian ruling elite knew very little about what was happening in the North Caucasus, and the bloody reminders brought them daily shudders. Chechen reality came as a shock to politicians who saw it. Gref went there for the first time with Putin in May 2004 and noted, "It doesn't look so apocalyptic on television." When his car hit a huge pothole on Grozny's main road, he said, "Give orders to have all this repaired immediately." He didn't think that the next land mine would create new holes in the repaired road.

The Russian regime seemed to do the very things that made Chechnya more implacable toward Russia. In April, the courts acquitted four Spetsnaz officers who had executed four Chechen civilians. In June, the appeals court acquitted two Russian officers who had killed three Chechen construction workers because they seemed suspicious. Those courts were generating more Chechen "black widows," who came to Moscow wearing "suicide-bomber belts" and blew themselves up along with innocent bystanders.

The next presidential elections in Chechnya were to take place on August 29, 2004. But just before the polls opened, about 300 rebels attacked a number of police stations in Grozny. The attack caught federal troops and Chechen enforcement forces that were loyal to Moscow off guard. Dozens of people, including civilians, were killed—this was the warning separatists were sending Moscow and its loyalists before the elections. And several days before the Chechen presidential election, Russia had suffered yet another blow from terrorists: Two domestic airplane flights were blown up simultaneously, 90 people were killed, and the whole act looked like an attempt to stage a Russian "9/11." Concerned about the possibility of new terrorist attacks, U.S. security officials ordered military jets to escort Russian flights into U.S. cities.

These gruesome blows did not change the political script in Chechnya, however. There were no surprises—the Kremlin candidate, Alu Alkhanov, was elected, winning nearly 74 per cent of the vote. Moscow and the Chechen clans loyal to it have learned how to guarantee the certainty of an election's outcome. But as the Kremlin candidate, Alkhanov is already a condemned man, like his predecessor, unless he breaks the inevitability of the Chechen drama, which dooms both those who fight Russia and those who serve Russia. At this stage of the endless Chechen bloodbath, the Chechenization of the political process—that is, the gradual transfer of power to the Chechens loyal to the Kremlin—appeared to be the only possible solution. Or—at least it was the only realistic solution, if we take into account the paradigm within which Putin had to operate. But this option could work, as Anatol Lieven has rightly put it, only under definite conditions—if Chechenization took place together with democratization and state building in the breakaway republic.[41]

The sad story was that the vicious circle of violence and desperation continued. The best-case scenario was that Alkhanov would succeed in keeping the war at least under some control and gradually start to rebuild the ruined Chechen infrastructure. However, the worst-case scenario was not entirely excluded: Alkhanov could fail to control the situation, and the rule of the ruthless Kadyrov clan would only trigger more terror and bloodshed. The nightmare would be if Chechen separatists were to join al Qaeda networks and the breakaway republic turn into a new haven for international terrorism, and there are signs that the once tolerant and rather soft Chechen Islam has started to evolve in this direction.[42] This, in turn, would provoke more brutal Russian reaction, this time supported by Russian society.

—————— ❧ ——————

Now let's take a look at another part of Russian life: the parties. The party system in Russia was paralyzed after the elections. At first, the Kremlin's idea to create a disciplined party to be the instrument of presidential policy seemed to be working. United Russia functioned like a well-oiled machine to confirm and endorse the decisions of the executive branch. However, the party had no stable electorate or clear-cut ideology. Besides which, by using the United Russia parliamentarians to formulate unpopular decisions, the regime was undermining the position of its party. It's quite possible that the Kremlin will have to think about creating a new tool for influence before the next elections.

However, the picture was even bleaker for the other parties. In June and July 2004, the Liberals and the Communists held their congresses, and that showed clearly that the party system of the Yeltsin era was on its last legs. Not only had the conflict between liberalism and communism, which supported political life in the 1990s, exhausted itself, so had the main parties of that era.

The Yabloko Congress on July 3, 2004, showed that despite a severe defeat and being forced out of public politics and into a hopeless situation, the Yabloko faithful were trying to find a dignified form of self-preservation. For the first time, there was an opposition group, but instead of pushing them out, Yavlinsky behaved wisely, stating that their presence revealed the party's viability.

Yabloko was facing its congress in hard times. There was no doubt that its liberal social philosophy would be needed. But it was not clear whether Yabloko would be able to express the interests of the social groups for whom the philosophy would resonate. Another party might come along, one better able to articulate the growing protest sentiments. The Yabloko people understood that the appearance of these sentiments was inevitable, and they began preparing for it, trying to move to a stronger opposition stance to the Kremlin. But the duality of their position remained. It was reflected by the fact that one of the leading Yabloko members, Igor Artemyev, was appointed head of the Federal Anti-Monopoly Service, becoming part of the government. This situation resembled the two-headed face of the Union of Right Forces (SPS), with some leaders attacking the regime even while Chubais was part of it.

The SPS Congress on June 26, 2004, demonstrated the total paralysis of the party. It was amazing that they even got enough people to hold a congress. The basic plotline of the congress was the leaders' attempts to keep the congress from electing a leader. This was another innovation introduced in Russia: Usually, parties have a struggle for the post of party leader, whereas the SPS leaders tried to prove that it's better not to have one. They barely managed to persuade the delegates to put off the elections. They did agree to organize primaries among the members and like-minded voters to elect the party leadership later. The lack of a leader means that the SPS will not be able to define its course or its attitude toward the regime. It all depended on Chubais, the real leader and financial backer of the SPS, who has not yet decided on his role in politics. Though the SPS's maneuvers looked like its death throes, in fact it had no niche left, because the right wing of United Russia had co-opted its liberal ideas.

Polling data indicate that after the elections of 2003–2004, Russians continued to be frustrated with existing liberal–democratic parties. In a February 2004 opinion survey, 24 percent agreed that "Yabloko" and the SPS "are doomed, but it is possible that some new democratic party will emerge and win sufficient support," while 19 percent argued that "in several years these parties will get stronger and assume their proper place in the country." It is worth mentioning that only 10 percent said that "democracy is alien to the Russian model of political life," and 6 percent said that "democracy and democrats in Russia are over and done with." Twenty-eight percent did not know what to think about the country's prospects for democracy.[43]

One can see that few respondents saw no hope for democracy in Russia. Almost a quarter of those polled hoped for the emergence of a new democratic party, but they did not think that their hope would be fulfilled any time soon.[44] During 2004, there were three notable efforts to create new democratic forums. These were the Committee 2008–Free Choice, led by the former world chess champion, Gary Kasparov; Irina Khakamada's Our Choice; and the democratic discussion club Democratic Alternative, formed by two independent Duma members, Mikhail Zadornov and Vladimir Ryzhkov. These tiny forums of intellectuals hardly had any serious chance to turn into popular parties, but they at least helped to keep embers glowing beneath the ashes of what was left from the democratic hopes of the 1990s.

What about the Communists? Their congress on July 3, 2004, was a farce. Schismatics in the party held their own congress and tried to take away the Communist Party brand name from Gennady Zyuganov. Zyuganov's people had their congress in the dark, because unknown wrongdoers pulled the electricity plug on the building. These surrealistic scenes gave the Communist Party's foes much to gloat over: Zyuganov reading his speech by flashlight, the grotesque shadows thrown on the wall by the members of the presidium, and hapless delegates wandering in dark hallways in search of the toilets.

The breakaway communists had their congress in comfort on board a ship and elected a new leader, the Ivanovo region's governor, Vladimir Tikhonov. Wagging tongues said that the schism in the ranks of the Communist Party was the work of the Kremlin spin doctors. Of course, the party's decline suited the regime, which worried that the Communist Party might get a second wind as social tension grew.

The most amusing event took place after the congresses of the competing communists. President Putin called each of the two rival chairmen and inquired, as if nothing were wrong, how things were going with the party. Either Putin has a strange sense of humor, or he was not fully informed about the technical details of Operation Anti-Zyuganov. Zyuganov began complaining to the president about his administration and the secret services, accusing them of trying to break up the Communist Party. This was certainly a joke: an opposition leader asking the regime to help him preserve his party!

In the end, Zyuganov stamped out the brush fire in the party and resumed control over his flock. But this was no longer the Communist Party that had threatened Yeltsin and until just recently had controlled the Duma. Even the party's traditional voters—the pensioners—were switching to United Russia. Though it was true that the Communist Party still controlled 12.7 percent of the electorate and that it was too soon to discount it totally, for the Communists to resuscitate even part of their former influence, they need to replace Zyuganov and move to harsh opposition.

As for the national-populist parties, the Liberal Democratic Party came in with its traditional 5 to 6 percent, and Rodina could count on 3 to 4 percent. To stop the shrinking of its support, the Rodina leaders tried using populist slogans and moving toward the social-democratic niche, in an attempt to attract the supporters of the Communists and Yabloko.

The Russian president seemed to have no reasons to worry about domestic politics: Russian political life was now easy to control and until 2006—when one could imagine that the real fight for power would start—the Kremlin could manipulate the scene without much effort. Yeltsin's political structure had been dismantled, and its heroes had been turned into ghosts still lingering on the scene but already written off by the new political and economic class. The crucial developments were unfolding in the economic area. Here, behind a quite rosy picture of robust growth that any industrial country could envy, unsettling signs were starting to emerge. The initial feelings that Mikhail Fradkov's government was not a consolidated team and had inherent sources of tension proved to be correct. The drafting of the 2005 budget provoked an open split in the cabinet; it became apparent that the prime minister and liberals had different agendas and systems of values, and that they were doomed to have conflicts. Their behavior during 2004 demonstrated that no one was ready to back and seek compromise, which made it difficult if not impossible to forge the government's priorities and cohesive policy. Besides, egos played their roles as well. Fradkov was not satisfied with the role of "technical premier," who would only have to endorse the course crafted in the leading ministries—first of all, the Ministry of Economic Development, headed by German Gref, Putin's favorite. Moreover, Fradkov was not ready to limit the state's control and to support the initiatives that Gref was advocating.

The future course of the government looked like a constant tug of war and chain of waverings. To defend their positions, the members of the cabinet would appeal to the president, and he would have to play the role of arbitrator and to make final decisions, which the president did not like to do. The president and not the premier or the ministers would be accountable for the government's agenda, and meanwhile, the cabinet members would pursue wait-and-see tactics. It was hardly the best possible option at a time when the government had only a two-year window of opportunity until 2006, when the new campaign starts and the issue of succession will dominate people's minds.

Meanwhile, in the summer and fall of 2004, Fradkov was moving in opposite directions. Thus, he mentioned the reform of Gazprom yet at the same time even more energetically highlighted the necessity to increase the role of the state in Gazprom activity. He had stopped the reform of the RAO UES energy holding, but soon after that announced that its planned reform had been delayed and that he personally would see to reenergizing it (!).

Having become frustrated with Fradkov's actions, German Gref and Alexei Kudrin did what they will definitely make a practice of doing—they went to see the president in Sochi, where Putin spent his vacation, and they complained. The last straw that forced them to openly take a step of disobedience and risk a public scandal was the premier's insistence on forecasting GDP growth in 2005 at 7.5 percent. Kudrin and Gref said "No," arguing that such high rates of GDP growth were impossible without reforming the energy and gas industries, transport, and the communal and housing services. The premier replied that he is undertaking only "sensible reforms, and not reforms for the sake of reforms." It was clear how the prime minister viewed the ideas of his liberal-minded cabinet members. Speaking about the role of the economic development ministry, the usually cautious Fradkov was for the first time openly harsh, saying that Gref's major task is " to create tensions with ministers." It was a difficult task for Putin to keep such a government together as a working team.

The cabinet members were bickering while the window for the next round of reforms was slowly closing. The task that Putin's second presidency was facing in the economic area was to start solving or at least mitigating the problem of Russia's resource dependence. It was becoming his toughest challenge. The negative consequences of resource dependence were evident: continuing rent seeking, increased corruption, and inequality of incomes—all of which were bound to undermine long-term performance.[45]

The Russian leadership faced a serious structural set of challenges, crucial among which was administrative reform, which would increase the accountability of the courts and the efficiency of the bureaucracy. Putin understood the challenge. But judging by his slow efforts to reform the bureaucracy, he was not ready to create enemies in his apparatus. No less important was the restructuring of large state-controlled monopolies in natural gas, electricity, and housing to create frameworks that would allow for competition. These were the real tests for the president and his team, which in the end will define what kind of mission Putin wanted to pursue in his final term.

Among other key priorities were banking reform; improving conditions for small and medium-sized business; and more effective fiscal policy, which meant increasing the task burden on resource sectors while reducing it on the rest of the economy. Nearly all these priorities had been on the agenda of Putin's first term. The fact that the government had failed to pursue them can be at least partially justified by the fact that Putin had to consolidate his grip on power. Now, in his second term, he had no excuses: He held all the power levers he wanted, and he either had to make a breakthrough with structural reforms or admit that by not doing so that he had other ideas on his mind or could not overcome the obstacles—first of all vested interests. If Putin wanted to embark on systemic reform, Fradkov's administration was hardly the ideal instrument.

Compared to the disarray on the domestic front, Russian foreign policy appeared much more structured. When Putin decided that the crisis in relations between Russia and the European Union had to end, he did what needed to be done. The basic points of contention were handled as if there had never been any mutual dissatisfaction that went as far as issuing ultimatums. On April 27, 2004, in Luxembourg, Moscow and the European Union signed a compromise that facilitated solving a cargo transit blockage between Russia's mainland and Kaliningrad. The sides agreed on an increase in quotas for Russian steel exports to E.U. countries and to slash commodity tariffs. The European Union made a pledge to monitor the situation with national minorities in the Baltic republics. This suggests that Russia's losses from the E.U. expansion will be minimal, and the whole story shows that Moscow can secure its interests without hysteria and threats.

Putin's course of compromising in the Moscow–Brussels relationship was confirmed during the thirteenth Russian–E.U. summit in Moscow on May 21, 2004. The sides signed a protocol according to which the European Union supported Russia's desire to join the World Trade Organization (WTO). The goal Putin had wanted for so long was becoming more realistic.[46] Once Brussels supported Russia, China and the United States could not block Russia's entrance into the WTO forever. It had taken Russia and Brussels six years to get there—with endless conversations, arguments, and cups of coffee. The two delegatio⸗s did not sleep the night before the signing. Gref and Pascal Lami, the European trade commissioner, worked all night ironing out the final details. Brussels agreed to support Moscow in the negotiations on the WTO in exchange for Moscow's promise to ratify the Kyoto protocol. Under Putin's pressure, the European Union rejected the "gas ultimatum"—that is, demanding an immediate price hike on gas in Russia's domestic prices, the liquidation of the Gazprom monopoly, and an assurance that private gas pipelines would be built. Russia agreed to a gradual increase in domestic gas prices.

At the signing of the protocol on the completion of negotiations between Russia and European Union, Putin, who could barely control his satisfied smile, turned to Romano Prodi, chairman of the European Commission, and said with great feeling, "Romano, thank you very much." Prodi almost wept. They embraced. The audience applauded. This was a moment when the pendulum swung to the positive side. But how long it would rest there, no one knew.

Since the expansion of the European Union on May 1, 2004, more than half of Russia's trade has been with the union. Russia covers more than a quarter of the union's energy needs. This demonstrates the economic interdependence of Russia and the union, which does not exist in the relations between Russia and the United States. But Russia and the union need to solve many practical issues dealing with border control, crime, illegal migration, lifting export duties, and equalizing prices for energy carriers. How quickly these questions can be resolved depends on how quickly Russia and the European Union find a formula for partnership in keeping with their new situation.

Not everything even in the field of foreign policy went smoothly, however. Russia's relations with Georgia, which for a long time had been a sensitive issue, became the source of a serious tension. With Mikhail Saakashvili as the new president, Tbilisi tried to restore the country's territorial integrity, which had been lost in the 1990s. The success of the new Georgian leader depended on Russia, which had supported separatist movements in Abkhazia and in South Ossetia and the independence of Adjaria, all constituent parts of Georgia.

Tbilisi began gathering up Georgian lands in Adjaria—whose leader, Aslan Abashidze, had close ties with Russia—first of all with the group of Moscow mayor Yuri Luzhkov. Almost every observer was certain that in a conflict between the Adjarian leader and Saakashvili, Putin would support Moscow's old ally. After a waiting period, the Russian leader sent the head of the Security Council, Igor Ivanov, to Batumi, the capital of Adjaria. He made such a convincing case for political asylum to Abashidze that the latter did not dare refuse. This was the determining step that obviated the danger of bloodshed in the separatist republic and permitted Saakashvili to restore control over Adjaria.

Like the compromise achieved at the summit with Brussels, the peaceful settlement of the Adjaria problem demonstrated Putin's willingness to take action that is not supported by the Russian political class. In solving the Adjarian conflict, Moscow worked with Washington, which kept Saakashvili from taking reckless action. True, it was not altruism that prompted Moscow to compromise with Tbilisi. The Russian military wanted a quid pro quo from Georgia: agreement to an extension of Russian bases on Georgian territory,[47] which Georgia, by the way, did not want, openly demonstrating its intention to squeeze the Russians out. Putin personally, it seemed, did not want to endanger his relations with the West, especially with the United States, and he was trying not to exacerbate tension in the Caucasus. But he hardly concealed his sour feelings toward Tbilisi.

Saakashvili, inspired by his swift success in the Adjaria blitzkrieg, decided to continue his success by trying to regain Tbilisi's control over South Ossetia. But here the situation was much more complicated.

Remembering Georgia's attempts to take Ossetian territory by force, the Ossetians did not wish to return to Georgia. They preferred living under Russia's protection, which is understandable: South Ossetia survived on its trade with Russia and on the pensions and benefits paid by Russia.

The impatient Georgians intensified the dormant conflict, which immediately mobilized the South Ossetian leaders. The stakes were high for Saakashvili. His political future was riding on this. Defeat in the struggle for regaining South Ossetia could be a blow against his presidency. But even South Ossetia was merely a step toward the real prize: breakaway Abkhazia. Further developments depended on Putin's position. Saakashvili admitted, "Putin told me he would let us meddle in Adjaria, but he would not allow us to do the same in Abkhazia."[48] Consequently, he had to negotiate with Moscow.

The tension on the border between Georgia and South Ossetia intensified in the summer of 2004, and military action seemed imminent. Volunteers, mostly Russian Cossacks and Abkhazians, arrived in Ossetia. A careless move could be the spark to ignite the entire region. It's unlikely that North Ossetia would sit idly by during an armed conflict between Georgia and South Ossetia. Karachaevo-Cherkessia, Adygeya, and Chechnya, all parts of Russia, would inevitably get involved if Georgia tried to take back Abkhazia. The Georgians and South Ossetians were already taking potshots at each other, and the first blood had been shed. This was a test of Moscow's ability to find a peaceful solution. And it was becoming a test of Putin's vision and cold blood.

Yet Putin still had not defined his goals in the Caucasus. As a pragmatic politician, he of course knew that Russia needed a stable Georgia. Therefore, Georgia had to solve its problem of territorial integrity. Moscow couldn't pursue a policy of double standards indefinitely: on the one hand, trying to rein in rebellious Chechnya; on the other, supporting separatism in Georgian breakaway republics. However, Russian political and military circles had apparently made promises to help separatists in unrecognized republics. Certain groups in Russia had their own commercial interests in Abkhazia and South Ossetia, which had turned into smuggling corridors. Putin also had to bear in mind that the Russian political class was strongly opposed to Georgia's pro-Western orientation. The impatience and even aggressiveness of the new Georgian leadership added fuel to the fire. But at the same time, Putin obviously wanted to avoid a new Caucasus conflict. Moreover, the Kremlin could not ignore the fact that a majority of Russians were strongly in favor of Moscow's neutral stance in the conflict between Tbilisi and South Ossetia; 63 percent of respondents supported Russian neutrality, 29 percent thought that Russia had to take a mediating role, and only 6 percent supported military support of the separatists.[49]

It was easier for Saakashvili than Putin, because he knew what he wanted. Putin had inherited problems that Russia had not seriously considered for a long time. "We can deal with each other," Saakashvili said after a meeting with Putin. The time had come to test just how well they could deal with each other. Even if they found a common language, they would have to make their policies fit the sentiments of the Russian and Georgian elites.

At this point in the story, I have to return to the phenomenon that became a puzzle for many observers: the "hot" Russian summer. In normal countries, summer is a time of relaxation. But not in Russia, where every summer something happens. This year, at a time of high oil prices, a bank crisis unfolded, for the third time in fourteen years. Crazed depositors stormed automated teller machines to take out their money. Stores stopped accepting credit cards. The panic of the depositors spread like wildfire to the banks, which stopped giving people their money and refused to meet their interbank obligations. Russia truly was unique if it could have a crisis in the midst of outstanding economic indicators.

Here is what happened. The Central Bank recalled the license of one of the medium-sized banks, Sodbiznesbank, suspecting it (not without foundation) of money laundering. But the clumsiness of the Central Bank's approach to the problem panicked its depositors. Soon rumors of the existence of lists of banks to be shut down multiplied, panicking depositors in other banks. And off it went: shaking the foundation of banks in the top 20, including Gutabank and Alfabank, which paid out $200 million to their depositors in a few days.

The banks unwilling to move to transparency were at fault. But the main responsibility for the crisis lies in the management of the Central

Bank and its chief executive, Sergei Ignatiev, who could not regulate the situation in time. The Central Bank should have solved the problem of undercapitalized banks a long time ago, but it allowed the messy situation to unfold.[50] The Central Bank's inability to take decisive action is to a larger degree the result of its contradictory role on the Russian market—it is supervisor and regulator of the banking system, while also being the majority owner of Sberbank, Russia's largest bank.

The banking crisis ended as unexpectedly as it had begun. The Central Bank cut reserve requirements twice, it introduced a bill guaranteeing deposits up to 100,000 rubles ($3,400), and Vneshtorgbank bought the damaged Gutabank. The president himself soothed depositors. The squall quieted down, albeit not without leaving victims. Once again, Russian private banks will have to rebuild the trust of their clients. The hardest hit were small and medium-sized banks. The state banks and financial institutions with ties to the state, as well as branches of famous Western banks, were the winners.

The new bank crisis demonstrated the need for banking reform and for clearing away banks with shady dealings. That requires the political will of the country's leadership and the determination of the Central Bank.

And now again, back to the foreign policy field. On July 12, 2004, Putin met with Russian ambassadors called to Moscow from all over the world. It was a routine meeting and at the same time a symbolic one. During such gatherings, the president usually reiterated the principles of foreign policy. This time, he presented the five main elements of the foreign policy strategy that he formulated during his first term. Let's list them as he did. First, foreign policy must become the instrument of the country's modernization. Second, relations with the newly independent states on the territory of the former USSR are a priority for Russia's foreign policy. Third, relations between Russia and Europe remain a "traditional priority." Putin responded to Russian great-power adherents by stating that "there are no alternatives to cooperation with the European Union and NATO." Fourth, Putin noted the need for partnership with the United States. Fifth, the president set the goal of initiating cooperation with the countries on the Asia-Pacific rim for the development of Siberia.

Russian foreign policy under Putin had become more defined. The Kremlin gave up the dilemmas that had perplexed it: West or East? Atlantism or Europeanization? Russia rejected not only pretensions to the role of one of the poles of international relations but also Eurasianism and the desire to become a bridge between Europe and Asia. "Economization," "new realism," "multivector" policy—these were the concepts driving Russian politics. In practice, the new foreign policy vocabulary meant a desire of the Kremlin "to domesticate" Russian foreign policy.[51]

Putin's multivector formula meant a few more things: first, a retreat from integrating Russia into the Western community in the near term; second, further correlation of ambitions with limited resources; third, an unwillingness to have confrontations with the West; and fourth, an attempt to assure Russia a dominant role in the former Soviet space, but by more flexible methods. Some observers defined Putin's search as an attempt to find a "third way" in international relations—one involving not integration but also not confrontation with the West.[52] I believe that he was thinking of "selective partnership" with the Western community while retaining Russia's principles of order. "Together but separate" might be the motto emblazoned on Putin's crest for this period. The policy's architects felt that, within this course, Russia could cooperate with some states and distance itself from others or oppose them, depending on what best suited Russia's interests. Dmitri Trenin, analyzing Putin's foreign policy, wrote: "Overcoming its identity crisis, Russia presents itself as an autonomous international actor, standing apart from the rest. This could best be described as an attempt to play the part of great power under contemporary conditions." Andrew Kuchins cleverly described the new formula for Russia's international role as greater interaction, rather than integration, with the West.[53]

The multivector philosophy was a way for Russia to adapt to the country's new geopolitical reality while its internal transformations were still not complete. It's quite possible that the policy of "together but separate"—which is oriented toward cooperation with the West for several crucial security and economic issues—could push Russia closer to liberal civilization. Another variant is also possible: an accumulation of mutual suspicion. It's unlikely that the Western community is interested in encouraging Russia's renaissance as long as the country retains a value system that is alien to the West.

During this same period, Moscow started to actively pursue the status of regional superpower. But this time, Putin wanted to downplay imperial aspects, which so worried Russia's neighbors and the West. Noteworthy in this regard was the meeting of the leaders of the Commonwealth of Independent States (CIS), headed by Putin, on July 19, 2004, in Moscow. For the first time, the Russian president criticized Russian policies regarding the CIS. He said, "It would be mistaken to think that Russia has some kind of monopoly on activity in that space."[54] The Russian leader stressed that, one, he was not interested in creating a superstate of the CIS, and two, he was planning to promote Russian interests in the region using market levers. He clearly wanted to find a new tie between geopolitics and economic interests. Nor was the Kremlin giving up the opportunity to use economic levers to secure a Russian military presence in the region. An example of this is the renewed military cooperation between Russia and Uzbekistan in exchange for Russian investments in the Uzbek oil and gas sector.

An indicator of Russia's search for ways to restore its influence in the post-Soviet space was the creation of numerous collective forms of economic and military cooperation with its neighbors.[55] But their very abundance evidenced their ineffectiveness. New unions were hollow from within because of the incompatibility of interests of their members. It seemed that only one thing united them: They could not sit at the table with advanced industrial countries, and that fact gave the integration projects in the post-Soviet space an air of disability. Russia was unwilling to be the donor to all its neighbors, but that eliminated their willingness to integrate; instead, they prefer to develop bilateral relations.

Despite Putin's pragmatism, the Kremlin was unable to free itself of Soviet thinking. Retaining Russian military bases in Georgia against Tbilisi's wishes; supporting separatist forces in the Transdnister, Abkhazia, and South Ossetia; and attempting to influence the presidential elections in Ukraine in 2004—all were manifestations of the attempts to preserve

Russian hegemony that contradicted Putin's stress on the economization of foreign policy. There were still influential great-power adherents inside the Russian political and military establishment, and they were not about to change their minds. They no longer set the vector of foreign policy, but they were able to complicate the reevaluation of Russia's role in the world. The influence of traditionalists on foreign and security policy was possible because neither the Kremlin's pragmatists nor liberals had a vision of Russia's new international role that would meet the needs of its modernization yet simultaneously not humiliate the nation, which was so accustomed to thinking in global categories.

And how were relations developing between Russia and its main partner, the United States? At the end of June 2004, an event revealed the attitude of the Kremlin toward the American administration. As the last session of the American commission examining the events of 9/11 began, Interfax, the official news agency, reported that "back in early 2002, Russian intelligence learned that Iraqi special forces were planning a terrorist act on U.S. territory....This information was given several times to our American partners in verbal and written form in the fall of 2002." This report did not make a splash, and so Putin himself said at a press conference in the Kazakh capital, Astana, "In fact, after the events of September 11 and before the start of military operations in Iraq, Russian intelligence repeatedly received information of this sort and passed it on to their American colleagues." He noted that George W. Bush had personally thanked the director of one of the Russian intelligence agencies for the information.

This statement could be seen as support for Putin's friend Bush when he was having trouble over the Iraq operation and its justification. But the question arose: If there were facts about the danger posed by Saddam Hussein, then why wasn't this mentioned during the discussions of Iraq in the Security Council and why did Russia vote against the military operation? To smooth over the contradictions in his statement, Putin explained that Russia's position against the war in Iraq had not changed. "There are procedures recognized by international law for the use of force in international affairs, and those procedures were not observed in that case," the

Russian president stressed.[56] In response to Putin's admission, the U.S. Department of State announced that it knew nothing of the facts mentioned by the Russian leader. Even Colin Powell knew nothing about this. Yet the Americans were going all out to find the slightest confirmation of a threat from the Saddam regime. This is a very strange story.

What does it tell us? That Putin took a chance and supported Bush in the presidential race—and that he will again do this on several other occasions. He showed the traditional Moscow preference for Republican presidents and its fear of Democratic ones. He also demonstrated that partnership with America was exceptionally important for him. He demonstrated other thing: He was giving a message to his allies in the post-Soviet space, which meant: "I have special relations with America. We are really close with Washington. And you, folks, don't even dare to dream about forming an independent relationship with the Americans. You have to deal with Moscow, as an intermediary." At least the timing and atmosphere of Putin's confession gave reason to interpret it this way.

But this demonstration of partnership was done in a way that bewildered Americans. And this sort of gambit would have put Moscow in an awkward situation if Bush had lost the election.

Russia was moving toward its new August, which has so often turned out to be for Russians a month of tragic dramas. August 2004 reconfirmed the worst forebodings—it was a really bad month for Russia. One terrorist act after another rocked the country. New guerrilla attacks on the Chechen capital, Grozny, ended with dozens of killed and injured among the federal troops and those loyal to Moscow Chechens. It was followed by the downing of the two airplanes full of passengers and the blast at the Moscow subway station, which again took dozens of human lives. Finally came the Beslan nightmare. A group of terrorists, mainly Chechens and Ingush, seized the school in the North Ossetian city, taking hostage of about 1,200 children and their parents. The seizure ended with massive deaths as a result of bomb blasts and shooting—more than 300 people, mainly children, were killed, and the death toll is still unknown and may reach 500 to 600 people. It was the worst world hostage disaster; Shamil

Basayev, the most radical leader of the Chechen separatists, took responsibility.

The world watched with horror unprecedented atrocities against the most innocent. Putin's "presidential vertical" proved to be totally helpless in dealing with the hostage crisis. Two officials who were closest to the president—Nikolai Patrushev, the head of the Federal Security Service, and Rashid Nurgaliev, the head of the Interior Ministry—secretly arrived in Ossetia but did not show up at the scene. The North Ossetian president, Aleksandr Dzasohov, who had been hand picked by the Kremlin, was close to hysteria and waited for orders from Moscow and rejected the terrorist offer to come to the school and negotiate. The president of neighboring Ingushetia, General Murat Ziazikov, went into hiding and broke the telephone connection. Putin himself hesitated in deciding what to do until the worst happened. Instead of thinking how to save human lives, officials shamelessly lied about everything: the number of hostages, the number of victims, the number of terrorists, and their ethnicity.[57]

The Northern Caucasus froze in anticipation of further drama. Ossetians—having waiting in vain for the official prosecution of those who had masterminded Beslan—started to prepare for revenge. As one of the Beslan people said: "We will retaliate. There will be bloody war!" Anger against neighboring Ingush and Chechen has been widespread among the Ossetians, because many of the hostage takers were representatives of these two groups. Besides, the animosity between Ossetians and Ingush had deep roots in the long-standing clashes in the early 1990s. The spillover of the conflict to other Caucasus republics, including multinational Dagestan, seemed inevitable. Putin was facing tough challenges in the North Caucasus.

The Beslan tragedy once again proved that the Russian regime of personified power cannot handle any crisis and gets paralyzed when quick and professional reaction and competence are needed. The centralization of power breeds irresponsibility from the top down: Local officials are waiting for orders from the top, and those in the Kremlin are not in a hurry to take responsibility either. Events in a small Caucasus town confirmed what had been apparent for a long time: that local bosses appointed by the Kremlin have neither influence nor respect among their population. In the midst of the hostage crisis, while the Kremlin loyalists were in hiding, it was Ruslan Aushev—the former president of Ingushetia who had been kicked out of power by Moscow for independent behavior— who met with the terrorists and freed 30 hostages, mainly small babies.

On September 13, after the massacre, Putin finally went on the air. He looked shaken and pale. His leadership had been tested, and he had to decide where he should go now. He could have used Beslan as the motive for reconsidering his course in Chechnya, for begging his society for forgiveness. National tragedy could have become a moment for him to rekindle his leadership of the nation on a new basis. But he stood his ground. He was not looking for forgiveness; he was looking for those whom he could blame for his failures. He vehemently rejected any criticism of his Chechnya policy. His message was: Beslan is about international terrorism and not about my policy backfiring.

"We are dealing with direct intervention of international terrorism against Russia," Putin insisted. He said that Beslan showed "that we are weak and the weak get beaten." Hence, from now on, Russia should be tougher. That meant one thing: keeping the Chechen war going. Putin's address to the nation contained a key phrase, which stunned all his buddies (his partners) in the West: "Some people want to tear from us a juicy piece of pie and others help them. They help in the belief that Russia—as one of the world's major nuclear powers—still represents a threat to someone. Therefore, this threat must be removed." Putin was vague about who exactly those enemies of Russia are. But the Kremlin's propagandists soon would explain whom the president had in mind.

Putin also said that there will not be a public inquiry into the events— just as there was no public inquiry into the Moscow theater siege of October 2002 and no inquiry into the *Kursk* submarine tragedy. The Russian authorities, trying to save the prestige of the state, continued to try keeping secret what was actually behind these Russian national tragedies. The truth often was so appalling that it really could change Russians' attitude toward their authorities.

On September 26, Putin addressed the nation about his new political initiatives, in the context of his response to the terrorist attacks. He announced that he was scrapping the elections of governors and introducing a proportional system for Duma elections. The Beslan massacre offered the Kremlin a convenient excuse to launch a long-planned strengthening of the executive chain of command. Under the proposed reforms, governors would no longer be dependent on their constituents. They would owe allegiance only to Moscow. And these were not the end of the Kremlin's initiatives: Now, the center will have to crack down on mayors as well; a bill was introduced to put the courts under the control of the executive, and the enlargement of the regions was discussed. Together, these changes amounted to an overhaul of the Russian Federation.

Putin's reforms undermined the Constitution, and once one constitutional block was removed, the whole constitutional structure became shaky. But who cared about the Constitution when the team of ruling elites had to achieve their more important goals—redistributing resources and self-perpetuating power. On October 13, Putin tried to reassure foreign journalists: "We shall seek in every way to build such a political system and such relations between the state and society which strengthen the system of democracy." He either had a strange sense of humor or an idiosyncratic understanding of democracy.

Soon, the deputy head of the presidential administration, Vladislav Surkov—the old Yeltsin hand who had remained to serve the new Kremlin boss—gave an interview on what sounded like the Kremlin's concept of a new course.[58] The concept sounded very much like updated Stalinist doctrine. Surkov reiterated that the Western powers were creating cover for the terrorists who attack Russia for the purpose of "feeding the predator with someone else's meat." He described their supporters and accomplices inside Russia as a "fifth column" that included "false liberals and real Nazis." "They hate what they call Putin's Russia, which actually means they hate Russia per se," he explained. Russia had to listen again to the forgotten song about the enemy at the gate: The enemy is everywhere; enemies are all those who have a different political position.

One could not believe that after more than 20 years of spontaneity and relative freedom, the Kremlin had decided to make this turn. I was telling myself: "This is a bad dream or this is a bad joke. Tomorrow we'll wake up and it will vanish." It did not vanish. The new reality was there, and it was sobering and frightening. The hunt started after the "enemies" of Russia, both inside the country and abroad. The talk of worldwide "conspiracy" became the main menu of the day for the political community. The remaining liberals and democrats, who had thought that they could linger in the ghetto left for them during Putin's first term, were now more pessimistic about their chances for survival.

The major enemy was still the United States and all those connected to Americans. The choice of the major enemy could be easily explained: The Russian political class could not admit its defeat by the Chechens. The enemy should be really big—the United States and the whole world outside Russia. It seemed that a new round of the Cold War was inevitable.

As for ordinary Russians, they did not believe that the authorities would stop terrorism. A total of 93 percent said that new attacks are likely, and 76 percent said that Russian leaders cannot protect the people from them. A share of 36 percent believed that Russian leadership reaction to the attacks showed "firmness and decisiveness," but 40 percent said it indicated that leaders were at a loss as to how to fight terror.[59] Insecurity again like after the apartment blasts in 1999 had an impact: Russians became suspicious of the outside world; 68 percent of respondents in October 2004 were convinced that Russia was surrounded by enemies, 25 percent said that the chief enemy was the United States, 7 percent said that the threat was coming from Arab countries or Islamic groups, and another 7 percent said that threat came from Chechnya.[60] This was nothing unusual; frustrated and insecure people under the pressure of official propaganda had started to look for an old recipe.

Contrary to expectations, after losing some points, Putin was trusted again—demonstrating his Teflon image. People disagreed with him but did not turn away from him. One third of respondents opposed Putin's tightening the screws. But this opposition did not affect his level of trust; 73 percent still trusted him, and among them, 21 percent trusted him entirely, 52 percent were more likely to trust him, and only 25 percent did not trust him—of whom 7 percent did not trust him at all. A lack of alternatives and fear of the worst are proving to be Putin's most enduring basis of support. A majority supported the idea of regional governor appointments; 55 percent of respondents were in favor of Putin's centralization. But about 36 percent of Russians disagreed with their president on the direction of his course and this said that the country was split.[61]

The Western community for the first time was really alarmed, openly accusing Putin of totalitarian policy. Ironically, criticism of Putin has united conservatives and liberals, former promoters of democracy in Russia and those who never believed in its success. Brzezinsky's comparison of Putin to Mussolini was only one example of how Putin was treated in the Western media. But despite the mounting criticism of Putin's authoritarianism in the media and among a wider audience in the West, it did not have an impact on friendly relations between the Russian leader and the Western leaders. The Western politicians were ready to forgive Putin for his undemocratic behavior if he continued to control the situation in Russia and remained an ally in the war on terrorism.

Putin let his propagandists to do the witch hunting and feed the anti American hysteria. He personally was cautious and left for himself the option of a softer policy. He created an impression that the Kremlin would try to mobilize Russia on the basis of the anti-Western rhetoric while the president would continue his engagement with the West. Thus he continued sitting on two chairs, trying to divide values and interests. He even took the steps to sweeten the pill—leveling the field for Gazprom shares, a move long sought by Western investors; and ratifying the Kyoto protocol to curb greenhouse emissions. This combinations of sticks and carrots suggested that Moscow would like to maintain constructive relations with the West. But not all in the West were mollified. Strobe Talbott was definitely among those concerned. "If we learned nothing else from the 20th century, it is that the nature of Russia's internal regime determines its external behavior. A Russia that rules its own people by force and edict rather than consent and enfranchisement is virtually certain, sooner or later, to intimidate its neighbors and to make itself one of the world's problems rather than a contributor to their solution," he warned.[62]

The start of Vladimir Putin's second term was darkened by events that made even the most stubborn optimists worry. The assassination of Kadyrov and the need for new presidential elections in Chechnya; the destruction of YUKOS and its ramifications for the Russian economy; the banking crisis; the social reform that was causing discontent in the public; the tension with Georgia; finally the escalation of the terrorist acts—all these were more than enough to cause serious concern. Nothing was threatening Putin's power for the time being. But quite reasonable questions arise: Can his potential last through a second term, and what will be the most formidable threats to his leadership?

President Putin began his second term by showing that he had a sense of his mission and was prepared to use his power to accomplish it. By this I mean, first of all, his decision to liquidate the state's paternalism. But the method he chose to solve social problems could give rise to social protest and undermine his political support at the very moment when the ruling team was seeking guarantees for its survival after 2008.

Putin was right to start administrative reform. But by giving his apparatchiks the task of restructuring the state, he himself turned his reform into imitation. He was right to try to tame the political ambitions and egoistic interests of big business. But in subordinating business to the bureaucracy, he was distorting the market, which he wanted to develop. He was right to cool Russia's great-power ambitions. But his hope that Russia could create a partnership with the West while keeping its traditional state was yet another illusion. In other words, each time the authorities tried to develop a modernist agenda, the regime they had formed blocked their efforts.

These were not the only Russian catch-22s. By turning toward hypercentralization, Putin tactically might have scored some victories by regaining full control over the provinces and the *cadry*. But strategically he was undermining his leadership and its legitimacy; from now on, he personally would be held accountable for all failures of his appointees in the provinces. Sooner or later, he was doomed to meet the same end that Yeltsin had encountered: Impotent Omnipotence—the inevitable outcome of any highly personified power. Hence, the major threats to Russia during Putin's second term were a weak state and a weak political regime that would try to imitate strength and toughness.

Putin's second term was only beginning, and life could take many unexpected turns. At the time of this writing, there were no forces in Russia that could offer an alternative strategy. Therefore, Russia had to follow the painful trial-and-error method, testing and rejecting one path after another. It is possible that Putin was fated to be the leader who will prove that Russia has exhausted its habitual forms of life, power, and thought in order for the next leader to take a different strategy.

In 2004, there was one more concern: the Russian president often looked as if he had lost his former vitality. He resembled a man who had run out of wind before reaching the finish line and who was moving mechanically, without the will to win. His eyes had dimmed. Whether this was a depletion of his spiritual strength, a loss of orientation, or only temporary weariness, which he would overcome, and if he does it—then for what purpose, we will have to see.

In any case, a lot of ambiguity still remained not in the Kremlin's policy, which has acquired a certain logic, but in its outcome, which could be different than the authorities anticipate. The popular political joke making the rounds in Moscow quite well characterizes Russian moods and perceptions at that moment: "A sick man picked up by an ambulance says: Where are you taking me? To the morgue, answers the doctor. But I am not dead yet. We are not there yet, was the response." Russia is "not there yet," and a lot still could happen before the end of Putin's second term

Chapter 13

RUSSIA'S UNFINISHED STORY

The West—means and goal. The Faustian bargain. Will Russia be able to reject the Russian System? Russia's hope.

T he reader who has been following all the ups and downs of Russia's transformation may be confused about the major trajectory of the country's developments, and reasonably might ask a question: Where in the end will Russia be moving—to a harsher authoritarian regime, even a dictatorship; or to linger in its hybrid bureaucratic authoritarianism and, after understanding the traps of this regime, starting to build effective democratic institutions, this time based on the rule of law and not unstructured freedoms? Hardly anybody could answer this question now. Indeed, after Putin's first term, the chances of preserving at least some political freedoms are becoming smaller and smaller. Besides, how democratic could mechanisms and institutions be whose main goal is to serve as window dressing for an undemocratic regime? Yet despite very gloomy Russian developments in 2003–2004, it is still too early to bury liberal democracy in this country.

Indeed, Russian society is still stumbling and lingering. Some Russians seek calm and tranquillity in personified power, approving Putin's hyper-centralization. But more and more, Russians are ready to walk forward without turning back. It took them twenty years, beginning with Gorbachev's *perestroika* in 1985, to reject quite a few traditions, patterns of life, and a mentality to which they had been accustomed—what constituted the Russian System, the form that used to embody Russia. It was nearly two decades—a long time in a human life, but a short period in history, just a flash. It is not clear, however, how long it will take the country to throw off the last waverings of the old system and what price it will have to pay for its final break with authoritarian rule and attempts to play a great-power role and to pursue "uniqueness."

Russians at the start of the new century have, I hope, rejected claims for Russia as the pole of an alternative civilization. But if the country is to move toward the West, it will have to discover what forms that movement can take and what routes it can follow. Russians must guard against fresh illusions and unreasonable expectations, as well as learn how to handle the inevitable frustrations and pain. Dialogue and even cooperation with the West during the 1990s did not preclude Russians' stumbling around in new delusions and neuroses, envying strong nations, and indulging in self-pity and unexpected outbursts of bitterness. Finally, Russians must overcome their major new temptation to pursue what seems the easiest road: to imitate the market and democracy in their surface aspects while underneath preserving patron–client relations, the rule of the few, and governance without accountability.

In the meantime, the alliance that Russia concluded with the West in 2001 contains not only the possibility of real partnership and Russia's integration into the West but the threat of a new Russian alienation. If there were a new misunderstanding or clash of interests with the West, Russia hardly would revert to its previous hostility toward Western civilization but rather would descend to a murky zone of disenchantment with everybody and everything—including Russia itself.

So far, the alliance Russia struck with the West has taken the form of a Faustian bargain. The essence of the bargain is simple: The West is including Russia in the implementation of some of its geopolitical interests—the war on terrorism, strengthening the security agenda, promoting an energy dialogue—while shutting its eyes to how far Russia still is from being a liberal democracy. Moreover, the West continues to view Russia's leadership as the major guarantee of its cozy relations with the West, thus endorsing Russian rule through personified power. In its turn, Russia is solving the problem of external resources for its modernization while retaining the old rules of the game domestically.

The Faustian bargain has its supporters among those who see Russia only as an ally in pursuing a few common goals; those who continue to view Russia as a hostile country, an embodiment of evil; and those who prefer to see Russia where it is now—at the perimeter of Western civilization, as a curtain dividing the West from rising China. In Russia, the Faustian bargain is supported by the advocates of authoritarianism and Russia's "uniqueness." Paradoxically, the current partnership between Russia and the West helps to preserve Russia's bureaucratic authoritarianism.

The inclusion of Russia in the Western orbit on the basis of certain coinciding geopolitical interests could be situational and merely temporary. Only a commonality of values would guarantee the genuine integration of Russia into the Western community. Russia would have to fully embrace liberal democratic principles, rejecting attempts to tailor democratic institutions to the needs of personified power and the bureaucratic state. Only then could Russia join in a "constructive partnership" with the West.

That partnership at first would inevitably have aspects of benevolent asymmetry, at least in the economic field. A serious challenge for Russia is to give up the notion of military parity with the United States, recognize its current limited capabilities, and channel its resources into building an affluent society—this time satisfying its people, not its vanity. Cutting excessive global ambitions now would not preclude the possibility of Russia's emergence in the future as an economically prosperous regional and, perhaps, world power. But for the sake of its future, Russia—and the West—will have to end the imitation game, which is humiliating for all participants and destructive for Russia.

Is the Russian public prepared to reject attempts to combine the incompatible: Westernization with Soviet-style superpower ambitions, democracy with personified power, the market with the regulatory role of the bureaucracy? Is it ready to reject great-power status based on military might? The data cited in this book suggest that by the late 1990s many Russians had matured enough to want to be integrated into a system of liberal values.

But many in the political class are not ready to give up their attempts to regulate, to reject patrimonialism, to leave behind the shadow networks, and to overcome nostalgia for the imperialist past. Those who consider themselves elites have been afraid to let go of the controls. They have no experience living in a free society. They are terrified of competition and have a fear of their own people and of any alternatives. They lean heavily on the police, the security services, the army, and the state apparatus, to which they look as their safety net and guarantor of survival. Their own helplessness, inadequate education, and lack of experience living in a culture of consensus and dialogue drive them to destroy the new sprouts around them, keeping potential rivals down. It is the political class in Russia, obsessed with self-preservation, that tries to reanimate the archaic elements of the public subconscious and heighten suspicion of the West, fear of openness, and nostalgia for lost empire. Superpower status and authoritarianism are the last bastions of those who do not know how to live and rule in a new way. The more the Russian political class loses its grip on the developments, the more it feels helpless and turns toward the traditionalist state and its instruments—coercion or the threat of coercion.

In the fall of 2001, Vladimir Putin forced the ruling class to accept his pro-Western shift. Cowardly and opportunistic elites followed the leader, as is usual in Russia. But to move presidential choice into the realm of concrete decisions, a new bureaucracy is needed, one that would leave provincial backwaters and servility behind and think in the imperatives of the modern competitive age.

In this situation, the Kremlin's choice in favor of the West cannot be fully realized. It has not become Russia's ideology and its elites' key mission. Moreover, the leader has not gone beyond the Faustian bargain. He remains the classic Russian modernizer, operating within the limits of the triad of autocracy, Western resources, and a market economy. Both President Putin and the Russian elites hope to join the West on their own terms—that is, while preserving the Russian System. Twenty years is not long enough to become accustomed to another tradition—to live, to work, to walk without a leash. Some have learned to do it; others are still afraid or reluctant.

The West, for its part, has not yet decided how much it needs Russia. Western governments are not prepared to integrate Russia into their space. This is understandable, for no one knows what it would do to Western civilization to bring in a weak (at the moment) giant, with all its complexes and pretensions, murky past, still-vague desires, huge ambitions, and enormous potential coupled with vestiges of Soviet and pre-Soviet legacies.

Yes, there is an understanding, especially in Europe, that fundamental issues confronting the world community cannot be resolved without Russia. But Europe is moving in its own direction, creating policy of a new kind—fashioning transnational governance, liquidating some functions of the nation-state, and destroying borders between countries. Russia continues building a traditional state with all its attributes and is again trying to lace civil society into a tight corset. I wonder how Russian modernism and European postmodernity can coexist. It may not be realistic to anticipate integration of entities with radically different views about the very substance of future development.

Besides, broad political forces in the West are currently out of sympathy with Russia. Western liberals resent Russia's global aspirations, Moscow's Chechen war, and the Kremlin's crackdown on pluralism and freedom. Western conservatives, however, are prepared to engage Moscow in dialogue, but within the framework of realpolitik, avoiding mention of Russia's domestic problems and regarding the country as innately alien and incorrigible.

Even those in the West who favor embracing Russia are still undecided about whether they should wait for Russia to complete its transformation into a democracy or start integrating without waiting for the outcomes of Russia's transformation. Western political circles hesitate, and many have reached the conclusion that it is better to wait. Europe still needs to absorb eastern Germany into western Germany, to incorporate Central and Eastern Europe and the Baltic states—and there is neither time for new worries nor money. Liberal democracies outside Europe have even less incentive to think about a sustainable marriage with Russia.

But Russia can transform itself only if it is part of the dialogue. The impulses from the outside world might even become the important factor needed for change. Russia's integration into the community of industrial nations should not necessarily mean membership in NATO and the European Union. Integration is a multistage process, and various forms of cooperation are possible—cooperation in strictly defined areas, adaptation, affiliation, mutual dependence, strong bilateral relations. Russia's setting its heart on full membership in Western international institutions could bring new disappointments to both sides if Russia is unable or unwilling to meet the requirements of that membership and continues to seek a "special status."

So far, the Russian ruling class has wanted to appear civilized in the eyes of the world by attempting to re-create in Russia the entire system of Western institutions, yet leaving out what it does not like and what really matters: definite rules of the game and uncertain results. What Russian political elites actually want is just the opposite: uncertain rules that can be changed at will, and predictable, certain results guaranteeing that they remain in power. Not only Putin and his team but also a part of Russian society still believe that a democracy managed from above by a small group of people is perhaps not just the best but the only form of government possible—at least at this stage.

Yet in the longer run, a system based on the absence of alternatives, on low expectations, and on high oil prices must be detrimental. All of Russia's political actors depend on loyalty to the leader, who in turn depends on his poll ratings. But let us imagine what would happen if the president's ratings plunged: It would shake the entire system or even trigger its collapse. A system built on shadowy deals and one-man rule is much more vulnerable than a system formed on the foundation of strong and viable institutions. Russia still must come to this conclusion, and this is the major challenge it is facing.

A combination of authoritarianism and economic liberalization may be perfectly adequate to drag a peasant country onto the road of industrialization. To meet postindustrial challenges, however, to move toward a high-technology society, a new type of regime is needed, one that makes room for social initiatives, local self-government, and individual freedom.

Issues that need answers have been accumulating. How could a dialogue with the West coexist with the desire to "seal up" society, depriving it of the freedoms to which it grew accustomed during the Yeltsin years? How could Moscow get out of the Chechen war and stabilize the Northern Caucasus? How could the Kremlin keep stability from again turning into stagnation? How would authorities deal with a social crisis? And how could Russians achieve a new breakthrough while avoiding chaos and disintegration? Questions, questions, very difficult questions. . . .

So far, the Kremlin's policy has been creating traps for Russia and for the presidency that might turn out to be disastrous for the current regime. On one hand, the policy permits the natural, albeit slow, growth of the middle class, of the new Russian generation ready to live and compete in the modern world. On the other hand, it cracks down on political freedoms. Sooner or later, conflict would be inevitable between the new social groups that strive for parliamentary democracy, local self-government, freedoms, and decentralization of power and those that support the current regime of the bureaucracy, the power ministries, and oligarchs.

It is difficult to tell what form that conflict would take—a pressure from the bottom, a gradual reform from the top, or a combination of both—or how it would end. The key would be solving the conflict without bloodshed or major social upheaval. No less important is avoiding the growth of marginal nationalist forces, which as old Europe has found, can happen even in stable, mature democracies. That would be Putin's task in his second term; or, more plausibly, it would be the task for another leader. In any case, the challenge of changing Russian mechanisms of governance is unavoidable.

———————— ❧ ————————

Russia's leader is influencing its future, and at some moments he is making the future even if he is often reluctant to take a position or is leading his regiment from behind. Is President Putin capable of comprehending that the rule he has created will not allow him to realize his goal—forming a civilized market economy and a modern state? And if he realizes that, is the founder of bureaucratic authoritarianism prepared to restructure his rule accordingly?

Starting with his second term, Putin has faced the dilemma: whether to stay a stabilizer of corrupt capitalism and of a country doomed to living in the waiting room of Western civilization, or to become a transformer and start building a new system that would allow Russia to become a full-fledged liberal democracy and enter the industrial world as an equal. Choosing the first path would mean a continuation of imitation and the construction of Potemkin villages, that is, the usual pastime of Russia's leaders and political class. It would mean a life of pretending: The authorities pretend to rule and the people pretend to obey. That path would mean slow degradation without a chance for Russia to get on its feet. An avalanche-like collapse, blown to bits by a bomb, unexpected ruin, disintegration—all these theatrical and frightening options are not—thank God!—for Russia. The gloomiest scenario for the country on this path is the slow spreading of rot, which might not always be visible but in the end would lead to the disintegration of the people's will, of the Russian spirit of adventure and of political and intellectual courage, and would mean muddling through for years and decades. That is the price of stabilizing current Russian reality.

For Putin personally, this first path might end with a repeat of Yeltsin's story—that is, with the "privatization" of the leader and the regime by a band of Kremlin conspirators. Any leader in Russia will be doomed if he has no strong institutions to support him. But in the historical context, the personal destiny of the leader, if he becomes a hostage of his entourage or of circumstances, will not be important or even interesting. He will remain a footnote to history—the leader who squandered his chance.

The second possible path for President Putin—reform of the regime—would be riskier, without guarantees of success, and with a likelihood that he might break his neck. If the political steering wheel is not turned carefully, reform could end up as Gorbachevism, with the leader losing control of power and events. Breaking one's neck while undertaking a historic task, however, is not the worst end for a world leader. There is honor in it. But Vladimir Putin could have been lucky. If he had decided to "dehermeticize" the regime and managed to cross thin ice without falling in, he would have accomplished what no Russian or Soviet leader ever had done: He would have begun building a responsible system of governance based not on the irrational and mystic power embodied in the leader but on the rule of law. That would have been a new chapter in Russian history. Overcoming the self and finding new impulses or a new destiny is enough to make any nation great and any leader worth remembering. But Putin has chosen the first path, preferring to stay with the tradition. He has not challenged the logic of history. No one in political history has done such a contradictory thing—no one has ever created an authoritarian regime only to consciously destroy it.

We may be demanding the impossible from Vladimir the Modernizer. We reproach him for his rule through personified power and his attempts to control the country's fate single-handedly. But at the same time, there is no sign that influential forces have formed in Russian society that could offer enough support for a completely new, democratic regime. Even the liberals are supporting the elected monarchy. Thus, for us to expect an authoritarian leader to democratize "from above" and voluntarily give up power to institutions in Russian society, which appears to be snoring quietly, would be beyond the limits of realism.

But leadership presupposes vision and the ability to see beyond the present day. The purpose of getting power is to be able to give it away; otherwise, it is not leadership but power grabbing. The rule of the personality in Russia is an atavistic remnant of the past, and it is high time to get rid of it peacefully. If any Russian leader at some point can come to understand this and has the courage and will to solve this problem, he will enter Russian history as Leader-Transformer.

Leadership is still the basic Russian institution. But sooner or later, Russians themselves will have to decide the country's fate. Sometimes this society's patience, conservatism, and inertness are astonishing. It seems hard to budge, turn, or reform. But Russian passivity and patience can be explained, if only partially, by common sense. There were so many opportunities for Russians to straighten their shoulders, shake off the bureaucratic midges enveloping them, and go on a rampage of destruction—in the Russian manner, without differentiation and with blood. But Russia under Yeltsin and subsequently under Putin, even unhappy and frustrated, has avoided hysteria and madness to this point and is still avoiding the worst. It did not crash, even though its ruling class pushed it to the brink many times. Now there is hope that Russia's most important reform the transformation of autocracy, splitting power into institutional pieces—will be achieved without bloodshed.

Russia can accomplish its farewell to its dramatic history, and the final systemic vestige of that history, if several factors come together: pressure from society, understanding among the political class that rule through personified power and the irresponsibility of elites are dangerous to its survival, and the intuition of the leader telling him that separation of powers and power sharing will make his rule more stable.

The history of Russia under Yeltsin and Putin has shown that during a time of historic transformations, many things must be regarded in a new light. What seems like an obstacle in normal development may turn out to be a blessing when a transitional society is seeking a new identity. Thus Russia is saved by the fact that a complete consolidation of society and rule is still impossible there. Today's reality, including the bureaucratic authoritarian regime, cannot be cast in concrete. Therefore, movement in a more positive direction is possible. Patients recovering from a virulent disease have occasional setbacks.

The conflicts and the struggle that have revived in Russia despite the Kremlin's attempts to control everything are more good than bad. The conflicts show that the country is alive, and interests are formed through the conflicts. Struggle does not permit the regime to ossify. An even more positive factor is the spontaneity present in the populace and its growing independence: When polled, 45 percent of the population said that the state plays no role in their lives at all.

Of course, it is not good for society and the state to travel on parallel tracks. But it is good that people are coming out from the shadow of the state leviathan and living independently. Soon they will have to build a new kind of statehood, serving their interests. In the meantime, Russia retains a certain unruliness and spontaneity that allow society to breathe. When I see how the state apparatus tries to control our lives again, I think: the more spontaneity, the better—for now.

In the final analysis, what happens in Russia in the next ten to fifteen years will depend on the generation that replaces the final echelons of the Soviet *nomenklatura*, diluted by pragmatists. Who will they be, the people who arrive on the scene in 2008 or 2012? They will be people who grew up in the eras of Gorbachev, Yeltsin, and Putin. We know that they are not interested in ideology, that they don't remember Russia's history of totalitarianism very well, and that they are uninhibited and liberated—sometimes too much so. Many of them are cynics or look like cynics.

But the important thing is that they are not cowed—they have never known fear. They don't have slaves' instincts anymore. This is an absolutely new phenomenon for Russia—its future elites will be free of the complexes and phobias that burdened the ruling classes of the country for centuries. It is not yet clear how they see the future of Russia. If Putin creates chances for their education, if he gives them the chance to bear responsibility for their actions, it will be one of his contributions.

For now and for a few years to come, Russian politics will see palace wars, highs and lows. There will be attempts to shape a political system to fit the needs of the political class that is trying to guarantee itself a future in an uncertain situation. Russia will have to pay for the training of its leaders and their teams again and again. Russia has to solve one more problem: the peaceful and legitimate transfer of power from Vladimir Putin to his democratically elected—not appointed, this time—successor.

Russians still have to learn not to never fall, but to rise up again every time they fall. Russia and the West will have to work on their relationship. And they are unlikely to avoid mutual hurts and suspicions. The Russian economy is still unstable and subject to shocks because it is now tied to the world economy and because it is still unstructured.

Unfortunately, we cannot discount the possibility of yet another experiment in Russia—with even harsher authoritarianism. It is not clear how the people who are running Russia will act in a crisis or in an attempt to hold onto their power. What if, feeling desperate and cornered, they decide that they can solve problems only by resorting to violence, and kick over the chessboard? The result of that experiment is clear beforehand: It will fail both because the authorities don't have the power to push society back into the cage and because society has grown accustomed to living in freedom, even if it is limited freedom. That certainty is promising.

And so we have reached the end of our ruminations. "Is that all?" the reader may demand, left with unanswered questions. People who are used to clarity and a lack of ambivalence will be confused. So, is Russia a democracy or a dictatorship? And who is Putin—a noble knight or an evil demon? Russia still defies clear answers. The country will be a hybrid for a long time. Both optimists and pessimists will find arguments to support their point of view on Russia. Both will be right—and wrong.

And what about hope? Is it still delayed disappointment, as it has always been in Russia? It depends on what we have in mind. My hope today is that Russia, for all its setbacks, passions, and tiresome scandals, is not only maintaining but also moving. Even when it is limping, it is moving . . . and, I believe, moving into the future.

NOTES

Chapter 1

1. Russia's oligarchs are the country's biggest businessmen. Their influence over state officials, often gained through blatant corruption, has allowed them to establish and advance their business empires, while degrading government power. The leading oligarchs of the Yeltsin era were Boris Berezovsky, Vladimir Potanin, Petr Aven, Mikhail Khodorkovsky, Mikhail Fridman, Alexander Smolensky, and Vladimir Gusinsky, known as the "seven bankers." In 1996, that group played a major role in Yeltsin's reelection to a second term as president. Its members were rewarded with extensive property (mainly in the field of natural resources) for which they paid almost nothing, in a deal that came to be known as "loans for shares." Under Putin, new oligarchs have emerged, among them Alexei Mordashov, head of the metallurgy conglomerate Severstal, Oleg Deripaska, who privatized Russia's aluminum industry, and Sergei Pugachev, a Saint Petersburg banker who allegedly was close to Putin's team. See Paul Klebnikov, *Godfather of the Kremlin: Boris Berezovsky and the Looting of Russia* (New York: Harcourt Brace, 2000), and David E. Hoffman, *The Oligarchs: Wealth and Power in the New Russia* (New York: Public Affairs, 2002).

2. Thomas E. Graham, *Russia's Decline and Uncertain Recovery* (Washington, D.C.: Carnegie Endowment for International Peace, 2002), p. 26.

3. Lebed was killed in a helicopter crash on April 27, 2002. The first person who attempted to play the role of Russian Pinochet tragically departed from the political scene. Lebed was a well-known author of aphorisms. A couple of them: "Pinochet— this is a Chilean problem. . . . To be exact it is not a problem—this is Chilean luck"; "You can't change horses while crossing the river, but you should change the assholes."

4. Primakov could not stand independent journalists and was suspicious of the press in general. But at the same time, in the dark days for Russia's independent television station NTV and later TV-6, he was one of the few politicians who was not afraid to come to the station and be interviewed by opposition journalists. Later, in 2002,

Primakov helped the team of independent journalists from the old NTV to build a new private channel TVS, becoming a member of its board.

5. Boris Yeltsin, *Prezidentskii marafon* [Presidential marathon] (Moscow: AKT, 2000), p. 246.

6. The president pushed Korzhakov out of his entourage on the eve of the 1996 elections. Korzhakov later wrote his memoirs, *Dawn to Sunset* (Moscow: Interbook, 1997), which revealed unflattering facts about Yeltsin and his family—unverifiable, whether true or not.

7. Roman Abramovich had at a certain point in his entrepreneurial career been under investigation on suspicion of embezzlement. Voloshin, Berezovsky's right-hand man, managed the structures which, so the newspapers said, siphoned funds out of pyramid schemes that had been created by Berezovsky.

8. Former deputy secretary of state Strobe Talbott drew my attention to a certain logic in Yeltsin's appointments as prime minister: young—old—young—old (Gaidar, Chernomyrdin, Kiriyenko, Primakov, Stepashin). Apparently, age had meaning for Yeltsin when he was thinking about breakthrough versus stabilization. For breakthroughs, he sought out young prime ministers; when he thought about stabilization, he turned to middle-aged politicians. Putin, however, did not fit entirely this logic.

9. Subsequently, Stepashin grew close to Putin and was appointed head of the Accounting Chamber. From this post, he initiated an attack on the oligarchs, obviously not without the president's knowledge, turning over materials on the machinations of the big businessmen to the prosecutor general's office.

10. The journalist Sergei Dorenko, a friend of Berezovsky's and one who was privy to much information, described the search process this way: "The name [Putin] was first thought of by Yumashev. It was supported strongly by Voloshin. Putin was received and they came to an agreement. Putin resisted for a long time and expressed unwillingness to be involved in this adventuristic undertaking. He was persuaded." S. Dorenko, "Statista Putina smenit general Shamanov" [Moderate Putin will be replaced by general Shamanov], *Moskovskaya pravda*, March 24, 2001. In turn, Berezovsky later declared more than once that it had been his idea to make Putin Yeltsin's successor.

11. Prosecutor general Skuratov was videotaped relaxing with prostitutes and then blackmailed. He refused to retire voluntarily and tried to prove that Yeltsin was firing him because he was investigating wrongdoing at the Kremlin. Putin unambiguously took Yeltsin's side in the matter, and his agency, the Federal Security Service (FSB), was active in coming up with compromising materials that hurt Skuratov. Later it became clear that some evidence against Skuratov had been forged.

12. The August 19, 1999, *New York Times* carried an article by Raymond Bonner and Timothy O'Brien, "Bank Activity Elicits Suspicion of Ties with Russian Organized Crime." According to Bonner and O'Brien, nearly $4.2 billion from Russia had

passed through Bank of New York accounts in New York City in the course of a year, and the transfers, they said, could be part of money-laundering operations of Russian criminals. Rumors spread alleging that the entire International Monetary Fund tranche given to Russia before the financial collapse of 1998 had been privatized by Russian bureaucrats and oligarchs and transferred to the West through the Bank of New York.

13. Russian officials instantly sprang to the defense of their own. The minister of foreign affairs, Igor Ivanov, declared, "We have no need to justify ourselves, and as for Russia's good name, we have it" (*Rossiiskii delovoi monitor*, September 4, 1999).

14. Mabetex is a construction firm that participated in the restoration of the Kremlin and was also involved in highly publicized corruption scandals with people from the Yeltsin circle, primarily Pavel Borodin, who headed the office of the president's affairs and was personally close to Yeltsin. The Italian newspaper *Corriere della Sera* of August 25, 1999, contained an exposé listing credit cards slips signed by Yeltsin and his daughters that were allegedly found during a police raid on the Mabetex offices in Lugano, Switzerland. The article alleged that Mabetex paid the bills on the Yeltsin family credit cards.

15. Rumors spread that right before the invasion Berezovsky allegedly met in France with Shamil Basayev, one of the Chechen separatist leaders who led the attack by the Chechen separatists on Dagestan, and Alexander Voloshin, the head of Yeltsin's presidential staff. Basayev is one of the most famous of the Chechen warlords, long suspected of having ties to the Russian secret services. See "Vnimanie, snimayu" [Attention, Camera!], *Profil'*, November 27, 2000, pp. 18–20.

16. Human rights activist Sergei Kovalev spoke about this openly, as did Chechen president Aslan Maskhadov, who, by the way, separated himself from the actions of the fighters who attacked Dagestan. In his interview with the Spanish newspaper *La Guardia*, Maskhadov said the following: "As for Dagestan, I can declare with full responsibility that Berezovsky, Voloshin, Magomedov [chair of the State Council of Dagestan], and Putin all knew. We absolutely did not need either Dagestan or the conquest of alien territory. It was all programmed by Moscow. Dagestan was an excuse for war." Cited from *Kommersant-Daily*, February 8, 2000.

17. One of the most suspicious episodes of this drama took place in Ryazan', where officers of the FSB were caught planting gexogen, an explosive used in the explosions in Moscow, in the cellar of the apartment house. The head of the FSB, Nikolai Patrushev, later declared that his people were taking part in "an exercise" (!). The Kremlin prevented any further investigation into what had happened in Ryazan'. See Pavel Voloshin, "Geksogen. FSB. Ryazan," *Novaya gazeta*, March 13–16, 2000.

18. In March 2002, Berezovsky, who had moved to London, organized the screening of a film he had commissioned from French journalists, which attempted to prove that the 1999 apartment building explosions were the work of the Russian security agen-

cies. The Kremlin responded by accusing Berezovsky of being mixed up in the Chechen separatists' invasion of Dagestan. This looked clumsy: If Moscow had proof of Berezovsky's involvement in the invasion of Dagestan, he should have been brought to justice long before. But the question raised in the film financed by Berezovsky and entitled "Assault on Russia" has never been answered.

19. "Zheleznyi Putin" [Iron Putin], *Kommersant-Daily*, March 10, 2000.

Chapter 2

1. The upper house of the parliament—the Federation Council—is formed from the representatives of the regions appointed by the regional authorities.

2. Putin showed support for the SPS in his characteristically restrained manner: He received Sergei Kiriyenko, one of the party's leaders, in the Kremlin and heard him out attentively in front of the television cameras, looking benignly at the thick program of the party that Kiriyenko had placed on a table for him. In farewell, Putin smiled and promised to study the program. That was all. But the very fact of the meeting was interpreted by the leaders of the SPS—and not only them—as a gesture of support from Putin, who did not contradict that interpretation.

3. After the parliamentary elections, Primakov became the leader of the Fatherland and All-Russia faction in the Duma. But he was obviously bored by parliamentary work. After lengthy negotiations with the Kremlin, he was appointed head of the Chamber of Commerce. He had requested the post of speaker of the Federation Council, the upper chamber of the parliament, but Putin gave that to his man from Saint Petersburg, Sergei Mironov.

4. Anatoly Chubais, who was in charge of the SPS election headquarters, described the party's election results as "a complete revolution in the political structure of Russia." On another occasion, he trumpeted: "SPS is tomorrow's power." As usual, he exaggerated.

5. Soon after, Sergei Kiriyenko, who accepted the post of presidential representative in Putin's new superpresidential regime, confirmed the evolutionary tendencies of the leaders of the SPS movement, whose aim was to have at any cost an official post that would give them the opportunity to engage in business. Chubais was already a state oligarch, having become under Yeltsin the director of RAO UES (Unified Electricity System), a "natural monopoly" that managed all of Russia's electricity.

6. According to a VTsIOM poll conducted January 6–10, 2000, 51 percent of Russians expressed satisfaction with Yeltsin's retirement, 27 percent surprise, 11 percent delight, 7 percent confusion, 4 percent each anxiety and regret, and 1 percent outrage; 12 percent had no particular feelings about it, and 1 percent had no opinion.

7. Notably, Yeltsin spoke about resigning even sooner and handing over power to Putin before the parliamentary elections. That might suggest that the ruling Family had already made its decision about the successor. It also suggests that the Kremlin was not very worried about the results of the Duma election, apparently feeling that they could control them. But obviously the failure of the pro-Kremlin movements to get a majority of votes in December 1999 could have led to corrections in the "succession plans."

8. In September 1999, according to VTsIOM, the desire to see Yeltsin retire predominated among Russians. Thus, 65 percent of those polled felt that it would be better for Yeltsin to retire and for new elections to be held, 21 percent felt that Yeltsin should stay on to the end of his term but not get involved in the work of the government, 5 percent felt that Yeltsin should keep all his powers to the end of his term, and 9 percent had no opinion.

9. See the analysis of Yeltsin's rule in Leon Aron, *Yeltsin. A Revolutionary Life* (New York: Saint Martin's Press, 2000); Peter Reddaway and Dmitri Glinsky, *The Tragedy of Russian Reforms* (Washington, D.C.: U.S. Peace Institute, 2001); Michael McFaul, *Russia's Unfinished Revolution* (Ithaca, N.Y.: Cornell University Press, 2000); George Breslauer, *Gorbachev and Yeltsin as Leaders* (New York: Cambridge University Press, 2002); and Lilia Shevtsova, *Yeltsin: Myths and Reality* (Washington, D.C.: Carnegie Endowment for International Peace, 1999), which is also available in a Russian edition, *Rezhim Borisa El'tsina* (a Carnegie Moscow Center publication; Washington, D.C.: Carnegie Endowment for International Peace, 1999).

10. I remember, in a film about Yeltsin shown in 2000, that Yeltsin's daughter Tatyana is watching former Soviet president Mikhail Gorbachev on television and says to her father, "How Gorbachev has aged!" Yet at that time, Yeltsin was a total ruin in comparison with the dynamic, youthful, still attractive Gorby.

11. Guillermo O'Donnell, "Delegative Democracy," *Journal of Democracy*, vol. 5, no. 1 (January 1994), pp. 59–62.

Chapter 3

1. Putin celebrated the New Year as acting president in notable fashion—he and his wife flew to war-torn Chechnya. It was yet another demonstration of his new, mobile leadership style.

2. *Moskovskie novosti*, January 5, 2000.

3. Oligarch Boris Berezovsky said, "Putin is a man who could guarantee the succession of power," explaining that he defined succession as "not allowing a redistribution of property." *Kommersant-Daily*, November 27, 1999.

4. *Nezavisimaya gazeta*, December 30, 1999.

5. *Izvestija*, February 25, 2000.

6. Lev Gudkov and Boris Dubin, "Vse edino: Rossiiskomu obshchestvu stalo zhit' khuzhe, stalo zhit' skuchnee" [All the same: The Russian government began to live worse and its life became more boring], *Itogi*, January 23, 2001.

7. Thus, in April 2000, only 2 percent of those polled felt that positive changes could be expected right after the election, 10 percent felt that such changes would happen after six months, 20 percent after a year, and 22 percent in two to three years; 20 percent felt it would take more than three years, 12 percent doubted there would be such changes under this president, and 14 percent had no opinion. VTsIOM, www.polit.ru, April 14, 2000.

8. VTsIOM, www.polit.ru, March 7, 2000.

9. VTsIOM, www.polit.ru, April 14, 2000.

10. Putin worked for Borodin for a time in the Office of the President's Affairs. After his election, he recommended Borodin for secretary of the Russian–Belarusian Union— a diplomatic position that gave him immunity. By making this recommendation, Putin was demonstrating his gratitude.

11. *Obshchaya gazeta*, February 9, 2000.

12. VTsIOM, www.polit.ru, November 2000.

13. Kasyanov was supported by 325 deputies—a record. The most influential prime minister before him, Yevgeny Primakov, got 317 votes.

14. Putin named as head of the Central Okrug Georgy Poltavchenko, lieutenant general of the tax police and Putin's close friend. The head of the North-West Okrug was to be Victor Cherkesov, an FSB comrade of Putin's in Saint Petersburg and the first deputy director of the FSB. Sergei Kiriyenko, a leader of the SPS faction and former prime minister, was named head of the Povolzhye Okrug. For the Siberian Okrug, Putin tapped Leonid Drachevsky, minister of affairs of the Commonwealth of Independent States. The head named for the North-Caucasus Okrug was General Victor Kazantsev, previously responsible for operations of the "antiterrorist operation" in the Northern Caucasus. The head of the Ural Okrug was to be Lieutenant General Petr Latyshev, deputy minister of internal affairs. For the Far East Okrug, the head was to be General Konstantin Pulikovsky, commander of federal forces in Chechnya in the first Chechen war. On Putin's Federation reform, see Eugene Huskey, "Center–Periphery Struggle: Putin's Reforms," in Archie Brown and Lilia Shevtsova, eds., *Gorbachev, Yeltsin, and Putin: Political Leadership in Transition* (Washington, D.C.: Carnegie Endowment for International Peace, 2001).

15. The first law gave the president the right to demand that the regional bosses obey the laws of the Russian Federation and to punish them by suspending the powers of the

law-breaking governors and replacing them with temporary leaders. Another law gave the same powers to the governors vis-à-vis local leaders. The third law covered new principles for the formation of the Federation Council, among them that governors and heads of local legislatures could no longer preside in the upper chamber and no longer had immunity from prosecution for criminal or administrative wrongdoing. The Federation Council would consist of regional representatives proposed by the regional authorities.

16. Writing in *Kommersant-Daily* on May 20, 2000, Ilya Bulavinov, Nikolai Vardul, and Azer Mursaliev declared, "There is yet another revolution in Russia. And once again from above. Of course, it is not clear whether it will achieve its goals. After all, not only are the disadvantages of the former administration still here, but new ones have appeared."

17. By 2002, the presidential representatives in the *okrugs* had basically fulfilled their positive role—thanks to the pressure on the governors, they had helped bring local laws in line with the Russian Constitution. But then they became an obstacle in the relations between the regions and the center, increasing its bureaucratization. Putin seemed to realize that, but he did not know what to do with his representatives.

18. Chubais's role in this period was contradictory. While trying to curtail Berezovsky and Gusinsky, he continued to support the oligarch Vladimir Potanin, who was close to the liberals at that time.

19. "Diktatura razrushit stranu: Obshchestvu est' chto teryat'" [Society has a lot to lose], *Obshchaya gazeta*, May 25–31, 2000.

Chapter 4

1. I observed this unequal battle close up—in 2000, I was a member of the Public Board of NTV, a consultative organ of the television network, headed by former USSR president Mikhail Gorbachev. The board included several well-known democrats of the first wave: Yuri Afanasyev and Yuri Ryzhov; writer Alexander Gelman; the editor of *Obshchaya gazeta*, Yegor Yakovlev; the editor of *Novaya gazeta*, Dmitry Muratov; and Mikhail Fedotov, a former press minister in the Yeltsin government. The Public Board tried to organize support for the persecuted journalists.

2. The results of another poll conducted by the VTsIOM in July 2002 are worth mentioning. In that survey, 39 percent were attracted to Putin because he was energetic and strong-willed, 19 percent thought he could bring order to the country, 9 percent thought that he was a leader who could lead others, 6 percent considered him an experienced politician, and 5 percent thought him a far-seeing politician. The rest selected other qualities in Putin—that outwardly he was nice, that he understood the

needs of ordinary people, and so on. When the same respondents were asked what they didn't like about Putin, 29 percent of them said that he had ties to the Yeltsin entourage, 12 percent that he had no clear policies, and 10 percent that his actions in Chechnya were solely to boost his popularity. Forty-three percent of respondents could not identify what they did not like about the new president.

3. Berezovsky, attempting to appear to be a defender of democracy, began subsidizing nongovernmental and human rights organizations. He even bailed out the Andrei Sakharov Foundation, named for one of the best-known Soviet dissidents, which was in a perilous financial state. Sakharov's widow, the human rights activist Yelena Bonner, accepted the money, albeit after some vacillation, thereby legitimating Berezovsky's new role.

4. But the intriguer remained faithful to intrigue—in his numerous speeches in that period, Berezovsky left open the possibility of rapprochement with Putin, if the president only called him. Berezovsky always said that there was no alternative to Putin in the presidential elections and that he would support him again.

5. After fleeing to London, Berezovsky created his party, Liberal Russia, which was joined by the well-known liberals and former members of the SPS Sergei Yushenkov and Victor Pokhmelkin. The oligarch took his place among the leadership of the party, which he financed. In April 2002, Berezovsky published "Manifesto of Russian Liberalism," one of the most eloquent attempts to set a liberal agenda for Russia. The former oligarch seemed to understand better than many other liberal politicians what Russia needed to resume its liberal reforms. Boris Berezovsky, "Manifesto of Russian Liberalism," *Nezavisimaya gazeta*, April 11, 2002. In October 2002, Berezovsky was expelled from his own party after trying to make friends with nationalists and communists.

6. *Kommersant-Vlast*, August 20, 2000.

7. When Russians learned from a note found with one of the bodies that some of the crew had remained alive for a time after the accident, 40 percent of those polled expressed outrage at the authorities, 25 percent expressed grief over the deaths, 16 percent said that the people had been lied to, 11 percent expressed sadness, 6 percent expressed no feelings, and 2 percent could not define their reaction to the event.

8. At that time, the Kremlin administration began examining the possibility of ending gubernatorial elections. The idea was fully consonant with the logic of the president's pragmatic authoritarianism, which was built on the lower echelons' dependence on the leader and not on the voters. Besides which, the people in the Kremlin were tired of expending energy and money supporting their candidates in the regions.

9. The president's political engineers began work on new electoral legislation. It proposed introducing proportional elections—following the model the Duma had created—in all the regional parliaments by 2003. That would change the political land-

scape in the regions, strengthening the center's control, because, in accordance with the law on parties, regional parties were in fact liquidated. The new laws on parties and on elections were supposed to be a new step in political reform that would establish the role of the Kremlin "party of power" (first it was Unity, later United Russia) and make it the ruling party.

10. In the fall of 2002, the pro-Kremlin party United Russia suggested that the threshold required for the political party to get representation in the Duma be raised from 5 to 7 percent (at the beginning, a 12.5 percent threshold was suggested). It was one more step toward a party system fully controlled from above that would keep the ruling team from having any unpleasant surprises.

11. The "Pristina dash" by Russian parachutists in 1999 during the Kosovo crisis (the purpose of the "dash" was to force NATO to guarantee for Russia a separate sector of responsibility in Kosovo) was organized by the head of the General Staff, Anatoly Kvashnin, and his deputy, Leonid Ivashov, without the knowledge of minister of defense Igor Sergeyev and most likely also without Yeltsin's knowledge. It could have created a real conflict between Russia and NATO

12. Unbelievable but true: In 2001, almost a million Russian service members continued to guard "mobilization resources" in case of global war; that is, they worked as warehouse guards. The warehouses they protected held enough old-style military topcoats to dress the entire male population of draft men.

13. Thus, in the course of the military reform initiated by Putin, the salary of officers went up by 300 to 500 rubles ($100 to $160), which would hardly have satisfied them.

14. Oleg Odnikolenko, "Skol'ko stoi profi" [How much do professionals cost], Itogi, January 22, 2002.

15. Every Russian man of age 18–27 years is required to serve two years in the military. But most get deferments for higher education and other reasons or exemptions for poor health. Others avoid the call-up by paying bribes or just fleeing.

16. In the heat of the 1996 reelection campaign, Yeltsin had pledged to form a fully contract military by 2000. But his promise was quickly disavowed by top officials, who said that such a project was too expensive.

Chapter 5

1. On the second Chechen war, see Gail W. Lapidus, "Putin's War on Terrorism: Lessons from Chechnya," Post-Soviet Affairs, vol. 18, no. 1 (January–March 2002), pp. 41–49; Anna Politkovskaya, A Dirty War: A Russian Reporter in Chechnya (London: Harvill Press, 2002); and Alexei Malashenko and Dmitri Trenin, Vremia Juga: Rossiia v

Chechnie—Chechnya v Rossii [The time of the South: Russia in Chechnya—Chechnya in Russia] (a Carnegie Moscow Center publication; Washington, D.C.: Carnegie Endowment for International Peace, 2002).

2. And only 17 percent felt that Russia was obligated to compensate Chechnya for war damages, while 73 percent were against it, feeling that Russia had enough of its own problems without the Chechens. Yuri Levada, "Rossiyane ustali ot voiny" [Russians are tired of war], *Obshchaya gazeta*, August 17–23, 2000.

3. Politkovskaya, *A Dirty War*, p. 21.

4. Ruslan Khasbulatov, "Situatsiya v Chechenskoi respublike" [The situation in the Chechen Republic], *Nezavisimaya gazeta*, December 29, 2000.

5. Quite a few Russians in the army, including officers, entered into a deal with Chechen units to sell Chechen oil illegally or to sell arms to the separatists Russia was fighting.

6. In April 2000, 60 percent spoke out in support of military action in Chechnya, but by October the figure was down to 44 percent. In April, 21 percent supported the idea of negotiations with Chechnya, whereas in October it was 47 percent. Yuri Levada, "Chto schitaem po oseni" [What we think in autumn], *NG–Stsenarii*, November 15, 2000.

7. In November, an International Monetary Fund mission came to Moscow and found the economic situation in the country so good that it concluded that Russia did not need new credits and could pay the Paris Club. This was a blow to the government, which had been counting on International Monetary Fund loans.

8. The price of Russian exports rose as much as 38 percent, while the cost of imports fell 14 percent. The index of industrial growth, compared with the same period in 1999, rose 9.6 percent. The growth in oil production continued. Real incomes rose 9.5 percent in ten months compared with the same period the year before. But they did not reach the 80 percent level of pre-crisis 1997. *Vedomosti*, November 27, 2000.

9. *Niezavisimaja gazeta*, November 17, 2000.

10. Polls showed that only 39 percent of Russians supported reinstating the Soviet anthem. The rest preferred other options, including the current anthem with music by Ivan Glinka (20 percent). *Vedomosti*, December 9, 2000.

11. *Komsomolskaya pravda*, December 8, 2000. Yeltsin spoke after Anatoly Chubais drove out to the dacha where Yeltsin was living like a hermit and persuaded him to protest the return to the Soviet symbols. It was obvious that Yeltsin was sincerely upset by Putin's decision to reinstate the old symbols.

12. The only possible path for Russia is to conclude a long-term strategic alliance with Asia, said Alexander Dugin, one of the ideologues of Eurasianism, a form of Russian nationalism. Available at www.strana.ru, November 14, 2000.

13. Strobe Talbott, *The Russia Hand, A Memoir of Presidential Diplomacy* (New York:

Random House, 2002).

14. Thomas Graham and Arnold Horelick, *U.S.–Russian Relations at the Turn of the Century*, Report of the U.S. and Russia Working Groups (Washington, D.C.: Carnegie Endowment for International Peace, 2001), p. 9.

15. Talbott, *The Russia Hand*, p. 4.

16. Jim Hoagland, "From Russia with Chutzpah, or How to Alienate a Partner," *International Herald Tribune*, November 23, 2000.

17. U.S. assistance to Russia was significant, but not as large as the Russian leadership expected. Between 1992 and 1999, the United States provided Russia with $7.67 billion in economic assistance (the European Union between 1991 and 2000 provided Russia with $2.28 billion). In addition, Russia got $8.89 billion in commercial financing and insurance from the U.S. government, of the $18.01 billion provided to the newly independent states. In 1999, Washington provided $905 million in official assistance to Russia. (The European Union provided $144 million, including Germany's contribution of $82 million.) Russia became the second largest recipient of American aid, after Israel. Esther Brimmer, Benjamin Schreer, and Christian Tuschoff, *Contemporary Perspectives on European Security*, German Issues No. 27 (Washington, D.C.: American Institute for Contemporary Studies, Johns Hopkins University, 2002). In the 1990s, the United States became the largest outside investor in the Russian economy, accounting for 30 percent of all foreign investments.

18. Yuri Levada, "2000 god—razocharovaniya i nadezhdy" [The year 2000—disappointments and hopes], *Moskovskie novosti*, December 26, 1999–January 2, 2000.

19. *Kommersant-Vlast'*, December 26, 2000.

Chapter 6

1. According to polls, only 15 percent of Russians at that moment wanted Russia to take "the path of European civilization common to the modern world," 18 percent wanted to return to the path followed by the USSR, 60 percent preferred Russia's "own special path," and 7 percent had no opinion. Lev Gudkov and Boris Dubin, "Rossiiskomu obshchestvu stalo zhit' khuzhe, stalo zhit' skuchnee" [Life is worse and less merry for Russian society], *Itogi*, January 23, 2001, p. 14.

2. Gudkov and Dubin, "Rossiiskomu obshchestvu stalo zhit' khuzhe," p. 14.

3. Alexander Tsipko, "Smozhet li Putin pereigrat' Gusinskogo?" [Will Putin be able to outplay Gusinsky?], *Nezavisimaya gazeta*, February 20, 2001, and Vitaly Tretyakov, "Bolshaya stat'ya o Putine i Rossii" [Big article on Putin and Russia], *Nezavisimaya gazeta*, January 31, 2001.

4. Gudkov and Dubin, "Rossiiskomu obshchestvu stalo zhit' khuzhe."

5. At the peak of the crisis with NTV in March 2001, 35 percent of those polled across the country expressed outrage over the events (in Moscow it was much higher—55 percent). In April, three-quarters of Muscovites said they trusted NTV. Almost half those polled in this period thought that the conflict surrounding NTV had been created because of the authorities' desire to liquidate independent television. Another 33 percent were blaming the company. Yuri Levada, "Vlast' sil'na no bespomoshchna" [The regime strong but helpless], *Moskovskie novosti*, April 10–16, 2001.

6. Part of the team from the old NTV, headed by Yevgeny Kiselev, moved to a different channel, TV-6, which by an irony of fate was owned by Boris Berezovsky. This is the drama of the Russian mass media—there were no alternative publicly financed outlets, and media that wanted to be independent of the state had to bow down to the oligarchs.

7. The former teams of *Itogi* and *Segodnya* soon began to publish the new journals *Ezhenedel'ny zhurnal* and *Djelovaya khronika*. But those journals had no previous popularity.

8. In 2002, the Kremlin began discussing the idea of forming the government on the basis of the dominant party, United Russia.

9. A number of active members of the Union of Right Forces (SPS), among them Sergei Yushenkov and Victor Pokhmelkin, created the new Liberal Party, in opposition to the Kremlin, with the active support of oligarch Boris Berezovsky.

10. Vitaly Tretyakov, "Putin, Chubais i SPS" [Putin, Chubais, and the SPS], *Nezavisimaya gazeta*, May 23, 2001.

Chapter 7

1. Now three disciplinary warnings were enough to get a judge fired. The mechanism for holding judges criminally liable was simplified. Ordinary judges and their tenures depended on the chairmen of courts, who were appointed by the executive branch.

2. In Europe, small and medium-sized businesses accounted for 70 percent of gross domestic product, whereas in Russia, they accounted for only 10 percent. *Novye izvestiya*, December 21, 2001.

3. The Putinists were also known as the Northern Alliance, a reference to Afghanistan's Northern Alliance and to the fact that these people had come with Putin from Saint Petersburg, Russia's "northern capital." The Putinists of that period included Nikolai Patrushev, director of the FSB; his deputy, Nikolai Zaostrovtsev; Igor Sechin and Victor Ivanov of the presidential staff; and Victor Cherkesov and Georgy

Poltavchenko, presidential representatives in the *okrugs* (new regional jurisdictions).

4. The leader of the Yeltsinites was first head of the presidential staff Alexander Voloshin. Prime Minister Mikhail Kasyanov was part of the group. They were soon joined by former privatization tsar Anatoly Chubais, who would for some time be the new inspiration of the old Yeltsin circle. Several oligarchs, such as Oleg Deripaska and Roman Abramovich, were part of the circle as well.

5. On United States–Russia relations under Bush and Putin, see Angela Stent and Lilia Shevtsova, "America, Russia and Europe: A Realignment?" *Survival*, vol. 44, no. 4 (Winter 2002–2003).

6. Other administration officials were less restrained. The secretary of defense, Donald Rumsfeld, said openly, "Russia is an active proliferator. It has been providing countries with assistance in these areas in a way that complicates the problem for the U.S. and Western Europe." And the deputy secretary of defense, Paul Wolfowitz, was even more frank: "These people seem to be willing to sell anything to anyone for money. I recall Lenin's phrase that the capitalists will sell the very rope from which we will hang them."

7. Right after the terrorist attacks on the United States, 52 percent of Russians polled expressed their support for Americans. A majority of 54 percent, however, thought Russia should remain neutral and not take part in the response to September 11; only 28 percent said Russia should give the West moral support, and 30 percent supported participation in United States–organized military operations aimed at terrorists.

8. Figures in this paragraph and the next are taken from "Rossiia v poiskakh strategicheskoi positsii" [Russia in search of a strategic position], posted on www.liberal.ru, October 2002.

9. "Rossiia v poiskakh."

10. At least a partial flare-up in the Russian public occurred during the Winter Olympic Games in Salt Lake City in February 2002, when the Russians began to lose. Some Russian media outlets tied these losses to a "conspiracy against Russia" with a bias toward the United States. Even Putin did not avoid outrage over "nonobjective judges."

11. Patrick E. Tyler, "In Spat on NATO and Russia, Powell Fends Off Rumsfeld," *New York Times*, December 8, 2001.

12. According to Public Opinion Foundation polls, 43 percent of Russians had negative feelings about the U.S. withdrawal from the ABM Treaty, 31 percent were indifferent, and 8 percent were positive (18 percent had no opinion). And 42 percent of those polled felt that Putin had to take action in response (only 28 percent felt that he should not). Posted on www.fom.ru, December 27, 2001.

13. Rodric Braithwaite, *Across the Moscow River: The World Turned Upside Down* (New

Haven, Conn.: Yale University Press, 2002), pp. 338–39.

14. Yuri Levada and Leonid Sledov, "Obshchestvenno-politicheskaia situatsiia v dekabre 2001" [The sociopolitical situation in December 2001], VTsIOM, December 27, 2001.

Chapter 8

1. Putin's constant vacillation increased the frustration of the liberal-minded people in Russia who had strongly endorsed his pro-Western shift. See Andrei Piontkovsky, "My Putin," *Novaya gazeta*, October 10, 2002.

2. Putin proved that he was consequential—he did not forgive and he did not forget his personal enemies as his predecessor sometimes had done. At that time, the president's chief enemy was Boris Berezovsky, who was waging his own vendetta against Putin and who continued to be the owner of TV-6. Having no possibility of reaching Berezovsky in the United Kingdom, where the oligarch found political asylum in 2000, the Kremlin cracked down on TV-6. But even without Berezovsky, independent television in Russia had no future.

3. *Moskovskie novosti*, January 8–21, 2002.

4. *Financial Times*, February 10, 2002.

5. Andrew Kuchins, *Summit with Substance: Creating Payoffs in an Unequal Partnership*, Carnegie Endowment Policy Brief 16 (May 2002).

6. In the spring of 2002, the United States withdrew from its steel agreement with Russia, increasing its tariffs, which was a painful blow to Russian producers: It cost Russian producers up to $600 million annually. Moscow reciprocated with a ban on American poultry—"Bush chicken legs" (as Russians called American chickens imported into Russia beginning during George H.W. Bush's presidency)—that affected American farmers in 32 states and cost American producers $800 million a year. In the end, the United States made exemptions on steel imports for its European allies. Those exemptions did not, however, extend to Russia. Meanwhile, Russia lifted its ban on American poultry.

7. *Nezavisimaya gazeta*, April 8, 2002.

8. Leon Fuerth, "On Russia, Think Big," *Washington Post*, May 1, 2002. Katrina Vanden Heuvel and Stephen Cohen criticized Washington policy for "treating Russia not as a real partner but as a helper when it suits U.S. purposes." Katrina Vanden Heuvel and Stephen Cohen, "U.S. Takes Russia for Granted at Its Peril," *Los Angeles Times*, May 1, 2002.

9. Robert Legvold, "Russia's Unformed Foreign Policy," *Foreign Affairs*, vol. 80, no. 5

(2001), p. 72. On United States–Russia relations after September 11, 2001, see Robert Legvold, "U.S.–Russian Relations Ten Months after September 11," paper presented at the 27th Conference of the Aspen Institute, U.S.–Russia Relations: A New Framework (Washington, D.C., August 15–21, 2002).

10. See *Current History*, October 2002, available at www.currenthistory.com.

11. Thomas Graham, *Russia's Decline and Uncertain Recovery* (Washington, D.C.: Carnegie Endowment for International Peace, 2002), p. 84.

12. Stephen Kotkin, *Armageddon Averted: The Soviet Collapse, 1970–2000* (New York: Oxford University Press, 2001).

13. On issues of order in Russia, see Richard Rose and Neil Munro, *Elections without Order: Russia's Challenge to Vladimir Putin* (Cambridge: Cambridge University Press, 2002).

14. *Vedomosti*, April 23, 2002.

Chapter 9

1. The Russian government retained other influential members of the Yeltsin group: Mikhail Lesin, head of the Ministry of Press and Information; Mikhail Zurabov, head of the Pension fund; Sergei Shoigu, minister of emergency situations; Vladimir Rushailo, head of the Security Council; and numerous less significant figures.

2. Mikhail Kasyanov made no efforts to flex his political muscles. He was too busy, according to his closest subordinates, with his own business. But he clearly would not have minded taking the most prestigious post in the land if it were offered to him and if all the dirty work needed to obtain it were done for him. What politician would mind it?

3. Address to the Federal Assembly of the Russian Federation, May 16, 2003. Available at www.kremlin.ru.

4. Russian observers expressed serious doubts about how things would develop after Saddam was removed. "No one doubts that the US is capable of destroying the Iraqi army in a few weeks," wrote Alexei Arbatov. "The problem is elsewhere: what is to be done after the operation is completed?" Alexei Arbatov, "Irakskii krizis: moment istiny" [The Iraq crisis: the moment of truth], www.politcom.ru.

5. VTsIOM, January 24–27, 2003.

6. Andrei Piontkovsky wrote: "The confrontation with America for the sake of confrontation and showing 'toughness' is not in the national interests of the Russian Federation. . . . For Russia, with its presently limited resources and the specter of security threats to the South and East, the properly phrased question is: how best to use

the potential of the only superpower in the world [i.e., the United States] to solve the problems of our own security." A. Piontkovsky, "Lovushka dlia prezidenta" [Trap for the President], *Novaya gazeta*, March 13, 2003.

7. L. Ivashov, "SShA terpiat politicheskoe porazhenie" [The USA is suffering a political defeat], *Nezavisimaya gazeta*, March 25, 2003.

8. Alexei Pushkov, "Printsipy—eto te zhe interesy" [Principles are just interests], *Nezavisimaya gazeta*, March 21, 2003.

9. *Le Figaro*, March 26, 2003.

10. Stephen Sestanovich, "Restoring US–Russia Harmony," *New York Times*, May 31, 2003. In turn, Dmitri Trenin wrote, "The events in Iraq could easily have led to a break between Moscow and Washington, but it did not happen. George Bush, apparently, decided that his relations with Putin were worth saving." D. Trenin, "Russian–American Relations Two Years after September 11," Briefing, Carnegie Moscow Center, August 2003.

11. Angela Stent, "Washington, Berlin and Moscow: New Alignment after Iraq?" *National Interest*, vol. 2, no. 29, July 23, 2003.

12. Leon Aron, *Russia, America, Iraq* (Washington, D.C.: American Enterprise Institute, 2003). Available at www.AEI.org/publications.

13. Pushkov, "Printsipy."

14. In 1993, both companies won a tender to develop the oil fields of Sakhalin-3 and even began investing in the development. But despite Putin's promises to settle the question positively with legal rights to the development, the Russian government decided to hold a new tender, annulling the results of the 1993 competition.

15. Angela Stent, "How Close an Embrace with Moscow?" *World Policy Journal*, vol. 20, no. 4 (Winter 2003–2004), pp. 76–77.

16. Sestanovich, "Restoring US–Russia Harmony."

17. FOM (Public Opinion Foundation), www.fom.ru.

18. During Desert Storm, Mikhail Gorbachev sent his emissary Yevgeny Primakov, who knew the Iraqi leader well, to Baghdad to help Saddam. This time, Putin sent Primakov to Baghdad right before the start of military action to persuade Saddam to give up power.

19. One of the warnings of the coming "anti-oligarch revolution" was the May 2003 report of the so-called Council on National Strategy, a Kremlin-created group of analysts. The report tried to show that Russia was in danger of an "oligarchic revolt," whose ideologue was allegedly Khodorkovsky and whose aim was the transformation of Russia into a parliamentary republic, controlled by big business. The revolt was to take place during the 2004 Duma elections, when a government headed by

Khodorkovsky would be formed. "An Oligarchic Revolt Is Planned in Russia." Report of the Council on National Strategy, available at www.apn.ru.

20. Putin's attitude toward Khodorkovsky became plain at the meeting between the president and the oligarchs on February 19, 2003, when Khodorkovsky expressed his doubts about the purity of Rosneft's acquisition of Servernaya Neft for $600 million. Putin responded by asking Khodorkovsky how YUKOS had obtained its super reserves. "The ball is in your court," the president announced, staring at Khodorkovsky unblinkingly and with such hostility that Khodorkovsky grew pale.

21. While in Washington, Khodorkovsky discussed the possibility of his going into politics with representatives of the American elite, and that fact was clearly no secret from the Kremlin. Visits to Washington have hastened the fall of important Russians in the past: Prime Minister Chernomyrdin lost his post because Washington began to see him as a pretender to the presidency.

22. At one point, Voloshin's circle tried to raise public concern and foment outrage against Putin's *siloviki*, hoping to stop the president from his anti-oligarchic move. But the attempt failed. Gleb Pavlovsky, an adviser to the administration close to Voloshin, had written a letter denouncing the Saint Petersburg group of *siloviki*—Sechin, Ivanov, and Pugachev—for trying to create their own power center in the Kremlin. See *Vedomosti*, September 8, 2003. But later Pavlovsky changed his position. Only the flexible survive in Russian politics.

23. Otto Latsis, "Zagryaznenie atmosfery" [Pollution of the environment], *Russkii Kur'er*, August 8, 2003.

24. *Vlast' i biznes: Leto 2003* (Moscow: Liberal'naya Missiia Foundation, 2003), p. 67.

25. In July, the members of the Russian Union of Industrialists and Entrepreneurs, the union of the oligarchs, wrote Putin a letter in which the tycoons stated that the main cause of their problems was the law and order agencies and demanded an end to the campaign "unleashed in the country by those forces who are threatened by stability." The initiator of the letter was Anatoly Chubais, who understood perfectly well that as soon as Putin's Praetorian Guard was through with the oligarchs, it would be his turn, as one of the most independent politicians and state "oligarch." The president did not like their letter, and the oligarchs wrote a second one, which was much milder and asked the regime to make a "civil contract" with them, in which the regime would pledge not to reconsider the results of privatization and business would guarantee to pay taxes. The president ignored this letter, too. And the courts kept the YUKOS managers in prison.

26. I remember my conversation with several major oligarchs, who were incensed by Khodorkovsky's behavior. In their opinion, he had endangered them all with his political ideas and attempts to wrest control of the Duma. They were afraid that the attack on big business would continue and they would all feel the blows. "He's gone

overboard," was the general reaction of Russian business. There wasn't a hint of sympathy for Khodorkovsky.

27. See www.liberal.ru.

28. See Marshall Goldman, *The Piratization of Russia: Russian Reform Goes Awry* (London: Routledge, 2003), on the character of Russian privatization.

29. *Vlast' i Biznes*, p. 31.

30. One of the most active proponents of this idea was Sergei Glazyev, from whom the concept of natural rent was borrowed by various political forces.

31. In his article "Liberalism: Without Democracy It Won't Work," Yegor Gaidar wrote, "The argument is that it's time to redistribute the assets, since they have become much more valuable. Naturally, redistribute it for the benefit of the people, even though in fact such attempts always end with redistribution for the benefit of the elite close to the regime." *Vedomosti*, April 16, 2004.

32. In June 2004, Paul Khlebnikov, editor-in-chief of *Forbes Russia*, was murdered in Moscow while returning home after work. Few people doubted that it was a contract killing. If so, looking into the pockets of hundreds of oligarchs, what Khlebnikov was doing, was really like walking in a minefield. Russian oligarchs still did not feel themselves secure and that means that privatization and with it Russian stability were not secure as well.

33. In 1993, the pro-Kremlin Russia's Choice got 15.5 percent, coming in behind the Liberal Democratic Party (22.9 percent). In 1995, Democratic Choice of Russia did not make it over the 5 percent barrier, getting 3.9 percent of the votes. The pro-Kremlin Our Home Is Russia came in fifth, with 10.1 percent. In the 1999 election, Our Home Is Russia got 1.2 percent, while the new pro-Kremlin party United Russia was second with 23.3 percent to the Communists' 24.3 percent.

34. Dmitrii Kamyshev, "Kremlya Palata," *Kommersant-Vlast'*, December 1–7, 2003.

35. VTsIOM polls in November 2003 showed that 26.2 percent would vote for United Russia, 19.6 percent for the Communist Party, 5.5 percent for SPS, 5.4 percent for Yabloko, 5.3 percent for LDPR, and 4.1 percent for Rodina.

36. See the analysis of the election results: Igor Bunin, Alexei Zudin, Boris Makarenko, and Alexei Makarkin, "Do i posle 7 dekabrya: razvitie politicheskoi situatsii v Rossii" [Before and after 7 December: development of the political situation in Russia], available at www.politcom.ru.

37. The Party of Pensioners and the Agrarian Party both got more than 3 percent—3.09 and 3.64 percent, respectively.

38. *Nezavisimaya gazeta*, December 11, 2003.

39. A member of the presidential administration noted in a conversation with me about

SPS and Yabloko: "We did not bother them. They couldn't stay afloat on their own." Yes, the Kremlin did not actually try to drown them. But the Kremlin created conditions in which swimming was very difficult.

40. It seems that the Kremlin spin doctors thought that their child Rodina would get 4 to 5 percent of the vote at best. But once Rodina got more, it began making demands. The Kremlin had no intention of satisfying the clone's demands, and it began turning off the oxygen supply, primarily of the most uncontrollable and ambitious Rodina leaders, Sergei Glazyev, who had presidential aspirations. Soon after the election, the pro-Kremlin part of Rodina, which was headed by Rogozin, got rid of Glazyev.

41. This fact was noted by Leon Aron, "The Duma Election," American Institute for Public Policy Research, Winter 2004, available at www.wei.org.

42. Yuri Levada, "2003—Events and People," *Moskovskie novosti*, no. 49, 2003.

Chapter 10

1. I. Bunin, A. Zudin, B. Makarenko, and A. Makarkin, "Prezident posledniego sroka: politicheskaya situatsiia v Rossii posle prezidentskikh vyborov" [The president of the last term: the political situation in Russia after the presidential elections], available at www.politcom.ru.

2. According to FOM (the Public Opinion Foundation, a survey institution close to the Kremlin), in February 2003 Putin would get 74 percent of the vote; Glazyev, 7 percent; Kharitonov, 6 percent; Khakamada, 5 percent; Mironov, 2 percent; Malyshkin, 1 percent; and Rybkin, 1 percent. Available at www.fom.ru.

3. Fradkov had worked at different jobs in USSR embassies, had been deputy minister and then minister of foreign economic relations in the Russian government, minister of trade, and director of the federal tax police.

4. According to the Levada Center, the popularity of Kasyanov's government was growing. The approval rating grew from 46 percent in February 2003 to 50 percent in 2004. Available at www.levada.ru.

5. The nomination of Ivan Rybkin and the business of his disappearance before registering as a presidential candidate were apparently related to the attempts of Boris Berezovsky, who was financing Rybkin, to discredit the election. In the end, after becoming the center of the scandal, Rybkin decided not to run.

6. Putin's speech to his representatives, *Izvestiya*, February 13, 2004.

7. Communist candidate Kharitonov got 13.7 percent (9.4 million votes); Glazyev, 4.1 percent (2.8 million); Khakamada, 3.8 percent (2.6 million); Malyshkin, 2 percent (1.39 million); and Mironov, 0.76 percent (588,000).

8. Michael McFaul and Nikolai Petrov, "What the Elections Tell Us," *Journal of Democracy*, vol. 15, no. 3 (July 2004), p. 29.

9. Gernot Erler, "Kak vospitat' 'khoroshuyu vlast'" [How to bring up a 'good regime'], *Nezavisimaya gazeta, Dipkur'er*, April 5, 2004.

10. Viktor Kremenuk, "Sovrashchenie sverkhderzhavy: Skandal vokrug pytok v Irake vysvetil opasnuyu transformatsiyu amerikanskogo obshchestva" [Seduction of a superpower: the scandal around torture in Iraq exposes a dangerous transformation of American society], *Nezavisimaya gazeta*, May 19, 2004.

11. The soft punishment of the Russian colonel Budanov, who had killed a Chechen girl and was caught red-handed, was only one of numerous cases that demonstrated the selective ways of the Russian court system.

12. VTsIOM poll, Interfax, May 14, 2004.

13. I have in mind the attempt of Dmitri Kozak, the deputy chief of the presidential administration, to push through his proposal to solve the Transdnistria conflict, which overruled the agreements reached with the mediation of the Organization for Cooperation and Security in Europe. After some vacillation, Kishinau rejected Kozak's plan, much to the embarrassment of the Kremlin. See the comments by Stephen Pfifer in *Rossija v global'noi politike* [Russia in global politics], vol. 2, no. 2, March–April, 2004, p. 116.

14. Michel McFaul, "Reengaging Russia: A New Agenda," *Current History*, vol. 103, no. 675, October, 2004, p. 312.

15. Ariel Cohen said in this context: "The fact that nationalists will exert considerable influence in the Russian legislature appears to sharply reduce the chances of a softening of Russian policy [in the post-Soviet space]." Ariel Cohen, "US Officials Warily Monitor Russian Policy Debate on Caucasus," available at http://eurasianet.org.

16. Alexander Vershbow, "Putin stavit kontrol' i poryadok vyshe svobody i ekonomicheskogo rosta" [Putin prefers control and order over freedom and economic growth], *Kommersant-Vlast'*, January 12, 2004.

17. D. Trenin, "Rossiia vkhodit v 'novy izolyatsionism'" [Russia is entering a 'new isolationism'], *Nezavisimaya gazeta*, December 8, 2003.

18. *Novaya gazeta*, June 28–30, 2004.

19. L. Grigoryev, A. Zagorsky, and M. Urnov, *Vtoroi srok prezidentskogo pravleniia V. Putina: dilemmy rossiiskoi politiki* [Putin's second term: dilemmas in Russian politics] (Moscow, Prava Czeloveka, 2004), p. 62.

20. James M. Goldgeier and Michael A. McFaul, *Power and Purpose: U.S. Policy toward Russia After the Cold War* (Washington, D.C.: Brookings Institution Press, 2003), p. 111.

21. Angela Stent and Lilia Shevtsova, "America, Russia and Europe: A Realignment?" *Survival*, vol. 44, no. 4 (Winter 2002–2003), pp. 121–34.

22. My personal meetings with Western politicians confirmed that Khodorkovsky was that last straw that made them change their minds about Putin. They weren't planning to refuse to deal with the Kremlin. But their resentment regarding the Russian leader and his team had increased, which could have political repercussions later. "We don't trust him anymore," said recent allies of the Russian president.

23. Jim Hoagland, "A Payoff for Putin," *Washington Post*, November 6, 2003.

24. Colin Powell, "Partnerskie otnosheniya: rabota prodolzhaetsya" [Partner relations: work continues], *Izvestiya*, January 26, 2004.

25. I confess that until recently I too had unjustified hopes for a more profound content in the Russian–American relationship. I saw every downturn in the relations as a harbinger of something incurable and dramatic.

26. Dov Lynch, "Russia Faces Europe," *Chaillot Papers* (Institute for Security Studies, European Union), no. 60 (May 2003), pp. 78–79.

27. But then, and not for the first time—as, for instance, in the negotiations over the Kaliningrad enclave—after issuing an ultimatum, Russia made concessions and compromised with Brussels.

28. Michael McFaul writes: "For instance, if Putin continues to roll back democracy and increase the state's role in running the economy, Russia's standing in the G-8 should be reviewed." McFaul, "Reengaging Russia," p. 312.

29. T. Bordachev and A. Moshes, "Rossiia: konets evropeizatsii?" [Russia: the end of Europeanization?], *Rosiia v global'noi politike*, vol. 2, no. 2, March–April 2004, p. 110.

30. L. Grigoryev, A. Zagorsky, M. Urnov, *Vtoroi srok prezidentskogo pravleniya V. Putinf: Dilemmy rossiiskoi politiki* (Moscow: Prava Czeloveka), p. 78.

31. Pekka Sutela, *The Russian Market Economy* (Helsinki: Kikimora Publications, 2003), pp. 257–58.

32. Poll, available at www.VTsIOM.ru.

Chapter 11

1. The metaphor "elected monarchy" (or "elected autocracy") that I used earlier in the book to describe Yeltsin's rule continues to reflect the content of that rule, accenting the contradictions between personified power and the elective method of legitimizing it. The concept of "oligarchic authoritarianism" has to reflect the direction of the evolution of the political regime under the first Russian president and its nature during the final stage of Yeltsin's presidency (1995–1999).

2. There were numerous attempts to define Russian political reality through the con-

cept of limited democracy, that is, "democracy with adjectives." Examples are Michael McFaul's "electoral democracy," Fareed Zakariah's "illiberal democracy," and Andranik Migranyan's attempt to define it as a plebiscite or "delegated democracy." These definitions allowed us to believe that there was democracy in Russia, but either not full or deformed. The deformation needed to be corrected, certain aspects of the democracy had to be strengthened, and then we could hope for Russia's movement toward total democracy. Evolution of Russian power under Putin has proved that this rule needs different categorization. Timothy Colton and Michael McFaul, *Popular Choice and Managed Democracy: The Russian Elections 1999 and 2000* (Washington, D.C.: Brookings Institution, 2003); Fareed Zakariah, "The Rise of Illiberal Democracy," *Foreign Affairs*, vol. 76, no. 6, November–December, 1997, pp. 22–23; Andranik Migranyan, *Chto takoje Putinism?* [What does Putinism mean?] (Moscow: Yedinstvo vo imia Rossii, 2004).

3. Of the definitions of the new Russian political regime, I find productive Michael Mann's "semi-authoritarian incorporation," which means limited civil society and pluralism but not polyarchy. Richard Sakwa developed the idea further, offering the useful option: "semi-authoritarian bureaucratic incorporation." Talk at Chatham House, "Putin's Second Term," March 2004.

4. Nikolai Petrov shows how Putin created the administrative construction in the center and the region by using people from the power structures to control personnel policy and implement orders from the center. Petrov calls it "grassroots activity." Nikolai Petrov, "Federal'naya reforma i kadry" [Federal reform and personnel], Briefing at the Carnegie Moscow Center, April–May 2004, www.carnegie.ru. Olga Kryshtanovskaya also wrote about the massive influx of people from the special services, especially from the former KGB, to the administration. Anatoly Kostyukov, "Vlast' tsveta khaki" [Khaki-colored power], interview with O. Kryshtanovskaya in *Nezavisimaya gazeta*, August 19, 2003.

5. Stephen Kotkin, "What Is to Be Done?" *Financial Times*, March 6, 2004.

6. The real gross domestic product (GDP) grew 7.3 percent in 2003, and 8 percent in the first quarter of 2004. The federal fiscal budget ran a surplus of 3 percent in 2004. Fewer than six years after the 1998 default, currency reserves increased tenfold, reaching $88 billion in March 2004. Inflation declined from 84 percent in 1998 to 12 percent in 2003. Export-oriented industries grew 7.8 percent and domestic manufacturing 5.6 percent in 2003. The share of investment in GDP increased to 21 percent in 2003 (from 19 percent in 2002). Foreign direct investment (FDI) increased 70 percent in 2003. Still, it amounted to $4 billion. Cumulative FDI since 1991 amounted to $21 billion. Personal spending grew 8–9 percent on the average, or 38 percent in four years.

7. For the first time after the economic decline of the 1990s, the fuel, nonferrous metals, and forestry resources sectors accounted for almost 70 percent of industrial growth

in 2000–2003, with the oil sector alone accounting for about 45 percent. In 2003, there was relatively strong growth in some parts of the food sector and a strong pick-up of growth in machine building. Organization for Economic Cooperation and Development, *OECD Economic Surveys: Russian Federation* (Paris: Organization for Economic Cooperation and Development, 2004).

8. In 2003, Russian GDP growth achieved a rate of 7.3 percent and with stabilized oil prices at $19 per barrel for the Urals, the growth would have been about 6.2 percent. *OECD Economic Surveys: Russian Federation.*

9. The resource-exporting sectors in 2004 accounted for 80 percent of Russian exports. The main investments continued to be in the oil and gas sector, totaling 21–22 percent of all investments (only 3 percent went into machine building).

10. Yegor Gaidar, "Ekonomicheskii rost i chelovecheskii factor" [Economic growth and the human factor], *Nezavisimaya gazeta,* April 30, 2003.

11. L. Grigoryev, A. Zagorsky, and M. Urnov, *Vtoroi srok prezidentskogo pravleniia V. Putina: dilemmy rossiiskoi politiki* [Putin's second term: dilemmas in Russian politics] (Moscow, Prava Cheloveka, 2004), p. 28.

12. V. Mau, "Okna rosta i prioritety ekonomiki" [The windows of growth and economic priorities], *Rossiia v global'noi politike*, vol. 2, no. 2 (March–April 2004), p. 56.

13. Pekka Sutela, *The Russian Market Economy* (Helsinki: Kikimora Publications, 2003), pp. 227–29.

14. Y. Yasin, "Strukturnye reformy ili ekonomicheskii rost?" [Structural reforms or economic growth?], available at www.liberal.ru.

15. "Quasi-state monopolies predominate in the energy and banking spheres," said Oleg Vyugin, "In such an economic structure, competition does occur. But its goal is control over the shares and satisfying the interests of the monopolists, not the production of any goods." "Makroekonomicheskaya situatsiia k nachalu 2003 g" [The macroeconomic situation in early 2003], Liberal Mission Foundation, www.liberal.ru.

16. "The reforms are blocked not by the resistance of the people but the rule itself," Vyugin said in despair.

17. Anders Åslund, "Russia's Economic Transformation under Putin," *Eurasian Geography and Economics*, vol. 45, no. 6 (September 2004), p. 417.

18. V. Mau, "Okna rosta i prioritety economiki," pp. 56–59.

19. Within the government, the most active proponent of economic growth was presidential adviser Andrei Illarionov.

20. Victor Polterovich, "Makroekonomicheskaya situatsiia k nachalu 2003 g," available at www.liberal.ru.

21. If the path of structural reform is taken, Yasin maintained, economic growth in

2005–2007 would fall to 2–3 percent. But by 2008–2010, it would go back up to 5 percent and perhaps higher.

22. Philip Hanson, "Putin and Russia's Economic Transformation," *Eurasian Geography and Economics*, vol. 45, no. 6 (September 2004), p. 425.

23. Grigory Yavlinsky, *Periferiinyi kapitalizm* (Moscow: Epicenter and Integral-Inform, 2003), p. 68.

24. In 2003, real household incomes, which by 1999 had plummeted to 49 percent of their 1990 level, recovered to 61 percent. Average annual income growth from 2000 to 2003 was 11.3 percent. The number of people living below the poverty line decreased from 37 percent in 1999 to 25 percent in 2003 and 20.4 percent in 2004.

25. Organization for Economic Cooperation and Development, *OECD Economic Surveys: Russian Federation*.

26. Mikhail Dmitriev, Gref's first deputy, explained the reasons that social reforms did not get off the ground during Putin's first term: "We did not have the resources. . . . We met with an overbureacratized process of taking decisions and an insufficient priority for social reform in key players." Besides which, even Gref's team, burdened with day-to-day paperwork, did not have time for "formulating policy," according to Dmitriev. *Profil'*, May 18, 2004.

27. Yevgeny Gontmakher, "Sotsial'naya politika v Rossii: evolutsiia 90-x gg i novyi start" [Social policy in Russia: evolution of the 1990s and a new start], *Pro et Contra*, Summer 2001, pp. 1–11.

28. See Vadim Radaev, "Kto pomozhet rabotayushchem bednym?" [Who will help the working poor?], *Pro et Contra,* Summer 2001; and Tatyana Maleva and Sergei Vasin, "Invalidy v Rossii—uzel starykh i novykh problem" [Invalids in Russia—the knot of old and new problems], *Pro et Contra*, Summer 2001.

29. As a result, there were situations in which the minimum pension was three times greater than the minimum wage; and when the neediest were left without the support of the state, while aid went to the less-needy.

30. Although the death rate (14 per 1,000 people in 2003) is still higher than the birthrate (10 per 1,000), the birthrate has slightly grown since 1999. Life expectancy for men in 2004 was still only 62 years, and for women 68 years. Russia faces the problem of a declining workforce starting in 2005.

31. Before 1999, Russia had only a few thousand HIV-positive people; in 2004, official statistics put the number at 280,000 and unofficial statistics at about 1 million.

32. In 2004, the number of illegal migrants in Russia was close to 5 million people, who had no status and were in dire straits.

33. The 2004 budget allotted 2.68 percent of the gross national product (2.34 percent in 1999) for national defense, 2 percent (1.28 percent in 1999) for law enforcement, 0.76

percent (0.52 percent in 1999) for education, 0.30 percent (0.025 percent in 1999) for health, and 1.05 percent (1.04 percent in 1999) for social policies.

34. *Russia's Engagement with the West: Transformation and Integration in the Twenty-First Century*, edited by Alexander Motyl, Blair Ruble, and Lilia Shevtsova (Armonk, N.Y.: M. E. Sharpe, 2004), p. 12.

35. See D. Trenin, "Realpolitik Moskvy," *Nezavisimaya gazeta*, February 9, 2004.

36. Yuri Pivovarov, "Russkaya politicheskaya kul'tura," *Pro et Contra*, Summer 2002, p. 38.

37. There is another form of simplification, the optimistic version. An example is "A Normal Country," by Andrei Shleifer and Daniel Treisman, *Foreign Affairs*, March–April 2004, which attempted to define Russia as a "a normal middle-income country" with a commensurate level of democracy. It is true that the level of economic development and well-being influences the quality of democracy, and that the problems that Russia had been experiencing are characteristic of many other transitional societies. But the question is how to understand "normal." Concluding that Russia is "normal" may justify a rejection of democracy. For if everything is going normally, as it is everywhere for everyone, there is no need for concern; democracy will come when income levels rise. This understanding of "normal" deprives society of stimuli for transformation. Incidentally, in an unexpected way, the adherents of such "normalcy" in Russia come to the same conclusion as the adherents of Russia's "special path," who maintain that Russia is not ready for democracy.

38. Richard Pipes, "Flight from Freedom," *Foreign Affairs*, May–June 2004.

39. T. Kutkovets and I. Klyamkin, "Normal'nye lyudi v nenormal'noi strane" [Normal people in an abnormal country], *Moskovskie novosti*, July 12–17, 2003.

40. *The Economic Elite of Russia in the Mirror of Public Opinion: Analytical Report* (Moscow: IKSI and Friedrich Ebert Foundation, 2004).

41. *Economic Elite of Russia.*

42. Kutkovets and Klyamkin, "Normal'nye lyudi."

43. Starting with 2000, 65–67 percent of Russian respondents were constantly against extending of Putin's rule. Data are from www.levada.ru.

44. Of the respondents, 29 percent trusted the president's administration; 14 percent, the government; 12 percent, the city administration; 6 percent, the Federation Council; and 5 percent, the State Duma. Data are from www.fom.ru.

45. The number of Russians who bought busts or portraits of the president has grown from 9 percent (2001) to 11 percent (2004). But 81 percent had no such desire. Only 15 percent thought that distributing pictures of Putin increased his authority, and 29 percent thought that this "invites mockery and puts the president in a bad light." Most of Putin's fans were young people, 18–24 years of age, with a high school education. Putinomania was a provincial youth fad. Young people from small towns wore T-shirts

with Putin's picture the way young people once wore Che Guevara T-shirts.

46. Research by the Public Opinion Foundation, known as FOM, available at http://bd.fom.ru. At the present time in Russia, according to Ministry of the Interior data, there are approximately 15,000 members of skinhead gangs, with about 2,500 in Moscow and the Moscow region. *Nezavisimaya gazeta*, April 2, 2003.

47. Yet the majority of Russians are sure that sooner or later they will live in a democracy. In 2003, 23 percent of respondents believed that Russia would be a democracy in 15–20 years; 13 percent, in 20–50 years; 10 percent, that it already was a democracy; 9 percent, that it would be one in 5 years; and 8 percent, that it would take more than 50 years. Only 18 percent thought that Russia would never be a democracy. Levada Center polls, available at www.levada.ru.

48. It is noteworthy that Russians know the value of their elites—48.9 percent feel that the interests of the population and the elites do not coincide (and only 4 percent believe that they do); *Economic Elite of Russia*.

49. Mikhail Afanasyev, "Nevynosimaya slabost' gosudarstva" [The unbearable weakness of the state], *Otechestvennye zapiski*, no. 2 (2004), p. 226.

50. See chapter 12 on the striving for democratization at the start of Putin's second term.

51. German Gref, after a trip to war-torn Chechnya, offered remarks in the same vein: "Chechnya looks like the set of a Hollywood blockbuster." It seems the authorities don't know how bad things are in a region they are constantly dealing with!

52. See Leon Aron, "The Putin Restoration," available at www.aei.org.

Chapter 12

1. Savik Shuster's talk show "Freedom of Speech" and Leonid Parfenov's "Last Night" were canceled by NTV in the summer of 2004.

2. Polls by Levada Center, May 2004; see www.levada.ru.

3. See Olga Anchishkina, "Burokratiia nachinaet, no . . . vyigryvaet li?" [The bureaucracy starts, but . . . is it winning?], *Otechestvennye zapiski*, summer 2004. Vitaly Kurennoi, "V poiskakh dostoinstv: smysl i logika administrativnoi reformy" [In search of merit: the meaning and logic of administrative reform], *Otechestvennye zapiski*, summer 2004.

4. One of the intended results was supposed to be a reduction in personnel. In 2004, there were 593,000 people working in Russia's federal organs and 217,400 in the regional ones. The reforms were supposed to reduce the number by 10 to 15 percent.

5. A U.S. senator is paid approximately 5 to 6 times more than the average American. After the salary raise, a Russian minister receives $43,600 a year; that is, his pay is 17

times more than the average annual salary in Russia ($2,500).

6. The decision was to replace benefits with financial compensation ranging from $5.10 to $53 a month, and $6 billion was budgeted for that in 2005.

7. Starting in 2005, the federal budget no longer was responsible for the salaries of the staffs of state-financed institutions, including teachers and doctors. Their salaries and pensions were to come out of regional budgets.

8. Mikhail Zadornov, "My riskuem sozdat' v Rossii 'Garlemy'" [We risk creating 'Harlems' in Russia], *Novaya gazeta*, July 12–14, 2004.

9. There were 156 kinds of benefits and aid that covered 236 categories of the population, or almost 97.9 million people (68 percent of Russia's population).

10. Municipal governments were getting 7 percent of the organizations—including day care centers, schools, clinics, and sanitariums—that had been in the federal budget. In view of the impoverished state of many regions, it was clear that all these institutions would be shut down.

11. M. Zadornov, "Budzhet nazval 'krainikh'" [The budget has named the 'marginalized'], *Moskovskie novosti*, June 18–24, 2004.

12. According to a survey, 38 percent of those polled had free public transport, 33 percent had reduction in rent, 21 percent did not pay their full telephone bill, and 91 percent had benefits for health care. Those people definitely were losing as a result of social reform.

13. *Nezavisimaya gazeta*, August 4, 2004.

14. Polls by the Levada Center, www.levada.ru.

15. Ivan Preobrazhensky, "Budzhet protiv budzhetnikov" [Budget against those subsidized by the budget], *Profil*, May 24, 2004.

16. *Novaya gazeta*, July 12–14, 2004.

17. Thus, in 2004, 57 percent felt that pension reform was not in their interest (24 percent thought that it was), and 64 percent felt that communal reforms would simply lead to higher prices (26 percent believed that it would improve the quality of communal services). Levada Center, www.levada.ru.

18. *Moskovskie novosti*, June 18–24, 2004.

19. See I. Bunin, A. Zudin, B. Makarenko, and A. Makarkin, "Novaya real'nost': osnovnye napravleniia razvitiia politicheskoi situatsii v 2004–2008 gg" [The new reality: basic directions of development of the political situation in 2004–2008], available at www.politcom.ru.

20. M. Khodorkovsky, "Krizis liberalizma v Rossii" [The crisis of liberalism in Russia], *Vedomosti*, March 29, 2004.

21. Another major stockholder of YUKOS, Leonid Nevzlin, who found asylum in Israel, had only a few months earlier still been ready to fight the regime and financed Irina Khakamada's presidential bid. He also wrote a letter to *Izvestia*, in which he announced that he was leaving the political struggle.

22. *Vremya novostei*, April 15, 2004.

23. *Financial Times*, April 16, 2004.

24. *Vedomosti*, April 16, 2004.

25. Neoconservative slogans were presented with the greatest clarity by Vyacheslav Nikonov, the ideologist of United Russia. They were reiterated in a more popular form by the film director Andrei Konchalovsky, who liked to say, "Russia is not ready for democracy and never will be."

26. Only 28 percent of those polled thought that Khodorkovsky's trial was objective and dispassionate, 49 percent thought it was not, and 23 percent had no opinion. Levada Center, *Moskovskie novosti*, June 4–10, 2004.

27. Delovye Novosti, *Kommersant-Vlast'*, July 6, 2004.

28. A reflection of these contradictions was this statement by Gerashchenko: "Inside the company and beyond it, both in Russia and abroad, there are groups of influence interested in prolonged conflict with the state in order to solve their personal mercantile interests." *Nezavisimaya gazeta*, July 15, 2004.

29. Dmitri Butrin, "Kogda v mogil'shchikakh soglas'ia net" [When the grave diggers disagree], *Kommersant-Vlast'*, July 26, 2004.

30. Yulya Latynina, "Konets okhoty" [End of the hunt], *Novaya gazeta*, July 26–28, 2004.

31. Soon, other Putin allies joined the boards of major natural resource companies: Vladislav Surkov was installed on the board of TransNeftProduct, the monopoly producer of pipeline hardware. Yevgeny Shkolov, another deputy head of presidential administration, was named to the board of Transneft, which controls Russian pipelines.

32. Denis Yermakov, "Non Free Fall," *Yezhenedelny Zhurnal*, August 29, 2004.

33. Before the YUKOS debacle started, Putin had approved the formation of TNK-BP. At the height of the hunt on YUKOS, Putin approved the sale of 7.59 percent of LukOil shares to U.S. ConocoPhillips.

34. Clouds were gathering over some of the "oligarchs." This time, there was talk of possible problems for Vladimir Potanin, the head of Norilsk Nikel, and Victor Vekselberg, the head of Sual-Holding.

35. I have in mind such organizations as the Union of Industrialists and Entrepreneurs, the Chamber of Commerce, Business Russia, and Opora (the Association of Entrepreneurial Organizations of Russia).

36. This tendency led scholars to speak of the appearance in Russia of a "neocorporative model." See Alexei Zudin, "Neokorporativism v Rossii" [Neocorporativism in Russia], *Pro et Contra*, vol. 6, no. 4, Fall 2001.

37. *Nezavisimaya gazeta*, April 21, 2004.

38. In 2003, until Khodorkovsky was arrested—that is, until the third quarter 2003—there was a net inflow of capital into Russia totaling $3.9 billion. In the third quarter of 2003, the outflow of capital reached $7.7 billion. The trend was continuing in 2004. According to the Central Bank estimates, $5.1 billion was taken from Russia in the first six months of 2004. Economic development minister German Gref made an admission that the net outflow of capital from Russia in 2004 will reach $12 billion. *Kommersant-Vlast'*, August 6, 2004.

39. Stephen Sestanovich, "Force, Money and Pluralism," *Journal of Democracy*, vol. 15, no. 3 (July 2004), pp. 41–42.

40. Actually, this time it also solved a long-standing problem: Kvashnin was an obstacle to army reform and had big ambitions. The new chief of staff is General Yuri Baluevsky, a man capable of strategic thinking and devoid of political goals.

41. Anatol Lieven, presentation at the Carnegie Endowment for International Peace, September 2, 2004.

42. Russian society continued to be split on Chechnya issue. A total of 55 percent of respondents said that the situation would not change after the presidential elections, 28 percent of those polled said the elections would help to improve the situation (and 8 percent said that situation would only worsen), 44 percent of those polled did not support the Kremlin's policy in Chechnya, and 41 percent said they supported it. The number of those supporting it has increased over the past two years. www.romir.ru, August 27, 2004.

43. Polls carried by the Analytical Service VTsIOM-A and can be found at www.levada.ru. After March 2004, the center was reformed as the Yuri Levada Analytical Center.

44. Yuri Levada, "What the Polls Tell Us," *Journal of Democracy*, vol.15, no. 3 (July 2004), pp. 50–51.

45. See Organization for Economic Cooperation and Development, *Economic Surveys: Russian Federation* (Paris: Organization for Economic Cooperation and Development, 2004), p. 51.

46. Half of Russian citizens—50 percent—felt that joining the WTO was in Russia's interests, 21 percent felt that it was contrary to its interests, and 29 percent had no opinion. Levada-Center, *Moskovskie novosti*, May 28–June 3, 2004.

47. Russia was supposed to withdraw its troops from Georgia and the Transdnister region in accordance with agreements made at the 1999 Istanbul summit of the

Organization for Cooperation and Security in Europe.

48. Arkady Ostrovsky, "How to Be a Founding Father," *Financial Times*, July 7, 2004.

49. www.wciom.ru, July 28, 2004.

50. Some observers in Moscow were convinced, however, that the banking crisis in the summer of 2004 was created both to clear the bank arena of unclean banks and to redistribute financial resources in favor of the state banks.

51. Sergei Medvedev was right when he wrote: "For the first time in Russian history, national interest is not linked to sheer power and territorial control, but rather to domestic reform." Sergei Medvedev, "Russia at the End of Modernity: Foreign Policy, Security, Identity," *Russia and the West at the Millennium*, ed. Sergei Medvedev, Alexander Konovalov, and Sergei Oznobishchev (Garmisch-Partenkirchen: George Marshall European Center for Security Studies, 2004), p. 511.

52. Richard Sakwa, talk at Chatham House, "Putin's Second Term," London, March 2004.

53. Dmitri Trenin, "Identichnost' i integratsiia: Rossiia i Zapad v 21 veke" [Identity and integration: Russia and the West in the 21st century], *Pro et Contra*, vol. 8, no. 3 (2004), p. 15.

54. *Kommersant-Vlast'*, July 20, 2004.

55. At the start of Putin's second term, the following integration associations that included Russia were active on the territory of the CIS: the Shanghai Organization of Cooperation, the Eurasian Economic Community, the Organization of Agreement on Collective Security, and the Single Economic Space.

56. *Kommersant-Vlast'*, June 21, 2004.

57. Masha Lipman, "Putin's Burden," *Washington Post*, September 9, 2004.

58. *Komsomol'skaya Pravda*, September 29, 2004.

59. www.levada.ru, October, 2004.

60. Data from www.moscownews.com.

61. From www.levada.ru.

62. Strobe Talbott, "The Strains of Putin's Clampdown," *Financial Times*, September 27, 2004.

INDEX

Abashidze, Aslan, 381

Abkhazia, 307, 381–82, 386

Abramovich, Roman: as Family member, 17, 27, 227, 421n4; as governor of Chukotka, 127; privatization of Sibnift and, 368, 369; suspicion of embezzlement, 410n7; YUKOS case and, 363

Across the Moscow River (Braithwaite), 219–20

Adamov, Yevgeny, 88

Adjaria, 307, 381

administrative reform: constitutional impact of, 390–91; under Fradkov, 297–98; as imitation, 394; in Putin's second term, 378–79; reduction in personnel, 434n4; salaries of officials, 355, 434n5; stability vs. transformation, 403; of state apparatus, 187, 190, 354–56; structural, 431n21

Adygeya, 382

Aeroflot, 366, 369

Afanasyev, Yuri, 415n1

Afghanistan, war in, 206–7, 210, 213

Agreement on Partnership and Cooperation, 317

AIDS/HIV, 334, 432n31

Aksyonenko, Nikolai, 88

Aksyonenko, Victor, 29, 191, 193

Aleshin, Boris, 355

Alexandrov, Alexander, 145

Alexii (Patriarch, Russian Orthodox Church), 56

Alfa, 87

Alfabank, 383

Alkhanov, Alu, 371, 373

All-Russian Center for Public Opinion Research (VTsIOM), 42, 73, 95, 120, 212, 295, 412n6, 413n8, 414n7, 415n2, 426n35, 437n43. *See also* public opinion

al Qaeda network, 373

alternative military service, 222

aluminum monopoly, 180

ambiguity, transitional, 5

Andrei Sakharov Foundation, 416n3

anthem, Russian, 144–46, 418n10

anti-Americanism. *See* anti-Westernism

Anti-Ballistic Missile Treaty (1972), 111, 155–56, 197–98, 200, 213–15, 234, 421n12

anti-Westernism: decline in, 211–13; great-power ambitions and, 174–76; Iraq war and, 268–69, 304–6; limited support for, 175–76; in military, 225; new Russians and, 174–75; in ruling class, 153–54, 234–35, 242, 399. *See also* Western world and Russia

apathy, 164, 359

Apatit, 275

apparatchik wars, 191

Arbatov, Alexei, 423n4

armed forces. *See* military

Armenia, 308

arms sales: to China, 201, 248; to countries sponsoring terrorism, 248; to Iran, 152, 199–201; U.S. disapproval of, 421n6

Aron, Leon, 271–72, 350

Artemyev, Igor, 374

Aslakhanov, Aslanbek, 283

Åslund, Anders, 217, 330

439

ABOUT THE
AUTHOR

———————— ✒ ————————

Lilia Shevtsova is a senior associate in the Russian and Eurasian Program at the Carnegie Endowment, working from Carnegie offices in Washington, D.C., and Moscow. She is one of Russia's top political analysts, an award-winning journalist, and a regular commentator for global television and radio networks.

Ms. Shevtsova has been a visiting professor at the University of California at Berkeley and at Cornell University, and she was a fellow at the Woodrow Wilson International Center for Scholars. She is a member of the executive committee of the International Council for Central and East European Studies, and a member of the board of the Institute for Human Science at Boston University. She also serves on the editorial boards of *Megapolis*, *Journal of Democracy*, *Polis*, and *Demokratizatsiya*.

Ms. Shevtsova is the author of six books, including *Yeltsin's Russia: Myths and Reality* (Carnegie Endowment, 1999) and *Gorbachev, Yeltsin, and Putin: Political Leadership in Russia's Transition*, edited with Archie Brown (Carnegie Endowment, 2001). She holds a doctorate from the Institute of International Relations and the Academy of Sciences in Moscow.

Carnegie Endowment for International Peace

The Carnegie Endowment for International Peace is a private, nonprofit organization dedicated to advancing cooperation between nations and promoting active international engagement by the United States. Founded in 1910, Carnegie is nonpartisan and dedicated to achieving practical results. Through research, publishing, convening, and, on occasion, creating new institutions and international networks, Endowment associates shape fresh policy approaches. Their interests span geographic regions and the relations between governments, business, international organizations, and civil society, focusing on the economic, political, and technological forces driving global change. Through its Carnegie Moscow Center, the Endowment helps to develop a tradition of public policy analysis in the states of the former Soviet Union and to improve relations between Russia and the United States. The Endowment publishes FOREIGN POLICY, one of the world's leading journals of international politics and economics, which reaches readers in more than 150 countries and in several languages.